CAP BADGE

CAP BADGE

THE STORY OF
FOUR BATTALIONS OF
THE BEDFORDSHIRE AND
HERTFORDSHIRE
REGIMENT (TA)

1939-1947

by
Major R H Medley, DL.

LEO COOPER
LONDON

First published in Great Britain in 1995 by
LEO COOPER
190 Shaftesbury Avenue, London, WC2H 8JL
an imprint of
Pen & Sword Books Ltd,
47 Church Street,
Barnsley, South Yorkshire S70 2AS
© RH Medley, 1995

A CIP record for this book is available from the British Library

ISBN 0 85052 434 2

Typeset by Phoenix Typesetting, Ilkley, West Yorkshire

Printed in England by
Redwood Books Ltd,
Trowbridge, Wilts.

Dedication

This volume is dedicated to all those who wore the cap badge of The 16th Foot, The Bedfordshire and Hertfordshire Regiment and The Hertfordshire Regiment, and served in the many theatres of operations around the world from 1939 to 1947. Besides those individuals mentioned in these pages there are many others no less worthy of a written record. Memories of those who gave their lives remain with us, and those who survive return to the battlefields of fifty years ago to pay respect to their fallen comrades. This dedication extends to the regimental family at home; parents, wives, and sweet-hearts whose steadfast support spurred on their loved ones far from home.

CONTENTS

FOREWORD

by

Major General A.J. Ward-Booth, OBE, DL.

This book brings up to date previous regimental histories of the Second World War and fills in a numbe of serious omissions in previous accounts. It is a substantial and detailed work but is in no sense difficult reading. The author and his contributors are to be congratulated.

The great strength of the book are the personal accounts of actions fought and the plethora of maps which enable the reader to follow the course of the battles with relative ease. The author apologizes for some duplication of personal accounts. There is no need, I found they usually gave another slant and certainly the smell and fog of war through strongly.

Whilst the book concerns itself principally with the story of the 2nd Battalion of The Bedfords and the 1st Battalion of The Hertfords, other chapters make fascinating reading and made me wish for more. For example I would dearly liked to have known more about how a Beach Group operated.

Lt-Colonel Whittaker and Major McMillen are masters of understatement. I found the former's account of training in England prior to the North Africa highly amusing and can imagine the soldiers' reaction to training for every eventuality! The latter's account of glider pilot operations leaves the hazards totally to the imagination of the reader.

The book reveals many acts of personal bravery and, I suppose, Frank Snape's conduct comes across most vividly. He appeared to seek out trouble and his conduct under fire was amazing. There is also the quiet courage displayed by Frank Sutton, the assault Pioneer Platoon Commander of the 2nd Battalion, and many, many more.

Private Scully's humour and descriptive powers are incredible. His story of the captive turned captor is worthy of a short TV film.

The book poses a number of questions such as who was the brigade commander at the battle of D'Jebel Aoud? Surely he must take the blame for having changed the plan at the eleventh hour. Also why was Lt-Colonel Whittaker's distinguished leadership not recognized? Could it be that he fought his own corner too hard with his superiors?

This is a history that will appeal to everyone in or connected with the Regiment and, I feel sure, to many others beside. The author can take pride in his work.

ACKNOWLEDGEMENTS

A story such as this is only possible because of the great number of individuals who sent me their personal stories. Material has been forthcoming from individuals as far afield as Australia, from generals and private soldiers, from pre-war regulars and territorial volunteers, and wartime citizen-soldiers, officers and men. I am most grateful to all those who have sent me their reiminiscences as it is the personal aspect which helps bring the text alive. My sincere thanks to one and all. The result is this story about four battalions during and immediately following the 1939–1945 War.

It is always dangerous to single out individuals by name but there are those whose records of events have helped round off some excellent material. I must thank Frank Snape, Frank Sutton and Bill Scully for their detailed accounts of life with the 2nd 16th Foot in Italy, Lt Colonel Jimmy Davenport and Lt Colonel Bill Whittaker for their view of actions in France in 1940, North Africa in 1943 and Italy in 1944, Brigadier Burke for his account of actions in Italy and Greece, Brigadier Bill Peters, John Evans and Sergeant Hart for their detail about the 1st Hertfords, Lt Colonel J Harper for the material about Number 9 Beach Group and the 2nd Hertfords, CSM Jack Leech for a mine of information about the Commandos, Tom LaFontaine for his war maps of North Africa, which, with the responses from Major Leslie Young and Jimmy Darville, helped me to present a more detailed account of the battle at D'Jebel Aoud, and Captain H.E.I. Phillips for his account of the experiences of the 5th Battalion in Malaya.

This story uses all the material made available to the editing team. Even with the material which has been forthcoming it is inevitable that there will still be ommissions.

I wish to express my thanks for the help given to me by members of the History Committee of the Regimental Association, all of whom spent many hours delving into records and collecting material. To Lt Colonel Whittaker, an old and respected friend, for his enduring interest and pertinent comments. To Jack Douglas for his study of Regimental and Brigade orders and records, and Frank Snape (Deceased) for collecting material on the Italian campaign. To Mr Eric Morris for guidance and advice on layout. Lastly but by no means least to Brigadier Angus Robertson for his great interest, assistance, and encouragement.

I am particularly grateful to Tom LaFontaine for allowing me to use his prints.

My sincere thanks also to Leo Cooper for his help and to his staff, especially Tom Hartman for his courtesy and patience.

This is a story of a British line regiment, a regiment proud of its history, and of the men who fought with its 'colours' during the Second World War.

The Regiment finally ceased to exist in October 1992 after three hundred and four years service to the Crown. It is fitting that this story be told.

INTRODUCTION

The cap badge worn on the headgear of the soldier identifies him as belonging to a particular organization or a member of a Regimental group. The cap badge of The Bedfordshire and Hertfordshire Regiment has as its background The Order of the Bath and The Star of the Garter, with the inscription 'Honi soit qui mal y pense' around the figure of a Hart. The title Bedfordshire and Hertfordshire is on a scroll below. The Hertfordshire Regiment (Territorial Army), whilst becoming a part of the Regiment in 1919, retained its own cap badge: a Hart couchant with the title 'The Hertfordshire Regiment' surrounding it and with the Crown above. The cap badge is emblazoned on the Regimental Colours. It is understandable because of the tribal nature of British Infantry Regiments why the cap badge has such meaning to those who wear it.

This story tells of the experiences of the infantry soldier, professional, TA volunteer and citizen in uniform, serving in The Bedfordshire and Hertfordshire Regiment and The Hertfordshire Regiment(Territorial Army). It tells of "Bedfords" who served away from their battalions with Special Forces. All individuals wore their cap badge with pride. The story covers all the theatres of operation ranging from the actions in France in 1940, in North Africa and Italy, Sicily, Singapore, Burma and Normandy to the 'Internal Security' tasks in Greece and Palestine. It shows how the infantry soldier, living as he does cheek by jowl with the man next to him, and sharing fear and danger, develops very strong bonds of friendship.

There is no barrier between officer, NCO and soldier; each develop a respect for the others. This bond is strongest within the boundaries of 'The Regiment', but it also extends across regimental boundaries. The infantryman is at the "sharp end" and he wears his 'Campaign

Medals' with pride. He well knows their cost in comrades killed and disabled. The expression PBI stands for 'Poor Bloody Infantry', but the infantry soldier is proud of being an infantryman. He is proud of himself and takes an inordinate pride in his regiment. He believes he is better than other soldiers. Awards to individuals in 'his' regiment and the award of 'battle honours' are equally cherished. It is this pride which instils in him the will to endure whatever the odds, and which sets him apart. It is a gem of great value envied by friend and foe alike. It may be that the ever-present need to conquer fear, and the face-to-face contact with the enemy, temper the infantry soldier into being over-modest. It is not British to be boastful so his pride is understated. In any case it is to be regretted that those outside the infantry brotherhood fail to appreciate its full meaning and value.

The response to the Editor's request for reminiscences has in some cases allowed further details to be set down. Some new material has been forthcoming about the period spent in captivity in Malaya by members of the 5th Battalion The Bedfordshire and Hertfordshire Regiment. More personal accounts have come to hand of experiences on the beaches at Dunkirk and of battles in North Africa and in Italy, supported by 'War Diaries' and maps. Further detail of the activities of the 2nd Battalion The Hertfordshire Regiment as a Beach Group has come to hand, as has a collection of material from "Bedfords" who served away from the Regiment. These reminiscences reflect the experiences of only a few but they help to show how 'Bedfords' were involved in many different theatres and types of warfare. This story has evolved from personal accounts set down by commanding officers, company and platoon commanders, warrant officers and non-commissioned officers as well as private soldiers. The story of a battle is presented as it was seen at these different levels. This leads to some repetition, but it is balanced by a broader understanding of events. Hopefully the discomforts, the terror, the guts, determination and cussedness, the comradeship and team spirit will be that much more emphasized and appreciated. This is the story of men who experienced war at the "sharp end" who wore our 'Cap Badge' with pride. It is a tribute to every member of the Regiment. Similar stories can be told of all the other infantry cap badges in the British Army. It is a story told with pride. It represents a small piece of our history.

MAPS

Map 5 is copied from an original drawn by Brian Pincombe who was the Battalion Intelligence Officer at the time.

The remaining maps supporting text in Chapters 1 to 13 are drawn from GS maps of 1940 for France, and 1943/44 for North Africa. Map 15 is copied from the original air photo overprint.

The maps in Chapters 29 to 37 are from original GS maps and overlays.

The remaining maps and sketches have been drawn by the author with the aim of presenting a clearer picture of events.

I

THE 2nd BATTALION
THE BEDFORDSHIRE AND
HERTFORDSHIRE REGIMENT

1

ENGLAND – SUMMER 1939

The 2nd Battalion of The Bedfordshire and Hertfordshire Regiment, the 2nd 16th Foot, was the home-serving Battalion of the Regiment. As such it received trained recruits from the Regimental Depot at Kempston Barracks, Bedford. The Battalion was responsible for sending reinforcements whenever necessary to ensure the 1st Battalion serving overseas in Palestine was kept manned at the designated strength. This requirement was no different from any other battalion serving in England but in time of peace it had the effect of denuding the Battalion serving at home. In the case of the 2nd 16th Foot it resulted in the Battalion being at a strength well below its authorized peacetime establishment.

It is of interest to note that the 2nd Battalion was to endure the experience of losing experienced officers and men as reinforcements to other units up to the time it deployed to Italy in 1944, in particular after the campaign in France in 1940 and after the North African battles in 1943.

The Battalion was commanded at this time by Lt Colonel J.S.Davenport, MC.

In the Summer of 1939 the Regular Army, which had moved to its training locations, received batches of Regular Army reservists who were to undergo training. The Battalion was based at St Martin's Plain, Shorncliffe under canvas.

At that time an officer served for three years as a 2nd Lieutenant, and was eligible for promotion to Lieutenant after three years, to Captain after eight years and to Major after seventeen years on passing the equivalent promotion exams. The age difference alone was sufficient to create barriers even without the very formal atmosphere which existed in an officers' mess. 2nd Lieutenants were the lowest form of life and the Commanding Officer was "God". The Adjutant, as the Commanding Officer's staff officer was held in respect, and the Regimental Sergeant Major struck fear into the hearts of all young officers.

The pattern of uniform had hardly changed since the 1914-1918

War. Working dress consisted of tunics, plus fours, puttees and boots. The tunics had brass buttons with the regimental crest and these had to be highly polished. A new pattern of web equipment had been introduced with pouches to hold magazines for the Bren light machine gun. There were straps and buckles so that if necessary the small pack and water bottle could be attached below the belt with the large pack on the back. In addition a gas cape was rolled on top of the back pack in such a way that it could be quickly released to drop down, enabling the soldier to envelop himself in it. Goggles to protect the eyes were carried in the top flap of the respirator, worn in its case on the chest, immediately available if required. Battle dress had not as yet been issued so soldiers wore denim fatigues for all outdoor exercises. In barracks officers wore tunics, plus fours and puttees, Sam Browne belt and sword, whilst Field Officers (majors and above and the adjutant) wore riding breeches and riding boots. Apart from teaching the new weaponry, time also had to be spent on learning how to piece all the bits of webbing together.

Pay for the private soldier was two shillings a day, to which an extra threepence could be added for efficiency awards such as shooting and a Second Class Certificate of Education. A 2nd Lieutenant was paid eleven shillings a day. These sums seem incredible to-day but with beer at fourpence a pint and ten cigarettes for twopence, a pie and chips in a pub for sixpence or a four course meal in a hotel for thirty old pence it was possible to enjoy the simple things of life.

Communications had changed little. The heliograph had been discarded with some reluctance, though the signalling flags were still part of the equipment. Signallers were required to be proficient at morse. Lieutenant Harrison, who had rejoined the battalion in February, was sent to Catterick on a signals course in May, having been selected after he had passed his promotion exam with distinction. He found the learning of the morse code something which was by no means his forte and was glad that the main means of communication from battalion headquarters to companies was by land line using phones.

In outline the battalion consisted of a Battalion Headquarters, a Headquarters company made up of specialists and administrative staff, and four rifle companies, each with its headquarters and three platoons. The Carrier Platoon in Headquarters Company with its lightly armoured tracked vehicles, provided the Commanding Officer with a fast, mobile reserve which could be used to protect the flanks or to reinforce danger spots. The 3" Mortar Platoon with two mortars provided local fire support out to sixteen hundred yards. This was minimal when a battalion often found itself responsible for a frontage of some two thousand yards.

Battalion Headquarters comprised the Orderly Room staff under the Adjutant, the Intelligence section under the Intelligence Officer (IO), and the Band and Drums. The former trained as stretcher bearers.

The 2nd Bedfords at this time only had two weak rifle companies each made up of a company headquarters and two understrength rifle platoons. Each platoon had a headquarters and three rifle sections. However, 2nd Lieutenant Medley records that even with the addition of reservists under training his platoon had no more than eighteen men, which meant that the rifle sections seldom had more than four men, including the section commander. This made realistic training difficult and much was left to the imagination.

Passive Air Defence (PAD) was a priority aspect of training. All troops were taught how to decontaminate themselves in the event of contamination by gas sprayed by aircraft. The battalion had a PAD centre set up with the entrances properly sealed off, receptacles to receive contaminated clothing, showers and decontamination materials. There was also the gas chamber to ensure every man knew how to adjust his respirator and know that it was working effectively.

Lt Colonel Davenport tells how he saw events. " Before the outbreak of war the 2nd Battalion was stationed at Milton barracks, Gravesend, but, with the exception of a small maintenance party left in barracks, the whole battalion were away on Collective Training in a tented camp outside Shorncliffe Camp, Folkestone.

"During this Training Season, two batches, approximately one hundred and fifty each, of Army reservists had been called up for a month's training with the Battalion – the second batch were actually still with the Battalion completing their training when war was declared. The Battalion had moved from Gravesend to Shorncliffe Camp by march route early in July after having taken a very full part in the Aldershot Military Tattoo, and under normal conditions would have remained at Shorncliffe with the rest of 10th Infantry Brigade until late September 1939.

"To the best of my recollection we had completed Battalion and Inter-Battalion Training and had just commenced Inter-Brigade Training, but, well do I remember that day in the field in late August 1939, half-way between Shorncliffe and Dover, when the Brigade Commander 10th Infantry Brigade (Brigadier E.Barker) was holding a conference prior to a night operation and the Staff Captain hastened up to inform the Brigadier that orders for the return of the Brigade to its peace station had been received. The Brigadier completed his conference, and telling us that he suspected that the next conference of a similar nature would be held under conditions of real war, he wished us all good luck, decided to cancel the Exercise, and ordered the Brigade to return to camp.

"The strides in general War Efficiency the Battalion made during this last Training season were magnificent, and I can say in all sincerity that no battalion in 10th Brigade had a higher standard. I know full well the wonderful confidence and pride which the Brigadier had in the Battalion.

"We all left the final peacetime conference with a feeling that our training for war had been completed, and that very shortly we should be able to put it into practice against the Germans.

"As we returned to camp our morale was very high, and we packed up our camp in record time and very shortly were off by road to Gravesend with that quiet and ordered efficiency which characterized the Battalion in all the vast number of moves which it had to carry out at short notice in the days to come. Back in Gravesend we completed our preparations – polished up our training – received the Mobilization Order – made up promotions – received our full quota of Reservists and stores, and were ready for war without any fuss or bother.

"I feel sure that none who were present will forget that Sunday morning, 3 September, when war was declared. The Battalion was paraded at 1100 hours for Church Parade on the barrack square, and the Prime Minister had just announced the declaration of war against Germany when off went the first air raid sirens. Our PAD Scheme immediately went into effect, and for high class work I never wish to see any scheme more effectively carried out. The Battalion merely dissolved to their appointed stations and jobs on the instant. I felt, I remember, extremely proud to command such a Battalion. I remember, too, mentioning it to the Area Commander (Major General Bond) at Chatham on the following day, and asked him what had happened at Chatham. He told me he was in church, and that most people hurriedly left the building. I asked him what he did and he replied, "I stayed where I was and prayed like hell"! No raid eventuated, but it was reported that German aircraft had been seen off the Thames Estuary.

"Shortly after mobilisation our A/Tank two-pounder guns arrived.

The platoon was selected and despatched to join the Brigade Company at Shorncliffe.

"On 20 September the Colonel of the Regiment (General Sir Henry Jackson) and the G.O.C. 4th Division (Major General D.G.Johnson, VC, DSO, MC) visited the Battalion. It was a great day for us all. It was an inspiring sight to see the Battalion complete in every detail for war drawn up for inspection on the football ground. After inspection the Colonel spoke to the Battalion, and was cheered by the Battalion. His letter to myself later, 'I am very proud of you all' expressed his feelings on that day.

"On 23 September the Battalion left Gravesend in two trains for Aldershot. The people of Gravesend were sad to see us go, and gave us a great send-off. The Mayor and Town Council bade us farewell at the station.

"At Aldershot we were quartered in Corunna Barracks, and in the course of the next few days the 10th Infantry Brigade, 4th Division and 2nd Corps were concentrated and ready to move. Those days at Aldershot were anxious and difficult ones. Intense secrecy as to the future was the order of the day. On 29 September the King and Queen visited Aldershot and met and spoke to all Commanding Officers on the Queen's Parade. I well remember the interest the Queen took in the Regiment and mentioned to myself that she was Colonel-in Chief of the Hertfordshire Regiment.

"On 30 September we left Aldershot in two trains for Southampton (at the time an unknown destination), and embarked on board SS *Biarritz*. The regimental transport did not accompany us as it had left for Newport, Monmouth, on 25 September. On board our ship (an ex channel steamer) was Brigade HQ, and the majority of 4th Divisional Staff. It was a crowded and uncomfortable trip as we sailed from Southampton at 1730 hours, and lay off the bar waiting for our escort until 12 midnight, when we finally sailed".

The key personalities in the battalion were Lt Colonel J.D. Davenport MC, the Commanding Officer, who had been severely wounded in the arm in the 1914-1918 War. The adjutant, Captain D.Rossiter, who had been awarded the MBE for gallantry in Palestine and the Quartermaster, Lieutenant Vosser, who had been a prisoner of war in Germany from 1914-1918. WO I Bluck was the RSM.

Lieut Britten remembers that one mobilization instruction directed that officers should sharpen their swords; this order was not implemented!

Reservists arrived at the barracks during the next three days, by which time the Battalion had been made up to its war establishment. A major reorganisation took place with the expansion to four rifle companies. There were promotions of warrant officers and sergeants and the introduction of the new rank of Warrant Officer Class III, Platoon Sergeant Major (PSM). The PSM was to command a platoon and a number of first class sergeants were promoted to fill the vacancies. It was a quirk of fate that there was no time for this rank to establish itself before mobilization. It was not long before the men so promoted were selected to go on officer training courses. Many of those remaining earned decorations for bravery during the war. Of those who survived Dunkirk three were given immediate commissions in the battalion.

At the same time as drafts of soldiers were arriving, a number of officers arrived in the Mess, some regulars from overseas who happened to be on leave and others from the regular and supplementary reserve. Major Wemys was posted away and Major Birch from the 1st/16th joined as battalion second in command. 2nd Lieutenants Sladen and Tasker Evans were posted to the Regimental Depot at Kempston Barracks Bedford.

Lieutenant Harrison was in the battalion orderly room when the code word for mobilization was received. The Colonel passed on the order and then instructed the orderly room quartermaster sergeant to burn the file "Command Secretariat". The file was thick with correspondence relating to expenditure of petrol in 1938, when the Battalion had visited the towns around the counties of Bedfordshire and Hertfordshire in celebration of the 250th Anniversary.

The days following receipt of the mobilisation orders were spent in packing up all unwanted kit for despatch to the Depot. As Junior Subaltern, 2nd Lieutenant Medley remembers being given the task of ensuring that the Colours were properly boxed and a certificate duly signed to that effect. Heavy equipment was crated, labelled and listed.

Lieutenant Britten, as MTO, found that after having met the demand for drivers for the carrier platoon and brigade headquarters, he had a deficit of thirty five. He was assured that the discharge documents of several reservists showed that there were more than sufficient drivers coming to meet his needs. The documents, however, did not say that the drivers being referred to had been horse transport drivers on their discharge from the Colours. Although some drivers were discovered there were not enough, and a further driver training course had to be initiated to cater for the demand, supplementing the course already nearing completion! The instructors worked around the clock and it was due to their diligence and enthusiasm as teachers, as well as the determination and application of the pupils, that the Battalion had one driver per vehicle, and a few reserves, when the transport set off to Newport in Wales on its long journey to France.

Mobilization also meant that the Battalion was earmarked to receive some thirteen "impressed" civilian vehicles most of which were quite unsuitable for military purposes, ranging from bakers and milk vans to a removal pantechnicon.

Before the war the Battalion had three civilian fitters, two of whom were Long (5'6") and Short (6').They were auxiliary members of the Royal Army Service Corps (RASC), although they never did any military training or visited the units to which they were attached. The inevitable happened and on mobilisation they were called up to report to their respective depots. Their departure was followed by a request that they be posted back to the battalion and they were returned at once! Private Long had been issued with uniform and equipment but had not been shown how to piece it together. He arrived back at the guard room at Milton Barracks and although he was inside his uniform, no one could have said he was wearing it. Pieces of equipment were carried over one shoulder and his boots hung over the other shoulder, whilst on his feet he wore civilian shoes.The sentry had been instructed to call out the guard when he needed assistance and he certainly thought this problem was beyond him, so, on his urgent summons the guard turned out. The corporal in charge, recognizing Private Long, thought that he merited a special welcome back so he ordered the "Present Arms".

One of the reservists called up was a Private Todd who was posted to "C" company as company clerk. On his desk in the company office he had put a notice written on a card. It said "Don't worry – it may never happen". Entering the company office a few moments after the Prime Minister had declared war on Germany the notice had been changed to read "Don't worry – it has".

Lieutenant Harrison was appointed to run the officers' mess which had a staff of one Corporal and one cook, the remaining personnel, in theory, being co-opted from officers' batmen.There was no provision for glasses, crockery or cutlery. Most importantly there were no secure containers for spirits or cigarettes. He recalls he slept with these valuables under his bed, and carried the cash round in a blue bank bag. Accounts were kept in a penny note book.

Whilst all these preparations were taking place, training of junior

NCOs continued in a cadre under the Regimental Sergeant Major, WOI Bluck. Officers were given talks by company commanders who described their experiences of patrolling against the Germans in the 1914-1918 War. They emphasized the need to pause and lie up and listen at frequent intervals so as to catch the enemy whilst he was moving. General Adam came down from the War Office to tell officers what was expected of them. Major Birch ran test exercises for platoons and ended his briefing by telling the platoon commanders that once the battalion was in action life expectancy for a young officer was but five days.

2nd Lieutenant Medley comments: "The attitude of the junior officers to the destined conflict was a sombre one and any piece of advice which might help to increase efficiency was welcomed. The achievements of the Regiment in the past provided an example to be followed. We had complete faith in our seniors; after all they had fought the Germans in the 1914 – 1918 War. We were part of a small professional army which had garrisons spanning the world. Although we felt anxious, because each one of us wondered how we would react under fire, our morale was high. The reservists who had rejoined the Battalion on mobilization were men who had experienced the local wars on the North-West Frontier of India against the hill tribes, as well as in Palestine against the Arabs. They knew what it was like to be shot at and had seen their comrades wounded and killed.

"We were unaware of the misgivings of Lieut General Alan Brooke, the Corps Commander, who, knowing that the 3rd and 4th Infantry Divisions had not completed higher formation training, had had little practice in firing their weapons and that in addition the gunners were still in the process of receiving their new 25pdr guns, requested time for training in Western France."

The battalion received three 1" Anti-tank guns forming a platoon which was placed under the command of 2nd Lieutenant McMillen. They left for France with the mechanical transport and joined up with platoons from the DCLI and RWK to form a brigade anti-tank company and never rejoined the battalion.

There were also the 2" Mortar, with smoke bombs – the high explosive bomb was not available – and the .5" Boyes Anti-tank rifle at each rifle platoon headquarters. First Line "A" echelon vehicles had been provided and there was a set drill for loading extra equipment so that it could be found in the dark should that be necessary.

On 23 September the Battalion marched out of barracks in field service marching order heading for the railway station. The streets were lined with the good citizens of Gravesend who had turned out to wish the Battalion "Godspeed". Families, including the wife of Private "Boy" Dearing of "C" company with a small child in arms, came to the station to say farewell.

The crossing to France on 30 September was rough and there were many very sick soldiers early next morning when the ship docked at Cherbourg. As Lieuenant Harrison stepped off on to the docks he spotted a ship from the merchant line in which he had served before joining the Army . He was about to set off to the ship when Colonel Davenport asked him where he was going. Harrison: "I am going aboard this ship." Colonel: "What for"? Harrison: "To get a case of whisky". Colonel: "What makes you think you will be successful?" Harrison: "The ship belongs to my father".

2

FRANCE – THE PHONEY WAR

Lt Colonel Davenport continues. "On 1 October we arrived at Cherbourg at 0715 hours and disembarked immediately. We were in France. As one who had landed in France in August, 1914, with the old 1st Battalion the atmosphere of our reception was most marked. Gone were the cheering crowds and tremendous enthusiasm of the local inhabitants and in their place we found complete apathy and an intolerant and non-cooperative atmosphere.

"A long and cold wait in the docks area until the early hours of 2 October, when we entrained, did not improve our feelings towards the French railway system, especially as the rolling stock provided was of poor quality and inadequate. A short stop at Caen for breakfast at 0530 hours – dinners at Le Mans and finally to Noyen where we detrained and marched to Malicorne-sur Sarthe. A few pleasant days billeted at Malicorne and off again by train to Carvin (Pas-de-Calais, half-way between Lens and Lille).

"A week or so later by road to the Belgian frontier in the Roubaix area, where we remained over Christmas and the New Year, until we moved to Lille late in January prior to our move to the Saar.

"Those months from October to January were spent mostly digging and preparing defence lines and in some cases filling them up and digging again. It was rather soul destroying work, especially in the Carvin area. Our billets were, to say the least of it, extremely indifferent, and at the start the inhabitants not too helpful. All Companies, helped by the Pioneer Platoon, soon got the billets into first-class order, and the attitude of the men, helped by concert parties, rapidly unfroze the hearts of the local people.

"Immediately we had made ourselves really comfortable and were on the best of terms with everyone from the Maire downwards, a move was ordered to another area and equally bad billets again. The weather

12

did not help. It rained incessantly and filled every trench or hole we dug with water.

"Early in December a representative party of 25 attended an inspection of 2nd Corps by H.M. The King. He made reference to his pleasure in seeing us again after bidding us Godspeed in Aldershot. On another occasion all COs were bidden to meet the Prime Minister (Neville Chamberlain). In the Carvin area the Duke of Gloucester frequently had his sandwich lunch with "A" Company HQ.

"It was aptly described as a 'phoney war' – all the discomforts were present with none of the excitements, but we enjoyed ourselves and kept on working and playing to prevent boredom. Strict orders had been issued to ensure the best possible relations with the French inhabitants and at times it was farcical when we had to beg permission to dig on private land or enter private property to make reconnaissance. Tactical considerations had almost to give way in the event of the owner's refusal.

"Training continued as opportunity offered and as a Battalion we did our best to defeat the static warfare complex which was becoming so prevalent.

"The Belgian frontier gave us a bigger thrill. Our line was intersected at intervals with French concrete pillboxes, which we took over on receipt from a French Battalion whose line we took over (Map 1). Their siting left a great deal to be desired, and here again we felt that tactical considerations had been sacrificed to the wishes of the proprietors of the land. It was a period that would try the enthusiasm of the best trained troops, but the Battalion stuck it magnificently, and their discipline, cheerfulness and conduct always remained highly exemplary.

"Nine days' leave was opened in late November on a small percentage basis. Twice we had our hopes raised that we would be off across the frontier into Belgium, and feverish excitement reigned for a day or two, but both were false alarms and we were bitterly disappointed. They kept us on our toes though.

"The rain turned to snow and ice, and Christmas in the Roubaix area was the coldest – but one of the most cheerful – we have ever known. Companies were very widely dispersed and we seldom got together as a battalion. Finally to our joy, we heard that the 4th Division were to relieve a Guards Brigade in Saar Force, and the Battalion were to be the first Battalion of the Division in the line with 10th Infantry Brigade."

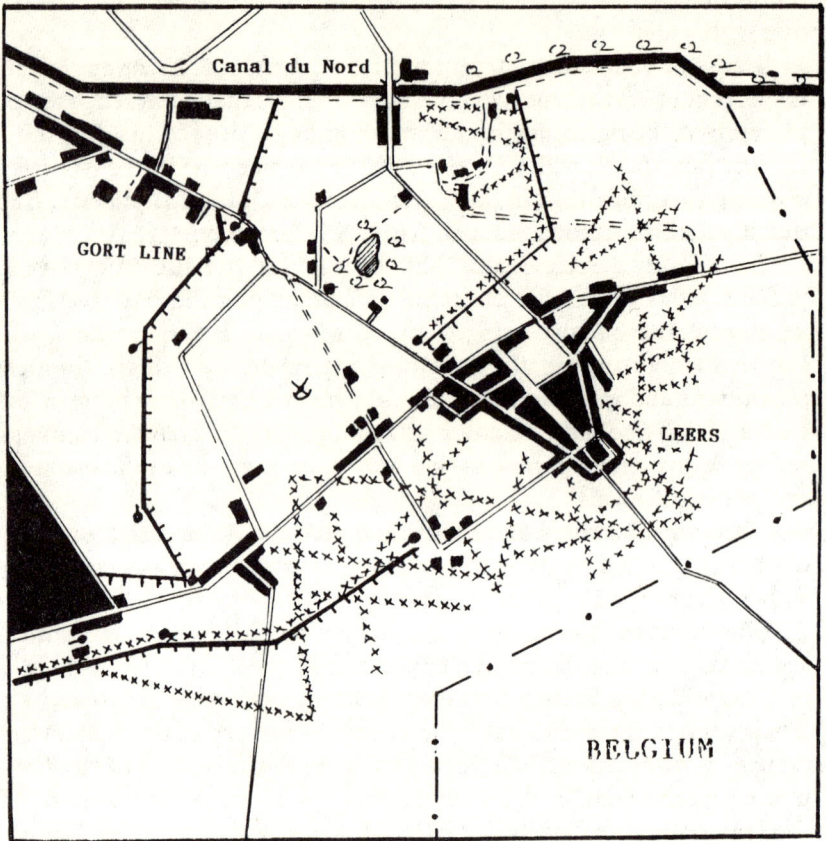

Canal du Nord

GORT LINE

LEERS

BELGIUM

0   1   2 Km

MAP 1

FRENCH FRONTIER – DECEMBER 1939 TO MAY 1940

The story is now taken up by Lieutenant Britten the MTO. The battalion transport which had left Gravesend for embarkation at Newport en route to France was having its own problems. It was remarkable that the transport platoon had no accidents considering that quite a few of the drivers had had no previous experience of driving in convoy and none at all of the treacherous cobblestone French roads.

Lieutenant Britten comments: "The impressed vehicles all presented maintenance problems. The worst offender was the MT stores vehicle, a furniture pantechnicon designed to carry a load of two tons, but upon which some five tons of stores were loaded. Privates Clarke, the driver, and Stead, the storeman, repaired some ten blowouts during the journey to rejoin the Battalion in France. The fact that this vehicle was still in service when the vehicles were destroyed prior to evacuation from France nine months later was due entirely to their determination and ingenuity. Great credit is also due to the fitters who worked miracles on that lorry, including the fitting of an additional axle and strengthening the springs. During the road journey from Nantes to Carvin it rained incessantly and all the motor cyclists, including myself, deplored the fact that the army issue waterproofs, consisting of a canvas jacket and a pair of canvas trousers, were made in one size. This size happened to be suitable for a very short man. All the motor cyclists were of average height upwards so when sitting on a motor cycle there was a gap between the bottom of the jacket and the top of the trousers! Even the boots became waterlogged. There was some solace as shoulders remained dry."

Meanwhile after disembarkation in France the Battalion enjoyed its first troop train ride through the French countryside with all soldiers travelling in railway carriages! The train stopped near Le Mans early the next morning and the soldiers under the guidance of Major Ashby quickly learnt how to brew tea in a dixie by taking hot water from the engine.

The Battalion detrained at midday and marched some five miles to Malicorne-sur-Sarthe where "C" Company found itself billeted in a leaking barn. Fortunately the weather was dry and quite warm. This was the first introduction to wartime billets. There was a liberal issue of straw!

Training continued with route marches to harden the feet, and anti-aircraft drill on the march. This was an activity which must have struck fear in the eyes of any observer. As the platoon marched along a road in threes a whistle would be blown by the platoon commander, followed by the order: "Aircraft left, " to indicate the attacking enemy aircraft was approaching from that direction. On this command every man would turn in the specified direction and place his rifle in his shoulder awaiting the order to fire. On receipt of the fire order the whole platoon would fire at the target in volley, continuing until receiving the order: "Aircraft about, " when the platoon would about turn and proceed to fire at the departing aircraft. This activity amazed the French farmers working in the fields and, suffice to say, the drill was never used in anger!

It was at Malicorne that Private Horne of "C" Company became the first man to be awarded field punishment. He had found his way one evening into an estaminet and settled down for a drink. The room he had entered happened to have been appropriated as the Mess for the local French Regiment. He was asked to leave, which he refused to do and was eventually collected by the regimental police and placed under arrest. Private Horne was a tall, well-built reservist who felt resentful at having had his life disturbed. He performed the rigorous tasks set him for his punishment almost with contempt and returned to duty. Over the next few months he continued to challenge authority and it was evident that restrictions had no effect on stilling his spirit. Captain Whittaker spent much time counselling him and this did seem to help, though the battle of wills continued throughout the winter. Once the battalion was engaged on more serious activities his leadership qualities and preparedness to take charge came to the fore. After Dunkirk he was deservedly promoted to Corporal and subsequently volunteered for the Commandos. He was a splendid man who, once he appreciated that there was serious work to do and that he could contribute, proved to be a natural leader.

The train journey north through France to the British Sector assumed the pattern for all subsequent train journeys. No longer were there coaches for the soldiers who now experienced the form of travel their forbears had known in an earlier conflict: cattle trucks labelled forty men/eight horses with a minimum of straw on the floor. The train set off in the evening and it was nearly twenty four hours later before it arrived at its destination.

On arrival in Carvin Lieutenant Harrison settled the mess into the Railway Hotel, a decision taken with little time to spare, as the Battalion was already arriving in the square. The French family did their best with the rations which were supplemented by the profit accruing from the sale of spirits and cigarettes. Occasionally the door to the hotel would open and soldiers from other units would appear, see the officers sitting around and escape as rapidly as they had arrived. It was only subsequently that it was discovered that the local brothel happened to be next door!

L/Corporal Major of "C" Company has vivid recollections of a "charcuterie" opposite his section billet which sold wonderful pork sandwiches.

The battalion was given a task to dig in on a line of defences and company, platoon and section commanders were allocated their areas. Each morning the troops were ferried out to the positions where the whole day was spent in constructing trenches to the pattern which had evolved from the 1914 – 1918 War. Initially work went well but then the rains came and the 'trench-works' filled up with water. There was nothing to do but to start afresh and construct earthworks above ground level – a timeconsuming task.

The company quartermaster sergeant came out each day with a hot meal and tea carried in containers. The meal was pretty basic, consisting of an all-in stew, some bread and a cup of tea. The all-in stew was more like a thin soup with pieces of carrots, potato, meat and fat. The Cockney sense of humour was shown as the chances of receiving more than two or three pieces of meat were remote. Thus it was that these delicacies were refered to as 'cap badges' and the pieces of fat as 'floaters'.

Lieutenant Britten remembers being admonished by the Commanding Officer whenever he came upon a vehicle which was not properly concealed in the digging area. He also recalls, after receiving a rocket, riding his motor cycle at a fast pace when he suddenly saw the Commanding Officer's car stationary in the middle of a crossroads just behind a company area. He was almost down the vehicle's throat before his bike came to a stop. He then heard a voice from the other side of the car say, "I am afraid this is my fault; I am sorry" and the Duke of Gloucester, wearing the uniform of a Major General walked round the end of the vehicle. He had been leaning through the passenger's window talking to the driver. As the liaison officer, he was paying a visit to see the Battalion positions on the ground.

PSM Kendall, the pioneer platoon commander, gave a classic example of the innate ability of the British soldier for improvisation. He designed and built double tier latrines. These were made in batteries, six up and six down with a smaller version of three up and three down. They were highly successful but the rush to get the vacant seat on the upper level was very understandable. This invention caused much interest on the part of other units and was often copied!

Whilst at Carvin there was a gas scare. A report came through that the Germans had developed a new form of chemical warfare agent and this necessitated all respirators having modifications made to them. Once these modifications had been completed the tense atmosphere which had prevailed amongst those in the know evaporated.

As has been described, the signal platoon equipment consisted of line and hand telephones. Harrison does not remember the signal flags ever being used and remarks that there were no tests while the Battalion was preparing the frontier defences. The Signal Platoon dug with the rest of the Battalion. No collective training took place as any exercises were of such limited time as to preclude the laying of line. Commanders controlled events by maintaining face-to-face contact. This involved a lot of walking on the part of company commanders, but did ensure that soldiers were led by example. The use of radio was still in its infancy and had not reached into the bastions of the infantry. This was not due to any reluctance on their part but to the fact that equipment was as yet not sufficiently light, small and robust to measure up to the standards required. The morse code was used as the means of passing information, and this required special training and was something which Harrison found was by no means his forte. The winter weather had set in and it was extremely cold. Leather jerkins were issued for wear over battle dress, and companies were issued with thickly lined special great coats for the sentries at company headquarters.

The ground froze solid so that it became all but impossible to enlarge the trench system. It was therefore a relief to hand over the positions to another battalion and move to Fives de Lille for a spell of training. Platoons were put through test exercises, and young officers were tested in taking charge of a company for an attack exercise. The Battalion was tested by Brigade in an approach march without transport and having to carry all first line ammunition . There was also much activity in learning to patrol, a task not made any easier as the snow was on the ground and there was a full moon so that it was almost as light as daylight. All that could be said was that it did mean that the drills could be seen by everyone and mistakes put right quickly.

3

FRANCE – THE MAGINOT LINE

One evening all officers, warrant officers and sergeants from the Brigade gathered in a local cinema. Brigadier Barker arrived and told the assembly that the 10th Brigade was to move down to take over positions in front of the Maginot line and that the "Bedfords" would go into the "Ligne de Contact" first. He then gave a detailed briefing on the layout of positions, the location of known German positions and the policy on patrolling. His aim was to ensure that we dominated no-man's-land.

Lt Colonel Davenport continues his story. "We moved to Lille late in January 1940 and spent a week at Fives, and then entrained for Metz and marched from there to the Ligne de Contact. It should be explained that the Maginot Line defences consisted generally of a forward zone called the Ligne de Contact – some 5 to 7 miles in rear came the Ligne de Receuil – a further 7 miles back the Maginot Fortress Line and some 5 miles behind this the Ligne d'Arrêt. The total depth of the defence system was therefore approximately 18 miles, and the main zone was, of course, the Maginot Line (Map 2). This line was permanently manned by French troops, all of whom were specially trained in the ingenious system of the defence and wore the Maginot Line badge "On ne Passe pas". The remaining lines consisted of field works only, and were very thinly held. The field works, in fact, were in a great many cases theoretical ones. The French relied entirely upon the devastating and accurate fire power which could be brought down on any given frontal area from the Maginot fortresses to destroy any hostile attack. The forts in the Maginot Line have often been described, and I think the best description of them is 'an underground battleship'. They were immense in size and fitted with every form of defensive device, but I think I am correct in saying that they could only function one way – to the front.

"A small area of the defence system (less the Maginot Line posi-

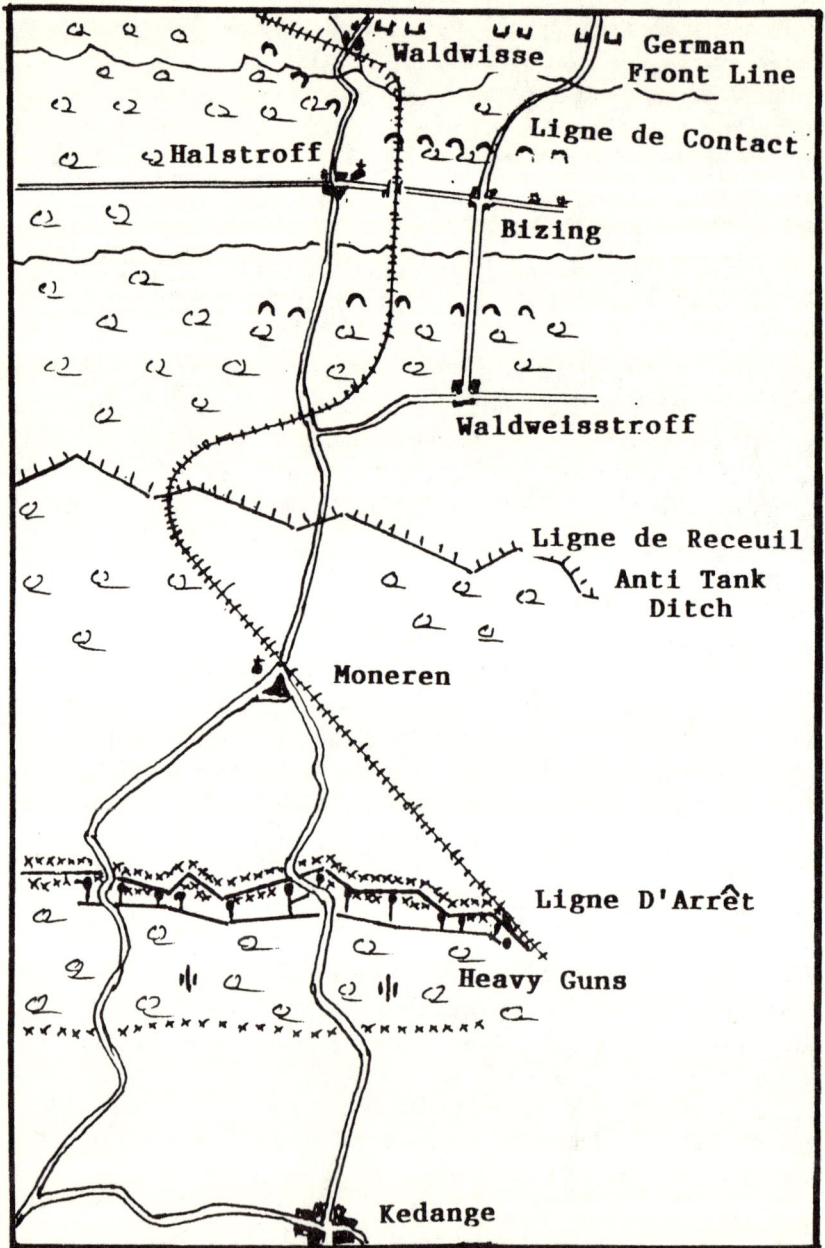

German
Front Line

Waldwisse

Ligne de Contact

Halstroff

Bizing

Waldweisstroff

Ligne de Receuil

Anti Tank
Ditch

Moneren

Ligne D'Arrêt

Heavy Guns

Kedange

MAP 2

SCHEMATIC–MAGINOT LINE DEFENCE LAYOUT

20

tions of that area) had been handed over to the British Expeditionary Force, and at the time that the 4th Division took it over only one Infantry Brigade did duty in the British sector. The tour was to the best of my recollection for 18 days which allowed each battalion in the Brigade approximately one week in each 'Ligne' in rotation. All British troops came directly under the French GOC of their sector of operations, but for administration came under British control. All supporting arms were entirely French (e.g., no British gunners, etc were in the line), and certain French infantry battalions were allotted for special jobs within the British sector. This is a rough and brief picture of the layout as it existed when 10th Infantry Brigade carried out their tour in the line.

"The British Sector was approximately 10 miles south of Merzig. The 2nd Battalion had the honour of first service in the Ligne de Contact, after which it handed over to the next British battalion in the Brigade and withdrew to one of the rearward lines. Each week therefore a general post took place until each battalion had served in each Ligne when the next Brigade in the Division came up and took over.

"The march up from Metz, although carried out in foul weather with extreme cold, was without incident. We had our first sight of completely deserted villages (an uncanny sight which has to be seen to be believed) in which we billeted for the night. I think it was at Moneren – a completely deserted village – on the way up, which had been left in an execrable condition by former troops (we were told they were French Moroccans), that I received orders to return to England on promotion and to report to Sevenoaks. The Brigadier agreed that I could remain until the Battalion had completed its tour of the Ligne de Contact. We made our number on the way up with the French fortress Commander of the Maginot Line and exchanged badges. At a later date a replica of the bronze regimental badge, which is carried on the Regimental L.M.S. Railway engine was sent to the Commandant as a presentation to his fort. I unfortunately forget the name of the fort (Ed. Fort Hackenberg). I trust this badge is still in its original position. We requested the Commandant to go easy on the trigger when we were in front, as he assured us that a special sign or code word would bring down an inferno of fire through which nothing would pass.

"We took over the Ligne de Contact from 3rd Guards Brigade (commanded by Brigadier Beckwith-Smith, who later died as a prisoner in Singapore), who regaled us with stories of punitive raids they had carried out against the Boches, who, they told us, were at first very tame but now seemed to have been relieved by good fighting troops. A story which amused us was a bet which one battalion of Guards made that they would enter Kedange in the face of Boche patrols and ring the church bells. They did ring the bells, to the fury of the local Boche.

"I should explain that for some reasons unknown to ourselves very strict orders had been given by the French High Command that all troops were to confine themselves to patrol work only, and that on no account was any larger operation to be carried out. It was indicated that any active operation against the Boche would be extremely unpopular with the French authorities.

"The line extended nearly 8000 yards – from Le Hartbusch Wood (north of Flastroff)- through Grindorff-Ewig and Bizing-NE of Halstroff, and thence NE to Le Grossenwald Wood to exclusive Waldwisse. A French Infantry Regiment was on either flank, and to ensure liaison, a complete section of French liaison NCOs (interpreters), who accompanied us, formed the flanking sections. Here I must mention M. Bouderon, our own interpreter. He was in ordinary life the maitre d'hôtel of the Dorchester Hotel in London. A splendid fellow in every way, and always of the greatest assistance to us. His English was so perfect that he was often suspect by his own countrymen. These French liaison officers and NCOs all did sterling work.

"All Companies (except HQ Company) were in the line, with A Company on the right and D Company on the left. The Mortar platoon was in position near Halstroff. The Carriers were by order not allowed near the front. Battalion HQ was at Waldweisstroff. Battle HQ with all battle fighting platoons of the Brigade (under command), were at Halstroff.

"Covering such an extended front, it was only possible for companies to hold certain key points, and in many cases these were only platoon or section localities, and were separated from each other in some cases by hundreds of yards. Other than what we could provide with our own limited signal equipment, there was no system of intercommunication provided. We took over these localities from our predecessors, and were appalled by the absence of wire and bulletproof cover. Many localities were extremely badly sited, and it was said that when the French, who originated them, retired in October across the Saar River (some mile or so to our immediate front) that they gave up more ground than was originally intended, and they therefore made the best of it.

"The Ligne de Contact had been made a sort of tourist centre, and parties from the rest of the front had been in the habit of coming to look (through glasses) at the German positions in the hope of seeing their first German. These tourist parties started to arrive again when we took over – often unannounced – and, standing about in the front waving maps and glasses, attracted the attention of German 5" mortar shells, which arrived among our inadequate defence after our visitors had departed. We decided to control these visits, and closed the line and started immediately to put the whole line in order. The Battalion worked magnificently and soon produced an excellent layout of their localities, and put in hours of really hard work under very difficult working and climatic conditions.

"At night everything closed down except for patrols. The combined battle patrols under brigade or battalion control carried out special tasks well ahead of the forward line into German territory, and companies within their own areas sent out patrols on a limited objective, normally up to the Hermsbach stream. It was excellent training and all enjoyed and benefited by it immensely. Many amusing and hair-raising episodes occurred, especially at night when the French units on our flanks started regular *feu de joie* shoots to raise their morale.

"Battalion HQ were virtually locked in at night at Waldweisstroff. On such a broad front German patrols could easily bypass our localities and penetrate through and past Battalion HQ.

"At 1800 hours each night at Battalion HQ a co-ordinating conference, with all local French supporting arms, was held to decide the next day's programme, but as the French ignored any requests, or even frequently failed to do what they had promised, such conferences merely provided us with a great deal of amusement. French 75 mm guns, used either singly or in pairs, would frequently appear quite unannounced along our front and start a shoot and then pack up.

"Conditions were at times not too easy for the British Battalion Commander, but it was essential to retain a sense of humour. I remember full well listening, in an agony of mind and bewilderment, when at night the whole front seemed to flare up with incessant fire, when I knew my patrols were out. There were, as I have said, no communications between companies or with Battalion HQ or flanking units, and I could only hope for the best, especially as one knew that the Boche opposite us were of a more pugnacious turn of mind than had been present before. One hoped, too, that the Maginot Line proper would not imagine the receipt of their eagerly awaited signal and start up too. In the early morning one found that the French had merely decided to let off steam at nothing, or that a French supporting battalion had unconsciously walked about in our rear lines.

"It was all good fun, and we enjoyed it all. As I have already said, it was first-class training for the Battalion, and such a relief after the previous months of boring digging.

"On 26 February (I believe it was), in response to a very direct order from GHQ, I said goodbye to the Battalion. I drove to Metz to catch the train for Paris and England. It was the saddest day that I have ever known. I hated leaving the Battalion and Regiment after 30 years. I handed over to Major J.C.A. Birch (Second in Command), and left behind the finest Battalion in the British Army and the most loyal team that any Battalion Commander could wish for.

"As the GOC 4th Division (Major-General D.G.Johnson) said to me later, 'I loved your Battalion. They were the finest lot of men I have ever known.' He told me that the proudest memory he had was when they marched past him."

The Brigade battle patrols were billeted in a frontier police barracks at Halstroff. Further down the road was the village church which had a splendid spire and this was used as a lookout post by the Intelligence section. The village had not been ransacked to the same degree as Moneren but there were hazards for the unobservant as grenade booby traps had been set up aimed at catching deep penetrating German patrols.

A typical company layout was for each rifle company to have two of its three rifle platoons in the front line with the third platoon in reserve located about eight hundred yards to the rear with the company headquarters. On the "C" Company front there was a gap in the region of six hundred yards between the forward platoons, which were sited on forward slopes or on the forward edges of woods. This meant that all movement by day was under full observation from the enemy trenches. The trenches themselves were also shallow and did not provide adequate protection. It was discovered that some sandbags were filled with old ration paper and broken biscuits! The ground had frozen so hard that it was not possible to deepen them. Each platoon was surrounded by wire and a further belt of wire stretched across the whole front. However the wire was often sited in dead ground and could not be covered by fire from the defensive positions, and in some cases this deficiency applied to the close in wire. Platoons closed up into their defensive perimeters by night and left any movement to patrols. It was still very cold.

Company commanders and their seconds-in-command visited the forward platoons at dawn and at dusk to receive any verbal reports.

The communication link back to company headquarters was by telephone over land line. These lines were very vulnerable as the Germans used to send out two men patrols with the sole purpose of cutting them. These patrols were made up of individuals who had lived in the locality before the war, had most probably made their living by smuggling and knew every fold in the ground. These patrols worked with dogs which alerted the patrol to any signs of movement coming in their direction. The patrol leader had a torch fastened on to a stick and this was used to find the telephone cables which could then be cut. The light of the torch could be seen hundreds of yards off but as soon as an attempt was made to get close the light was switched off and the patrol vanished into the darkness.

The Battalion took the aim of dominating no-man's-land seriously and as many as four or five reconnaissance patrols and listening posts operated in front of the company positions. 2nd Lieutenant Medley went out with Sergeant Everett, Privates Reynolds, Allot and Todd to inspect a wire fence some five hundred yards in front of the company positions. " There was thick cloud and it was a very dark night, quite the opposite of the full moon and snow reflecting the light when training back at Fives de Lille. Two men lost contact before the patrol had even reached the defensive wire. The leading scouts were halted and a search was made to try to locate the missing men, but they could not be found. The patrol moved on without them to carry out its task, arriving at the wire late. Negotiating a wire obstacle in pitch darkness proved to be a major problem. The patrol now moved down the slope towards the stream in the valley, moving with long pauses to lay up and listen before continuing to proceed. At one point, after a long halt the patrol heard a cough and discerned movement. Private Reynolds excitedly got up and pointed in the direction of the noise. As surprise had been lost the patrol moved away as fast as possible. The tasks of checking the wire and depth of the stream were carried out. The patrol then lay up for two hours during which time there were active exchanges of fire on the flanks of the Battalion, a number of Very lights were put up, and there were exchanges of artillery fire with the German artillery replying to the French 75mm guns."

Imagination plays odd tricks and there were two separate incidents which are worthy of the telling. The first was at twilight during the evening stand-to when Private Brace, who had stayed at the rear edge of the wood manned by 14 Platoon, signalled PSM Fidler that he had sighted something. He proceeded to give a detailed description of a German officer whom he said had run down the railway embankment and taken cover in a dugout. Scrambling down the railway embankment the dugout was searched but there was no evidence of any life. It was apparent that there never had been any German officer in the vicinity.

On another occasion during the visiting of sentry posts by night the sentry signalled for quiet. He told the visiting officer that a troop of German cavalry had ridden past in front of his post, dismounted at a tree to his front and then mounted and ridden off. It was quite impractical for any cavalry to have operated in the area with all the many wire obstacles, and inspection of the ground next morning did not reveal any hoof prints or horse manure!

The eyes at night do play tricks and a bush or tree can easily seem to be an enemy patrol. It was therefore important to ensure the tightest control on the firing of weapons and no excuse was accepted for firing at shadows. This attention to fire discipline was an important lesson learnt whilst down the Saar and helped steady nerves for future operations.

The last morning the Battalion was holding the forward line 2nd Lieutenant Pincombe, the Battalion Intelligence Officer, arrived at "C" Company headquarters in the morning and asked for two men to go out with him to patrol along the dead ground some five hundred yards in front of the forward positions to check and see the state of the barbed wire fence running along the bank of a stream. Privates Horne and Allison volunteered for this patrol. As the patrol would be out of sight in dead ground, it was decided to provide a small covering party forward of the defensive wire where it could observe and give covering fire should this be needed. The patrol found that the wire had been cut in several places along the whole front!

Patrols such as these, undertaken by all the companies, gave the Battalion useful experience. Communications, which relied on land line, were exasperating as links to forward platoons were cut every night and signallers spent many hours searching to find where the lines had been cut. The requirement to use morse with the fullerphone link to Battalion Headquarters caused long delays while patrol reports were sent before an acknowledgement came back. In fact the Signals Officer, Lieutenant Harrison, commented that it was often quicker for him to take a message on his motor cycle.

The spell in the line had helped the Battalion to learn to adapt to events. Fire discipline had become an accepted norm and the enemy was real. Lessons were learnt on patrol work, which ran contrary to training doctrine. The practice of having leading scouts was discarded and the patrol leader from now on led from the front.

Organizational changes took place. The strength of the British Expeditionary Force had been built up to some ten infantry divisions over the winter months by the arrival of some six Territorial Army Divisions. In April a redistribution of Regular Army battalions took place and the 1st RWK left the 10th Infantry Brigade to join a Royal West Kent Brigade in the 44th Home Counties Division. They were replaced by the 1/6th Territorial Battalion of the East Surrey Regiment.

The pace of activity seemed to be gathering momentum; there was a sense of purpose in the training and morale was high.

4

THE GERMAN ATTACK, MAY, 1940

The morning of 10 May was different, as sounds could be heard of more air activity than had been usual, but there were no immediate signs of being at war. News of the German attacks was picked up on the radio and the Battalion awaited orders. One result of the new state of affairs was that all movement of individuals away from billets called for the wearing of field equipment with the respirator on the chest, goggles to protect the eyes from any gas sprayed from enemy aircraft, and a gas cape rolled on the shoulder ready to be released and wrapped round the person. Apart from this, there was a dearth of news and the Battalion waited. There was a Bofors anti-aircraft gun sited on a hill only a few yards away from "C" Company officers' mess and 2nd Lieutenant Medley recalls the sight of a stream of tracers rising into the sky like a chain of graceful fireworks on the first occasion the gun fired in anger. The shells appeared to be floating at such a seemingly slow pace it was difficult to appreciate they were set on a deadly mission.

Lt Colonel Birch was on leave in England with Lieutenants Britten and Vosser, and the Battalion Medical Officer, Captain Bell, when he heard the news on his fourth day of leave. He caught a train and boat and made it back to the Battalion by 12 May. The Battalion was still awaiting orders.

Lieutenant Britten had only just arrived home when he heard the news of the German attack on the radio, and an announcement advised those on leave to complete their leave before returning to France. He decided to return at once and found the journey via Southampton slow and tedious, taking five days. During the course of this travelling he met up with some eight soldiers from the Battalion who had also foregone their leave to hasten to rejoin the Battalion.

Two of these soldiers were of Irish stock and bitterly resented the fact that they had only had time to drink a few pints of Guinness during their brief stay in Dublin.

On 13 May an advance party set forth. Meantime at company level orders were received at 2230 hours to assemble at 0400 hours ready to move on 14 May.

Reveille was at 0300 and the Battalion collected itself together awaiting transport. Billets were inspected to ensure they were left in a clean and tidy condition, and as a check that nothing was left behind. A hot meal was provided and haversack rations issued as no one knew when or where the next hot meal would be possible. Then the inevitable, the start time for the move was put back to 0745 and the first period of boredom and inactivity was spiced with the tension of wondering what lay ahead.

When the Battalion eventually set off in convoy with a space of three hundred yards between each vehicle it was a glorious sunny day. On crossing the border into Belgium the countryside seemed to be fresher and the houses benefited from fresh coats of paint. As the vehicles progressed through the villages and towns the local population cheered each vehicle, waving flags and throwing flowers. Often young girls ran alongside and when possible gave the soldiers a kiss. As yet we had not seen any evidence of the misery of war. The route forward passed dumps of ammunition which had been brought forward and was now dispersed under tarpaulins and camouflage nets. There was no sign of any enemy air activity to delay the advance into Belgium. The journey passed through Oudenarde, where soldiers of the 16th Foot, fighting under Marlborough, had earned a Battle Honour and memories were stirred and spirits fired. Next the route passed by Alost, which had been bombed so that the route had to be changed to avoid craters, and Belgian Boy Scouts aided in acting as traffic controllers. It was here that the Battalion saw the first evidence of the mass movement of civilian evacuees with endless streams going in the opposite direction, rich and poor, young and old, in motor cars, in buses, in carts, on bicycles and on foot, literally carrying all their possessions with them, driven from their homes and striving to escape from the invading Germans, an experience remembered by those who had seen it all in 1914, a sobering sight which moved the senses, made more disturbing as there was nothing that could be done to help alleviate the misery, a sight to be seen again and again during the next few weeks and one which left a lasting impression on all who were witness to it.

The convoy drove on and reached a de-bussing point outside

Brussels at Grimberghem at about 1600 hrs. The Battalion formed up and began to march down a hill on either side of a wide street towards Vilvorde. As the Battalion marched downhill the middle of the road was filled with Belgian troops, infantry and horse-drawn artillery coming in the opposite direction! They all looked utterly exhausted and dispirited. Although it was a hot, sunny day all the soldiers wore their greatcoats with a leather belt round the waist from which was slung the ammunition, while they carried their rations and water in a haversack slung round their shoulders. The rifles looked pretty antiquated.

While marching down this road there was the sound of anti-aircraft fire and the noise of approaching aircraft. Looking to the flank it was possible to see three German bombers flying along the line of a canal at low altitude and heading in our direction. A Bofors gun which had opened fire scored a direct hit, tearing the wing off one of the planes. The other two took immediate evasive action and flew out of sight. This first sign of action was very good for morale.

Arriving in Vilvorde the Battalion was met by the advance party guides and shown allocated areas and given instructions to set up Bren guns in an anti-aircraft role to defend key points against air attack. Billets were allotted for soldiers and officers. On dumping his kit at a house listed as a billet 2nd Lieutenant Medley remembers that the good lady burst into tears, remarking that three British officers had already come to her door and that not one had stayed longer than four hours. She was very distraught as her husband had been killed two days before.

The company quartermaster sergeant, CQMS McGann, had set up his cook house and it was not long before the men of "C" Company had a hot meal. Meantime, outside there was the constant sound of aircraft and distant bombing. Hardly had the Battalion had time to settle down than the Commanding Officer called for company commanders to go with him on a reconnaissance of new positions. Major Anstee was to confirm orders for a move to company seconds-in-command. The prediction of the tearful lady had come true. The battalion moved out of Vilvorde in just on four hours.

After receipt of orders it was dark by the time the Battalion set out on the march to Saventhem, where it was to take up a defensive position nicknamed "The Brussels Loop", to protect the flank of the 3rd Division. The march started at 2230 hrs on 14 May arriving in the early hours of 15 May. Again on the march forward the Battalion passed columns of Belgian soldiers marching in the opposite direction. As "C" Company deployed in its nominated location, 14 Platoon had a brush with a Belgian army post which had no idea of the deployment of British forces in its area. Captain Johnson billeted the Company in a modern school shortly before dawn.

Daylight comes early in mid-May and with it came the first signs of air activity. A German aircraft drew anti-aircraft fire, and this was followed by the sounds of fighter aircraft gunfire enough to wake everyone up and cause a rush to see what was happening. High in the sky a plane could be seen with a red glow beside one of its engines. The aircraft began to falter and a dot appeared from the rear section. Shortly a parachute opened and the figure started the long glide to earth. No further figures escaped from the aircraft which spiralled down and crashed in flames in the DCLI battalion area away to our left. Belgian troops throughout the area fired their rifles at the airman; it was almost a Brocks firework display. It was rumoured that the wretched airman had been hit but once in the leg.

As there had been little chance of sleep for the previous twenty-four hours a routine was established to ensure that everyone went off to have four hours sleep on a roster basis, meantime the remainder of the troops were digging trenches. The "B" Echelon transport with the CQMS and the cooks withdrew during daylight under brigade instructions to the rear area leaving a haversack meal to keep the troops fed by day. The company quartermaster sergeants appeared at dusk with a hot meal in hay boxes, stayed with their companies to cook breakfast, which was issued before first light with the haversack ration for the day. The cooks' lorries then beat their retreat, repeating the procedure daily.

It was at Saventhem that the Battalion experienced the first deliberate reconnaissance flight by a Fieseler Storch plane of the German Air Force. It flew over at a height sufficient to ensure it was outside the range of small arms fire, cruising sedately back and forth and spotting the spoil from our earthworks. He was undisturbed in his work and eventually departed back whence he came. When dusk came the sounds of gunfire and heavy machine-gun fire from Louvain, where the forward elements of the British forces were fighting could be heard quite distinctly. The Battalion suffered its first casualty, a soldier of "B" Company was accidentally shot in the hand, PSM Scales cannot remember his name. On 16 May air activity increased but the land battle was still in the Louvain area. CQMS McGann of "C" Company arrived before dusk with his vehicle and the company gathered to collect the hot evening meal. At the critical moment when the issue of food was half complete the sky was filled with eight German bombers flying over at about two thousand feet. Spotting activity, the aircraft began to circle and fire their machine guns. The Company responded by engaging the aircraft with all its Bren guns, firing them over the shoulder of the number two on the gun. Meantime the remainder of the company dispersed at a fast double to platoon positions. It was said that a strike was seen on one aircraft and that an engine was set on fire. Be that as it may a squadron of Spitfires appeared and the sky was soon empty of enemy aircraft! One German aircraft was seen descending towards earth as it flew away with smoke trailing from an engine. The Royal Air Force could not have arrived at a more propitious moment. Recalling this incident Lance Corporal Major comments that "the rations consisted of good old Machonachies".

While this activity was taking place the company commanders were at Battalion Headquarters receiving orders for the next action. Captain Johnson returned to "C" Company and called his Orders Group together. He started his orders in typical manner by saying, "Something dreadful has happened. The British Expeditionary Force is withdrawing according to plan." He then proceeded to explain that the situation was such that forces on our flanks were withdrawing under pressure and that the British had to pull back to conform. The Battalion was to man its positions, as units of the 3rd Infantry Division, who had been fighting at Louvain, were pulling out and would pass through our lines during the night, and we were to pull out ourselves at 0930 the following morning, 17 May. The forward troops made a clean break and the remnants of a company of the Coldstream Guards passed through at about 0200. They halted for a break after passing the checkpoint. They were very tired but discipline was splendid.

Next to the checkpoint was a landmark in the shape of a water tower. (This tower still stands and can be seen from the railway line on the bounds of the International Airport.) Privates Daley and Le Maitre of the Intelligence Section remember being on duty on this tower which was being used as an observation post. Although the height gave extra vision, the ground ahead was very wooded so that vision was somewhat limited.

Dawn came and the Battalion awaited the arrival of the Germans as the cavalry rearguard passed through about 0830. The withdrawal started on time without seeing the enemy. The withdrawal from Louvain had apparently achieved a clean break. In spite of the warlike activities, quite a number of civilians had chosen to remain in their homes rather than join those who were fleeing from the battle zone.

These people were not at all impressed to see the British troops pulling out without even having fired a shot in anger. There was the sight of a little old lady armed with an umbrella soundly belabouring the wretched PSM Wilson of "C" Company around the head accompanied by a stream of voluble invective. This incident was witnessed by a number of soldiers and did nothing to help morale.

The route led down to the canal which flows through the outskirts of Brussels where there were pontoon bridges to allow the troops to cross over to the friendly forces' side. Royal Engineers were blowing up any bridges and blowing holes in all craft which could assist the enemy in crossing the water obstacle. There were soldiers digging in and the Battalion now passed through and continued its march to the rear. Initially the route passed through some suburbs; then it began to climb steeply up a wide road through a landscaped park. The scene was incredible: row upon row of marching soldiers as far as the eye could see, and, in between the marching columns, guns towed by their "Quads" and light tanks and reconnaissance vehicles. As Lt Colonel Birch recalls, the lines of vehicles moving slowly up this hill were double-banked. This great mass coming up the hill out of Brussels was a dream target: luckily no enemy aircraft put in an appearance. Eventually, after a march of some sixteen miles, the Battalion dispersed in a park at Wemel, where feet were inspected, a hot meal was provided and companies received their first, and last, issue of Belgian Francs. As PSM Scales commented, "There were no shops or stores open to spend the money in". During this spell of quiet three Messerschmitt fighter planes flew over just above the treetops, causing an unseemly dive for cover into the nearest ditch. By the time all administrative aspects had been completed it was well into the evening and company commanders had gone off to receive further orders. In effect this meant a night march starting at 2200. 2nd Lieutenant Pincombe noted that the orders for this withdrawal were received too late for the Battalion to set off at the correct time. Initially, as Colonel Birch stated in his report on the actions of the Battalion, the troops had to march along the uneven sides of minor tracks as the road space was taken up by a congestion of vehicles all using the same route. This tortuous progression lasted for some two hours before the routes separated and it was possible for the infantry to march in threes along good roads. This was as well as tiredness was catching up and quite a few individuals were all but walking in their sleep. The march continued through the night and as dawn broke the columns broke up and dispersed along each side of the road. Eventually at about 0600 the

Battalion left the hard road and approached a village with a church whose tall spire could be seen across the fields. It was named Maal and was different from other villages as there were thick hedgerows.

On arrival, companies dispersed to billets and looked forward to a rest. Each man really knew what it felt like to be totally exhausted after having marched thirty three miles in under twenty one hours. The Battalion had arrived tired but marching in step each man by his example encouraging the remainder. Not one man fell out.

Company Commanders had been called to go to an Orders Group. Having found billets for the men of "C" Company Medley relaxed under a duvet and revelled in the chance of removing his boots. After about 30 minutes Private Woor woke him to say that the Battalion had to stand to as German tanks were approaching. Dressing quickly, he checked that "C" Company was deployed and that each platoon knew its tasks, subsequently checking on the tie-in with flank companies. Eventually after an hour the order came to stand down and fall in ready to march on. Fortunately the march was but a mile or so as transport was parked waiting for the Battalion to embus at a village named Erpe. The sight of those vehicles was so very welcome, and the order to embus was received with a feeling of relief and deep gratitude.

5

AVELGHEM ON THE ESCAUT
18 – 22 MAY

The Battalion embussed at Erpe at about 1030 and the convoy moved off passing through Oudenarde where fresh troops could be seen digging trenches to defend the river/canal obstacle. It was a hot sunny day and the convoy eventually drew up with the vehicles dispersed at intervals along a road in the vicinity of Knock. Time passed and no orders came down as to what to do. More columns of vehicles arrived facing the opposite direction and military police appeared on their motor cycles but still no orders. Eventually after a halt of nearly two hours the convoy began to move once more arriving at dusk at Avelghem. What was not known at the time was that troops of the 4th Infantry Division had been sent to the assembly area of the 44th Infantry Division, a mess-up that took time to sort out. At Avelghem "C" Company was billeted in the local cinema and after a hot meal the troops settled down to a refreshing six hours of sleep, much needed after the events of the previous forty-eight hours. Orders had been received and companies marched out at 0600 to deploy to their allocated defensive positions. The companies had been given a cooked breakfast and haversack rations and water bottles had been filled. There were still quite a number of the civilian population around and they began to evacuate when they realized their town was to be in the front line.

Avelghem and the Escaut Canal were overlooked on the far bank, the enemy side, by a high feature named Mont d'Eclus, and this feature dominated the Battalion frontage (Map 3). There was also a railway and a road bridge crossing the canal and neither of these had been blown up. The Battalion therefore was deployed with three rifle companies forward of the canal on Mont d'Eclus and "C" Company was tasked to defend the bridgehead at Escanaffles covering the road

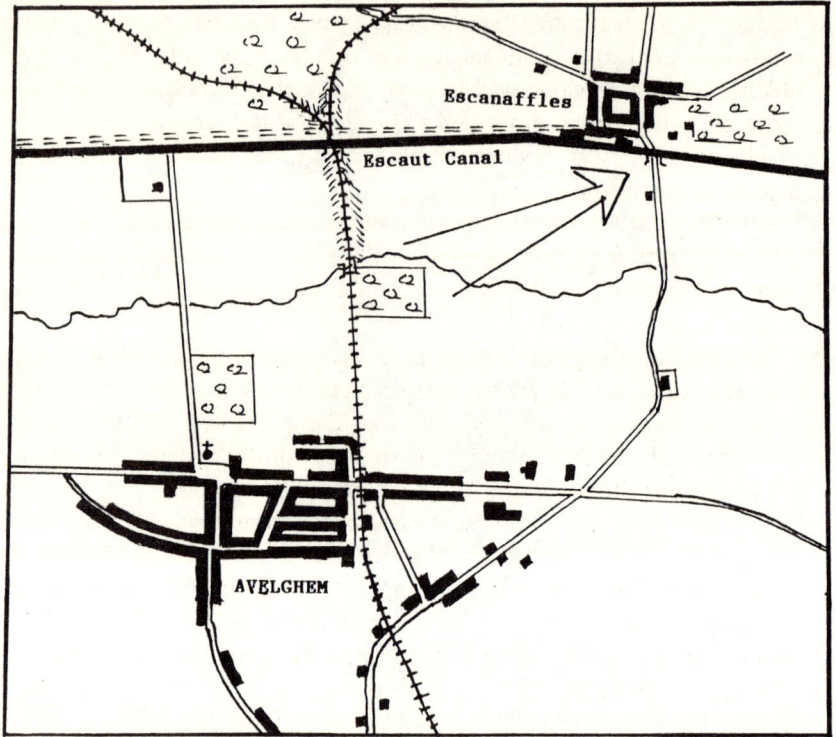

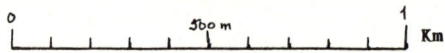

Escanaffles

Escaut Canal

AVELGHEM

0   500 m   1
|_____|_____| Km

MAP 3

AVELGHEM ON THE ESCAUT – MAY 1940

bridge. "C" Company headquarters was established in a small estaminet near the road bridge on the friendly side of the canal obstacle where it was possible to overlook the demolition party and blow the bridge in an emergency should that be necessary.

The weather was becoming hotter and the task of constructing defensive positions was exhausting and thirsty work. An inhabitant of Escanaffles was very irate because holes had been knocked into the wall of his house to provide fields of fire down a street. Preparations went well and by the afternoon some strong positions had been made ready.

During the afternoon a loud bang indicated that the railway bridge over the canal had been blown up. Meantime the Royal Engineers were continuing to lay charges and complete the wiring for the demolition on the road bridge, which was soundly constructed of concrete. During the afternoon new orders came in which required the urgent withdrawal of the three forward rifle companies, "A", "B", and "D" through "C" Company to take up defensive positions to deny the crossing of the Escaut to the Germans. "C" Company was to hold its bridgehead position until all troops had passed through. Major Anstee, the Battalion second-in-command, came forward to pass on these orders and informed "C" Company that German tanks had been reported in Renaix ten kilometres away an hour earlier. He gave orders that the road bridge was not to be allowed to fall into enemy hands and had to be blown even if our troops were still on the enemy side of the obstacle. The atmosphere was strained whilst "C" Company held its positions and waited for the other companies to pass through. "A" and "B" appeared quite soon and crossed over, but there was no sign of "D" Company. Eventually after a long pause when the situation was becoming very tense "D" Company appeared marching towards the bridgehead perimeter. Once they were passed through, "C" Company thinned out and crossed over itself. Medley was standing beside the trench where the sapper sergeant was waiting for the command to fire the charges to blow the bridge. "Eventually the last section under the command of Lance Corporal Major came doubling over the bridge followed at a distance by the head of a column of refugees. The sapper sergeant called upon the civilians to go back but they paid no heed. He then told the troops to run flat out and he would press the plunger in a minute. Lance Corporal Major and his Section then completed an Olympic 100 metre dash when there was a deafening roar as one and a half tons of explosive charge erupted and bits and pieces of bridge were thrown high into the sky. Large chunks of debris fell down beside the estaminet which was some two hundred yards away from the blown bridge! The owner had decided to leave during the day and had all but emptied the beer barrels. However, a pint was drawn by the CSM and issued to those around. Regrettably the innkeeper had left his dog tethered in the yard and the animal was going wild in the heat and trying to bite anyone who went to unleash it. It was decided that the kindest thing to do was to shoot the animal and this was done. Cows which had been left to roam the fields were lowing and demanding to be milked".

Private Doug Ansell of "C" Company was a milkman by profession and Lance Corporal Major states that he always helped augment rations by taking two or three mess tins of milk whenever cows were around. There was no doubt that the cows were happy to be relieved.

The Battalion now deployed along the line of the Escaut with "B" on the right, "D" centre, "A" left and "C" in reserve, having spent an abortive day preparing positions which were never used.

Having completed its task of ensuring that the road bridge was blown, "C" Company marched back into the outskirts of Avelghem and found the CQMS with his cooks set up in the railway station. Everyone was fed and platoons deployed to their new positions. Captain Johnson then called an orders group. Those involved sat in a small room with the windows covered to ensure no light was evident outside and with light provided by an old oil lamp. The atmosphere was hot and humid and after the strenuous activities of the day heads began to nod and individuals had great difficulty in staying awake in spite of urgent reminders. Platoon commanders acknowledged orders but vehemently denied having received them the next morning.

Lance Corporal Major recounts that, having taken up positions near the railway station, his section procured three chickens, and acquiring carrots and onions brewed up a tantalizing stew in a lovely copper. The order then came to move before the stew could be enjoyed.

"B" Company found that the trenches dug on the friendly side of the Escaut were overlooked from some industrial buildings at Escanaffles on the enemy side and suffered their first casualties from sniper fire. Initially at daybreak PSM Scales recalls seeing a marching column of Germans approach the canal bank. They were engaged by rifle and Bren fire suffering heavy casualties. At about 1100 12 platoon came under heavy mortar fire and PSM Warren was severely wounded. CSM Harrison distinguished himself in helping to evacuate Warren. PSM Scales fired Very light signals to call down our own artillery fire and it was not long before shells were falling in Escanaffles and one shell passed through a tall chimney stack. An anti-tank gun fired two rounds at a half track heading for the blown bridge, stopping it in its tracks.

On rejoining the Battalion from leave, Lieutenant Britten was ordered to take over the transport platoon. This was late at night and in the small hours of the next day he was told to send a vehicle forward to collect some bodies. He decided to accompany the vehicle and, on arrival at "B" Company headquarters, collected two bodies one of whom was one of the Irishmen who had rejoined the Company a few hours earlier, a Private Corcoran.

During the morning a Lysander reconnaissance aircraft flew low over the Battalion positions and it was possible to see the pilot and observer clearly. What was not appreciated at the time was that in all probability the aircraft had been captured by the Germans and they were plotting our positions. This was evident during the course of the day when enemy artillery fire was directed against our lines of communication and on roadways running through Avelghem.

The forward positions on the Escaut were all overlooked by the enemy and sniper fire was pinning down troops. A decision was made that the forward line would withdraw to a secondary obstacle some six hundred yards back from the canal during the night. The reserve battalion of the brigade, the 1/6th East Surreys, came up and helped dig trenches for the forward companies to fall back to. The move was carried out without incident and all troops were in their new positions before morning stand-to on 21 May. It was not long before the Germans discovered what had happened and they quickly began to filter men over the blown bridge to form a bridgehead which caused an immediate reaction from the Commanding Officer and Brigadier. It was decided to organize a counter-attack as soon as practicable to evict the enemy and secure the position. This task would be undertaken by a platoon of "C" Company with a second platoon providing covering fire, and ready to assist if required. 2nd Lieutenant Muirhead and 15 platoon were selected with fire support being provide by PSM Wilson and 13 platoon.

Muirhead was called to company headquarters to receive orders from Captain Johnson who had an Artillery Forward Observation Officer helping to agree the artillery fire support. The Commanding Officer and the Brigade Commander sat in and listened to the plan. The attack was to start at 1200 and approach the bridge from a flank. 13 platoon was to give small arms fire support covering the flank exposed to the enemy. Artillery fire would start at 1200 with 25 pounder guns firing onto the canal bank and around the bridge. Twelve minutes was allowed for the assaulting troops to arrive on their objective when the artillery would lift to fire onto Escanaffles and would be assisted by 60 pounder medium guns.

Once the plan was agreed Muirhead set off to brief his platoon. There was a feeling of despondency in the air as so far the battalion had not seemed to have had much success and Sergeant Theobald commented that was the last that would be seen of 15 platoon.

The guns fired bang on time and the ground around the target area erupted with explosions, but as yet the attacking troops could not be seen as they were hidden from view. After some eight minutes the attacking platoon came into view with the soldiers advancing steadily, rifles and bayonets across their chests and with the leading sections widely deployed. It was a splendid sight and, as far as could be seen, there were no gaps in the lines. Meantime the artillery was pounding the objective and 13 platoon was firing on to the enemy bank of the canal with their Brens. Bang on time as the assault charged in the guns lifted and the din of explosions increased as the 60 pounders joined in and hurled their shells against the enemy for a further four minutes, giving 15 platoon time to deploy and firm up on its objective. After sixteen minutes the guns stopped firing and there was a sudden silence. The only indication of what had gone before was the pall of smoke rising around the village of Escanaffles. The owner of the property who had complained two days earlier about having holes knocked in his walls had much more reason for complaint.

Captain Johnson, who had gone forward to observe the assault, came back to company headquarters and reported, that as far as he could see, the objective had been taken without suffering any casualties. 13 platoon and 2nd Lieutenant LaFontaine of "D" Company, who had watched the attack going in, stated that the enemy evacuated the position as soon as the artillery fire started to come down and crossed back to their side of the canal. The success of this small assault was extremely good for the morale of the Battalion and everyone now felt that they had the edge on the Germans.

Plans were made to take rations up to 15 Platoon after dark and Medley was given this task with a party of five soldiers. "The food was in bulky containers which had to be carried on the back and which inhibited action on the part of the individual carrying it. Accordingly I asked for an extra four men to act as escort; this request was refused.

"After dark the resupply party set forth, checking in at B Company headquarters, meeting Captain Onslow and Lieutenant Lofts and advising them of the route being taken through their forward lines. On the way forward the party met a group of engineers at a crossing over a dyke, who were preparing a charge to blow a small bridge. Arriving in the vicinity of 15 Platoon position, the party halted and having set them in a defensive posture, I set out with Private Woor to locate 2nd Lieutenant Muirhead. We lay down and observed the position as two figures had been seen moving in the location where the platoon should have been. A figure approached – silence – it was Muirhead, so the rest of the food party were called forward. Just then there was a blinding light and a large explosion. It was the bridge being blown by the Engineers. There had not been time to warn all the men of 15 Platoon of this activity so the event was a total surprise. There was the sound of movement and a section of men were seen charging towards platoon headquarters in extended line. Muirhead ordered everyone to stand-to and be prepared to use bayonets. Fortunately, on being challenged the unknown force proved to be Corporal Edwards and his section, who, not knowing of the demolition, led his section at the double towards platoon headquarters. The platoon was fed and Muirhead reported on the success of the attack and that he was now firmly established to prevent any further attempt by the Germans to force a crossing at that point. There had been no further attempts by the Germans to counter attack. The platoon was fed and my party returned to company headquarters without further incident, arriving back at about 0130 hrs."

It was just about the time that 15 Platoon was receiving orders for its attack that Captain Whittaker rejoined "C" company and reassumed the appointment of second in command.

It was now 22 May and shelling activity built up during the day. Battalion headquarters was heavily shelled but suffered no casualties. In spite of the observation provided by Mont d'Eclus the Germans sent up an observation balloon beyond the range of our anti-tank guns. There was sporadic artillery fire during the morning and sounds of heavy automatic fire away to the right flank. The shelling increased in intensity during the afternoon and "A" company on the left was subjected to a creeping barrage which ranged back and forth for some four hours. A direct hit on one trench had killed Medway, who had distinguished himself earlier by taking a reconnaissance patrol on to the enemy side of the Escaut. The Germans had established a foothold across the Escaut further to the left of the Battalion and 13 Platoon under PSM Wilson was sent to strengthen "A" Company. The shelling continued and was now falling in the reserve areas.

Company commanders were called to attend an Orders Group, and the Battalion was directed to withdraw after dark, beginning the move at 2200 hrs.

The signal platoon had laid its full complement of line from battalion headquarters to the rifle companies. The task of reeling in took three hours. There was no time available when the order to withdraw was given and the complete stock of line was abandoned on the Escaut.

Private Rayner of "C" Company had acquired a goat which helped to supplement the milk ration. He was determined not to leave the animal for the benefit of the Germans; accordingly he set off on the march leading the goat on a rope. Arriving at a checkpoint Capt Johnson ordered the goat to be released. The Brigadier, who as was his wont, was at the checkpoint seeing his soldiers through and offering words of encouragement, retrieved the situation by having the goat lifted in the back of his vehicle.

The long march back became more exhausting as the Battalion was following the East Surrey territorial battalion who were marching at a very slow pace with constant breaks. As time progressed the pace became slower and slower. A shot rang out and it transpired that one of their soldiers had shot himself in sheer desperation. The Bosyut Canal was crossed by the last men of "C" Company, who were the rearguard at 0235 hrs and the bridge was blown. Eventually the route left cross-country tracks and followed metalled roads and the pace improved. The Belgian – French frontier was crossed at about 0700 hrs and companies found guides awaiting to lead them to company areas. The CQMS's were to hand with a very welcome hot meal.

6

THE FRENCH FRONTIER –
NEUVILLE EN TERRAIN 23/27 MAY

The Battalion was now back on the French frontier, but not in the locations which it had spent so much time preparing during the long winter months. It was an excellent position with two anti-tank ditches and a number of new pill boxes. (Map 4). A major road crossed the frontier in the middle of the battalion frontage. To add to the difficulties "A" Company had been allocated an area which housed a large hospital right in the front line and time was spent in knocking off the tiles with the international red cross markings painted on them. 2nd Lieutenant Whitworth recalls that civilian patients were being evacuated as the company started to prepare their defences around the hospital. The Pioneer Platoon assisted in helping remove the tiles from the roof and making loopholes in the walls. It was a three or four storey building and I thought our portly Pioneer Sergeant looked somewhat precarious on the roof. No sooner were the crosses removed than the buildings came under fire from enemy mortars and Private Fuller was wounded."

PSM Scales of "B" Company found that there was an abandoned NAAFI truck close by his platoon position with plenty of cigarettes and other sundries, also an abandoned stores vehicle with clothing and footwear. His men acquired clean clothing and a jar of rum.

Initially "C" Company was in close reserve and dug positions along the side of a rifle range. Digging continued throughout the day. In the afternoon a Gipsy Moth airplane carrying the colours of the Belgian Air Force flew overhead at less than 100ft. As the Belgian Army was on our flank this activity did not raise any doubts, though it is most probable that it was being used by the Germans. The Carrier platoon under Lieutenant L.C. Young deployed forward of the Battalion on a ridge named Risquons Tout covering the occupation of the new

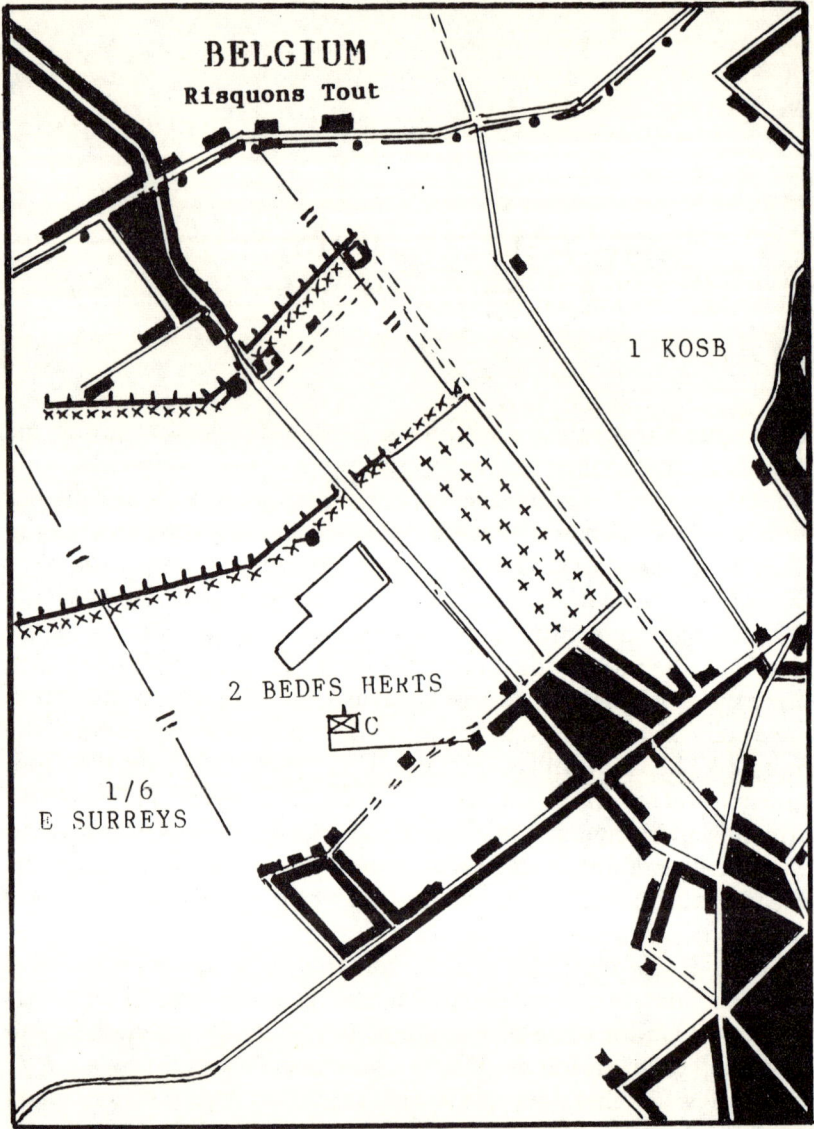

MAP 4

FRENCH FRONTIER NEAR RISQUONS TOUT 23–27 MAY 1940

positions. In the late afternoon German cyclists made contact and then withdrew. That night Lance Corporal Major remembers settling down to sleep in a convent, only to be woken up to go out on patrol as protection to a wiring party.

The Battalion continued to dig in on 24 May and sent out a number of daylight patrols. Several enemy were killed and general movement of the enemy was reported heading Northwards. One of these patrols was led by Muirhead with two sections of 15 Platoon who stayed out for about three hours. They suffered one casualty, Corporal Edwards, who was wounded in the leg.

Further patrols were sent out that night. One patrol of these was led by 2nd Lieutenant Medley with Corporal Taylor and four men. Initially just after having passed through the forward positions it was desperately noisy as there was so much glass and debris strewn about as a result of the demolition work; it was impossible to find a clear area underfoot. "Our presence could hardly have been announced more boldly, and our task was made that much more difficult as an enemy aircraft was dropping parachute flares. We continued the patrol and identified an enemy position which was reported upon return to our own lines."

On 25 May enemy activity increased in the shape of continuous shelling, apart from that there was little enemy ground activity. A mortar bomb landed alongside Captain Johnson as he was standing at a street corner near 15 platoon billet but he survived unscathed. A shell holed the roof of the house being used as "C" Company headquarters. In spite of this activity civilians were still moving around and it is likely that there were fifth columnists among them indicating positions to the enemy.

A large enemy patrol was encountered by a fighting patrol led by Captain Peters, who had been joined by 2nd Lieutenant P. Young, the battalion liaison officer, and a spirited action took place. Young received a minor wound in the foot. A little later the Intelligence Officer 2nd Lieutenant Pincombe with three men made further contact with the enemy. As a result of these actions Pincombe was given the immediate award of the Military Cross. Apart from these skirmishes the enemy was not at the time in direct contact with the Battalion. News was received that the Belgian Army was withdrawing to the north which created a possibility of opening up a gap in the defences on the left.

On 26 May the radio announced that the Germans were fighting around Boulogne, and instructions came through that ammunition and food was to be rationed. The Battalion line was adjusted to help the KOSB on the right. Artillery fire could be heard to the rear and the situation on the left was becoming grave as the Belgian Army was being driven back towards Menin. There was increased enemy artillery fire and PSM Reedman of "D" Company was killed whilst visiting his sections.

On 27 May the shellfire was more pronounced and "C" Company positions were overlooked from high ground which had been captured by the Germans. Carriers were sent to reinforce the line at Risquons-Tout inflicting casualties on the enemy before one carrier was hit by anti-tank gunfire and the driver was killed. Privates Waring and Roberts leaped out and continued to fight until killed.

Information was received that the Belgian Army had capitulated and orders came for 10th Infantry Brigade to move and come under command of the 5th Infantry Division which was fighting somewhere near Ypres. This order involved withdrawing troops who were not in contact and leaving a composite force under Major Ashby, who was now battalion second in command. Major Anstee had been sent to take over command of the 5th Northamptons whose Commanding Officer had been killed. This composite force comprised two platoons from "A" under Captain Lewis, two platoons from "B" under Captain Onslow and one platoon of "D" Company under 2nd Lieutenant LaFontaine. 2nd Lieutenant Pincombe stayed as staff officer, as well as Captain Bell the Medical Officer. The remainder of the Battalion pulled out of their positions at 1430 hrs and embussed for a move along congested roads through Armentières, Neippe, Neuve Eglise and thence towards Ypres.

As the convoy progressed dusk was beginning to fall. There was continuous shellfire falling in the fields on all sides and as it grew darker the flashes of the explosions grew brighter showing up vividly in the half-light. The battalion party debussed near to Wytschaete and awaited orders.

Meantime the rest of the Battalion on the French frontier came under heavy shellfire starting at 1600 hrs. Force headquarters was severely shelled and during this incident 10 Platoon of "B" Company suffered heavy casualties losing 2nd Lieutenant Bousefield the platoon commander. Half of Burgoyne Farm was demolished. PSM Scales left his platoon, went over and resited the Brens in the rubble and then commanded both platoons and beat off a fierce enemy attack, inflicting heavy casualties on the enemy. The Germans used high velocity anti-tank shells which pierced the steel shutters of the pill boxes. A lance corporal of "A" Company was hit in this manner, and, although mortally wounded, continued firing until he collapsed. Eventually the Bedfords Force was relieved by the Coldstream Guards at 2400 hrs and moved to rejoin the rest of the battalion which was now deploying on Messines Ridge in front of Wytschaete.

7

WYTSCHAETE – MESSINES RIDGE
27–29 MAY

It was fully dark by the time Captain Johnson returned to find "C" Company resting in its assembly area at Wytschaete. The Company was to deploy along the line of the Ypres-Warnetan road with all three platoons forward holding the line. Dispositions were PSM Wilson and 13 Platoon on the Left, 2nd Lieutenant Lockhart and 14 Platoon Centre, and 2nd Lieutenant Muirhead and 15 Platoon on the Right on a frontage of some fifteen hundred yards. (Map 5). The company was to relieve elements of the Royal Irish Fusiliers and the Cameronians who had returned from fighting the Germans on Vimy Ridge. The Royal Irish Fusiliers were reduced to five officers and 127 men.

There were two routes leading out of Wytschaete and 13 and 14 Platoons headed off into the night down one, whilst 15 Platoon and company headquarters went down the other. Very lights were going up all along the front and there was continuous artillery fire exploding alongside the roads from German medium guns. "C" Company headquarters found a position some four hundred yards to the rear of 15 Platoon on a reverse slope and immediately began to dig in. Captain Johnson went off to visit the platoons and returned to say all platoons had established themselves and were digging in hard. 15 Platoon, hearing sounds of movement to their front and receiving no response to their challenge, opened fire. Regrettably the target was a friendly fighting patrol belonging to the relieved unit. Its location and activity had not been disclosed on hand over of responsibilities, an indication of the exhausted state everyone was in. Casualties were

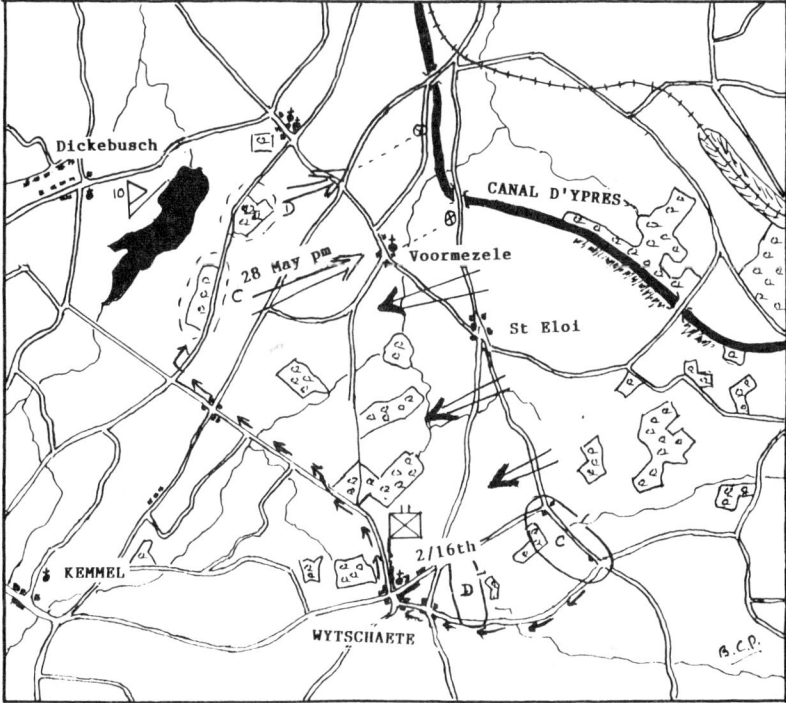

SCALE:- 1" = .623 miles

MAP 5

WYTSCHAETE AND MESSINES RIDGE 27/28 MAY 1940

inflicted before identification was established. It continued to be an active night with continuous shelling.

An initial probing attack came in soon after dawn but this was repulsed. The carrier platoon under Lieutenant Young came to help cover the flanks of the company which was now in an exposed position as the troops on the left had fallen back. St Eloi was in the hands of the Germans who were pressing the DCLI hard. There was a lot of British artillery available and this was responding to the heavy fire being directed at the forward positions, approach routes and Wytschaete itself. Columns of earth were erupting some fifteen feet into the air and this harassing fire was continuous. At about 1100 hrs the forward platoons were blasted but no attack developed. A further bombardment followed at 1300 hrs with an assault by enemy infantry which was held off. Captain Johnson returned to "C" Company headquarters after making a round of the platoons to say that PSM Wilson was missing, believed wounded, and that a direct hit by a shell on a 14 platoon trench had killed Lockhart and three men. Sergeant Everett had also been wounded. A message was sent advising that the company position could not be held much longer as ammunition was running short.

The shelling continued and the farm animals grazing in the fields caught the brunt of this fire. The lowing of cows heavy with milk and terrified at the noise of exploding shells was added to the sounds of battle. Shells landed close to "C" Company headquarters but the only casualty was a cow grazing fifteen yards away.

At about 1500 hrs the order arrived for "C" Company to withdraw and Medley was sent to pass on these orders to 13 and 14 Platoons on the left. "Passing through a German 1914-1918 war cemetery I came under machine-gun fire and dived for cover over a wire fence into a ditch. Working my way forward I found a number of Royal Inniskillings lying in the open facing towards the front and, continuing forward, found the two platoons. The order to pull out was given and a rendezvous some two hundred yards to the rear was indicated. Number 2 Section under Corporal Pitchers set off and was not seen again having missed the rendezvous. All the remainder managed to extricate themselves and came back in extremely good order, especially as quite apart from the bombardment, small arms fire and enemy attacks it had been a cold wet day more than enough to sap anyone's morale.

"The Company marched back through Wytschaete in pouring rain and eventually deployed in a wood where the noise of shrapnel in the branches of the trees was particularly unnerving. Orders came through for the battalion to move forward and seize positions as a firm base from which to patrol and check whether the Germans had effected crossings over the Ypres canal."

Dusk was settling as the Company set forth and Capt Whittaker gave the command of 13 Platoon to Medley and told him to lead the Company forward. A patrol of the East Surrey Regiment was meant to be in Voormezele but as the leading men of "C" Company entered the village all was quiet, the windows of the houses were shuttered and lying beside the road were five very dead British soldiers. The company quickly dispersed to take up defensive positions. It was now almost fully dark. Just at that moment a doorway was opened slowly in a house across the road and a priest came out to inform Captain Whittaker that he had a wounded soldier inside. On inspection he proved to be the officer who had been in charge of the patrol which had been ambushed by the Germans. There was little that could be done to help as there were no stretcher bearers with the Company. The Company settled down into positions which defended the village from all directions. After dark Very lights were being fired by the Germans to indicate their positions to their artillery and it became evident that "C" Company was located behind the German lines. "D" Company meanwhile, which had been sent off to perform a similar task on the left of "C" Company had met with enemy fire and had not advanced so far. Unbeknown to these two companies the orders for these movements had been cancelled with an order to pull out towards Einhoek but they had been committed to the advance before the countermand was received. "D" Company was located and given the new orders which it complied with. However it missed the checkpoint and did not rejoin the battalion again in Belgium.

It took time for Captain Johnson and Sergeant Calcutt of the Intelligence section to locate "C" Company who were ordered to quickly assemble and march off down the road as fast as possible. This gave little time to gather in the dispersed soldiers. Before this happened a section of 14 Platoon had a brush with an enemy patrol. Also, at some time during the night, friendly artillery started to shell the village. It was almost dawn as "C" Company set off at a forced march which was kept up without a halt for two hours. The route led along a road strewn with abandoned vehicles, but in spite of the close proximity of the enemy at Voormezele the Company had managed to make a clean break.

At about 1000 hrs the Company had caught up with the rest of the

Battalion and took a ten-minute break by the side of the road.

The Battalion deployed into an assembly area where it was fed and issued with rations, a most welcome meal as it was the first cooked meal in twenty-eight hours. It was also directed to dispose of all baggage other than that which could be carried. There was a slimy green pond nearby and much kit was thrown therein. Other kit was set on fire but this caused smoke to rise and the fires were quickly put out. Close by two sixty pounder medium guns were firing off their rounds. All documents other than the soldiers' conduct sheets were burnt. Having emptied the company box CSM Goodall of "C" Company detailed two soldiers to collect stones, which were placed in the box. The CSM then wrote a note which he locked inside which said "I hope you have carried this for miles you bastards." Numbers were now reduced so that somehow the troops were able to scramble onto the first line transport which headed for Furnes.

8

THE DUNKIRK PERIMETER

Major Ashby was leading the convoy, as the Colonel and Company Commanders had gone forward to the next location. At one crossroads a military policeman diverted the convoy and after a while the route became clear of traffic and signs of life. As it appeared that the direction was heading towards the enemy Major Ashby turned the convoy round and headed back to the crossroads once more. There was no sign of the "Bogus" military policeman. The convoy now passed lines of marching troops among them Lance Corporal White who had been posted from "C" Company to the Pioneers in December.

As the convoy passed through the Belgian countryside there was the sight of white sheets being displayed at every window of the houses alongside the route. Belgium was out of the war. Far from depressing the Battalion this action had the opposite effect. It was now known that the responsibility was ours alone and this had a tonic effect on morale.

At Furnes the order was given to abandon vehicles before crossing the bridges over the canal. The vehicles were driven into a field to join row upon row of vehicles, all of which had been abandoned. Orders were given to wreck the vehicles as much as possible. Radiators were drained and the engines left running, tyres were slashed and bullets fired into the cylinder heads. Sandbags were filled with tinned food from an abandoned NAAFI van even though this meant increasing the load to be carried. Lieutenant Britten, the Transport Officer, confirms that the vehicles had water poured over the cylinder blocks and that sledge hammers were used with a will. Anything which might have been of use to the Germans was smashed. He remembers a signaller smashing his radio set with tears running down his face and swearing freely with every blow. He explained that he was so upset because he had been fined £5 earlier that month towards the cost of repair after he had been adjudged guilty of causing damage by neglect.

After completing this task Britten rejoined "A" Company as second-in-command. Leaving the field with the wrecked transport behind, he came to a canal bridge where he met Colonel Anstee who directed him on his way. Colonel Anstee was his imperturbable self but what was the more remarkable was that he was resplendent in Service Dress, Sam Browne, and highly polished brown boots.

The Battalion now marched some six miles to Oost Dunkerke carrying all its kit, picks and shovels. In spite of the trauma of having destroyed all surplus equipment and vehicles, and in spite of being very weary, the march discipline remained at a high standard and the sections filed along the roadside at a steady pace with the step being well maintained. What was not known was that the Germans were already on the banks of the canal which the Battalion was to defend and that it had been intended that transport was to have been used to move to the new area. Initially the route passed through the centre of Furnes where the Germans were just across the canal. The route crossed roads which were under direct automatic fire and these had to be crossed at the double. Fortunately these obstacles were all passed without any loss and eventually the troops deployed to an assembly area near the church at Oost Dunkerke. The town was being shelled and tension rose whilst waiting to deploy.

Eventually orders came down the line and the companies moved forward to take up positions along the Nieuport/Furnes canal, with "C" Company on the right at Wulpen (Map 6). The march forward started at dusk and it was dark by the time the canal was reached when positions were selected, sections given their tasks, and digging began. Medley deployed astride the road at Wulpen and was relieved to find the bridge demolished. Having seen his sections start their tasks he sought to find where the troops were on his flank and was perturbed to find that apart from a machine-gun post, there appeared to be a void. He went back to company headquarters to report this situation to be told that troops were coming up to fill this gap. Returning to his platoon, he became aware of a noxious smell akin to gas. It transpired that a sewage unit had been hit by shell fire, hence the abominable smell.

It was now fully daylight and a dead despatch rider was found lying in the ditch beside the road, who had obviously been there the night before when the platoon came to the area. The identity discs were sent back to company headquarters. An enemy machine gun at Wulpen across the canal continued to fire at anything or anyone crossing the road. Apart from this activity there were no signs of any attempt to

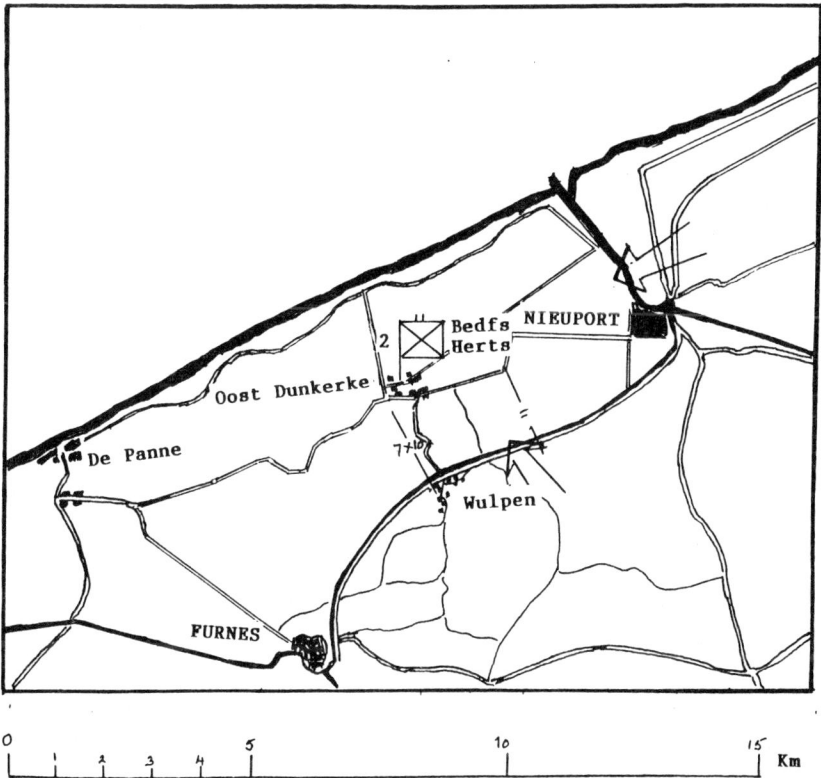

MAP 6

DUNKIRK PERIMETER – NIEUPORT FURNES CANAL
29–31 MAY 1940

force a crossing. At about 1100 hrs a truck drove up much to everyone's amazement and was ordered to "Get out of it fast". The driver, Private Carlton of "A" Company, did a very quick reverse and turn and accelerated off the way he had come, followed by a long burst of fire from the Germans. It was learnt later that this burst of fire had hit the left side of the vehicle breaking all but one of six bottles of whisky and shaking the passenger sitting on the opposite side of the truck. How the vehicle had managed to get past a road block was a mystery. To confound the issue further another vehicle drove up in a similar manner about an hour later. This time the Germans reacted more quickly and the first burst killed the driver as he was reversing into a turn. There were two more bursts of fire as the passenger leapt out and ran for cover in the buildings at the side of the road. Medley and Chandler set out to find this man and searched the houses along the side of the road. A sound was heard upstairs in one cottage and a figure appeared coming down the stairs with a revolver clutched in bloody hands which he pointed at Medley. Fortunately his wounds prevented him from shooting as he was convinced he was in enemy territory. Subsequently it was discovered that as he made his dash for cover, the first burst of fire broke the straps of his steel helmet, and the second burst had cut through his hands which he had raised to hold the helmet on his head. He was a very lucky man. He was evacuated after dark.

It was thought that the enemy had an observation post up a church spire which was engaged by our anti-tank guns. The enemy was becoming more active, an officer appeared briefly in the doorway of a warehouse across the canal, and soldiers ran across a gap between two brick walls. "The lack of high explosive bombs for the 2" mortar was infuriating as there was no means of hurting them". The forward trenches were under observation and any movement drew immediate automatic fire and Lance Corporal Major confirms that his section was pinned down.

A message came up after dusk to say that "C" Company was to hand over to a company of the East Yorks that night and to move back into battalion reserve. A check round all the sections found everyone in good heart. Furniture and sheeting were placed across the road to provide a shield for the next day so that the German machine gunners would not see when anyone was crossing from one side of the road to the other. The relieving company did not arrive until 0200 hrs on 30 May. By the time the handover had been completed it was nearly 0300 hrs and light was breaking as the company marched into Oost

Dunkerke. New positions were allocated and trenches were available, which had been dug previously by the Royal Engineers. Captain Johnston ordered a stand down and rest for six hours. It was now after 0500 hrs.

At about 0600 hrs there was the familiar sound of incoming shells, and from the sound of explosions these were mediums. A lateral road ran close behind the positions and it was evident that this and local road junctions were the targets. It was also obvious that rest was over and the most sensible thing to do was to man the trenches. The trenches provided were sited right out in the open in the middle of fields, providing no natural cover and isolating the soldiers occupying them. Accordingly Medley sited platoon positions behind hedgerows and left the other trenches vacant. Fortunately the ground was sandy and a complete trench system with linking communication trenches was dug in two hours. While this digging was taking place the platoon came under sniper fire from a fifth columnist. The platoon had been strengthened by a section from the carrier platoon, which was now foot-bound as the carriers had been destroyed.

"The Battalion was now on hard-tack rations consisting of bully beef and naval biscuits. Activity was building up and there was continuous enemy artillery fire. The response from the British side was minimal as the shortage of ammunition meant that the guns could only fire one round every 30 minutes. The Germans sent their planes over to drop bombs, and a Junkers 52 flying at five hundred feet headed straight for 13 Platoon. It was so low it was possible to see the bombs strung out below the wings and the first set of five bombs started their fall. Everyone tried to get deeper in their trenches. There was the crash of the first string whose last bomb settled centrally between two trenches with the bomb crater on the edge of these trenches. Miraculously no one was hurt. There had been a small delay before the second string was released and the first bomb of this string fell behind platoon headquarters dug in inside a hen coop. The hens did not lay extra eggs. Lance Corporal Major discovered that one of the two tins of bully beef issued to his section had been buried as a result of the bombing.

"The Germans had once again launched an observation balloon to gain an even better view of the battle ground. The pattern of shellfire continued and a few of the enemy managed to cross the canal."

It will be remembered that the Battalion anti-tank platoon had joined the 10th Infantry Brigade anti-tank company at the outbreak of war. The platoon was commanded by 2nd Lieutenant T.D.B.

McMillen with Sergeant Day as platoon sergeant and Sergeants Munday, Percival and Corporal Muskett as detachment commanders. McMillen takes up the story.

"We had not fired a shot in anger during the retreat to Dunkirk until we took up defensive positions near Bray Dunes. Up to that time we had been plagued by German observation balloons, flown behind their lines, which saw every move we made and brought down artillery fire even if two people walked along a road together. My platoon of three 25mm Hotchkiss anti-tank guns, which fired solid shot, had dug into a position in a hedgerow on the brigade left flank and were overlooked by two of these insolent observation balloons. I thought that we ought to do something about them so decided to have a go myself. I cleared the crew of one of the guns away to safety and with Sergeant Percival as loader and with maximum range on the telescopic sight fired at the nearest balloon. The third round must have scored a hit as the nose cone deflated rapidly and the balloon was hauled down even more rapidly.

"Sergeant Percival and I dived into our adjacent slit trenches and cowered under the answering enemy artillery fire. When we surfaced later I found that my binoculars, which I had left on the lip of the slit trench, had been shredded by enemy fire.

"Brigadier 'Bubbles' Barker was delighted with this result and turned the whole company of nine guns on to counter balloon fire. This resulted in five more balloons being destroyed and the whole lot being withdrawn so far back that they became ineffective. We had several opportunities to fire, mainly at enemy strongpoints in houses, before being withdrawn to Dunkirk. Activity during these two days had been constant with little chance to relax, continuous shellfire, and no hot food."

PSM Scales recalls sniper fire as being troublesome throughout this period. Lance Corporal Wellard had a bullet through the side of his steel helmet, and another soldier was badly wounded. A Section commander in 15 Platoon was hit by a high-velocity 22 bullet which entered his chest and came out at his buttocks.

2nd Lieutenant Pincombe noted that the enemy had succeeded in building a bridge near a factory West of Wulpen opposite the DCLI. The enemy were filtering across the canal in small numbers with MG supporting fire. There was plenty of sniping in rear areas and forward companies were constantly harassed by snipers, probably fifth columnists. "B" Company repulsed an attack and reoccupied positions on the canal bank supported by the last six rounds of one 3" mortar.

There was also an unreal atmosphere as there were a great number of civilians caught up in the battle. On a visit to Battalion Headquarters Medley was approached by two nuns as he was passing a school and asked to go in and see the wounded. A large room was filled with dead and wounded lying on the floor, young and old, men, women and children. There was an urgent need for medical supplies but there was nothing that could be done to help, a most distressing fact of life.

Orders were received that the Battalion was to withdraw to the beaches that night. The forward companies, "A" and "B" were to evacuate their positions and clear "C" Company by 0130 hrs. "C" Company was to hold on until 0230 hrs and cover the withdrawal of the remainder of the Battalion. 13 Platoon, which sat astride a track leading from the canal was to pull out last. At dusk there was a splendid view of some forty Bristol Blenheim bombers flying in over Nieuport to bomb the German lines which cheered everyone up considerably. The shelling continued and the explosions set houses on fire along the route to be taken. The shelling was very methodical and it was possible to determine when to run the gauntlet past the target area and as a result all troops passed the danger spot without suffering harm.

The disengagement went without a hitch and the forward companies fell back through "C" Company and set off on their march to the beaches. The next hour passed with no let up in the German harassing bombardment but there was no sign of any patrols or infantry advancing towards the defended positions. Eventually the time came for "C" Company to pull out and Lance Corporal Dilley and his section moved off with the platoon commander at a steady run. Captain Senior, the Adjutant, was at the rendezvous, near the place where battalion headquarters had been, with transport. Reporting all troops safely back, the convoy set off for De Panne. The journey was like a Brock's firework display. The German artillery fire along the route was constant and the sight of the exploding shells was all the more terrifying as the sound of their approach was drowned by the noise of the vehicle engine until the very last moment. There was nothing that could be done but hope that the vehicles would escape being hit. Nevertheless this experience gave a sense of utter hopelessness as the individual had no control over events. As the convoy neared a town, which turned out to be De Panne, the road became congested with abandoned and burning vehicles. Shells were falling and striking buildings and masonry was falling down on to the road and it became impossible to drive any further. Trams were halted and ablaze and the overhead cables were entangled round trucks as many of the supporting pylons had been blown down. It was a sight which almost defied description. The noise was indescribable and the burst of exploding shells seemed to be never-ending.

The convoy halted as it could go no further and it was with some relief that the company debussed, and, deploying into platoons, was guided down by Captain Johnson through a street lit by burning buildings which led through to the beach. There was no other way. There was a constant bombardment at the exit to the beach with four shells exploding every minute. Fortunately the timing of these salvoes was exact and there was time to rush through in the interval between each salvo. Captain Johnson spaced the platoons out and ordered them to charge through the gap on his command between the salvoes. 13 Platoon was the last to go, having seen the other two platoons disappear through the gap and further shells explode hiding them from vision once they had run the gauntlet. There was no knowing what to expect once on the other side. At last 13 Platoon lined up in threes and, on the signal, charged through to the other side. It was an eerie experience as the beaches were in total darkness, or so it seemed after the blazing light in the town. The sand dunes reached right up to the promenade and the enemy bombardment stopped at the high water mark. It was now about 0300hrs on 1 June.

Lieutenant Britten was sent by Captain Lewis to make sure that a platoon which had been out of contact since early morning on 31 May withdrew in accordance with the company timetable. He set off with a soldier and carried out an extensive search but could not locate the platoon. Realizing that the other two platoons had already withdrawn he reluctantly set off on the road to De Panne.

Pincombe, the Battalion Intelligence Officer commented that the roads to De Panne were heavily shelled and that the move was slowed up by the congestion of transport in De Panne.

9

THE BEACHES – 1 JUNE

13 Platoon had come through the previous three days without suffer-ing any casualties and much of this was due to the readiness to dig fast and deep as soon as new positions were agreed upon. Having survived this far and reached the beaches Private Davis was hit by shrapnel on the dunes and had his nose removed. Lance Corporal Major put on a first field dressing and got him into a boat.

It was evident that the German artillery was ranged at the high water mark so platoons headed down on to the sands. The beaches were filled with masses of soldiers milling around. The time gaps between the platoons rushing the gap made it difficult to link up with those who had gone ahead but 13 Platoon met up with Captain Whittaker and 14 Platoon and this party gathered itself together. Looking around there appeared to be lines of dark objects on the fore-shore. Out to sea it was possible to make out the silhouettes of some large ships. Added to the noise of the ground battle was the sound of the guns of the Royal Navy ships firing in support of our troops still holding the line. As the light grew, the lines on the beach were seen to be orderly columns of soldiers in threes, waiting as the head of their line climbed into small boats to be ferried the five or six hundred yards out to the larger ships. The whole beach seemed to be filled with these well-disciplined lines waiting patiently for their turn to be ferried out. Not far away a company of the Grenadier Guards was lining up under the company sergeant major who was ensuring their drill would have done credit on Horse Guards in Whitehall.

It was evident that the chances of being evacuated from this stretch of beach were not good so Whittaker decided that "C" Company, as it had been collected up, should march down the beach to see whether the possibility of finding a boat were better away from the congestion off De Panne.

Light was growing rapidly and no sooner was it daylight than the sky was filled with a squadron of Messerschmitt 109 fighter aircraft who dived on to the beach and started strafing the soldiers. The aircraft peeled off at a height of some five thousand feet and dived down with their guns blazing. Levelling off, they flashed at zero feet over the tops of the soldiers' heads. The only thing that reduced casualties was that, as the planes were flying level, many of the bullets went overhead. Nevertheless it was a frightening experience. Captain Onslow, who had been wounded getting on to the beach and was lying on a stretcher, was caught in this fire and killed.

Once this attack had started "C" Company took cover in the dunes and escaped casualties. The air attack was over very quickly and the planes flew off. The march down the beach continued until a Royal Navy officer came up to Whittaker and offered him a large ship's lifeboat. He gave orders that all weapons had to be thrown away. He would not allow anyone to set out for the ships who was armed, as it was more important to save trained soldiers and without weapons more men could be carried. The tide was coming in over the flats and it was necessary to wait for sufficient depth of water to ease the boat out into the tide before taking on any passengers. The Bedfords worked with a will and found themselves joined by a mix of soldiers from every Arm of the Service and with guidance from the Naval officer they pushed the craft out against the incoming tide. It was quite a task as the boat was about twenty five feet long and was driven by propellers which were connected by shafts to ten poles with seating on each side. The art was to seat soldiers facing one another holding a pole which was then pulled vigorously back and forth to provide the drive for the propellers. It was essential that the teams responsible for this all pulled and pushed in unison. The first attempt met with failure as soldiers anxious to get aboard clambered over the sides before the drill had been learnt and the incoming tide drove the boat back onto the beach. Captain Whittaker then ordered that only he and his batman would climb aboard, from whence he would direct the floating operation and tell individuals when to climb aboard. The first aboard were given the task of manning the drive poles and were directed to pull and push on orders, somewhat like ancient galley slaves. The British soldier is amazingly adaptable and this time the boat began to make way against the incoming tide. By ensuring that embarkation was delayed as long as possible the shore line was left behind. Medley, dressed in battle order over his greatcoat, was so weighed down with sodden clothing that it took four men to drag him aboard. Had weapons been carried it is possible that men would have been drowned with the extra weight.

There were two destroyers lying about 1200 yards off shore and Whittaker decided to make for the nearest. The lifeboat was some four hundred yards from the nearest destroyer when a squadron of Stuka dive bombers came into view flying at about ten thousand feet overhead. The planes peeled off and came down in a steep, screeching dive, attacking the destroyer, which, as soon as the planes appeared, had made steam and opened up with all its weapons. The squadron had split up into flights which approached their target from different directions so as to evade the defensive fire. One large bomb was clearly visible below the belly of each aircraft. Once this bomb was released the pilot pulled his plane sharply out of the dive into a steep climb. The Stukas seemed everywhere and at the bottom of the dive it was possible to see the features of the pilot and his gunner. One of the destroyers took a direct hit – there was a blinding flash of light followed by a massive explosion. When the smoke cleared there was no destroyer. This had all happened so suddenly that the mind could hardly take it in. As all the Stukas had dropped their bombs by now they were intent on making their escape and flew off inland.

Things settled down and the surviving destroyer had stopped about a mile further out to sea. So with a number of other small craft the lifeboat headed towards it. Pace through the water was not fast and before contact could be made the drone of approaching aircraft was heard. The Stukas had bombed up and come back for another attack. The destroyer got up steam and managed to evade the bombs aimed at it. This time the German aircraft began to attack the small craft full of soldiers. Captain Whittaker deemed it wiser to return to shore and seek to escape elsewhere, especially as it was highly probable that the Stukas would rearm again and look for new targets. The thought of being in an open boat without being able to retaliate was not an attractive one. The boat beached some thirty minutes later at about 0800 hrs. The squad formed up and started to march down the beach towards Dunkirk. There seemed to be so much bombing and artillery bombardment in that direction that the possibility of marching on to Calais was considered as an option, oblivious of the knowledge that Calais was now held by the Germans. It was a hot sunny day, which helped the sea-sodden battledress to dry out quickly. Arriving at Bray Dunes at about 1000hrs "C" Company met up quite by chance with Battalion Headquarters which was established in a house by the sea front. There were some 180 Bedfords and orders were given to split up into parties of ten men under an officer or non-commissioned officer and to march down the beach at two-minute intervals.

It was an exhausting slog through soft sand with constant interruptions from bombing and artillery fire. Some sixty bombers came over flying in different directions in threes, dropping bombs in the dunes. Whenever these attacks developed everyone took cover and waited for the raid to pass. While these attacks against the ground forces were taking place, the Stukas were constantly diving down on any shipping in sight. The effects of lack of sleep and short rations had their effect and Medley fell asleep during one of these air attacks and could not be roused. He awoke two hours later and found his batman 300 yards further down the beach and the Regimental quartermaster sergeant, RQMS Gayleard, close by also resting. Waking them up, the march towards Dunkirk continued. Captain Whittaker, who had also fallen asleep, joined up with this small party. The march down the beach passed burnt-out vehicles, anti-aircraft guns with their muzzles split by demolition charges and innumerable abandoned vehicles. Some of these had been driven out into the sea to form jetties to help soldiers to embark in small boats. Coming into Dunkirk the sky was blackened by the smoke from burning oil tanks. A French officer was firing his rifle at a German plane well out of range. There were soldiers sitting at cafés watching the saga while waiting for ships to take them off.

All troops coming into Dunkirk were directed toward the mole, which Whittaker and his party reached at about 1800 hrs. All junior officers were detailed in charge of a party of fifty men from every regiment in the British army and sent off down the mole at two hundred yard intervals. The Germans were shelling the port but their fire was falling short. Across the dock were about 150 prisoners of war, mostly German Air Force, with the incoming artillery fire falling onto the defences behind them. Whittaker walked down the mole with Medley and his party of fifty men. After some 400 yards there was a huge gap resulting from earlier German bombing attacks with the sea water swirling below. This gap was bridged by two planks, somewhat precariously balanced, over which it was necessary to pass to reach the waiting ships and craft. In normal circumstances anyone would have thought twice before risking this passage, but everyone crossed over and headed on down the mole. Tied up alongside was a large paddle steamer with Colonel Birch and a number of Bedfords aboard. It was about to cast off and Whittaker was allowed to jump aboard.

Medley and his party climbed aboard a fishing trawler and were sent below into the hold. Four further parties came aboard. At the time a flight of three Spitfires were patrolling over the harbour and not one German bomber showed up. As soon as this flight withdrew at dusk the bombing attacks started again. The thump of bombs exploding alongside in the water could be heard but the soldiery were soon all fast asleep. Next morning the boat arrived at Ramsgate. It had been taking on water in the bilges and although everyone had been sleeping with water round their seats not one had woken up! The harbour was chock-a-block with boats disembarking troops who had been brought back from France. The WVS were dishing out cups of tea. As individuals came off the boats they were sent to the railway station and put aboard trains. Once a train was fully loaded it was sent on its way and another train was brought in ready to receive passengers. The whole operation worked smoothly and efficiently.

2nd Lieutenant Muirhead had led 15 Platoon of "C" Company through the enemy artillery fire at De Panne and on reaching the dunes had discovered his men were not with him. There was a mass of individuals milling around and the noise of the bombardment by the Royal Navy together with the German artillery was such that his calls to rally went unheeded. He decided to head down the beaches and took cover when the Messerschmitt fighters strafed the beaches shortly after first light. Moving on, he met up with PSM Kendle of the Pioneer Platoon who had found a small craft. They teamed up and with much laboured effort paddled out to a destroyer which they went aboard.

Pincombe commented: "The beach was constantly bombed and shelled during the day. The enemy aircraft seemed to have complete air superiority. There appeared to be a complete lack of organization to facilitate embarkation of units."

Private LeMaitre joined up with Whittaker's party marching down the beach and recalls the fun and games in trying to float the lifeboat. Once ashore again he headed off down the beach with Private Fry of "B" Company, who was subsequently taken prisoner at Singapore. Private LeMaitre was wounded on the beaches and Private Fry assisted him to Dunkirk where he was evacuated to England.

Lance Corporal Major of 13 Platoon remembers the dash to the rendezvous and the convoy to De Panne which he recalls being under heavy shellfire and burning fiercely: "Filtered through to the beach and the inevitable 109s came strafing. Told my chaps to scatter. From then on a hazy recollection of walking, miles of sand, strafing planes and shelling, many vain attempts to get on boats. Eventually reached jetty at Dunkirk and in between attacks by aircraft I was lucky enough to board the destroyer Worcester as she was casting off. Attacked by bombers and fighters during the crossing, many dead and wounded on the ship. The ship was disabled and taken in tow by another warship. On reaching Dover the Worcester collided with the Maid of Orleans and rolled steeply; many went overboard including Sergeant 'Spot' Davies of 15 Platoon who was drowned. By train to Aldershot, sleep, then to Yeovil." Private R. Day of "A" Company recalls getting off the beaches with a Private Oliver and helping to carry a wounded soldier along the mole and on to a ship.

PSM Scales of "B" Company received orders to withdraw from his position on the canal line by midnight 31 May, and make for the beach. He passed Captain Onslow at the company rendezvous. In the shelling he and Private Collins were wounded. Private Collins was evacuated in an ambulance. Private Baldock stayed with PSM Scales until a Royal West Kent carrier came by and lifted him to the beach, where he was placed in a boat and taken aboard a destroyer. Arriving at Dover, he was transferred to a hospital train . At Horton Emergency hospital he recalls being visited a couple of times by 2nd Lieutenant P. Young.

Shortly after first light on 1 June Lieutenant Britten came upon some members of the battalion on the beach West of De Panne. After failing to find any members of "A" Company among them, he sat down under the side of an old hulk and fell asleep. He had been on his feet continuously for over twelve hours. When he awakened all the Bedfords had gone, including the men who had been with him. There were a few men of other units trying to empty a beached boat which was full of water.

There were a number of abandoned vehicles about and, after examination of them all one was found which was lacking a distributor. It took very little time to replace this with one from another vehicle and after collecting all the men from the beach set off for Dunkirk with Britten driving.

"The lorry had a bench seat supported by a wooden board which served as a lid for a tool box. This ran the full width of the vehicle. On the edge of Dunkirk we came upon a road block manned by what we thought were French soldiers. As I slowed down the shock of going through a small crater caused the wooden lid over the tool box to collapse and the three of us sitting in the front dropped down. When we suddenly disappeared from view the men on the road block thought that we were hostile and opened fire! By the time I had managed to regain control we were through the knife rest and some sixty yards away from it. As the lorry was still under fire and the men in the rear compartment were still in danger I carried on to the beach. No one was hit although the windscreen had been riddled with bullets. On reaching Dunkirk there was a sizeable vessel alongside the mole so we carried the wounded aboard. The mole had been breached half-way along and the gap, about three yards across, had been bridged by a ladder. It was a bit tricky getting the wounded over but it was achieved without mishap. There were no problems after that."

2nd Lieutenant La Fontaine of "D" Company, who had arrived at the beaches direct from Whyschaete, received the order to embark with his men on any boats available. "Sergeant Fullick and half a dozen or so of "D" Company did not make it the first evening. Not much evacuation went on that night. Also not much the next day in spite of the sappers building a jetty of lorries to help things. There were long queues for boats, some of which were swamped by the incoming tide, as frequently boats did not return for a further load. When the sea mist aided by smoke began to clear later in the day there was some low level enemy activity, but we were not under shell-fire. Our group managed to get hold of a small boat. There must have been thirty or forty of us by now, many lost souls having tagged on. A queue rapidly formed and the only way was to detail the two men by name who were to row the boat back for the next load. I like to think that after getting off we left behind a going concern. Sergeant Fullick was quite excellent. The only interesting bit comes now. When I got on to the destroyer I was shown to the wardroom – given a pink gin and a small triangular sandwich reminiscent of peacetime tennis tea parties. A steward came up. 'Follow me Sir'- and took me to the first officer's cabin. 'I'll dry your boots Sir'. I lay down on the first officer's bunk and woke up in Dover. The best channel crossing I have ever had. I was most certainly the most junior officer in the wardroom and was lucky to get VIP treatment. I cannot remember the name of the destroyer."

2nd Lieutenant Whitworth went aboard a coaster off De Panne which was attacked by Stukas and holed so that the soldiers returned to shore and started their long march down the beach to Dunkirk. Arriving at the mole he boarded a vessel in mid afternoon but the vessel did not leave until dark. During the daylight hours there were constant air attacks. On arriving at Dover the following morning on a beautiful sunny day he recalls seeing a company of Coldstream

Guards form up on the quayside and after a formal "Right Dress" marching at the slope on to the railway station platform. The WVS were everywhere whenever the train stopped with refreshments and hot cups of tea. Eventually he found himself in a reception camp at Aldershot. He considers his most abiding memories were the miraculous weather, flat calm sea, the warm sunshine and the all prevailing wonderful spirit of comradeship and mutual help, the "Dunkirk Spirit".

Private T.H.Morley was wounded in both arms at De Panne. He remarks that if it had not been for Major "Ted" Ashby who ordered him to march to Dunkirk he has no doubt he would have been taken prisoner. He made it and was carried aboard HMS Warwick to England where he went into hospital. On discharge he was posted to the Middle East where he joined the 1st Battalion.

Captain Senior, the Adjutant, rounded up any stray Bedfords he saw and led them down the beach, insisting that they march properly – no slouching. He bumped into Brigadier Barker, who told him a boat was expected shortly. Returning to his small party they promptly abandoned a brew up and headed for the anticipated craft which they boarded. Captain Senior can not recall anything of the trip back as he fell asleep. On arrival in England he was awakened by his men with a cup of tea. These few personal reminiscences all emphazise the extreme fatigue of those involved. Individuals who fell asleep were so tired that no amount of shaking had any effect. Soldiers who tried to wake officers up received no response, in effect an example of being "dead tired".

2nd Lieutenant McMillan tells of the Anti-tank Platoon: "We dumped our guns and transport in the outskirts of the town and having removed the breech blocks of the guns and poured sand into the sumps of the vehicles, left them with the engines running at maximum revolutions. We marched down to the sands and were allotted a position adjacent to the mole. After what seemed a lifetime the destroyer HMS *Shikari* drew alongside and we embarked dry-shod. I went to sleep while we were being bombed by a German-manned Blenheim bomber, still wearing RAF roundels, and woke up in some unknown port. Our train took us to Porthcawl in South Wales where we were treated like a victorious army instead of a defeated rabble.

"I lost two men during the entire operation, Privates Rex and Dockett."

10

HOME DEFENCE 1940–1943

The German onslaught, which had broken through to the Channel coast, had forced the withdrawal of the main British Forces back to the United Kingdom where they were being prepared to return to the fray at the earliest possible time. It was intended that these battle-experienced units would join other British forces already fighting the Germans on the Somme. The tide of events moved so fast that these plans never bore fruit and with the collapse of the French armies these latter forces were evacuated to the United Kingdom in their turn.

Britain, defiant, stood alone. The whole attention of the army was now turned to the defence of the homeland. Initially there was a grave lack of equipment as vast resources had been lost on the continent. Led by the Prime Minister, Winston Churchill, the nation took up the challenge and set to prepare defences against invasion. Initially it was a case of deploying along the coastline to defeat any invasion attempt with but few mobile reserves available to support any threatened location. Gradually, as time went by and with the defeat of the German Air force in the Battle of Britain, the situation changed and the emphasis in role changed from one of purely defence to one of training for aggressive operations.

Overseas the Italians had invaded British Somaliland and were poised on the frontiers of Egypt. However campaigns in the Middle East and Abyssinia overran the Italian forces and caused the Germans to despatch troops to Greece, Crete and Libya. In June, 1941 the Germans invaded Russia and the threat of an invasion ended. The main theatre of operations was in the Western Desert where the Eighth Army fought a series of see-saw actions with the German and Italian forces.

The role of the Battalion changed from defensive on the coast line to the counter-attack role and thence to amphibious training.

In the Middle East in October 1942 the British Eighth Army had defeated the Axis armies at the Battle of Alamein and was now pursuing them along the North African coastline. The Allies were not yet ready to attack Germany across the English Channel. The thrust was to be from the South with an Allied force landing in Morocco and Algeria in November 1942, to advance eastwards to join up with the Eighth Army. The 2nd Battalion would join the 1st British Army in Algeria in March, 1943.

This chapter takes the reader through this period of repetitive training and preparation from the arrival back in the country from Dunkirk to the participation in the landings and campaign in North Africa in 1943.

Medley arrived back in England on 2 June. "It was hot and sunny. The reception organization at Ramsgate sent the troop trains off as soon as they were loaded and there was no waiting around. As the train steamed towards London there were signs and posters displayed in the gardens of houses alongside the railroad saying 'Welcome home boys' and 'Well done boys'. This reception was not expected, the Germans had defeated the British Expeditionary Force! I found the welcome home totally incredible. At Catford the train stopped and WVS ladies dished out tea and sandwiches. I felt embarrassed as I had no English money and did not expect to be given free rations. There were also girls from the ATS, who came and asked if there were any messages to be sent to close relatives. Again the lack of cash caused concern, but after reassurance messages were given and passed efficiently to the phone numbers given.

"The train eventually stopped at Shrewsbury. The soldiers, from an assortment of regiments and units, were sent to Copthorne Barracks where some 2000 soldiers were housed in pretty cramped conditions, while the officers were billeted in hotels in the town.

"It was about 1800 on 2 June and after a meal the comfort of a bed seemed too wonderful to resist. Fatigue of the previous weeks took charge and it was 2000 hrs the next evening when I awoke. Reporting to the barracks the next morning and expecting a rocket I found that I was free to depart and occupy my time until the next day. The summer was at its best and boating on the river with others awaiting instructions to rejoin their units was a wonderful means of peaceful relaxation. The staff at Copthorne Barracks had the unenviable task of sorting out the mass of soldiers and officers into units by formation and despatching parties off to their divisions in the order of priority determined by the War Office, who were at that time trying to build up a second expeditionary force to go to France."

After about a week Medley and seventeen soldiers of the 2nd Battalion, The Bedfordshire and Hertfordshire Regiment, were sent off by train to report to the 4th Division assembly area near Yeovil arriving late in the evening. Most of the officers who had survived were already with the Battalion; there were only two who rejoined afterwards, Captain Johnson and 2nd Lieutenant Pincombe.

Losses in the battalion compared with other infantry battalions were light, and a great number had been suffered on the beaches and during the evacuation, with soldiers being presumed lost aboard ships which were sunk. Five of the twelve platoon commanders were killed, and a further two wounded. Captain Geoffrey Onslow was killed on the beaches lying on a stretcher already having suffered a severe shrapnel wound to the jaw as he was approaching the beaches. Lieutenant Vosser, the Quartermaster, who had been taken prisoner in 1914, was wounded and captured again. He was to spend the whole of another war in a German Prisoner of War camp!

The next few days were spent in reorganizing and everyone was sent off on 48 hrs leave. Fighting was still going on in France and the Battalion was expecting to receive orders to join the forces there at any moment.

Brigadier "Bubbles" Barker visited and thanked the Battalion for what it had done saying, "Now you all know what it is like to be really tired. In spite of all difficulties you did everything ordered of you." The Battalion gave three loud spontaneous cheers, something which showed the affection and respect all troops felt for him. Throughout the battle he had stood by the road at each battalion checkpoint until the last soldier was through, during every withdrawal, before driving off to his new headquarters.

Reinforcements arrived and the Battalion sent drafts to the territorial battalions, receiving men from them in exchange. There followed a move to a tented camp at Fareham where time was spent on getting to know the locality and preparations to repel enemy parachutists. One morning "C" Company was called out at 0200 hrs and sat in buses for three hours as there had been a parachutist scare. A week later the battalion deployed to the Bognor Regis area of some three and a half miles manning defensive positions along the coast.

It was a long hot summer and there were holiday makers, who being banned from the beaches, sat across the road from the esplanade watching the soldiers digging defences. It all seemed a little unreal as France had surrendered, but the British public was not going to forego a holiday that had been planned ahead.

Man for man the soldiers felt that they were better than the Germans, and, strange as it may seem, were all the more confident now that the British were on their own following the defeat of France.

It was not long before the German air attacks began and raids came in nightly over the Downs heading for Portsmouth. RAF Tangmere was only a few miles away and the Battalion area was overflown by the squadrons as they took off and returned from sorties. The daily routine was wearying. Morning Stand to was at 0230 hrs until 0400 hrs, followed by a return to bed. Reveille at 0630 hrs and after breakfast down to the beaches to dig trenches, with a short break for a haversack meal at midday. Digging finished at 1730 hrs when the soldiers returned to billets with a hot meal at 1830 hrs. Platoon commanders held short training sessions for their section non-commissioned officers each evening on return from digging.

Companies were required to submit a daily state of the development of the defensive positions. Evening Stand to was from 2130 hrs to 2300 hrs and so to bed. Companies were billeted in available houses in their respective areas and each platoon had double sentries on every night. In "C" Company it was the responsibility of an officer to man the telephone in the company office in case of a call out to repel enemy parachutists. Practices were held to ensure that response times were rapid and as the effect of the daily routine was wearying, these training exercises kept everyone on their toes. On one such practice the company was called out at 0230 hrs and bussed out to an assembly area where it deployed and launched an attack against an enemy parachute group. The exercise over and Captain Harrison was to be seen gathering up mushrooms which were growing in profusion in the fields! There were also practice exercises of section movement making use of all available cover benefiting from the experiences gained in France. The emphasis of the training was on rapid movement and deployment to attack and destroy enemy parachutists before they had time to organize themselves on the ground.

The Battle of Britain was being fought in the skies overhead and some nineteen aircraft were brought down in the Battalion area. There was a big attack by Stukas on RAF Tangmere. The enemy aircraft flashed at roof level over Bognor Regis and out to sea hotly pursued by Hurricane fighters and cheered on by our soldiers.

One edict of the battle in France was that all officers under the rank of Brigadier were to be taught to ride a motor cycle. Brigadiers would ride pillion. Instruction consisted of a short ride on the pillion behind the MT Sergeant who then changed places. After this short introduction the learner was sent off on his own!

A number of changes took place and the key officer appointments were now as follows:

Commanding Officer	Lt Colonel Birch
Second in Command	Major Ashby
Adjutant	Capt Pincombe
"A" Company	Capt Lewis
"B" Company	Capt Whittaker
"C" Company	Capt Harrison
"D" Company	Capt Peters

Captain Johnson left the Battalion as did Captain Harrison who was posted to Headquarters 38th Division. On his departure Captain "Streaky" Yate-Lee took over "C" Company. Lieutenant L.C. Young departed to join the Recce Corps, and 2nd Lieutenant P. Young joined the newly formed Commandos.

PSMs Clayton and Rayner were given immediate commissions as Lieutenants and stayed with the Battalion.

The full schedule of work, training and alertness continued and was having its effect. Efforts were made to relax the pressure a little and a small number of men were given passes for the evening. Company canteens were set up and were managed by volunteer members of the Women's Voluntary Services.

Work continued on improving the defences and Corporal Todd devised his own obstacles in the shape of broken bottles cemented in in front of the defensive wire. Artillery fired ranging shots into the sea. Rockets were placed on the pier, which were to be set off to give warning to all and sundry in the event of a German invasion. Medley was made responsible for this task!

Gradually the battalion was being re-equipped with weapons. Each rifle section was given a Browning automatic rifle in addition to the Bren LMG. Platoons received their 2" mortar. The Battalion was issued with two Vickers heavy Machine Guns. There was also the placement of a six-pounder gun to strengthen the beach defences. These issues raised morale considerably and Corporal Todd was all but praying for the Germans to invade so that he could eliminate them. As the summer months passed, and the tempo of the air battle increased so did the tension build up on the ground. Trenches were manned along the coast line and the Battalion watched the sea. One evening there was a general alert and boots remained on all night and respirators were kept ready fastened to the chest. All the conditions were favourable for the enemy to attack, the tides were right and the wind was blowing off the sea. German aircraft flew overhead along the line of the coast dropping flares at periodic intervals during the night, an activity which had not been experienced before. Dawn came and with it a relaxation of orders.

In spite of these diversions the main action was taking place in the air and there was a feeling of frustration at not being able to hit at the enemy. Volunteers were called for and 2nd Lieutenants Medley and Fawssett, having applied for overseas service, were accepted and left the Battalion.

Lt Colonel Birch had gone away to attend a course and Major "Ted" Ashby became responsible for running the Battalion in his absence. He remained in command until Lt Colonel E.C. Pepper assumed command in February, 1941. In the meantime the Battalion had left Bognor and spent time between Arlesford and Totton training and taking part in numerous exercises.

Lt Colonel Pepper handed over to Lt Colonel D.S.W. Johnson in February, 1942, by which time the Battalion was in GHQ reserve.

In March the Battalion moved to Inverary to learn and practice assault landings and pursued combined operations training through the following months. Key appointments were now as follows:

Commanding Officer	Lt Colonel	D.S.W. Johnson*
Second in Command	Major	W.A.Whittaker *
Adjutant	Capt	E.S.Jenkins
Intelligence Officer	Lieut	J. Douglass
Quartermaster	Capt (QM)	H.T.Beasley
"HQ" Company	Major	D.F. Yate-Lee*
"A" Company	Capt	S.F.Rayner*
"B" Company	Capt	M.H.Lofts*
"C" Company	Major	L.C.Young*
"D" Company	Capt	S.F.Charkham*

The asterisk denotes those who were with the Battalion during the campaign in France in 1940.

The story is now taken up by Lt Colonel W.A.Whittaker, who, it will be seen was second-in-command at this time.

"A joke often repeated is apt to wear a little thin, but when the joke involves the granting of leave, it is acceptable at all times. It was in something of this mode that the 2nd Battalion, part of the 4th Infantry Division, whose composition had remained the same since leaving Belgium, received news of yet another embarkation leave early in January, 1943. We were though becoming impatient.

"Since returning from Belgium in 1940, most of southern England and almost the whole of Western Scotland had fallen to our victorious arms. Under Field Marshal Montgomery, then Lieut-General, we had studied Desert Warfare on Salisbury Plain in December and had fought our way in box formation through mud and pouring rain to gain the Pusey Oasis without which the Division was threatened with disaster through lack of water. We gained it, soaking wet, and Sergeant Parker's exhortation to his Platoon, "Now then, we're in the fertile country now, keep your thieving fingers off them bananas," shows we knew how to exercise restraint in moments of victory.

"We had crossed narrow rivers, wide rivers, slow, fast, deep and shallow rivers, we had landed from most types of landing craft on many different coasts penetrating deeply inland. We had co-operated with artillery, tanks and aircraft, a twenty mile route march was of course routine, whilst ten miles in two hours in full equipment which was not to be undertaken for the fun of the thing, occasioned no undue alarm. Two men apprehended in a field one evening in gym shoes and with rifles, maintained stoutly that they were only settling an argument as to whether you could get from 'A' to 'B' without being seen from 'C', so well ingrained was the principle of use of ground.

"We had three lots of embarkation leave, we had prepared and been equipped to go to very cold countries and to very hot countries but we remained quite firmly in a very wet one. South West Scotland, to be exact, was very wet. Thus it was that the Battalion accepted this new embarkation leave in the spirit of which it assumed it had been given, and while all the routine preparations proceeded any undue enthusiasm had been regarded as rather naive. This impression was strengthened shortly afterwards by a brigade adjustment when we exchanged camps with the 1/6th Surreys about twelve miles away at Carrenbridge. Having installed ourselves in our new location we set about energetically with ambitious schemes to make the new camp as comfortable as possible, this being the only course open to us to encourage an early move. All this work was not in vain. Towards the end of February the Division was honoured by a visit from His Majesty the King and we then knew that this time we were off.

"Enthusiasm was no longer naive but natural and universal. The transport moved off on 26 February and on 11 March the main body of the battalion left Carrenbridge for Glasgow on the first stage of its journey. Our destination was, of course secret, but as we had been part of First Army and had originally been intended to land with them, only to have to our place taken over by Americans at the last moment, North Africa was a strong favourite and so it turned out to be.

"If travelling in HMV Orion with over 6000 troops on board and boat stations four or five times a day can be regarded as uneventful, then it must be recorded that the voyage was uneventful. I say almost because the ship was 'dry' and the sight of Colonel Johnson enjoying his last lemonade before turning in must be recorded as an event and I am sure he would wish it so. Johnny had taken over from Colonel Pepper about a year previously, it is always difficult to succeed someone superlatively good at their job, but Johnny's terrific good humour and enthusiasm carried the Battalion through a period in which it might well have become stale. His energy and unwillingness to spare himself made everyone feel that the best they could do could scarcely be good enough. Headquarters Company was commanded by 'Streaky' Yate-Lee, he seemed to have been commanding it for ever, presumably there was a time when he took over, (Corporal Mayes would know), but whenever that time was it was so lost in antiquity as to be unimportant. 'A' Company had been commanded by Rayner by this time for two years. About a year previously it had won an exhaustive competition as the best company in the division, this speaks for Rayner. 'B', 'C' and 'D' Companies were commanded by Michael Lofts, Porky Young, with the same zest with which he did everything else, and Charkham respectively. There are very many others I would like to mention, of all ranks, the only difficulty would be to know when to stop but I will content myself with saying that a visitor who knew the battalion in 1939 would still have had no difficulty in finding plenty of faces he knew."

11

NORTH AFRICA 1943

The landings in Algeria and Morocco in November, 1942, which were planned to clear the African continent of Axis forces caused an immediate reaction from Hitler who despatched thousands of extra troops and aircraft. These reinforcements built up in strength fast enough to take advantage of the hostile terrain and the battle inexperience of the Allied Forces to prevent the seizing of Tunis. It forced the despatch of further Allied formations to this theatre of operations and prolonged the battle. The end result when it came to pass was a resounding defeat for the Germans with hundreds of thousands of men taken prisoner. All this was in the future when the 2nd Battalion arrived in North Africa, Colonel Whittaker resumes his account of events.

"On the 23 March, we arrived off a port which we were informed was Algiers, and disembarkation commenced without delay. We then had a seventeen mile march to a staging camp at Camp Matafou. Conditions there were, to say the least, indifferent but Sergeant Thoms soon had a cookhouse going in a barn, and to Sergeant Waller and his pioneers and to Corporal Finch with his sanitary section, this was merely another challenge to their ability which they dealt with in the usual way.

"On the 29th at 1130 hrs we entrained for Bone where we were to link up with the transport. Troop trains seldom end up at the destination for which they set off and this was no exception. We did not go to Bone but to a small village Ghardimou about fifty miles inland from Bone and at about an equal distance behind the front lines, where we arrived on the afternoon of the 31st. On the following morning a warning order was received that we were to take over a section of the line forthwith and Colonel Johnson with company commanders and the intelligence officer went forward. The transport started to arrive during the afternoon and continued into the night. They'd had a pretty tough time coming over the frozen mountain roads from Bone

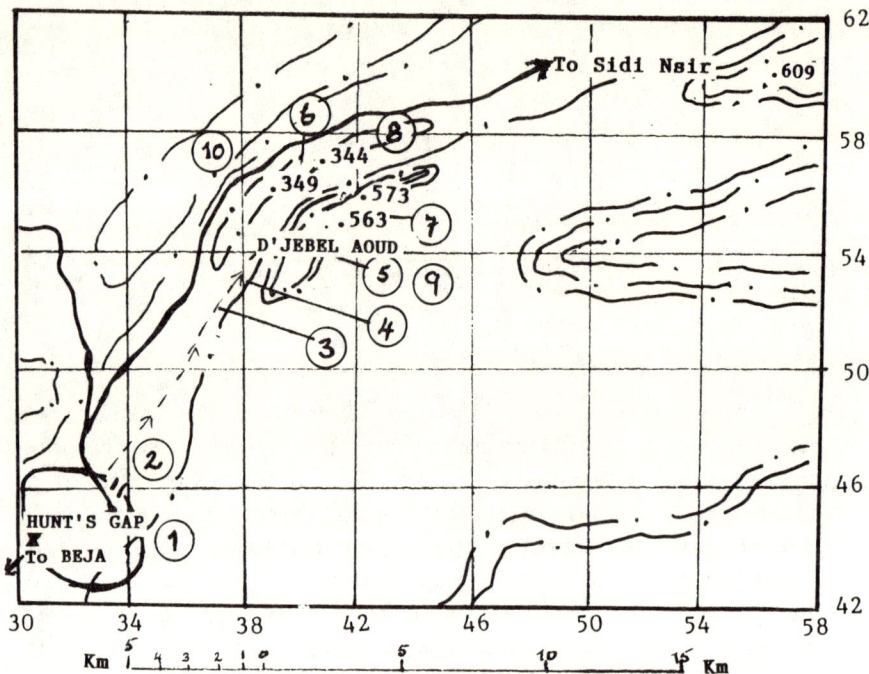

MAP 7

2ND BEDFORDS BEJA–SIDI NSIR 4–19 APRIL, 1943

1. 4 April Battalion takes over in line at Ksar Mesonar.
2. 11 April begins advance at 0430 hrs. Objective Point 609.
3. 1530 hrs Commanding Officer killed by enemy artillery fire.
4. Battalion leaguers for night. Advance continues 0630 hrs 12 April.
5. Forward companies held up. CO gives orders at 1500 hrs for night attack on Points 573 and 563.
6. 2200 hrs. Brigade orders Points 344 and 349 also to be captured by 0600 hrs 13 April.
7. Points 563 and 573 captured by 0530 hrs and prisoners taken.
8. Germans counter-attack and recapture Points 563 and 573.
9. Battalion consolidates on existing line and holds position until relieved by US 26 Combat Team on 19 April.
10. Surreys held up by strong enemy defensive position.

through a storm but they all arrived. The following night we relieved the 1st Hampshires and by 0440 hrs on 3 April we were in position in Hunt's Gap at the mouth of the Sidi Nsir valley in front of Beja, (Map 7). We had been a long time getting near the battle, but once near things had moved quickly. The seven days we were in position were fairly uneventful. A certain amount of mortaring and shelling went on and there were a few unpleasant fighter raids mostly on the Battalion Headquarters area. 'C' Company who were forward in a rather exposed position had some casualties from sniping. Operations were proceeding further to the north as a result of which it was expected that the enemy would withdraw and nightly patrols were sent off to test this. On the night of the 9th there were signs that this was happening and unusually heavy shelling during the night made it appear sufficiently certain to warrant sending out day patrols on the 10th and these confirmed that the enemy had gone from his previous positions. 'A' and 'D' Companies were ordered to move forward to cover the commencement of mine clearing and orders were issued for a brigade advance astride the Beja – Sidi Nsir road the following morning.

"This was the only road in this part of the country. It ran through a wide valley with rugged hills rising abruptly from the valley base several hundred feet on either side. These hills were very broken, barren and rocky with long razor ridges, and going was bound to be very difficult. Such was the nature of the ground on the ridges that digging was all but impossible. Recourse had to be made to using any available loose stone or rock to provide some form of protection from enemy fire.

"The Bedfords were to move through the hills to the south of the road and the Surreys to the north. It was not anticipated that the whole road would be opened up for some time. The general appreciation was that the enemy was not strong and that reasonable risks could be taken in the interests of speed. When contact was made, movement should be away from the road rather than towards it.

"At first light on 11 April the advance commenced. The Bedfords objective was Point 609 about seven miles ahead. The battalion plan was for an advance in two columns. On the left 'A' and 'B' Companies, the anti tank platoon and carrier platoon and two sections of the mortar platoon with a detachment of sappers for mine clearing. This column was under the command of Major Whittaker, the Battalion second-in-command, and was to move initially up the main road. 'C' and 'D' Companies with advanced Battalion Headquarters and

Colonel Johnson were to move through the hills to the right of the road. The two columns were to link up at crossroads some miles ahead.

"It was apparent from the outset that movement along the road was going to be very slow indeed: the road and fields to either side were heavily mined and booby trapped and mine clearance was slow. Captain Browning and five soldiers became casualties from mines during this phase. Meanwhile the column on the right was making much better progress after some initial difficulties with mines and tracks marked on the map which no longer existed. At about 1400 hrs it was decided the the road should be abandoned and that the left-hand column should turn off the road and follow the route taken by 'C' and 'D' Companies through the hills accepting the difficult going for vehicles and tracks. Meanwhile the right-hand column continued its advance and had reached the area of Ben Hederich (3753) when it came under heavy shellfire and Colonel Johnson was, most unfortunately, killed.

At about 1530 hrs Major Whittaker arrived with the leading elements of what had been the left column and assumed command. As it was now getting dusk, and the Battalion was very dispersed, the positions reached were consolidated for the night. Our tail was drawn in and necessary steps taken to recover the large number of vehicles and tracks which had become casualties from both columns during the advance.

"At first light the next morning the advance was resumed along the next series of features and in the shallow valley to the west of D'Jebel Aoud. The advanced guard commanded by Major Yate-Lee consisted of 'D' Company, the carrier platoon and two detachments of the mortar platoon. Contact with the enemy was made at about 0800 hrs and 'D' Company came under heavy small arms and mortar fire suffering a number of casualties in endeavouring to get on. After a visit to 'D' Company's positions and a recce to the right and east of D'Jebel Aoud I ordered 'A' Company to advance along the next series of features about half a mile to the Right. They came under mortar fire and suffered casualties but pressed on until they also were halted by small arms fire.

"In the early stages of the contact battle such as this, information about the enemy dispositions and strength is necessarily very sketchy. As it was getting into the afternoon and as a day attack in this country could not have been contemplated without careful artillery preparation, which would also have betrayed our intention, I decided

1. L/Cpl Major returns to the bridge over the Escaut Canal in 1990 (p37).

2. The Escaut Canal today, new buildings on both banks (p37).

3. "Medley deployed astride the road at Wulpen" (p54).

4. Wulpen today looking down the street from the German side of the canal. A footbridge has replaced the blown road bridge (p54).

after another recce to put in a night attack on the dominating feature of the enemy position and another feature to its right. This was to be carried out by 'B' and 'C' Companies respectively. At the same time 'D' Company was to make ground on the left of 'C' Company, whose objective directly controlled the area in which 'D' Company was being held up. After these objectives were gained 'A' Company was to send a strong fighting patrol out through 'B' Company to a small pass about eight hundred yards beyond, which would govern our next advance and give early warning of any enemy reaction. The attack was to be silent, but an artillery plan was prepared in case of need.

"Orders were given out to company commanders on the ground at 1500 hrs and a co-ordinating conference ordered for 2200 hrs. Zero hour was 0300 hrs, (Map 8 A).

"Whilst the co-ordinating conference was actually taking place at 2200 hrs, further orders came over the air from brigade. I was also to capture by first light the following morning two other features, Point 349 and Point 344, about a mile and a further half mile to the left and nearer to the road (Map 8 B).

"I protested that it was now dark and this would involve a further night attack for which I had made no preparations. I knew nothing about the ground in between. Further more it would leave the Battalion extremely dispersed. I was told that the other two features had to be captured. I said in that case I would have to abandon the attack I had already laid on and was told no, that must remain as well.

"This was all an extremely ambitious project. I thought the only thing to do was to cancel the strong fighting patrol going out from 'A' Company, to cancel the movement forward of 'D' Company on the left of 'C' and to hold these two Companies back in reserve to carry out the attack on Points 349 and 344. This phase of the attack would follow once "B" and "C" Companies had achieved their objectives. The Surreys were in the hills some six thousand yards on the other side of the valley beyond the road. They had been held up on much the same line as ourselves. To the right the nearest own troops were some miles to our rear. The Brigade was very dispersed.

"The attacking companies, 'C' on the left, 'B' on the right, crossed the start line at 0300 hrs. The approach to the objective and the attack was excellently carried out and took the enemy completely by surprise. Twenty six prisoners were taken and about the same number of Germans were killed. Our casualties were one officer and five soldiers wounded.

"By 0500 hrs both companies were able to report in position on

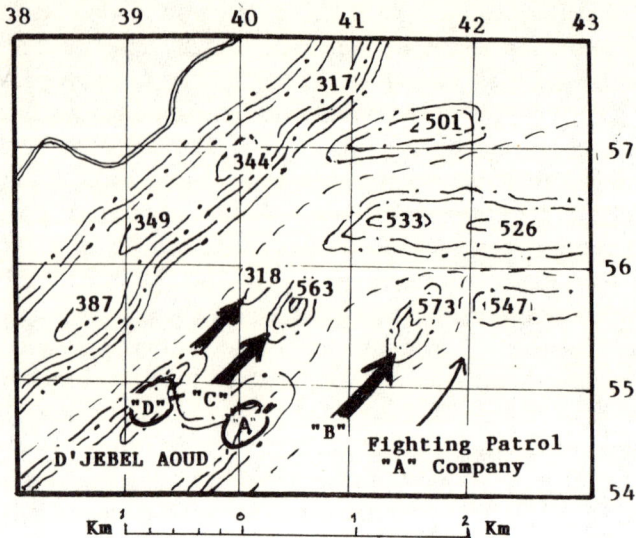

MAP 8A

COLONEL WHITTAKER'S ORDERS AT 1500HRS

"B" and "C" Companies to seize Points 583 and 573. Silent night attack, Start Line to be crossed at 0300 hrs. "D" Company to protect Left Flank and patrol from "A" Company to protect Right Flank, "A" Company remain in position at FirmBase.

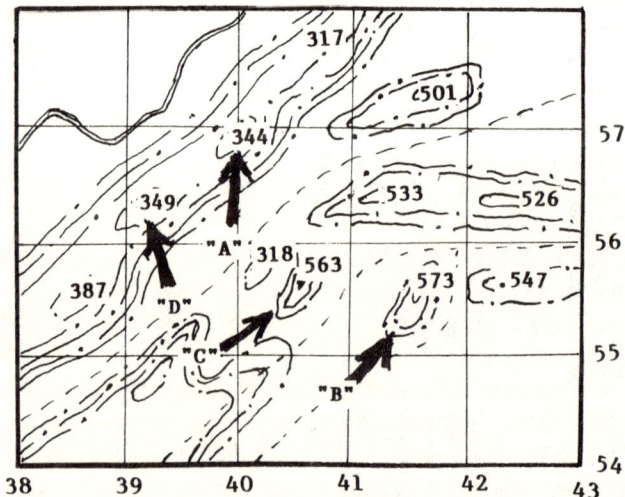

MAP 8B

CHANGE TO PLAN ORDERED BY BRIGADE AT 2200 HRS.

In addition to task to seize Points 583 and 573, Battalion was to attack and seize Points 344 and 349 also by 0600 hrs. "A and "D" Companies were given this task and previous flank protection instructions cancelled.

their objectives. A warning order was sent to 'D' and 'A' Companies to stand by to move to their new objectives. Shortly afterwards the Germans started mortaring the whole area and this fire was particularly accurate on 'C' Company positions. This seemed to suggest the possibility of reaction on the part of the enemy and I did not feel justified in releasing 'D' and 'A' Companies for their new tasks leaving the battalion with all four companies forward, widely dispersed in very difficult country, until the situation immediately in front of us had settled. I had been up to 'A' Company to assess the situation when I received a message that the Brigadier had been on the air and wished to discuss the position with me. On my way back to Battalion Headquarters, shelling resumed on the forward positions and very quickly a powerful counter attack developed from the left which completely overran 'C' Company and part of 'B'. For a time this threatened to envelope our right flank completely. This threat was averted by 'A' Company under Major Rayner who moved to cover the withdrawal of the remains of 'B' Company, though he too was eventually forced back to the original positions on the D'Jebel Aoud.

"Corporal Winter of 'A' Company was seriously wounded in a forward position and refused to allow his section to carry him back as he felt that this would hamper their own chances of withdrawal. 'D' Company was ordered to withdraw to conform with 'A', and carried out a very well controlled withdrawal in the face of the enemy. The carrier platoon was further deployed on foot on the right to prevent further penetration.

"It was most unfortunate that throughout this counter-attack the gunner liaison officer was unable to contact his guns to provide any defensive fire. It must be said that this was not 22nd Field Regiment, with whom we had trained extensively and had a close relationship but a converted Yeomanry Regiment attached from another division. 22nd Field were very upset when they heard about it.

"At this time it was not understood how this powerful counter-attack could develop so suddenly and apparently without warning. It was not until later when some of those taken prisoner were recovered that the tragic explanation appeared. It will be remembered that the plan for attack given out at 1500 hrs on 12 April had to be changed at 2200 hrs as a result of orders received from Brigade. By the time the company commanders rejoined their companies from the orders group at 2200 hrs 'B' and 'C' Companies were already on the move up to the start line and the change of plan did not get down to all ranks. In the early hours of the 13th the forward troops of 'C' Company heard and apparently saw movement in the half light and mist of the early morning. They assumed this to be 'D' Company moving up on their left, or as some said the fighting patrol going out. They therefore took no action and did not report it. This counter attack by the Germans was therefore apparently able to be prepared and to move into position without any interference.

"Had the original plan remained, the Left of 'C' Company would have been protected by 'D' Company and the fighting patrol from 'A' Company. The mortars which caused 'C' Company so much trouble would have been flushed. A subsequent visit to the battlefield made all this clear."

The story as seen from "C" Company, which bore the brunt of the enemy counter-attack is narrated by Major L.C. Young who was commanding "C" Company. "The advance continued at 0530 hrs on 12 April and after about two miles the carriers reported casualties from enemy mortars sited in the village to our front. 'D' Company managed to get through the village and take up positions on the north side where they were held up by machine-gun and mortar fire. In the meantime the Germans shelled and mortared the main body and Major Whittaker decided to send 'A' Company off to the right flank. They advanced through a valley in the hills and reached their objective by about 1500 hrs.

"Major Whittaker now took the company commanders of 'B' and 'C' up to 'A' Company's position to look forward over the ground ahead. The Commanding Officer favoured patrolling forward to gain information on the ground and about the enemy positions. We returned to our companies. However orders were subsequently received from Brigade to push on with all possible speed and Major Whittaker called for an 'Orders Group' comprising himself, the Intelligence Officer, the Gunner battery commander and company commanders to meet him back in the 'A' Company positions at 1500 hrs.

"The Commanding Officer confirmed the night attack and 'C' Company was tasked with seizing a hill feature to the left front of 'A' Company. 'B' Company was to move along a high ridge to the right with the task of patrolling forward with a platoon into a valley approximately one and a half miles further ahead where some enemy movement had been observed. 'A' Company reported that 'C' Company's objective was very lightly held and that no movement had been seen on 'B' Company's ridge.

"I was called to Battalion Headquarters for new orders at 2200 hrs.

Further orders had been received from Brigade directing that in addition to the two features we were already tasked for two further features forward and to the left of 'C' Company's objective were to be seized. This meant an alteration in plans with 'A' Company staying put and moving through 'C' Company once we were established on the ground. It was also decided that a platoon of 'A' Company would support me.

"There was little enough time left now for me to give out orders to platoons and just before we moved off the Company Sergeant Major reported that there were no 36 grenades. My plan of attack was for two platoons forward in the assault with 15 Platoon and the 'A' Company platoon in reserve. Company Headquarters under the second in command was central in the formation and I was with the leading platoons.

"We had travelled about half way to the objective, some 1200 yards when the enemy fired on us from our left. The position was obscure and as the leading platoons were not under fire I decided to press on leaving the second in command to deal with this problem. This meant that we had to make a deeper sweep to the right to get on to our objective and we were not at the base of the hill until about 0400 hrs. 13 Platoon on the left cleared out an enemy Observation Post capturing two occupants whilst 14 Platoon discovered enemy M.G positions. The follow up platoons were arriving on the hill which was almost sheer rock at about 0430 hrs just as light was breaking. The 'B' Company ridge was off to our right where fighting was going on. To our left was the high ground which was to be the objective of 'A' and 'D' Companies later on.

"I made a quick reconnaissance to decide where to place my platoons, considering first where they would be best able to support 'A' Company and second where they could get the maximum cover from enemy mortar fire as the hill was devoid of cover. I also had in mind my orders concerning the 'A' Company platoon which had suffered casualties including the platoon commander, Lieut Carter. The Company suffered twenty casualties during the advance, including Captain LaFontaine.

"My final decision was to place the 'A' Company platoon strengthened with a Bren Gun group on the extreme left and on the base of the hill where they would be able to get back to 'A' Company if orders came for them to do so. 13 Platoon were on the right of the company also facing towards the 'A' Company objective. 15 Platoon were on the Left with Company Headquarters between. 14 Platoon were on the other side of the hill facing half-right towards 'B' Company (Map 9).

"Communication was difficult as the 38 sets were not working and we could not contact Battalion Headquarters on the 18 set. I sent word back with two prisoners that we had reached our objective. I arranged for messages to be relayed by shouting between sections.

"There was no chance of digging in at all with the exception of 13 Platoon which occupied the O.P. Platoons had to get as much cover as possible behind small boulders which they found in the shape of section posts. By this time it was quite light and 'B' Company could be seen on their ridge with two platoons facing our position and with the third platoon presumably on the ridge itself. At about 0600 hrs we were mortared by light mortars which seemed to be in a position behind a small hill to our left rear facing the 'A' Company platoon. 13 Platoon tried to take on this target with their 2" mortar but the range was too great. Shortly after this a heavier mortar opened up on us. It was impossible to locate any of these as they were firing at us by groups from three sides. Any movement on our part was greeted by machine-gun fire.

"13 and 15 Platoons soon suffered casualties. I tried to move two sections of 15 Platoon to the other side of the hill but had to give up as there was no better cover there than where they were. We had by now managed to contact Battalion Headquarters on the 18 Set and I asked for artillery support on the enemy mortars and on anticipated forming-up places for any attack. I was informed the Commanding Officer was doing all he could to get this fire support for us.

"At about 0900 hrs following a succession of Very light signals, the Germans attacked on our left flank and got on to the hill behind the 'A' Company platoon. Lieutenant Lemon was hit by a mortar bomb splinter and died shortly after, which possibly explains why I received no word back at the time of this attack. At the same time I could see 'B' Company being attacked from all sides. Small arms fire was con-tinuous and the German mortars were still in action.

"The first intimation I had of the seriousness of the attack was the news that 13 Platoon were being attacked on their right flank and two men of the right section of 15 Platoon were seen standing up in their position with their hands up. I scrambled out of my scrape and threat-ened them with a rifle and was narrowly missed by automatic fire directed in my direction from about thirty yards range. Company Headquarters had their enemy well enfiladed and did good work hold-ing them back but the enemy were working round to the rear of 13

MAP 9

"C" COMPANY AT SIDI NSIR
13 APRIL 1943

1. Enemy fires on "C" Company fropm Left. 2 i/c and reserve platoons directed to deal with this.

2. 14 Platoon moving round Right of hill.

3. 13 Platoon capture Observation Post and two prisoners.

4. 14 Platoon capture enemy MG post.

5. All platoons on feature – casualties Capt LaFontaine Lieut Carter, the platoon commander of the "A" Company platoon attached, and 18 others.

6. Heavy enemy mortar fire. Lieut Lemon killed and two Brens knocked out.

7. Enemy attack on all fronts and overrun company headquarters. Privates White and Jenkins killed, Private Broom wounded.

8. 14 Platoon under heavy fire from Right, short of ammunition.

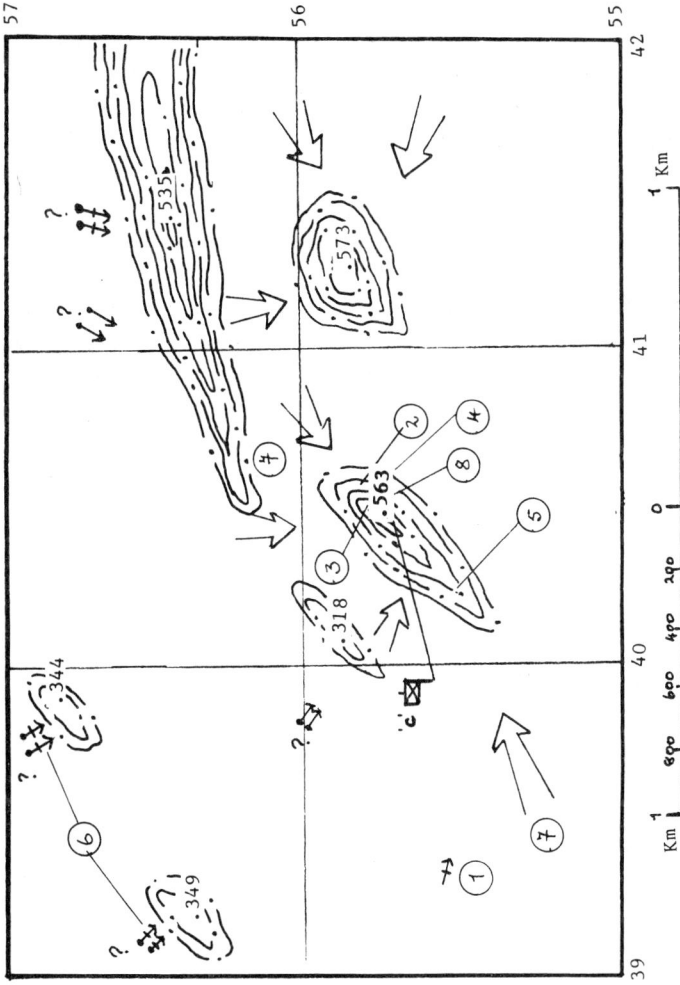

Platoon. Suddenly Germans appeared in front of and behind our trench and opened up with an automatic. Privates White and Jenkins were killed instantly and Private Broom was badly wounded. There was nothing more I could do against this new threat and I surrendered the trench. 14 Platoon was now exposed to fire from the hill above them and were enveloped by the assaulting German force.

"The nature of the ground makes it difficult to estimate what casualties were inflicted upon the Germans. We were handicapped by the lack of No 36 grenades and both 13 and 15 Platoons lost Bren Guns by direct hits from enemy mortars. Private Bryant of 13 Platoon attacked an enemy MG post single handed firing from the hip and put it out of action. The stretcher bearers also did excellent work; two of them were killed. Private Haston carried out his duties under fire in an exemplary manner. Lieutenant Crouch of 13 Platoon was wounded during the initial stages of the attack but carried on commanding his platoon. All platoons were short of ammunition towards the end. Soon after the attack started the No 18 Set went off the air and contact was lost with Battalion Headquarters. We had no supporting artillery fire throughout the action. It eventually came down on the forming-up positions on which I had called for fire after the Germans had overrun the position."

Lieutenant Turner remembers the confusion caused by the change of orders which did not give sufficient time for him to fully brief his men. He confirms the ruggedness of the terrain and the rocky features which prevented the construction of adequate defensive positions. When the attack started shortly after dawn the Germans seemed to be on all sides with the advantage of supporting fire. This was his first major action and the speed of events was almost hypnotic.

Lieutenant Darville was a platoon commander with "B" Company. "I recall some of the events of 12/13 April. Major Lofts, the Company Commander took platoon commanders forward on a reconnaissance to a point where the objectives could be seen. This was early evening on the 12th. The start line was crossed on time and initially everything went well. Some enemy fire was encountered and overcome and our objective was taken before dawn. At first light some mopping up took place and a number of prisoners were gathered and sent back. Some of these were used as stretcher bearers.

"The ground on the objective, a steep sided mountain, was rocky and digging was impossible. There were a few shallow sangars and these we used to provide some scant cover. The whole ridge was very exposed to higher features to our front and flanks. At this stage we had no contact with Company Headquarters and no wireless communication. Contact between platoons was by runner. I could see 'C' Company over to my left on a higher feature.

"I expected orders to either continue the advance or stay where we were and that other troops would pass through. The German attack against 'C' Company began and almost at once 'B' Company came under attack. It was not long before 'C' Company was overrun and fire was directed against "B" Company from all sides. The nature of the ground made any movement impossible and it was not long before the Germans had seized the high ground and taken the position. During the whole of this time there were no communications with Company Headquarters and only by voice between sections. Lieutenant Collins was wounded in the leg and foot and subsequently repatriated by the Red Cross late in 1944.

"I remember vividly our own artillery fire coming down after I had been taken prisoner. It came down about four hundred yards away in what had been the enemy forming-up area. It was thirty minutes too late!

"Lieutenant Selby escaped in Italy and made it to Switzerland in September 1943. I escaped in September 1943 and spent three months on the run before being recaptured in civilian clothes. I eventually arrived in Mahnisch Trubau in January, 1944, where I met up with Lieutenants Collins, Crouch and Turner of 'C' Company. Major Young escaped on 9 September, 1943, in Italy. The last I saw of him he was dressed in Italian civilian trousers which ended some two inches above his army boots, a shirt which barely reached down to his trousers and a small cap perched on top of his head. Looking exactly like an escaped POW he strode off into the vines. I understand he made it to the Allied Lines."

The story of this battle shows what can go wrong when basic principles are flouted. Higher command issued new orders after dark for an attack to be completed by dawn over ground which had not been, and could not be reconnoitred. This necessitated the alteration of orders already issued, which put the Battalion in a precarious position leading to a disastrous result. A study of the map of the area shows that the Battalion was separated from the battalion advancing on the far side of the Beja – Sidi Nsir road by some 5000 yards and had an open flank on the right. The task given to the Bedfords necessitated dispersion over a frontage of 3000 yards in inhospitable terrain. The distances involved caused difficulties in maintaining radio links and the forward troops did not receive artillery support when the enemy counter-attack came in. Companies could not provide each other with mutual fire support as the range was too great.

Colonel Whittaker resumes the story. " In the meanwhile, on the other side of the valley, the Surreys had made several attacks without success and the DCLI who had been in reserve were ordered to regain the objectives we had gained and lost the previous night. This order was later cancelled and the Brigade was ordered to consolidate on the line on which we stood. The Battalion dug in in the hills just South of Sidi Nsir having advanced just under six miles.

"We remained in this position until 19 April and during this time recovered, by night, six carriers from between the lines which had been knocked out in the earlier battle. This was a most commendable effort on the part of the carrier platoon and the various covering parties. The main activity apart from patrols was artillery fire from both sides. There was fairly consistent shelling but we were well dug in and suffered few casualties. The Intelligence Officer, Jack Douglas, was wounded but insisted on remaining at duty despite the fact that he was forbidden in that case by the medical officer to ride his motor cycle which we, and I think he himself, had come to regard as part of him. There was also a certain amount of air activity and we had the unique experience of shooting downwards at German planes as they manoeuvred in a valley below, unfortunately without success.

"On the 17th we had orders to send a recce party to the 6th Gordons who were in front of Medjez el Bab and a recce party arrived from an American formation which was to take over from us. The American party was not at first inclined to take seriously our warning of the inadvisability of moving about in groups. They had, I believe, the feeling that we were rather windy, but a very sharp and extremely accurate stonk by German mortars as they were leaving Battalion Headquarters soon put them right on this score, unfortunately reducing their party somewhat at the same time.

"The best method of taking Point 609 which remained their objective was discussed and the senior American officer, the second-in-command of the division, gave it as his opinion that the best plan would be 'To blast that 609 until it's 202 and then rush it." It is of some interest to note that the Americans later went through this area. Point 609, which had been our objective, was then the objective for an American division.

"We were relieved on the night of 18th/19th by an American unit and on the 19th after receiving reinforcements to bring 'B' Company up to strength we moved to Medjez el Bab to relieve the 6th Gordons. We were in position in front of Medjez by 0300 hrs on 20 April."

12

MEDJEZ EL BAB

The road running east out of Medjez el Bab separates in a fork just clear of the town. There the diverging roads run through fairly flat country for about three miles until at a point where they are about four miles apart they pass through an area of large rocky features. After which they emerge into a plain again on the far side.

Major Whittaker continues: "The area taken over by the Battalion was along this line of hills between the two roads and was just over four miles long. There were no transverse roads or good tracks and physical communication within the Battalion other than on foot was only possible by the roads back through Medjez. The area had been the scene of bitter fighting earlier on but recently had been very quiet. Owing to its length the position demanded four companies forward each with an allocation of battalion support weapons under command. "C" Company, not yet being reformed, the Carrier Platoon slightly strengthened was incorporated as the fourth company. The Germans were about two miles away on the other side of the open flat valley and were not very active.

"The Battalion layout was as follows, starting with the road on the left. There was a gap of about half a mile to "A" Company in a fairly compact area. A further half mile to two platoons of "B" Company with the third platoon about three quarters of a mile to the right. Then another gap of nearly half a mile to the Carrier Platoon position. A further half mile to the right and on the other side of a deep gulley was "D" Company's position on a big feature D'Jebel D'Jaffa. This position extended in three platoon posts for about three quarters of a mile when there was a gap of half a mile to the road on the right. (Map 10). Battalion Headquarters was about 400 yards behind "A" Company on the Left where it was accessible from the road.

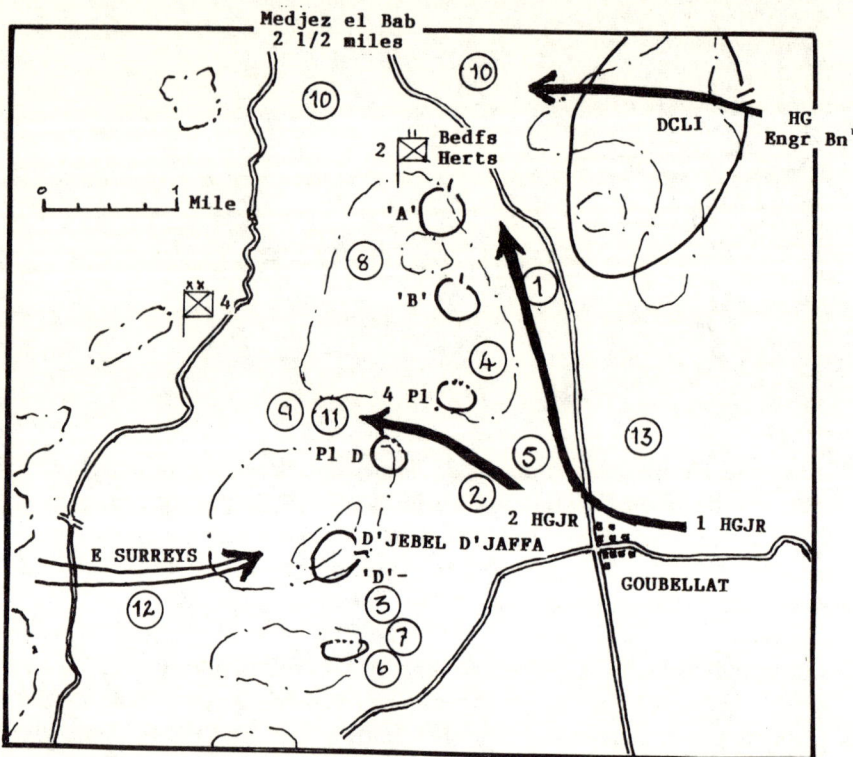

MAP 10
MEDJEZ EL BAB 20 APRIL

1. 0030 hrs – "A" and "B" companies report sounds of tanks.
2. Tank movement reported.
3. 0200 hrs – Heavy rifle and mortar fire on Right.
4. "B" company patrol fired on from Carrier platoon position.
5. Enemy attack with main thrust in Centre.
6. 0300 hrs – "B" company report no contact with 12 platoon.
7. Patrol from "B" company fired on from 12 platoon position.
8. 0400 hrs – Company of 6th Gordons to reserve position.
9. 0500 hrs – Enemy tanks moving through gap in lines.
10. 0900 hrs – Tank battle on plain in rear.
11. 1200 hrs – Enemy tanks start to withdraw.
12. 1500 hrs – E Surreys start counter attack.
13. 2100 hrs – Enemy tanks withdrawn from front.

"The brigade area was taken over at this stage necessarily on the previous appreciation and layout, which meant our Battalion anti-tank guns were with and under command of the DCLI on our left. It had been considered there was no tank run through our area. We were somewhat concerned that these positions had been occupied for a long time, more especially as the Germans had carried out some successful raids when the Americans had been there a month or so previously. Furthermore the Germans themselves had held this area for some time earlier and knew the ground in detail. We therefore decided to consider the possibility of alternative positions at the first opportunity.

"The relief was completed by 0300 hrs on 20 April and the remainder of the day was spent in reconnoitring alternative positions.

"Lt Colonel K.J.G. Garner-Smith arrived at Battalion Headquarters and took over command. I had been in command since the death of Lt Colonel D.S.W.Johnson.

"The foothills were patrolled at dusk. Further patrols destined to go further afield were preparing at 2200 hrs when a warning was received, in clear and urgently over the radio, that a strong enemy attack was imminent.

"At 0030 hrs on 21 April 'A' and 'B' Companies and the Carrier Platoon reported sounds of movement of tanks to their front, with 'D' Company and the carriers reporting movement of tanks in their area at 0100 hrs. At about 0200 hrs heavy rifle fire was heard from the right. No reply could be received from the Carrier Platoon. With the wide separation between positions, some penetration seemed inevitable and so a patrol was sent out from 'B' Company to ascertain the situation. This patrol was met by heavy small arms fire as it approached the Carrier Platoon position and was forced to withdraw. Attacks now developed along the whole of the battalion front, the main effort, apparently, being directed at the right centre in the area of the gully. At about 0300 hrs 'B' Company reported that it had lost contact with its right flank platoon, No 12. A patrol sent out again came under fire from 12 Platoon area. No contact could be made with 'D' Company. At about 0400 hrs a company of the 6th Gordons appeared, led by their commanding officer, who was going to plug the gap between 'A' and 'B' companies and assume a counter-attack role should 'D' Company's position be lost. The Gordons had not gone out of the area but were lying up just in rear of the Battalion. This was very fortunate and particularly useful later on.

"At about 0500 hrs more tanks were reported moving through the gap now existing between 'B' and 'D' Companies. Further heavy shelling and sporadic attacks developed upon 'B' Company but they retained their position, stood firm, and these attacks were repulsed.

"We now heard from Brigade that 'D' Company had made contact with the Hampshires on their right. Their left platoon, by the gully, had been overrun in the early part of the attack, but, though for some time completely surrounded their remaining positions, were holding. The Germans had, however, established themselves in some strength on D'Jebel D'Jaffa. At about 0900 hrs 'A' Company, Battalion Headquarters and the whole area came under small arms fire from positions now held by the Germans. At the same time a tank battle developed in the plain between the company positions and Medjez el Bab.

"The position was now very confused and it was impossible to obtain reliable information as to what was actually happening. It seemed that at about 1200 hrs the enemy tanks were getting the worst of the action and were beginning to withdraw. At about the same time we received a signal that the Surreys would be launching a counter-attack at 1400 hrs to recover that part of D'Jebel D'Jaffa held by the Germans. This attack went in across difficult country meeting strong resistance and the situation was still uncertain by 1800 hrs. The German tanks had withdrawn by 2100 hrs and the whole area was quiet. It was not until the following morning, the 22nd, that the Surreys were able to report D'Jebel D'Jaffa clear of the enemy and took over defence of the feature. 'D' Company now moved over to occupy the position previously occupied by the Carrier Platoon.

"It became known later that this had been intended by the Germans as a strong spoiling attack to disrupt the preparations for the final attack on Tunis. The fact that this had only been partially successful was due in no small measure to the spirited defence put up by the battalion particularly by 'B' Company and 'D' Company on the D'Jebel D'Jaffa."

Captain Douglas comments: " On the afternoon of the 22nd the battalion reorganized after the traumatic losses it had suffered first at Sidi Nsir and now on D'Jebel D'Jaffa. It seemed an odd time to receive a new commanding officer, Lt Colonel Garnons-Williams, who came from the Gordons but it was a strange war in North Africa. To me it seemed like all I had imagined the North-West Frontier to be like with isolated pockets occupying hill forts miles apart, except there were no forts and there were no tanks and aircraft and mines on the North-West Frontier."

The story is now taken up by Lieutenant P.F.Huckle, a platoon commander in "D" Company. " Moving from the Sidi Nsir sector to South of Medjez el Bab the Battalion took over the positions of the 6th Gordons at D'Jebel el Mouhra. 'D' Company was given positions on D'Jebel D'Jaffa and on the other two slightly lower peaks of D'Jebel el Mehirigar, about a mile away S.W., a frontage of some 2500 yards.

"The Gordons had allocated two platoons to defend D'Jaffa and one each to the secondary hills; company headquarters was at the foot of the central hill, a comfortable dugout but untenable in the event of attack.(Map 11).

"In view of the fact the company would have fewer troops available than the Gordons, permission was asked for the entire company to be concentrated on D'Jebel D'Jaffa, the most dominant feature, which overlooked the entire surrounding countryside for five or six miles. This request was refused. 17 Platoon under Lieut Harrowell was then given D'Jebel D'Jaffa, 18 Platoon with Sergeant Bryant the central hill and 16 Platoon were on the right. The defences on each crest were slit trenches blasted from solid rock by explosives and surrounded by wire. It was not possible to man all the trenches on D'Jebel D'Jaffa with the smaller number of troops and to keep all the surrounding wire under observation.

"It had been the practice to man the defensive positions on D'Jaffa during the hours of darkness only with a standing patrol in the pass between D'Jebel el Mouhra and D'Jebel Jaffa. There was a gunner observation post on the forward slope of D'Jaffa with a concealed communication trench leading to the rear of the crest which was manned in daylight. Other known friendly troops within the company area were some anti-tank gunners commanding the pass. No 4 Carrier Platoon was on the left of the company the other side of the pass, with the 2nd Hampshires on the right, somewhere to the south.

"On 19 April the Company was busy checking positions and carrying ammunition, grenades etc, up the steep slopes of the D'Jebels to the positions. About 2200 hrs a radio message from Battalion Headquarters reported tanks had been identified moving across the Battalion front. Captain Charkham ordered a full 'Stand to'. Soon after midnight we too could hear tanks and heavy small arms fire from the area of the pass and on towards Commando Farm.

"I was sent out with the company clerk on a reconnaissance patrol to identify the penetration, knowing that Commando Farm was occupied by various units including a Field Ambulance. Moving down a small wadi alongside the track from our position to Commando Farm

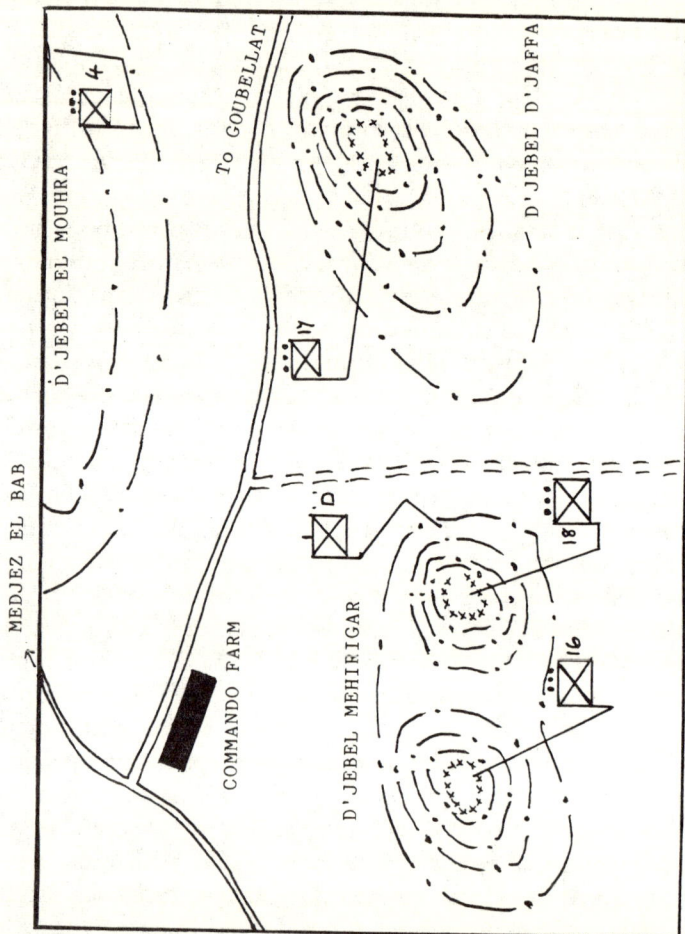

MAP 11
ROUGH SKETCH MAP BY MAJOR HORACE HOLLICK DSO.

"D" COMPANY POSITION D'JEBEL D'JAFFA 20/21 APRIL

we soon met a party of Germans identified by their silhouettes of two light machine guns carried on the shoulder, some fifteen to twenty strong, shouting excitedly in German and English with recognizable swear words. We threw grenades and made a wide sweep southward to try to reach the farm. In a second deeper wadi on the far side of the company area we found a light anti-aircraft detachment who had only just arrived and were interested to hear of the proximity of the enemy. Continuing towards Commando Farm there was again firing of light and heavier weapons and the area appeared to be overrun by significant numbers of the enemy. At the same time we could see gun flashes and firing on the crest of D'Jebel D'Jaffa and it was obvious that 17 Platoon was under heavy attack.

"Returning to company headquarters, now based on 18 Platoon position, we found Captain Charkham had taken most of 18 Platoon to go to support Jim Harrowell. After some time the firing ceased on D'Jaffa though there was still plenty of activity in the valley below us.

"Daylight showed no sign of our people on D'Jaffa and our radio was out of action. Thinking it possible we had lost half the company I left Company Headquarters with the Company Sergeant Major and went up to 16 Platoon to pass on information and check their situation. They were in good heart under Sergeant Wimshurst and had taken over a Vickers heavy machine gun, found it serviceable, and were ready to use it. Whilst we were with 16 Platoon a reconnaissance patrol from the 2nd Hampshires made contact and I asked them to pass a message back to our Battalion Headquarters that we had to assume that 17 Platoon may have been pushed off D'Jebel D'Jaffa but that our other positions were intact and that we intended to stay put unless otherwise ordered.

"Back at Company Headquarters a few men from 18 Platoon began to filter back with Sergeant Bryant. Their counter-attack had been checked by heavy machine-gun fire and our troops had been forced into the dead ground on the eastern steeper side of the D'Jaffa after having been pinned down on the open southern sloping face. Soon after Captain Charkham came in with most of the rest of the platoon. Some time later Jim Harrowell, with a few men from 17 Platoon also got back, having had a sticky journey via the plain and through the enemy still attacking Commando Farm.

"A tank battle was developing on the open plain with much manoeuvring in the uneven ground. There were several casualties on both sides and the battle continued until dusk.

"Our Company Quartermaster Sergeant happily managed to reach the company with a truck and rations and did much by his action and example to raise spirits. Meanwhile the Surreys were mounting an attack on the D'Jaffa starting from our position on D'Jebel el Mehirigar. Supported by tanks and artillery fire they advanced up the long sloping face that 'Butch' Charkham had tried earlier before being stopped by heavy fire from the crest. Later a second attack, led personally by Lt Colonel Bruno, advanced close to the wire. Lt Colonel Bruno and the platoon commander, Lieut Marlow, were killed during this final assault. The remainder were withdrawn under cover of smoke from the gunners back to our positions while the carriers picked up the wounded.

"Next morning we heard that Major Maggs of the Surreys had made a lone reconnaissance of D'Jebel D'Jaffa at first light and found it deserted except for one wounded German who said the remaining garrison had pulled out just after the second Surrey attack when they thought the smoke screen presaged a further attack.

"Our reconnaissance of the company area showed all the positions, including Company Headquarters, had been entered. Personal possessions, equipment and stores ransacked and strewn around. All the troops in the area on the reverse slopes appeared to have been killed or taken prisoner including the gunner observation post team. Our standing patrol was also missing.

"We received orders towards the end of the day to move into reserve. The Company assembled at Commando Farm and moved to new positions prior to the final assault on Tunis."

13

TUNISIA – THE FINAL BATTLES

The Battalion had been in action continuously since it had deployed near Hunt's Gap on 4 April. In the battle at D'Jebel Aoud on the road to Sidi Nsir it had lost eleven officers and 142 soldiers including the Commanding Officer. A further four officers and eighty soldiers were lost in the battle at Medjez el Bab. In the latter battle the Battalion had held on to widely dispersed positions against the counter attack by tanks and infantry of the Hermann Goering Division. Having withstood this attack, the battalion held its position until 26 April.

On 27 April the Intelligence Officer was ordered to "pace out" the distance to Goubellat with a view to a night patrol and to find out if there were any enemy in the vicinity. As he set forth on this task Captain Douglas was fired on by one of the the forward sections. He spent some hours pacing the route stirring up a column of dust on a cloudless, windless day there and back. There was no visible evidence of an active enemy at Goubellat, who if they were there were uninterested in his dust trail. Reporting back at 1700 hrs he was in time to join the Commanding Officer in a trip to Brigade to receive orders to pursue the enemy along the Medjez el Bab – Tunis road. This role did not materialize. Over the next few days there followed a succession of reconnaissances and orders as the Battalion moved to keep up with the pace of the pursuit and a series of moves whilst preparations were completed for the push for Tunis(Map 12).

On 2 May "C" Company was reformed under Major Lofts and that night patrols went out to the Snakeridge area. No contact was made with the enemy.

On 4 May the Battalion Reconnaissance Group proceeded to a Royal Artillery Observation Post on the 1st Infantry Division front to view the approaches via Montarnaud to a feature Point 151. The Battalion concentrated in the area of Snakeridge by 0600 hrs on May the 5th and company reconnaissance groups went forward to the same

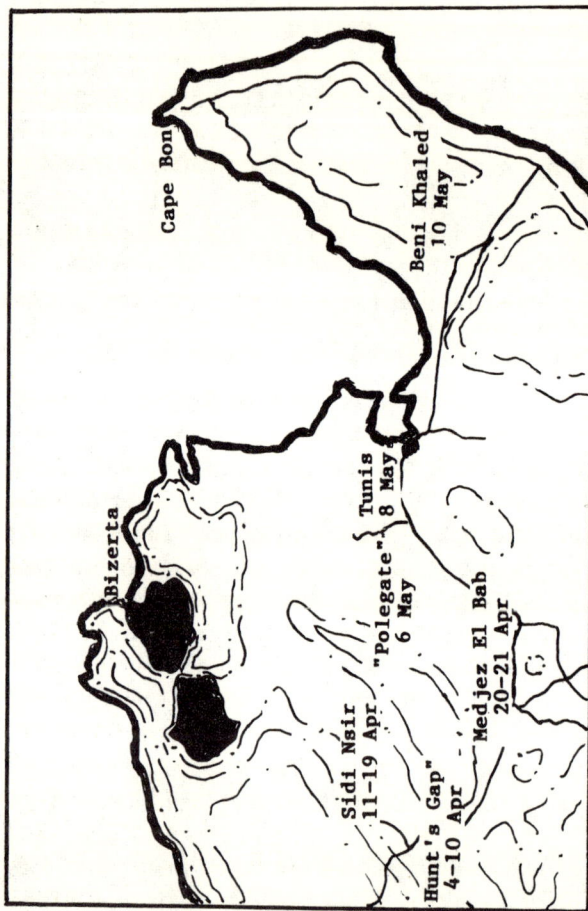

MAP 12

NORTH AFIRCA – THE PUSH TO TUNIS

This map shows the dates and locations of the actions in which the 2nd Battalion was engaged in the North African campaign in April and May, 1943.

Cape Bon

Beni Khaled
10 May

Bizerta

Tunis
8 May

"Polegate"
6 May

Sidi Nsir
11–19 Apr

Hunt's Gap"
4–10 Apr

Medjez El Bab
20–21 Apr

Miles

Royal Artillery Observation Post. At 1730 hrs Captain Douglas with his patrol from "C" Company and his Intelligence section had collected a load of reels of marking tape some 1500 yards in length in all. The start line was to be marked by tape to enable the first attacking battalions to advance under the artillery barrage next morning. This was a new experience and stemmed from the arrival under the 1st Army command of the 4th Indian Division, which had moved over from 8th Army command and was very experienced in attacks in the Western Desert. In that terrain there were literally no geographical features and attacking troops lined themselves correctly with the artillery barrage along a tape laid for that purpose.

Captain Douglas, who was the battalion Intelligence Officer at the time, was responsible for laying out the tapes to mark the start line for the battalion's night attack as part of the combined 4th British and 4th Indian Divisions' attack.

He tells his story. "The Bedfords' tape laying party consisted of my Intelligence Section and a patrol from "C" Company. The party from the 4th Indian Division comprised the same number under a Captain. The plan was for us to await dusk and then move down a track, which was the boundary line between our two divisions, for a predetermined number of paces. Having reached this point we were both to turn outwards and move with our respective parties on compass bearings laying tape diametrically opposed to each other. For our part we were to continue until we hit a track which was the right-hand boundary for the attack. Arriving at this point we were to turn to our right and report the task completed to the first unit in line contact with its own headquarters, proceeding thence to brigade and finally to rejoin the Battalion.

"Silence and secrecy were paramount and we were not to engage the enemy for fear that the start line and plan would be discovered.

"The reels of tape were clumsy and a hindrance, but I had set my compass, had it checked by my sergeant and off we went towards Montarnaud. With several hundred paces to go I could see an olive plantation. I knew from my visit earlier to the Royal Artillery Observation Post that the forward edge of this plantation was the line on which the artillery barrage was aimed to begin. I could hear, and my opposite number from the 4th Indian Division confirmed, the sound of digging in the olive trees. We checked our count of paces and agreed. I knew that I now had to estimate, in the dark, one hundred yards back from the olive trees and lay our line from there. Having agreed this with my opposite number, we shook hands, and laying our tape plunged into waist-high corn with more thistles than corn stalks. The corn and thistles were quite a feature for us all as we had been issued with khaki drill shorts that morning and our knees were sunburnt and tender.

"I looked back and to my consternation saw that the 4th Indian Division line was at an appreciable angle to our own, running towards the barrage. My first reaction was to ask myself how I had made such a cock-up and went quickly down his tape to check the bearing with him. His was different and appreciably so. I believe he had begun to think I was unreal but I was very worried. Suddenly a flash – magnetic variation. Our maps were old and a considerable allowance had to be made from the map to line up with the compass. I asked him and I am sure he did not know what I was talking about. In the desert the compass reading was used universally; without features and few or no maps, what else? I was already worried in case the bearing I had taken from the map using the edge of the olive plantation (because this was the gunners target) lined up with what I now had decided must have been new planting since the map survey. The gunners used aerial photos which did not distinguish between old and new. All this in the middle of a wet cornfield one hundred yards from a very much awake enemy and still my argument had not prevailed with my opposite number. We were both captains so I pulled the seniority card and got him to give me his date first. I lied to become his superior and gave him an order. So back to my own wet miserable party, who had listened and observed and now had something to show me.

"I saw and heard no sign of their German patrol until we got up to move on. As we moved they moved, when I stopped and hunkered they did likewise. After three separate one hundred yard moves with the same reaction I stopped my party, dispersed into the corn, pulling the corn behind each of us and waited, looked and listened. I waited it seemed for some time hearing nothing and seeing nothing, fully realizing that if they moved in our direction the tape would give our plan away. We had prepared to shoot it out as our last resort (there were more of us) in the hope that confusion would leave some of us able to complete the tape laying and advise the probability of compromise.

"Time was running away. I got up, pulled all my party in, stepped up the pace and laid the tape. The track when we reached the edge of the field was most welcome. We turned and moved towards our own lines when a password challenge came out of the night and the sound of a rifle bolt loading a round. I didn't recognize the password but I knew the response but when the strange challenge was repeated I realized with dread we had left the Battalion the previous afternoon. It was now 0145 hrs and we hadn't got the new password for the day, neither had the troops watching the front been apparently told of our tape laying operation.

"We heard the sound of a German infantry support aircraft approach and open its bomb doors right above us. I waited until I reckoned the bomb was about to hit, rushed forward and fell upon the soldier (who was from the 1st RWK as it turned out) as the bomb exploded. I think he thought the last trump had sounded. I found myself apologizing to him. We soon reported in, almost in the nick of time joining the Battalion just before it set off for the start line. At least I had time to collect a pair of long khaki drill trousers and the correct password.

"I discovered subsequently that the Germans had indeed been digging new positions at the forward edge of the olive plantation at Montarnaud. They had moreover sent a screen of patrols forward to prevent us from discovering these new positions. Their orders were the same as ours – no provocation.

"I never heard from my 4th Indian Division Captain. He probably is convinced that all Bedfords are barmy. Sometimes when I think of the holes we got ourselves into and out of I think we were."

On 6 May the Battalion took part in Operation 'Polegate' as part of the thrust by the 6th and 7th Armoured and 4th British and 4th Indian Divisions towards Tunis. The Bedfords' final objective was to seize and hold Point 156 which dominated the route. The Battalion moved to the forming-up point prior to the attack, arriving there at 2200 hrs. They set out for the start line at 0230 hrs, only thirty minutes after the taping party had returned to the Battalion. At 0300 hrs the leading companies, "A" and "D" crossed the start line under the covering fire of the heaviest artillery barrage since El Alamein. In spite of this fire support the enemy fought fiercely and MG, mortar and shellfire caused casualties among the assaulting companies. The leading companies were on their objective, Point 156, ten minutes ahead of schedule. Enemy MG fire during this assault inflicted casualties, as did shell and mortar fire on the objective itself.

Lieutenant G.C.LaFontaine (the brother of Tom LaFontaine already in hospital recovering from wounds) was killed. Capt Rayner and Lieutenants Harrowell and Shaw were among the wounded. "B" company joined the forward companies on the objective at 0610 hrs with Vickers guns and Anti-tank detachments.

At 0830 hrs tanks from the 6th Armoured Division passed through towards the village of Bordt Frenj. At 0930 hrs the Battalion was relieved by the 1st Northumberland Fusiliers and moved to Brigade reserve west of Point 175. "B" Company was shelled during this relief and sustained casualties. Through the afternoon the Battalion was dive-bombed and shelled, with "D" Company sustaining casualties. In the evening the Battalion relieved the 6th Black Watch on Point 161 and dug in for the night after a very eventful day.

Further orders were received on 7 May to be prepared to move in troop-carrying vehicles to support 6th Armoured in pursuit of the enemy and an attack was ordered for the following day. This order was later cancelled and the Battalion was now ordered on 8 May to advance with 10th Infantry Brigade to an area south of La Mohamedia behind 6th Armoured.

On 9 May a brigade reconnaissance party, which went forward to look at the ground for an attack on D'Jebel Ressas, came under enemy shellfire and Lt Colonel Garner-Smith was wounded and evacuated. Command of the Battalion devolved once again on Major W.A. Whittaker. Such was the pace of events now that the attack was cancelled. The enemy seemed to be moving backwards as fast as the Allies were moving forward.

Major Whittaker takes up the story once more. "Meanwhile on May the 8th the 6th and 7th Armoured Divisions had occupied Tunis. The 7th Armoured then continued north towards Bizerta whilst the 6th turned towards Hamman Lif at the base of the Cape Bon peninsula. The peninsula, about forty-five miles miles long and twenty-five miles wide, had been the base area for German operations in this part of North Africa. The German withdrawal appeared to be towards Cape Bon, and it was thought that they might be preparing to make a last stand there" (Map 12).

"On 9 May the 6th Armoured Division was held up by strong defences at Hamman Lif on the coast at the north-west end of the neck of the peninsula, whilst the 1st Armoured Division was similarly held up at Cretenville, on its approach to Hammamet on the coast at the south-east end of the neck. The country in between was semi mountainous and rugged. The Battalion, as part of 10th Brigade, was concentrated near La Mohammedia, about five miles south-east of Tunis, preparing for an attack through this central area, when, on the night 9th/10th the 6th Armoured Division carried out a most determined moonlight attack and broke through at Hamman Lif. They continued across the neck of the peninsula towards Hammamet, supported by 12 Brigade. The 10th Brigade's planned attack was cancelled and the Brigade was ordered to advance through Hamman Lif into Cap Bon in the hope of breaking up the German forces before effective resistance could be organized, The Brigade advance started at 1400 hrs on 10 May and, after passing Hamman Lif, continued for some twelve miles before adopting defensive positions for the night between Menzel Bou Zelfa and Beni Khaled.

"At 0600 hrs on 11 May the advance continued with the DCLI following the coast road on the north-west side of the peninsula, and the Bedfords branching off across the centre eventually arriving at their final objective, the airfield at Menzel Temimi.

This was about two thirds up the south-east coast of the peninsula. This objective was reached by the morning of 12 May. During this advance the Battalion suffered only a handful of casualties from shell-fire in the early stages. Resistance where it occurred was little more than token. "This was, however, a rare, if not unique period in the history of military operations. The North African Campaign had from early days been something of a private war, and, no doubt, aided by the cartoon 'The Two Types' in the Union Jack and the eccentricities of some commanders, and later with General Montgomery's cricket references, had always had a fair leavening of sporting overtones. And so it ended in an atmosphere for all the world as if the final whistle had blown and the game was over. Groups of men, who less than twenty-four short hours before had been determinedly intent only on killing each other, and would be so again in changed circumstances, met, and whilst there was no fraternizing, neither was there as much apparent hostility as one might find at the end of many a professional football match. It all started shortly after we had left Beni Khaled in the early morning, with individual groups of men surrendering as we approached, and increased during the day, until by midday some thousand or so prisoners had been passed back. As we continued to advance Germans and Italians came streaming in from every direction to surrender. Groups of individuals; whole sub-units with officers and NCOs; the great yellow diesel lorries with their trailers carrying fifty or sixty in each, with their baggage and swathed in white flags; staff officers in their cars, including two Regimental Commanders with their batmen and ADCs and all their kit. Quite early on the Intelligence Officer, Jack Douglas, was heard on the air to Brigade asking for the nearest prisoner of war cage. On being told where to send them, 'with minimum escort', he replied, "These chaps don't need an escort, all they need is a guide". Later it was learned from interrogation further back that the German soldiers had in general felt that they had put up a good fight, which indeed they had, and could surrender with honour when it became obvious that the game was up.

"On 12 May the 2nd Battalion settled for a peaceful night's sleep with a company at each corner of the airfield at Menzel Temimi. It seemed unnecessary for each to mount more than double sentry posts. There were more than 1000 prisoners in the centre of the airfield, but with the Mediterranean on one side and the desert on the other, they were not going anywhere.

"The Battalion now had the task of combing an area of some 200 square miles, to collect in any remaining Germans or Italians, deal with any pockets of resistance, and find out what military installations there were, including of course hospitals. A high priority was to bring in all vehicles that were runners. The intention was that these would be passed on to the Free French, who were woefully short of equipment.

"Parties were sent out in all directions – on foot, in carriers, on wheels and on motor cycles. Shortly reports of dumps, technical stores and, in our view most important of all, an enormous Italian ration store. This obviously merited special attention and the Quartermaster was duly despatched with a few three ton vehicles. Meanwhile a number of German trucks that were runners were being brought in but the yield was disappointingly small, as the Germans had made most of them unserviceable, just as we did in Belgium in 1940. Major Yate-Lee, however, acquired a car for a brief period and those who remember him will have no difficulty in visualizing him in the back seat of a German General's Mercedes looking, for all the world as though he were the rightful owner.

"A few days later an American airfield maintenance unit arrived. One must hand it to them – within twenty four hours German vehicles were running in from every point of the compass. I sent for their commander and told him they must hand in all these vehicles. He was most unhappy. The following day he appeared again. A man of his unit had found a truck. All that it needed was just a little nut. That man has gone all over Cap Bon, he pleaded, until he found that little nut. He did and now he's got the truck going. Now do I have to tell that man to hand that truck over? Sadly I told him he had and he left a broken man. War can be very cruel.

"I had been visiting Italian and German hospitals reported in our area to ensure that they had adequate supplies for the moment. At one, a very large tented German hospital some half-mile long and several hundred yards wide I arrived at the main square and sent for Herr

Commandant. In due course he appeared with his staff, a very Prussian type of Colonel, even complete with monocle. He presented his staff with great ceremony and considerable clicking of heels. After discussing his supply position and having a brief tour of the camp, we were about to leave when he asked, 'Could you please send me some soldiers to guard my camp? Now that they know we are beaten, robbers are breaking in and stealing.' I had to explain that having just one battalion and being fully operational this was not possible. The German colonel then said, 'Well, if you cannot send me some soldiers, will you send me some weapons so that we can guard ourselves?' I was so impressed with the high standard of discipline that was obvious throughout this camp and also by the fact that this German colonel now regarded himself as completely under our orders, that I readily agreed. We sent some rifles and ammunition from one of our captured dumps together with a note saying we were now responsible for the civilian population so we must have his assurance that these weapons would not be used except to assure the safety of his property and personnel. We had the reply, 'I can assure you. I think. that they will not be used at all. So long as they know we have them, other people won't come near us.' So far as we know they were never used.

"On 16 May those Bedford prisoners who had been captured by the Germans in earlier battles, who were still alive and fit and had not been evacuated to Italy by the Germans, were returned to the Battalion.

On 20 May the Battalion took part in a victory parade through Tunis. General Eisenhower took the salute. But the same day we suffered a severe blow, we were ordered to despatch four officers and 248 other ranks as reinforcements for the 1st Division. By now the airfield was getting busy, and on the 22nd the Battalion moved to Kelibia some ten miles further up the coast. Mopping up continued as reports of Germans continued to come in, but few were found. On 2 June the Battalion lined the road at Grombalia for a drive past by the Prime Minister, Winston Churchill, the Foreign Secretary and the Chief of the Imperial General Staff. This was in a way disappointing. We had a very early start, a long drive and quite a long wait lining the road and when the party came, they went by at such speed that there was scarcely time to realize who was there.

"At about this time Boubaker Saafi, the head of the Dar Saafi, the largest tribe in this part of Africa, announced his intention to entertain 'Les Officiers de l'Armée Anglaise glorieuse' and on 11 June Brigadier Hogshaw, commanding the 10th Brigade, with his three commanding officers and their adjutants proceeded to Boubaker's village in the mountains. The entertainment was to take the form of a demonstration of falconry followed by lunch. Unfortunately in deference to the convenience of 'les officiers Anglaises' the falconry was set to start at eleven o'clock, by which time the sun was well up and it was very hot. The birds released as prey only flew two or three hundred yards and settled, obviously preferring to risk death rather than try to fly in that heat, to the evident disgust of our hosts. The meeting was therefore abandoned and the party adjourned to the more congenial, but almost equally lethal fate waiting us. The lunch was very well arranged and some excellent food, beautifully cooked, with some interesting wines, all no doubt influenced by the French Consul who was present. But fifteen courses! It was not possible to deny any dish, since each was said to be an offering of a particular branch of the Dar Saafi. At course eight a whole roasted lamb was carried round the table. The Brigadier murmured, 'They could hit me on the head with a hammer now, I wouldn't even notice.' It was a very generous gesture on the part of the Dar Saafi but after living on army rations for four years our stomachs were scarcely prepared for such feasts and the party left eventually feeling very much as French geese must feel on their way to becoming foie gras.

"On this day another blow was dealt to our morale when we were ordered to send some of our equipment and weapons to 78 Infantry Division.

"On 18 June the Battalion lined the road at Turki for a drive past by His Majesty King George VI, and on the 22nd the brigade received a warning order for a move.

"After handing over to the 6th Gordons, the road party left on the 25th and the Battalion, together with the DCLI, left by rail from Tunis on the 26th bound for Djidjelli, some 200 miles west on the Algerian coast. The train proceeded in the usual hesitant way, until, to everyone's surprise, it arrived at Constantine early the next morning. Surprise, because Constantine was not on our intended route. The Railways Transport Officer appeared and explained that our destination had been changed. The Battalion destination was now Bougie and would the officer commanding the train come to his office and sort out the arrangements. I went along as OC train, taking Lt Colonel Musson commanding the 2nd Battalion DCLI and our two adjutants. While the RTO was on the phone, discussing the future with some distant authority, the tail of the train was suddenly seen to be disappearing in the distance. Our party piled hastily into a truck and set out in hot pursuit. There was, of course, little difficulty in catching the train. This occurred as the engine was taking a breather before attempting an incline which lay ahead. There, the men of the two battalions had the delight of seeing both their commanding officers and adjutants chasing across fields after the train, which had left them behind. They were not of course without encouragement. In later years Geoffrey Musson became the Adjutant General of the Army."

14

NORTH AFRICA – BOUGIE

Colonel Whittaker continues his account of events. "The journey continued in the same vein, with a series of hilarious incidents until the train arrived, on the morning of the 28th, not at Djidjelli or Bougie, but at Philippeville. Troop-carrying vehicles awaited us there and, as though to preserve the whole spirit of the move, as the vehicle column left the station yard it became entangled with our own MT column, which had left Tunis three days earlier.

"After exchanging expressions of good will with the engine driver, who was, by now, virtually a member of the regiment, the Battalion embussed for Bougie, where we arrived on the afternoon of 29 June.

"Bougie turned out to be a fairly undistinguished coastal town midway between Algiers and Philippeville and we set up our tented camp just outside the town by a road heading inland to nowhere. We were now a long way from the action and consequently rather uneasy about our next role. Particularly so after the large draft we had had to send away before leaving Tunisia. However, we were encouraged by the information that a flotilla of a new type of Landing Craft Infantry was on its way to Bougie. We were to familiarize ourselves with these craft and prepare a programme of combined operation training.

"Combined operations and general training continued with special emphasis on physical fitness. At the same time a special non commissioned officers' cadre continued throughout this period. Reviewing recent operations, I felt that the wide dispersal which came about, and was likely to continue in future operations demanded a high standard from the most junior commanders, the Section Commanders. A programme was prepared which had two objectives: firstly to increase the confidence of junior, and potential, non-commissioned officers and secondly to give them plenty of actual practice in the physical command and control of a section. This training covered all aspects of war covering various operations using live ammunition and as far as possible under battle conditions. Captain Bricknell, who had done his initial training in the Guards and had absorbed their philosophy and methods, was put in charge of the cadre. He was assisted by two very capable and enthusiastic sergeants, Kennedy (later CSM) and Plant. The splendid work put in by these three, with not a little 'Theatre', paid dividends later in Italy. At the end of the three-week course I attended the passing-out tests with all the company commanders.

"On 2 August a change in battalion organization was decreed. The Pioneer, Carrier, Mortar and Anti-Tank platoons broke from the administration of Headquarters Company to form a new Support Company. Captain La Fontaine, who had been wounded at Sidi Nsir and had recently returned to the Battalion from hospital, was appointed to its command.

"Some reinforcements had been arriving, sixty-five in July and on 2 August thirty five. The latter were mostly returning casualties. Then on 3 August a draft of four officers and 189 men. Included in this draft was Captain Hollick, a long time member of the Regiment who was later to distinguish himself in battle. At about this time Lieutenants Sutton, Kemsley and Ord also joined. All three played important parts later. Sutton, who had experience with explosives, became Pioneer Platoon Commander, as did Kemsley with the Signals, whilst Ord became an outstanding Transport Officer.

"Things were now looking up. Training continued with renewed enthusiasm and we confidently awaited orders for a return to active operations.

"Orders duly arrived on 10 August to despatch ten officers and 275 soldiers to the Infantry Reinforcement Training Depot. This was a bitter blow, but worse was to follow. Further orders came to despatch twenty-three soldiers on 8 September, and another ninety-six on 21 September. We were now sending away men we really wanted to keep. All infantry units of the 4th Infantry Division, camped at different parts of the Algerian coastline, were similarly affected and the utmost gloom descended. The hammer blow came on 30 September when orders came to despatch a further four officers and 110 soldiers.

"Long and anxious discussions took place in company offices and finally the orderly room as to who should be posted away. The overriding principle had to be to keep those who would contribute most to the reconstruction of the Battalion, when, as we continued to assume, that would take place. Personal factors were also brought into the balance. So and So's wife was about to have a baby, someone else's young son had recently been killed in England. Private 'X' might not have much to offer but had a record of long unblemished service with the Regiment. All these and many other matters were considered before lists were drawn up and we had to say goodbye to many who had put in good service with the Regiment.

"This was a most unhappy period made worse by the fact that we had no idea what the future might hold. It was perhaps just as well that we did not know what the intention was at this time.

"It will be remembered that the 4th Division was a mixed division consisting of two infantry brigades and one tank brigade. High Command had decided that a mixed division did not fit into the pattern of operations taking place in Italy and that the 4th Division should be broken up and used as reinforcements. Blissfully unaware of this, we continued in the firm belief that this was only a temporary hiccup. Training continued, mostly operational, active, and where possible competitive. All ranks were left in no doubt that they had been selected to form the nucleus around which, and with whose help, the Battalion would be reconstituted when it would be made up to strength again. The trouble was that we did not know when that would be. We did not contemplate *if*.

"Early in October I met, quite by chance, Colonel Brookes who was commanding 48 Royal Tank Regiment, still part of the 4th Division with whom we had trained in England. We hatched a plot together for a full-strength composite company of Bedfords to set up camp alongside the tank regiment at Bone. This was on the coast about one hundred miles east of Bougie. The plan was to carry out a number of combined exercises and to get to know as much about each other as possible. The company moved to Bone on 23 October and stayed there for about a month during this time the infantrymen acted as tank crews and the tank crews as infantry. Many Bedfords learnt to drive a tank and others had the chance to fire the tank gun. The outcome was that the infantry decided they preferred to go to war on their feet whilst their opposite numbers expressed a strong preference to remain in their tanks. This training period was excellent value both in itself and as a break from normal training.

"Meanwhile at Bougie we had received orders to prepare our camp for the coming winter. This did little to raise our spirits. However, the great majority of those remaining in the Battalion, officers, warrant officers and soldiers, had by this time, served in close association and under active service conditions for so long that a splendid spirit prevailed. The prospect of the Battalion breaking up was so unthinkable

5. "The whole beach seemed to be filled with well-disciplined lines" (p61). Painting by T.S. LaFontaine.

6. "Some of these had been driven out into the sea to form jetties" (p64). Painting by T.S. LaFontaine.

7. "Johnny's terrific good humour and enthusiasm carried the battalion through a period in which it might well have become stale" (p76). Painting by T.S. LaFontaine.

8. C Coy HQ, Montange Hunt's Gap, April, 1943, by T.S. LaFontaine. (p79)

that we had no alternative but to await the future with expectation.

"Mention must be made of the three key members during the whole of this period. Jack Douglas had taken over from Jenkins as Adjutant shortly after we arrived at Bougie. He had taken to the appointment like a duck to water and his efficient, cheerful and understanding approach was a most important factor in the maintaining of morale. In this he was ably assisted by RSM Roberts. Then Harry Beasley, the Quartermaster, always helpful, never at a loss for a solution to any problem that fell in his domain. We were lucky.

"The company which had been on detachment with the tanks at Bone returned on 25 November and preparations for winter continued."

Captain Douglas comments : "It is difficult to convey the state of depression which pervaded through all ranks when draft after draft of soldiers were posted away after the closing stages of the North African campaign. It was sad to see the posting away of so much new found experience and battle wisdom. I know that I am obsessive about this but to watch a good unit die the death of a thousand cuts and to suspect that it was destined for final extinction was extreme desolation. I know that my own disillusionment with the Army was great and growing. Training and regimentation were the only antidotes, apart from being the only way to fulfil the duty we owed to our soldiers.

"To have the Battalion snatched from the maw, trained, exercised and quickly thrown into battle was indescribable elation. To then witness it biting the bullet, time after time, was to be made prouder than all the rest of the Army."

Colonel Whittaker continues: "The signal arrived on 28 November: Prepare to receive reinforcements sixteen officers and 428 other ranks early December. We were also warned that we would have little time to absorb them.

"Five officers and 203 other ranks arrived on 5 December from our own 9th Battalion, followed shortly by two officers and eighty-one other ranks from the Infantry Reinforcement Training Depot, seven officers and ninety-seven other ranks from the Royal Norfolks and a mixed contingent of two officers and 128 other ranks. In all a total of sixteen officers and 509 other ranks.

"To say the camp buzzed would be an understatement. Intensive organization and training was the order of the day and everyone played his part with commendable enthusiasm. We didn't have much time. December the 15th found us on our way to Algiers where we embarked on the *Llangibby Castle* for Port Said.

"Arriving at Port Said on 22 December the Battalion moved by train to Kabrit in the Canal Zone where, once again, we started combined operations training. Between 1 and 15 January the Battalion took part in five separate brigade exercises across the Bitter Lakes, assaulting the shore of Sinai, visualizing different conditions and consequently different loadings. That concentrated effort completed, it seemed an anti-climax to return to standard training and I ordered a sports fortnight. The Quartermaster was despatched to NAAFI to get all the equipment he could, officers were appointed in each company in charge of each sport and everyone had to put his name down for at least one sport including athletics. Platoon and company teams competed and for a period the Battalion area looked like a school's sports finals. We had one cricket mat stolen. The theft was reported to the military police and a weary voice inquired 'Were you playing on it at the time?'

"Early in February the Battalion was again on the move, this time to Amerya near Alexandria. It was fairly obvious where our next move was going to be. All who had served with the Battalion since our arrival in North Africa were sent off on forty-eight hours leave. Everyone returned on time.

"On 14 February the Battalion embarked in the *Letitia* for Italy." This latter period at Bougie was exceedingly frustrating as it threw a heavy responsibility upon the Commanding Officer and his key subordinates. Not only was it essential to pursue an effective programme of training but it was important to maintain the morale of those officers, NCOs and soldiers selected to stay and form the nucleus on which a full strength unit would be built. The Commanding Officer decided to place emphasis on the training of section leaders and junior leaders.

On 15 December the Battalion sailed to Port Said, where training continued in the sands around Kabrit. This move to arid desert wastes caused some comment at the time on the mountain warfare training; however, on deployment to Italy the hardening up proved beneficial.

The North Africa campaign was really the last time when enemy aircraft caused any worries for the allied ground troops. Although the 1st Army had spent many months in hard training in the UK prior to deployment to North Africa, they found themselves up against a battle hardened enemy who had the advantage of terrain to assist him in his defensive battles. The German commanders also had battle experience honed over the years, whereas Allied commanders, at all levels, were adjusting afresh to the realities of live ammunition. War is a hard learning ground and it was not long before commanders realized that "pressing on at speed" which had been emphasized in training did not pay the dividends anticipated. Planning needed to allow time for full preparation to ensure that orders were understood by all down to the individual soldier in the forward rifle company. Initially commanders and staffs ignored this aspect with resultant foul-ups.

The Battalion had lost its colonel in the first action, and suffered the effects of an enemy counter-attack when, due to communication problems, the forward companies were without any artillery support. The distance between company objectives also meant that mutual support between companies was not possible.

It had subsequently, only a few days later, withstood a tank and infantry assault by the Hermann Goering Division again when dispersed in positions over a wide frontage. It had held this assault without its anti-tank guns, which were deployed to aid a neighbouring battalion, as higher command thought there was no tank threat on that part of the front.

The Battalion received reinforcements and took part in Operation "Polegate", the final major assault towards Tunis, where the attacking companies seized their objectives ahead of schedule against determined resistance.

Once the battle was won the Battalion faced the disappointment of exclusion from the invasions of Sicily and Italy, withstood the constant loss of drafts to other units, and set about rigorous training to remain fit for battle.

Suffice to say the key staff met this challenge and when at long last the call came the Battalion was ready.

15

ITALY FEBRUARY 1944 –
THE GENERAL SITUATION

Such was the threat to Germany posed by the invasion of Italy and the defection of the Italians that reaction had been fast and positive. The German Army, by mid October, 1943, had deployed nineteen divisions against the Allied thirteen. Not only did the Germans enjoy the advantage of interior lines of communication, the terrain was much to their advantage. A deep defensive zone had been developed across the breadth of Italy which made use of the dominant features as artillery observation posts, from which they overlooked the valleys below. This defensive barrier was called "The Gustav Line". In the west the pivotal post was the massif of Monte Cassino.

There were two Allied Armies in Italy. The Fifth Army under the American General Mark Clarke was on the west coast. This Army, besides having American divisions, also had Polish, British, Free French, Indian, Canadian and New Zealand formations under command. On the east coast and linking with the Fifth Army was the British Eighth Army under the command of General Sir Oliver Leese. This Army had Canadian, Indian and Greek formations, besides the British divisions.

The general front line ran from Ortona in the east across the central mountain features to Minturno on the west coast, (Map 13). Monte Cassino dominated Route 6 the main trunk route North to Rome, and Monte Cairo rising behind it overlooked the Liri and Garigliano valleys. The structure of Italy with the central spine of rugged mountains favoured defence. Streams running down off the mountain slopes towards the sea formed deep ravines. Rains and melting snows increased the hazards as flood waters made streams and

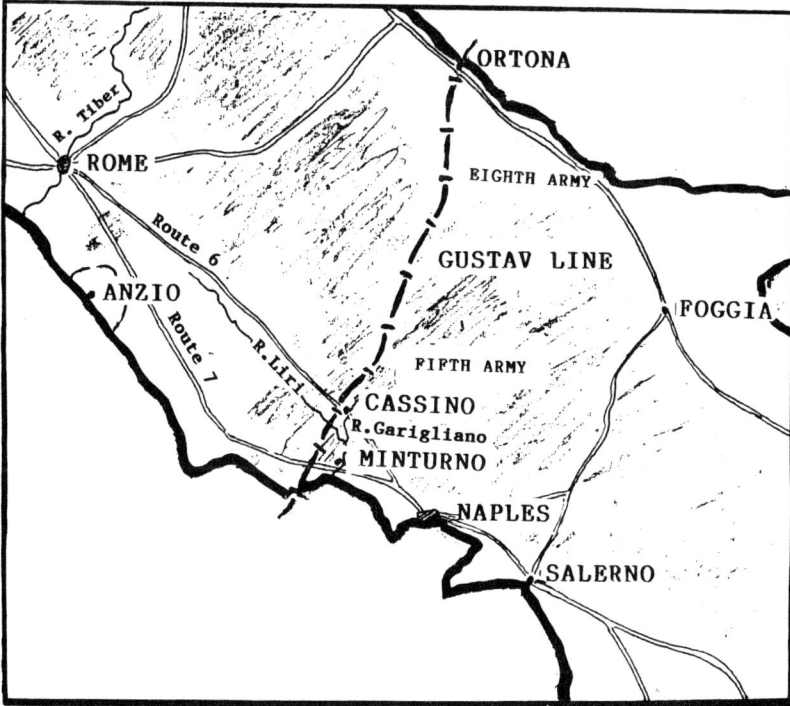

MAP 13

ITALIAN FRONT – JANUARY 1944

rivers impassable obstacles washing away pontoon bridges and cutting off forward troops from vital supplies.

Each of these natural obstacles was sufficient problem in itself, without the addition of man-made hindrances in the form of mines and booby traps covered by defenders in well-sited concrete bunkers and weapon pits. To these had to be added the extra logistical headaches of having to open up supply routes to the front line troops, and the task of ensuring that the soldiers of different nationalities and creeds received ammunition of the correct calibre and their own rations.

The initial battles for Cassino fought through the winter months had developed into a slogging match. Attempts to force a crossing of the River Garigliano at Sant' Angelo by the US 36th Division on 20 January had been repulsed by the Germans with heavy losses.

On 22 January an Allied force landed at Anzio behind the German defensive front with the aim of thrusting towards Rome and drawing troops from the Gustav Line. German reaction was swift. Drawing three divisions from the quiescent east coast and a further four divisions from the north, this threat was held without the Germans having to withdraw any forces from the front at Cassino.

Further attacks in late January by the US 34th Division, had fought forward as far as Cassino town and on to the lower slopes of Monte Cassino. Again the Germans held on. The first battle of Cassino had ended.

The second major assault in February was spearheaded by the 4th Indian Division transferred from the Adriatic coast. The plan was for the 4th Indian Division to attack and capture Monastery Hill above Cassino, whilst the New Zealand Division captured Cassino Station a heavily fortified position. The earliest launching of this attack was forced upon the commander so as to relieve pressure of a determined counter-attack by the Germans against the Anzio bridgehead. The attacks went in and fierce hand to hand fighting took place on Monastery Hill which the Germans held. The New Zealand Division stormed and seized the station but they were driven back by infantry supported by tanks. The second battle of Cassino was over, with the Germans still in command of the key position on Monastery Hill.

Although the attacks against Cassino to open up Route 6 and the way north up the Liri valley had not met with success, a bridgehead had been seized across the River Garigliano nearer the coast by the 46th and 56th British Divisions. A foothold had been established on the craggy mountains beyond the river below Mount Majo and Mount Faito on Cerasola Ridge.

The 4th Infantry Division, from Egypt, joined the Fifth Army to relieve the 46th Infantry Division, which was defending the bridge-head over the River Garigliano on the left centre of the front. The 4th Division now comprised three infantry brigades; the 10th and 12th which had been part of the Division since the initial battles in France and Belgium in 1940 and throughout the campaign in North Africa, and the 28th Infantry Brigade which had been brought in to replace the 21st Tank Brigade.

The scene is now set to resume the story of the 2nd Battalion, which had arrived in Italy from Egypt.

The part played by the 2nd Battalion in the initial battles and the battle at Cassino have only been covered in outline in Volume II of *The Story of The Bedfordshire and Hertfordshire Regiment (The 16th Foot)*. The period from June to November 1944 has been covered in some detail based on the account provided by Lt Colonel B.A. Burke. This story utilizes fresh material covering this early phase of the battles in Italy and adds to the detail of the later battles. In expanding the account of this phase of the war use has been made of individual memoirs which have become available, and which provide further insight into the fighting spirit of this Battalion. These narratives have not been altered. There may be repetition as the stories show the picture of the battle as it affected individuals in different companies.

The tone of a battalion is set by the commanding officer assisted by his key officers. It is interesting to note that a listing of the key officers at this time shows that the commanding officer and three company commanders had served with the Battalion in France in 1939/40 and in North Africa. The adjutant, quartermaster and a further company commander had been with the Battalion since October 1940. The same was true of the senior warrant officers and non-commissioned officers where again a strong nucleus had been retained. Thus the leaders and key members of the battalion team had served, trained and fought together over a period of years. The Battalion had on numerous occasions been required to provide drafts of soldiers for other units, but the retained core of officers and NCOs enabled the Battalion to absorb and train new drafts to a high standard. The leaders had experience and confidence, and this had its effect upon the morale of the soldiers who responded to the demands placed on them. Evidence of this response can be found in the descriptions which follow of battles and by the awards for bravery earned in those actions.

16

ITALY FEBRUARY–MARCH 1944

The Commanding Officer, Lt Colonel Whittaker, tells how he saw the initial battles once the battalion deployed in Italy.

"The Battalion disembarked at Naples on 21 February confident, after all the combined operations training it had done in England in 1942, and now the recent intensive period of combined operations in Egypt, that it was on the way to staging an asault landing somewhere. It was, therefore with some mild surprise that it found itself, less than forty-eight hours later in the Valley de Sujo, the first staging post on its way into the mountainous country of the Garigliano bridgehead south-west of Cassino. The 4th British Infantry Division was to take over from the 46th British Infantry Division.

"The Bedfords were to conduct the first relief and on 25 February marched up the mountain tracks to the second staging post at 'Cheshire'. On the 27th after an exhausting five-hour march up tracks which grew progressively narrower, rockier and steeper, the Battalion relieved the 2nd Battalion the York and Lancaster Regiment on the summit of Monte Cerasola, the highest and most distant feature on this part of the front. It consisted of a long razor backed ridge of which we occupied one side just below the ridge, the Germans the other. The mountains were of rock and barren and digging was impossible, the only shelter and protection available being small sangars, built from surrounding rocks, and bivouacs. It was February and the whole area was under a foot of snow.

"Three rifle companies, 'C', 'B' and 'D' were deployed along the slope just below the ridge, 'A' Company and forward Battalion Headquarters were about four hundred yards to the rear at the opposite edge of a shallow basin (Map 14).

"The relief was completed by about 2330 hrs on 27 February and at 0400 hrs the enemy greeted our arrival with a 'Stonk' which landed

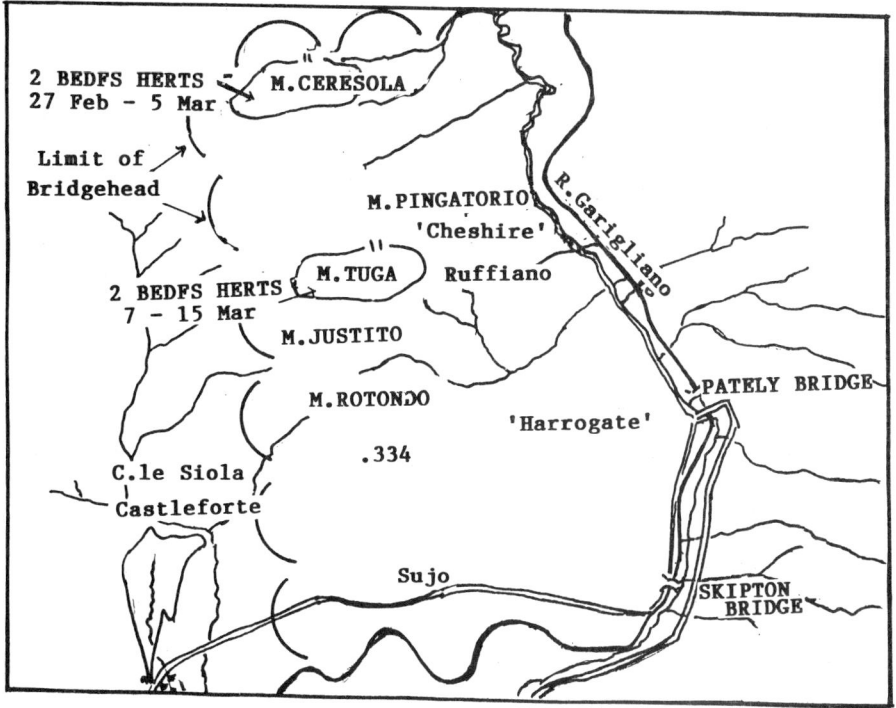

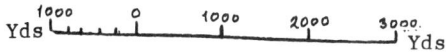

2 BEDFS HERTS
27 Feb – 5 Mar

M.CERESOLA

Limit of
Bridgehead

M.PINGATORIO
'Cheshire'

R.Garigliano

2 BEDFS HERTS
7 – 15 Mar

M.TUGA

Ruffiano

M.JUSTITO

M.ROTONDO

'Harrogate'

PATELY BRIDGE

.334

C.le Siola

Castleforte

Sujo

SKIPTON
BRIDGE

Yds 1000 0 1000 2000 3000. Yds

MAP 14

LOWER GARIGLIANO BRIDGEHEAD

121

directly on Battalion Headquarters, killing both signallers on the Brigade set, wounding fourteen others and knocking me out cold.

"The opportunities for ground action here were obviously severely limited, but a high degree of alertness was essential with the enemy in such close proximity. That this view was shared by the enemy became obvious one day when two sergeants of "D" Company decided ' to have a go' on their own. They had scarcely cleared the ridge and both fell dead under a hail of bullets. This brave but misguided effort was a sad waste of two valuable NCOs.

"Great care had to be exercised when moving about the slopes, since the rattle of dislodged stones invariably attracted grenades from the other side. This of course worked both ways.

"A small amount of patrolling around the edges of the position, including one by Lieut Calvert, yielded valuable information. Activity was, in the main, confined to artillery and mortar exchanges. These were fairly continuous, particularly by night and in the barren setting there was a small but regular daily quota of killed and wounded.

"The evacuation of casualties was extremely difficult, as will be evident from a description of the supply system. From the B Echelon base at Rocamonfina, jeeps moved on a rough track to a pontoon bridge over the Garigliano and then to the first staging post named *Skipton*. From there supplies were carried up, by mule train to the second dump, *Harrogate*, in 'The Valley of Death', thence by another mule train to *Cheshire*, from there by native porter to rear Battalion Headquarters, and finally by unit porters to the forward area. All movement in both directions was necessarily by the single narrow track and since, for its entire length, it was subject to frequent intermittent shellfire, not to mention the snow which persisted most of the time the Battalion was there, rigid control was necessary.

"However, we are told every cloud has a silver lining. In this case it was the rum issue. As we were over 3000 feet up we were eligible and the Battalion discovered that, after a wet cold miserable night as dawn comes up, there is nothing to compare with a mug of hot sweet tea liberally laced with rum. The Battalion was relieved on the night of 5/6 March by the 3rd Battalion Grenadier Guards and, after a long and difficult progress down the tracks in heavy snow, spent the rest of 6 March resting in the Valley De Sujo. The Battalion had lost on Cerasola ten killed and thirty wounded. General Hawksworth, who had commanded the 4th Infantry Division in North Africa, and was now commanding the 46th Infantry Division visited the Battalion. He expressed himself well satisfied with the conduct of the Battalion in the very difficult conditions on Cerasola and on the high state of morale. A few days later there appeared an article on the front page of The Crusader (the 8th Army newspaper) describing how the Guards had struggled through the Valley Di Sujo in a snow storm to relieve an infantry battalion on Cerasola. It sounded very dramatic. Their public relations was obviously better than ours.

"On 7 March we moved again to relieve the Surreys above *Cheshire*. The situation here was similar to the last but considerably less demanding as there was more cover, some digging was possible and the enemy was at the other side of a small valley, instead of a few yards away. The supply situation was also considerably easier. There was active patrolling on both sides in the course of which a number of enemy positions were identified. A battle patrol which was sent out to take prisoners was, however, less fortunate. It ran into what appeared to be an ambush and had two officers and three other ranks missing and four wounded. Casualties were certainly inflicted on the enemy but it seems unlikely we had the better of this encounter.

"On 12 March the Battalion carried out a mutual relief with the Royal West Kents, still lower down the mountain, and on the night of 15/16 was, in turn relieved by the 6th Surreys and found itself once more in the Valley Di Sujo. Shelling continued to be the main activity on both sides and further casualties were suffered – no doubt by the enemy also."

The story is now related as seen by other members of the Battalion. Sergeant Snape recalls that the sun shone brilliantly as the ship steamed into Naples bay. "To starboard the Isle of Capri in the wonderful blue of the Mediterranean seemed like a green heaven. Ahead Naples looked very lovely and peaceful with Vesuvius standing like a sentinel gently smoking in the background. Drawing nearer to the quay the results of bombing marred the beauty. The harbour was littered with upturned vessels and partly submerged wrecks so the ship tied up alongside an upturned ship across which were laid duckboards to bridge the gap between ship and shore.

"The trucks to lift the battalion arrived without canvas covers and the journey after the balmy air experienced on the voyage seemed intensely cold. The Battalion deployed in the Valley Di Sujo on 23 February. It was in the rear area of the 46th Division which was to be relieved by the 4th Division.

"The next move forward was to a rest area prior to taking over in the line from the 6th Yorks and Lancs of the 46th Division the following night. The positions which the Battalion was to occupy were in a bridgehead across the Garigliano River. The first five miles of the journey was by road to the truck-head, and from thence the route followed mule tracks up and down hills over country across the area of the Valley Di Sujo. The weather was cold and rainy and the paths were steep and muddy."

Lieut Sutton states " When I arrived at mule-head. where my platoon was to stay, shelling started. I had just selected a nice, deep sangar for myself when it received a direct hit while I was a few yards away. I quickly moved to another sangar. These sangars were built up with rocks above ground as it was too rocky to dig. They gave good protection against shell and mortar fire."

John Bricknell comments upon the scramble up the mule tracks: "The stench of rotting bodies, animal and human, in this valley is still a vivid memory". It was obviously out of the ordinary as Sergeant Snape remarked "It (the stench of rotting flesh) was horrible we didn't know whether it was human or mule, probably the latter. It lent wings to our feet and we moved on at a cracking pace."

A description of the "A" Echelon task is appropriate. Supplies were brought up by jeep train under the arrangements of Division from Roccamonifina, over the River Garigliano to the base of the mountain range – known as *Skipton* (Map 14). Jeeps could not go any further forward and that sure-footed, patient, temperamental and maddingly obstinate beast, the mule, took over.

Led by Algerian or Italian muleteers, with British NCOs in charge, the mule train would load up and set out on the first stage of its strenuous journey – the forty-five minute climb to Dump 2 *Harrogate* which was established in the Valley Di Sujo. Water was taken on here and the second stage a two-hour back-breaking climb to Dump 3 *Cheshire* began. At this stage the supplies were transferred to porters both native and British, who, equipped with Everest packs and a stick, would stagger on the last lap to the forward positions. The stick was an essential aid and prevented many a broken limb. Porters from the Battalion were provided by men from the Anti-tank and Carrier Platoons.

This daily task was performed often in pouring rain, sometimes in hail and snowstorms, always in soft, clinging mud which effectively concealed the boulders and pot holes that constituted the surface of the track. The Germans added to these difficulties imposed by Mother Nature as harassing fire was laid down regularly and with commendable accuracy. The Bailey bridge over the river was hit on more than one occasion, and jeeps using the track to *Skipton* often ran through

124

artillery fire. A grimmer note was when a train of fourteen mules with seven muleteers and an NCO were mortared on the narrow track between *Cheshire* and *Harrogate* on the return journey. Five of the muleteers and twelve mules were casualties. Those animals which had not been killed by the mortaring had to be shot and pushed off the track as it was impossible to get them down to *Skipton* or *Harrogate* for any attention. Casualties among the porters on this stretch were fortunately light, although for the greater part of its length it was under enemy observation and shelling. The track here was so bad that all journeys had to be made in daylight.

"A" Echelon during this phase of operations was divided into two main parties. At *Skipton* Lieutenant Gammie with twenty men carried out the offloading of jeeps, the breaking of bulk supplies, and the loading and escort of the mules.

The Headquarters Company Commander, Captain Denis Mole, the Regimental Quartermaster Sergeant and all the Company Quartermaster Sergeants and a handful of men from Support company were located at *Cheshire*. Major Powell was in charge of this second part of "A" Echelon. Their task was to receive the mule trains, offload and re-sort the supplies where necessary, and start off the porters on their daily journey forward.

This pattern of logistic support forward of "B" Echelon describes the supply system which would have been repeated across the whole British sector of the front and illustrates the planning and physical aspects involved. The reader should be aware of the detailed planning and organization needed to bring these necessities forward from the ports, through the depots by train and truck to be broken down for carriage to the lorry-head. At each level supplies would be sorted and labelled to ensure the soldier in the forward position was fed, watered and fully equipped.

The Battalion deployed on Cerasola ridge with three rifle companies forward; the company in the centre was on a ridge within thirty yards of the enemy. Sergeant Snape found that half his section was in a reverse slope position, whilst at night the remainder held a post on the forward slope which they withdrew from at daylight. Having taken over, he settled down in a sangar just big enough to allow him to stretch his legs when in the sitting position. At daybreak he found three dead Germans close by and on inspection found their personal documents had not been removed. Everything was intact including Italian and British Military money which he collected and sent back to Battalion Headquarters.

There was a thick mist which began to disperse with rain so withdrawing the forward element behind the crest Sergeant Snape took up a position with binoculars on the crest and scanned ahead. As the low cloud cleared he had a good view of a German setting up a machine gun across the valley some five hundred yards away. Frank Snape was not the only one to observe activity from the German lines. Reports from the forward companies during stand-to told of German soldiers getting out of their sangars, stretching and shaking out blankets in the far distance.

Private Scully, telling the story of this first night's action, recounts: "D Company was on the right with two platoons holding a ridge. We had a raised plateau to defend. In between ran a deep long gully. Jerry held one half and us the other. At night we had to man the Observation Post with a Bren gun while round the bend separated by a few strands of wire festooned with empty tin cans sat two Jerries with a Spandau. It was eerie, I can tell you. In moments of silence you could hear them coughing. The place reeked of German corpses. In the daytime we used to pull out, then a Vickers machine gun a few hundred yards up the gully would take over and every now and then it would fire bursts down into the gully just in case Jerry decided to visit us, for the gully ran round the back of our defences. On the ridge our sangars were some sixty feet and in some cases only forty feet from the tip of the crest. We could hear Jerry coughing and bringing up ammunition. Periodically he would throw hand grenades depending how thick the mist was. Number 18 platoon sergeant, Sergeant Le Fanu, waited for the mist to come down and with Corporal Cox ran up to the crest and surprised a group of Germans preparing to attack our sangars. They engaged the enemy, killing some before being killed by Spandau fire. A stretcher bearer, Private Riscom, who went to see if he could help was also shot by a sniper."

As Pioneer Platoon Commander Lieutenant Frank Sutton took his men out to improve the footpaths, which were rocks and stones glued together by sticky mud. These routes were shelled at irregular intervals. Just below Battalion Headquarters there was a first aid post in a tent. A few yards further down was a row of German graves. Alongside was a gully and where it crossed the path seemed to be an aiming mark for the German artillery. The blast of falling shells had uncovered the jackbooted feet of the dead. Looking into the FAP tent Frank Sutton saw Captain Tom La Fontaine waiting for a stretcher party. This was the second time he had been wounded during the first night of action. He had earlier been wounded in North Africa. There was heavy shelling and mortaring of the Battalion positions throughout the night and Lieutenant Carey was wounded during the night also.

Both Sutton and Snape comment on the weather, which after the warmer clime of Egypt was particularly trying. Cold, rain and sleet made life miserable. "It rained throughout the day and although we had gas capes and ground sheets it was inevitable that parts of our clothing were saturated. In the late afternoon the rain stopped and the air took on a frosty nip. During the night it froze our wet clothes and chilled our bones."

Conditions in the front lines were such that movement in the open in daylight was restricted; there were no sanitary arrangements and as the area had been occupied by troops for over six weeks the smells were not too pleasant. The rations were repetitive.

After a week the Battalion was relieved by the 3rd Battalion, The Grenadier Guards. The casualties during this short stay in the line were two officers and three men killed and two officers and nine men wounded.

This period saw periodic enemy shelling and mortaring and the exchange of small arm's fire with the enemy by both "C" and "A" Companies. Reconnaissance patrols were sent out which located and confirmed a number of enemy positions.

The following is Frank Snape's account of a handover in the line. "At the end of a very trying and uncomfortable week we were told we were to be relieved by a company of Guards. The handover was due to commence at 2000 hrs and be completed by midnight. During the day we had the usual rain but towards evening the weather did not appear to be turning as cold as hitherto. We rejoiced at this but had we known what the apparent warmth foretold we would have been less cheerful. Soon after dark the light rain turned to snow and big feathery flakes started to carpet the ground. With amazing rapidity everything left lying was covered by snow and there was a danger of losing equipment.

"I went round the platoon and instructed the section commanders to have men completely dressed and ready to make a quick withdrawal. By this I hoped to ensure that everyone had his equipment and lessen the danger of loss.

"The time moved on and at 2000 hrs there was no sign of the relieving troops. We started to get anxious but consoled ourselves with the thought that the snow would have delayed them but as the hours passed without any word or even an advance party arriving hope of moving that night flagged and the troops, still dressed in full equipment, became restless. However, at about midnight Lieutenant Frank Sutton, platoon commander of the Battalion Pioneer Platoon, arrived with the relieving platoon commander. My platoon commander had gone on the advance party to the rest area so it fell to me to hand over the positions. While Frank was introducing the relieving platoon commander the Germans started one of their periodic bouts of shelling. The shells went over and fell harmlessly in the valley below.

"Frank left us and I took the relieving commander into the platoon headquarters sangar. This was a little more luxurious than the rest of the ones in the platoon. It was covered over and had a blanket at the entrance so we could have a light inside. I started to explain the positions but the officer interrupted me and said, I leave all that to my sergeant. I went outside and met the platoon sergeant who had halted his men on the edge of the platoon area.

"I took him round and showed him each of the positions and then accompanied him when he put his sections in position. As each of my sections was relieved I moved them away on to the track leading back which we had come up eight days before. It took about an hour to complete all the details of the handover and then I reported to the Company Commander".

Private Scully of "D" Company now tells of the withdrawal from the Cerasola ridge positions. "The leading platoons have already put Cerasola heights well behind them. 18 Platoon being the last platoon to pull out are still being sorted out and counted. At last the NCOs give the order to move off. The air at a height of nearly 4000 feet above sea level was fresh as our boots squelched in the mud of the mule track.

"We have to reach the dip before daylight for to be caught on the tracks in daylight draws fire from the German artillery. Light showers of rain follow our progress down the slope. The showers become heavier, colder and more frequent. Soon we are soaked to the skin. At about 0200 hrs the rain changed to sleet and there was mud everywhere, at times a mess of liquid filth in which we waded up to our ankles. Time passes and it is now six hours since we set out. I had hardly the strength to drag one foot in front of the other. 'Keep going, keep going we are nearly there,' cries a voice somewhere to the front of us but conditions become worse and the line of marching men lengthens. The weight of the Bren is buckling my legs. We are stuck in a bottleneck of mud. At long last we are able to rest."

Sergeant Snape, having handed over his platoon was ordered to proceed to the Valley Di Sujo. The journey up to the positions had been difficult, going back was a veritable nightmare. The snow was covering the track with thick slush and the troops during the week of sitting on the hill side had become soft where marching was concerned. "I constantly stumbled back and forth along the platoon chivvying, encouraging or cursing according to the known temperaments of the men. Just before dawn we arrived back in the valley and were met by guides who took us to the bivouacs pitched on the side slopes of the valley. We got into bed but alas, not to sleep. The snow of the higher hills had turned to a gentle persistent downpour of rain and we found water flooding the hillside and washing through our bivouacs. The blankets were not just damp, they were downright sodden. As soon as it was daylight everyone was trying to get warm by walking up and down. The Company Commander, John Bricknell, got the cooks working to produce hot tea. Seldom was it more welcome and soon everyone was cheerful again.

"After we had had breakfast we moved to the farmhouse ruin which we had occupied before going forward, and when we had settled in, went by platoons to some natural hot sulphur baths at the roadhead. It was heavenly to take off boots and clothes, which had not been removed in their entirety for about fourteen days, and wallow in the luxury of warm, soft water. At length we retraced our steps to the valley and were greeted with the news that the Commanding Officer's batman had been killed by a direct hit by a shell on the house occupied by Battalion Headquarters. It was damnable luck to spend a week in a forward position where shells were bursting almost continuously and not get a scratch and then, when one had moved back to an area considered relatively safe, to be killed by the only shell that landed in the valley that day.

"The Battalion spent two days in reserve in the valley checking equipment and weapons and becoming battleworthy again before moving forward to take over from the 1/6th East Surrey's on the Tuga Tulino feature. This position was not quite so far forward and it was fairly quiet. 10 Platoon headquarters was luxurious by comparison with the last positions. There was room to stand and the blackout was such that the residents could smoke at night! The biggest hardship was a shortage of water each man being rationed to one water bottle a day for all purposes.

"Lieutenant Derek Calvert left 10 Platoon and went to Battalion Headquarters as Intelligence Officer and was replaced by a New Zealander, 2/Lieut A.K Jameson, who had been a Sergeant in the Western Desert."

On the fifth day in the line Sergeant Snape was sent for by Major

Jenkins, his company commander, and told to take out a listening patrol to the forward slopes of the hill on which the company trenches were on the reverse slopes and remain there until 0430 hrs. If any suspicious noises were heard a warning would be given by firing Very lights. The lying-up position was reached by walking a given number of paces on a compass bearing. At this time compasses were in short supply as so many had been lost. The one issued had only arrived that day from the quartermaster. During this listening watch the Company was to withdraw to reserve positions and the patrol was to rejoin at a given time. All went well and the patrol arrived in position and settled down to wait. There was the sound of rattling mess tins during the night, which confirmed reports of previous patrols that the Germans had a hot meal brought up during the hours of darkness.

When the time came to withdraw, Sergeant Snape reached into his pocket for the compass and found it had gone. While crawling from place to place the compass had fallen out among the rocks and there was no chance of finding it. Defining the direction of the enemy, Snape turned his back to them, selected a star as a beacon and led his patrol back finally stumbling over the hill at company headquarters. Reporting the loss of the compass Major Jenkins remarked, "Oh dear, I don't know when we will get a replacement. They are so difficult to get."

The Battalion remained in this area for a week during which it again patrolled actively gaining information about the enemy and confirming locations. It then received orders to move back to the Valley Di Sujo again. The march back to the roadhead showed the effect of three weeks in the hills. Feet had become soft and swollen in their boots.

Private Scully tells how his feet became swollen due to the conditions in the sangars and lack of movement. Lifting a sodden boot out of four inches of water, he reported his "foot was on bloody fire". He was told there was nothing that could be done and he faced an eight-hour slog carrying a Bren. On advice of a fellow soldier Private Scully took off his boots. At that moment Corporal Jones arrived and reminded him that it was contrary to orders to remove boots in a forward position. The task of fitting the swollen feet into the boots proved an impossibility and makeshift sandals were created.

The order now came to move out and by the time "D" Company hit the main track the white direction tapes had been obliterated by the leading companies. "The first few miles wasn't too bad, then we hit the boulders. Jagged teeth of broken rock of all shapes and sizes protruding everywhere and here's me with no boots on my feet. The straps which held the makeshift footwear on my feet caught in these obstructions and I tripped up and fell down. As the dawn began to light up the track I could see it continually dipping through gorges and clinging perilously to outcrops over ravines. The strange ruggedness of the scene gave an impression of dignity and great age to every rock, stump and crevice.

"We have been on the march for eight hours and not a single man belonging to 18 Platoon has dropped out. We feel rather proud of ourselves. I think Corporal Jones feels proud of us too. The track ahead is stonked by enemy artillery and we take cover. After a while we carry on, the whole Battalion strung out along both sides of the road that wends its way through 'Purple Heart Valley'. I expect when the push comes we need the likes of Corporal Jones to drive us on. We marched on with straps cutting into our shoulders, heads held high, no slouching and no moaning. Corporal Jones looked at my ragged feet. 'Well done private Scully, I'm proud of you.' This return march was a nightmare in slow motion.

"I never made it on my two feet: I was picked up by a jeep. As we passed our gun lines an artillery major saw my feet and ordered me to climb in. At battery headquarters I was given hot food and my feet were bathed in warm water and then sent on to the Battalion assembly area."

17

ITALY MARCH–APRIL 1944

On 15 March a new assault was launched against the Cassino fortifications. The 4th Indian Division attacked along the ridges north of Cassino towards the monastery. There was bitter fighting and the Germans held on to their positions. At the same time as the Indians were assaulting the heights, the New Zealand Division forced a crossing of the Rapido near Cassino town. German armour counterattacked before the bridgehead was secure and forced the New Zealand forces back. The wintery weather was adding to the hazards with drenching rain and mud. This and the well sited concrete defensive posts caused a stalemate. This third attack had failed.

Colonel Whittaker continues: "This time we were off. On 18 March after a march back over the Garigliano to San Carlo, the Battalion embussed and in due course arrived at Guiliano on the outskirts of Naples. On the night of our arrival we were treated to the magnificent spectacle of Vesuvius in full eruption. It was really awe inspiring, the whole smoke filled sky reflecting the glowing crest of the mountain from which leapt jets of scarlet molten lava to fall and join the rivers of dull red molten rock creeping downwards, turning it to a sort of evil purple as they descended.

"It had been decided the 4th Infantry Division would now move over to the Adriatic coast and come under command of V Corps. On 21 March advance parties set off for Lucera and preparations were put in hand for the move but on the 22nd these orders were cancelled. The 4th Division was now to join XIII Corps in the Cassino area. The advance parties left for Dragoni followed by the main body of the Battalion on 24 March.

"The area to which the Battalion was now to move was the wild and mountainous country of the Upper Rapido River just north west of Cassino. The sector represented the high water mark of an allied attack which had broken against virtually impregnable mountains, leaving, under the eyes of the defenders, troops who could advance no further. From Monte Cifalco to the north through the tremendous peak of Monte Cairo, more than five thousand feet, to Monte Cassino itself. German positions dominated the whole area. From such observation posts they could bring down accurate artillery fire to bear over most parts of the Division's forward area. Needless to say all troop movement was by night, and very little movement of any sort went on by day.

"The 4th Division was to relieve the 3rd Algerian Division and once again the Bedfords were to conduct the first relief. The positions to be occupied were in the mountains on the north side of the valley about two miles wide enclosed on the east by mountains held by the Germans and to the west by Cassino itself. This approach had to be through mountainous country to the south, following the line of the Inferno stream, a tributary of the Rapido, across the open plain and the Rapido and up into the mountains on the other side.

"On 26 March I left with the brigadier to reconnoitre the new positions and at 1400 hrs on 27 March the Battalion left in troop-carrying vehicles for Aquafondata where it arrived at 1725 hrs. Then on foot to a lying-up area, behind where the Inferno stream emerges into the valley, where it arrived at 2215 hrs.

"At 1900 hrs on 28 March the Battalion moved off to cross the valley to relieve the 3rd Regiment Tirailleurs Algérienne on Monte Belvedere. It was an eerie feeling marching across the open valley with the knowledge that, by day, the whole area was under observation from all round and that by night a random 'stonk' might arrive at any moment. There was a road junction which the Germans had registered well. There were a few jeeps available if the valley had to be crossed by day and each driver had his own theory about this junction. Some would stop suddenly a hundred yards or so short and wait a minute or two before continuing, others would approach slowly and accelerate. Either way the feeling was that the jeep would not be where the observation post thought it would be when the shells arrived. Whether the Germans ever thought it worth shelling a single jeep, or whether the idea worked is not recorded.

"As we approached the Rapido evidence of recent heavy fighting emerged. A tank on its side in a ditch, a listing Sherman bogged down in the waterlogged fields, the permeating charnel stink of the battle field and the swollen carcasses of dead animals, the shattered trees.

"The Battalion was fortunate to cross the valley without incident and, after an exhausting climb up steep mountain tracks the relief of the French was completed by 0400 hrs on 29 March. We lost one killed and three wounded. Our orders in this area, which we did not understand at the time, but the reasons for which became apparent later, were that, whilst we could take appropriate action if the enemy were aggressive, they were not to be stirred up unnecessarily. There is therefore little of note to record. Three escaped prisoners of war, taken at Tobruk, suddenly presented themselves to 'A' Company one night and were despatched under escort and not without suspicion to Brigade. We were showered by German planes with leaflets in French and Arabic extolling the benefits of placing our future in Hitler's hands, but since we had few students of French or Arabic they did little to relieve the monotony.

"On 7 April we were relieved by the 2nd Battalion King's Regiment and retraced our steps via the Rapido Valley, and the Inferno to Aquafondata where we embussed for Barracone. There we spent five days training, mainly at night, ending on 11/12 April with two night river crossing exercises.

"On the 13th April we were lifted back to Aquafondata where we first relieved the 6th Surreys in a reserve position. Then on the nights of the 17th and 18th moved up again by the same route as previously to relieve the 2/4th Hampshires in a different sector on Monte Belvedere.

"At dawn on 19 April Major Jenkins, 'D' Company, reported they had seen, silhouetted against an early dawn sky, German troops moving out of positions near the crest of the spur of the Colle Abate, a feature a few hundred yards in front of and considerably higher than our position. This seemed almost certainly to be alternative positions occupied by the Germans by night, though it was unusual for German troops to be as careless as this. Anyway, that day the gunner liaison officer with me registered on a point from which they could accurately adjust on to the spur in question. At 2030 hrs Major Jenkins reported that the enemy could be seen moving in. The artillery fire landed with devastating accuracy. No further movement was seen on that spur. The Germans responded with some very heavy shelling from which we assumed ours had been pretty effective, We had no casualties. This time we were bombarded with American leaflets urging the Germans to surrender!

"Going on my rounds one night I missed a track junction and was proceeding rapidly out of our lines towards the enemy when a rather startled cough from out of the darkness alerted me and I was respectfully advised that it would be unwise to proceed further.

"We had come under command temporarily of the New Zealand Division, who were taking over the area from the 4th Division, and on the night of 22/23 April we were relieved by a New Zealand battalion. The relief was punctuated by two unusual incidents, In the first we had to secure the release of one of our soldiers who had been captured by a Maori unit which had moved in on our left. In the second the Commanding Officer was asked by the Commanding Officer of the relieving unit, as the relief was nearing completion, if he would leave the two most forward companies in position until the following night, as after the move up the mountain his men were in no condition to take over. This is noted not in any sense to denigrate the New Zealanders who were indeed loyal and gallant allies, but in justice to the British infantryman whose trumpet is seldom heard but who, as this incident shows, can be as tough as any when the military situation requires.

"Once again we returned to Aquafondata where we embussed, this time for Presenzano."

Incidents experienced by Battalion members give further background to this phase of the battle.

After a short rest near Naples the Battalion went forward on 28 March to relieve the French, who were holding a Sector just north of Cassino and took over from the 3rd RTA of 103rd Régiment d'Infanterie, which occupied positions in and around the village of Belvedere. The mule company supporting the Battalion in the line was French. The difficulty which immediately presented itself was the liaison which had to be carried out with the French, as none of them had any knowledge of English, neither had any of the Battalion jeep-head party more than the usual "Tommy's" knowledge of French. The pioneer platoon sergeant managed to achieve results with his *"Ong avec les mulies"* and *"Chargey les mulies la-bas"*. These two gems of the French tongue delivered in the most confident manner on all possible occasions usually produced the desired results.

After nightfall the Battalion moved from a lying up position at Inferno by route march across the plain through a hamlet named Cairo to the north of Cassino. The road here was in good condition and headed straight through the German lines. One or two vehicles had driven straight on and landed up in the bag. Again the stench of decay, sickly sweet and overpowering in strength was noticeable. After Cairo which was shelled regularly every twenty minutes, the Battalion turned off the road and started for the hills waiting for the guides to lead the companies forward.

Sergeant Snape found a mound on the ground and rested his head on it allowing his aching shoulders to relax. "After a time I turned my head and looked around and saw at one end of the mound a pair of small ammunition boots. Thinking it odd that they should be there I looked at the other end of the mound and then realized to my horror that I had been using the grave of a Gurkha soldier as a pillow. I quickly shifted my position and saw there were several such graves all with boots at the foot. Later I discovered that the Gurkhas always placed the boots of dead soldiers in readiness at the foot of the graves.

"Soon we moved on up the hill and after a climb started to move along a side track towards occupied positions. Any takeover should be as quiet as possible so the enemy is unaware of what is taking place. On this occasion the troops whom we were relieving came out of their sangars and met us with handshaking and an appreciable amount of noise. We discovered they were French troops. With much kicking of tins and stones we eventually took over the positions and were greatly relieved when the French went away and relative silence reigned once more. At daybreak the next morning an amazing sight met our eyes. The French had been supplied with American rations and the whole area was littered with tins and packets, in the main empty, but some unopened. It appeared these French troops did not like vegetable mayonnaise, biscuits, souppowder or Nescafé."

The troop positions were in the main on reverse slopes and the pattern of activity, apart from a twenty minute bombardment just after the evening stand-to, was an occasional shell burst. Activity was quiet on 30 and 31 March with only slight mortaring and shelling. The name of 5770897 Private Pickess. W. is listed as being promoted to Lance Corporal. (Ed: Extracts from his account of activities appear later in this story). On 1 April shelling and mortaring increased on 'A', 'B' and 'D' Company areas.

The Pioneer Platoon was ordered up to lay a small minefield in front of "A" Company to protect a forward platoon on Point 856 from being rushed, as the Hampshires, who had been holding this position, had suffered casualties from a German raiding party using flame throwers. Frank Sutton went up and prepared a set of American jumping mines to block the approach route. Sergeant Waller detailed Privates Worboys and Jarvis for this detail. They reported carrying Tommy guns and Sutton had his pistol and two grenades. This party arrived at "A" Company Headquarters at 2200 hrs and were briefed by "Ginger" Rayner, the Company Commander on the company layout. "A very steep climb, over stones and rocks, got us to the top of

856. We seemed to be making a frightful noise and my heart was in my throat. When we got to the top we were quietly challenged from two sides. I then realized we had been covered by Brens and Tommy guns for some time. The section positions were well sited among the rocks and Lieut Howley, the Platoon Commander, described the situation to us in whispers. I was asked whether I wanted an escort, but I said I preferred a Bren gun at the top of a gully to fire over our heads in case we had to beat a hasty retreat. Stirling, the Platoon Sergeant, said he would man this Bren gun himself.

"We started down the gully. Luckily, there was some high grass and so we made no noise. Although we went down only a short distance I was scared we should bump the enemy in the dark. I thought we were now far enough away from our own positions to start laying mines. The mine laying drill went off very well. We fixed an irregular pattern of trip wires on our way back. This was slow uphill work. With the mine block completed we hurried to the top and went down the other side to company headquarters. It was getting lighter; or whether it was the noise we were making in our haste to get out of it, Jerry started to snipe from a flank followed moments later with automatic fire from a Spandau."

"A" Echelon had their spot of fun during the take-over on the 28 March and Dennis Mole records the following incident."Mules and guides were to meet the Battalion party at jeep-head to carry forward rations, blankets, ammunition etc. The Arab NCO was there with twenty mules, but protested that the column had arrived so late that the remainder of the mules had been dismissed to their lines and that his mules should not make the trip to Battalion Headquarters because the "Sales Boche"would shoot him up if he was caught on the journey in daylight. This was disastrous as it meant a tired, hungry Battalion just going into the line would have to spend the next twenty four hours without rations, water or ammunition, and heated protests were made in execrable but forceful French that with dawn at 0430 hrs there was still time for at least one trip to be made. The NCO was adamant and Captain Mole had decided force would be needed to reach the required solution when Lieut Frank Sutton, the Pioneer Officer, who had been sent down by the Commanding Officer to find out why no rations had been sent up appeared out of the darkness like Aladdin's genie. Sizing up the situation, he directed a torrent of fluent French at the startled NCO emphasized by a short burst of fire from his Tommy Gun at the man's feet. The mules did the trip and were back in their lines before daybreak.

"While the Battalion was in the line a German aircraft flew over dropping propaganda leaflets on the nights of 3 and 4 April. These were all printed in French!

"After a comparatively quiet week the Battalion was relieved by the 2nd Kings and moved back to a camp beside the Volturno River spending the time cleaning up and carrying out river crossing training and exercises."

Tom Brown, the Mortar Platoon Commander, remembers when he took over from the French that although he had his mortars there was no ammunition. The French had been using the American Army mortar which used a fuzing mechanism different from the British. They had left hundreds of rounds behind. Deciding that some bombs were better than none he set about adapting them for use. Carrying out all the initial trials himself he eventually was able to produce a range chart. Having completed this task he reported his efforts to Battalion Headquarters. About two months later he was visited by two staff officers from Divisional Headquarters and told that he had been acting contrary to King's Regulations! He heard no more about the matter but some six months later a formal amendment was issued detailing his procedures.

On 15 April the Battalion took over a position on the lower slopes of Monte Cairo. This position was overlooked by the Germans so no movement was permitted by day. Sergeant Snape was in a small cottage which had only one room. It was so tiny the men had to sleep sitting up propped against one another. A lookout was in the roof but had the enemy attacked the position would have been untenable. Tea was brewed in a biscuit tin on a communal basis for the whole platoon and this provided a mug for each of the twenty four men. By night section positions were manned round the outside of the cottage and carrying parties fetched supplies from Company Headquarters.

The position was close by the Germans and these forays to collect supplies were not without risk as there was the ever present danger of walking into an enemy patrol or into an ambush. On the first night it was necessary to make two trips to collect supplies and Sergeant Snape detailed the carrying party and led them back to Company Headquarters. On returning to the Platoon he ordered the party to turn round and go back to fetch the next load. The trip was uneventful.

On 19 April "B" Company sighted a platoon of enemy to their front and engaged them successfully with mortar fire. Propaganda pamphlets addressed to the Americans were dropped by shells in the company area. Active patrolling continued across the battalion and an enemy prisoner surrendered to "A" Company on 20 April. Further enemy activity was observed on the 21st and an enemy platoon was fired on by our artillery. There was heavy shelling in and around Battalion Headquarters on 21 April and this activity increased on 22 April.

18

CASSINO – TOPOGRAPHY AND THE DIVISIONAL PLAN

The Commanding Officer continues his story. "Cassino, with its monastery perched on top of its mountain, providing marvellous observation over all approaches from the south, its strong, long-prepared defences and forward positions covering the swiftly flowing Gari and Rapido Rivers, had already become something of a legend in Italy by May 1944. It commanded the entrance to the Liri Valley, the traditional approach to Rome from the south, and described by General Alexander in his despatches to Winston Churchill as the only practicable approach for a large force.

"It had been regarded by the Italian General Staff, before the war, as an exercise example of an impregnable position, and as though to prove them right previous to May , 1944, three full scale attacks had failed. Some progress had been made against more distant defences some six miles to the south over the Garigliano River, and two miles north over the upper reaches of the Rapido. The Battalion had already served in both these areas in a defensive role (i.e. Cerasola to the south and Belvedere to the north) as described in Chapter 16. By May, 1944, Monte Cassino still dominated all approaches to Rome.

"After the failure to break through the German defences in the three earlier battles General Alexander determined that the next assault would have sufficient strength to achieve the task. The greater part of the British Eighth Army were brought over from the east coast to link up with the Fifth (US) Army. There were to be two armoured divisions ready for the breakout and a vast concentration of artillery.

"The British Eighth Army was to attack in the northern sector with the Polish Corps storming the ridges to seize Monastery Hill. The XIII British Corps, comprising the 4th and 78th British Divisions and the

8th Indian Division, were to force the Garigliano/Rapido and cut Route 6 depriving the Germans holding out in Cassino town an escape route.

"The Canadian Corps of an armoured and an infantry division were in reserve to exploit the breakout into the Liri Valley.

"Further south the French Corps were to break out of the bridge-head over the Garigliano River at Cerasola, attack over the mountains, and approach the Liri Valley from the south. The American II Corps was to attack past Minturno along Route 7 parallel to the coast. Towards the end of April in company with other Commanding Officers I was summoned to Divisional Headquarters where under conditions of the highest security we were informed that a major assault on the Gustav Line right across Italy was shortly to take place. The spearhead of the attack was to be carried out by the 4th Division against Cassino itself. This information was not to be passed on for the time being.

"After the relief by the New Zealanders on Monte Belvedere the Battalion moved back to Presenzano and then on 24 April to Alife for a brief period of further training in close cooperation between infantry and armour with the Lothian and Border Horse. This was followed by three days refresher training in assault river crossings back at Presenzano.

"During this time the Brigade Commander met me on the ground and discussed the brigade plan for the attack. A brief description of the ground is appropriate. The town of Cassino nestles at the base of Monte Cassino which rises sharply some 1800 feet above it. Cassino is roughly midway between Naples and Rome about fifty miles from each. Route 6 running north-west from Naples crosses the Rapido River just outside the town and bears sharply south-west in the cen-tre of Cassino round the base of the mountain before turning north-west into the Liri Valley to continue towards Rome.

"The Rapido River runs into the Gari just outside the town and the Gari continues roughly south-west for about one mile at a distance of four to five thousand yards from Route 6 before turning south to join the Garigliano River. It was in this area that the 4th Division attack was to be launched with the intention of isolating the town by cutting Route 6 and subsequently taking the town from the flank.

"It was known that the whole area over which the attack was to be made was defended in great depth and that there would be determined resistance. A considerable extra force was placed under command to strengthen the Division, including 26th Armoured Brigade Group,

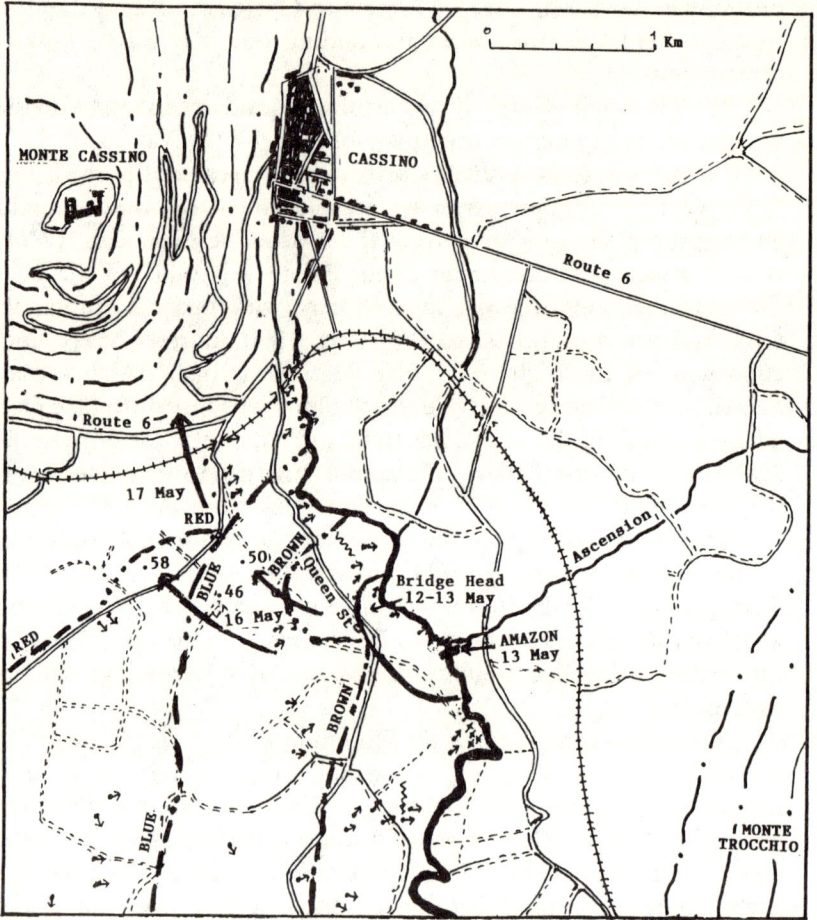

MAP'15

2nd BEDFORDS CASSINO 12–17 MAY

1st Guards Brigade Group, an additional Artillery Group and two Air Support Tentacles.

"Major General Ward was the Divisional Commander and his plan was that the initial assault and river crossing was to be carried out by 28th Brigade on the left and 10th Brigade on the right. The 1st Guards Brigade were to contain the Germans in Cassino and protect the flank of 10th Brigade. 12th Brigade was held in reserve to exploit success. Thirty assault boats were allotted to 28th Brigade and forty-two to 10th Brigade.

"At the same time as this assault the Polish Corps was to attack over the mountains from the direction of Belvedere with the monastery as their objective.

"4th Division's assault was in three phases. The first was the river crossing and advance to the first objectives, a line some thousand yards beyond the river to be known as *BROWN* line.the second, some twelve to fifteen hundred yards further on, followed the line of high ground the capture of which would shield the river crossing places from direct ground observation, but not from Monte Cassino, to be called *BLUE* line, (Map 15).

"On reaching *BLUE* line the position would be assessed and further orders issued for the advance to *RED* line which dominated the route out of Cassino.

"Each brigade was to set up three ferries in its sector with cableways and rafts capable of five to eleven ton loads for vehicles, supplies and the evacuation of wounded. As early as possible the sappers were to build a Bailey bridge in each sector capable of carrying tanks.

"There was an elaborate artillery programme on a massive scale along the whole of the Eighth Army front involving counter-battery work to silence the enemy guns and mortars before the assault boats were launched and to soften up the enemy defences covering the crossing places. A carefully synchronized plan of barrages followed, designed to precede the infantry to their successive objectives on a timed scale. The infantry would lose the barrage if they fell behind schedule as the whole plan was too elaborate to be altered.

"Brigadier Shoosmith, the commander of 10th Brigade, planned to assault with two battalions forward crossing in succession over a single crossing point named WHISKY, divided into two sections about one hundred yards apart. This crossing point was on the right of the brigade sector. Close to this point and on the enemy side was a ridge some eight hundred yards long roughly at right angles to the river. This ridge was known to be honeycombed with caves and to contain several enemy positions.

"The East Surreys were to cross first with the task of clearing this ridge. The Bedfords were to follow fanning out at an angle to seize the line of the road – BROWN line. Following this task the Bedfords were to advance a further fifteen hundred yards to BLUE line. This road was to form the start line for the Bedfords main attack. However enfilade fire could be brought down on this advance to BLUE line from the ridge and it was therefore stipulated that the Bedfords should not advance until the East Surreys had cleared the ridge.

"Artillery softening up was to commence at 2300 hrs on 11 May. The first wave of assault boats were to be launched at 2345 hrs and the barrage to carry the infantry from BROWN to BLUE line to start at 0141 hrs on 12 May.

"In the meantime the Battalion was back at Presenzano blissfully unaware of what was in store and enjoying a relatively relaxing time including the occasional film show and concert party.

"In the early days of May the Battalion was required to carry out two rather unusual moves. Opposite Cassino and about one thousand yards our side of the river rises the great whaleback feature Monte Trocchio, almost as high as Monte Casino itself. On the evening of 3/4 May the Battalion embussed and moved off after dark to behind Trocchio where it debussed and proceeded to dig in on the reverse slopes. Early on the 14th all work was camouflaged and the Battalion embussed and moved out after first light back to Presenzano. The first part of this move was in full view, though distant, of observers on Monte Cassino. Vehicles were of course well spaced out. This procedure was repeated the following night. All of this of course attracted a fair amount of adverse comment from the soldiers who felt practising the digging of slit trenches by night was something of which they were not in urgent need. It was not till later that all was revealed. This was, of course, intended to make the Germans think that troops were moving out of the sector, and was part of the overall deception plan. It is worth noting that such moves would not have been possible had we not had command of the air.

"I had by now prepared my own operation order and this was issued to the Battalion Orders Group and other units involved on the morning of 10 May. A sand table model of the area of operations had been prepared by the Intelligence Officer and company commanders and others had the rest of the day to study that in conjunction with maps,

9. "Jeeps using the track to 'Skipton' often ran through artillery fire" (p124) (See also Map 14). (*Imperial War Museum*)

10. On the way up to Ceresola, by T.S. LaFontaine. (p125)

11. 'Cheshire' Dump. Socks being washed and darned (p125). (*Imperial War Museum*)

12. "*Chargey les mulies la bas*". The mule company supporting the battalion was French (p135). (*Imperial War Museum*)

aerial photographs and traces of known enemy positions. They also studied the artillery fire support plan.

"An opposed river crossing is always a rather dramatic affair requiring most careful preparations. In this instance the number of large units and sub units moving about at the same time in a limited area demanded the closest control of routes and timings. The plan broke the operation down into four phases.

"Phase I

A march of about ninety minutes round the base of Monte Trocchio from the battalion assembly area on its reverse slope to a railway cutting on its forward slope about one thousand yards from *WHISKY*. The East Surreys were due to start crossing at 2345 hrs and the Bedfords were to be at the cutting by 2300 hrs. The purpose for this was to allow companies a short rest before embarking on the crossing and also to allow any slack either way to be taken up in the timing. The railway cutting afforded good cover.

"Phase II

The move from the cutting to the forming-up point where companies wait to be called forward in boatloads to the crossing point. To avoid confusion the Bedfords were not to enter this area until the Surreys were clear.

"Phase III

Crossing and advance to start line. The objective for this phase was to get to the start line ready for the next phase, not simply to get across the river. Companies were only to move forward to the crossing point when called forward by the beachmaster. Once over the river 'D' Company on the right would have about five hundred yards to the start line; 'B' Company on the extreme left had about nine hundred yards, having to move off at an angle. Maintaining direction in this advance would not be easy especially if there was opposition. Later in the advance to *BLUE* line Bofors guns would fire tracer over the axis of advance to help the infantry to maintain direction but in the first part of this attack leaders had to rely on their compass, knowledge of the ground gained from the sand table model and ability to control.

"Phase IV

The attack to the *BLUE* line. The objectives of each company involved an advance of some fifteen hundred yards. The barrage supporting this attack was to open at 0141 hrs by which time all companies should be ready on the start line of the road.

"That then was the plan as company commanders pored over the sand table with maps, aerial photographs and intelligence reports preparing their own plans and committing every possible detail to memory.

"The key personalities at the time were: Ginger Rayner commanding 'A' Company had been commissioned from the ranks, unusually for those days into the same regiment, after the return from Belgium in 1940. Always cheerful and with a joke for most situations he had by this time been commanding his company for two years. 'Jenks', (one almost forgets his real name was Jenkins) joined us in 1940. His sound judgement and reliability led to his becoming adjutant in 1942 and to command 'B' Company in 1943 at the end of the North African campaign. 'C' Company was Graham Martin who had only joined us at Bougie with the reinforcements, but his tremendous enthusiasm and total commitment had rapidly made him a very welcome member of the family. 'D' Company was in the hands of 'Butch' Charkham. He had joined us in France in 1940 and so had already seen two campaigns. Solid and unflappable he and Rayner had already shown courage and skill in handling their companies in difficult operations in North Africa.

"Administration was in the capable hands of Jack Douglas, who had taken over as adjutant from Jenks about a year previously. His dedication to the Regiment was an important factor in maintaining morale and spirit during the lean months in Bougie in 1943. He also maintained a high standard of discipline without forfeiting the good regard in which he was held by all ranks.

"At 2000 hrs on 10 May the Battalion again embussed at Presenzano and by 0100 hrs on the 11th was safely in the area already prepared on the two previous visits to the reverse slopes of Monte Trocchio. Later in the morning the company commanders gave out their orders to platoon commanders who, in turn assembled their platoons and put every soldier completely in the picture as regards everything that was intended. The rest of the day was spent in relaxation and general preparation. A lot of letter writing was done and the padre elected to hold a short service for each company. The numbers who chose to attend would surprise many people. Walking round the companies I found everyone in good heart but rather sombre mood.

"The Battalion paraded at 2115 hrs and, after marching round the base of Monte Trocchio arrived in the railway cutting just before

2300 hrs. Punctually at 2300 hrs the artillery programme started. In an official history of the 4th Division it is stated that over five hundred guns took part over the whole front. The effect was quite extraordinary. I was not conscious of any particular discharge or group of discharges but suddenly the whole sound level was dramatically raised and I found myself shouting to be heard by someone only one yard away.

"Information soon began to arrive that the Surreys were having a difficult time at the crossing and everything was well behind schedule. The battalion therefore did not move off from the cutting until 0030 hrs when it soon ran into a thick fog with visibility down to two or three yards. It was said this was due to the dust and smoke of battle mixing with the mist rising from the river, but, whatever the cause, it added enormously to the difficulties of communication. The Battalion was halted again just short of the forming-up point and, on going forward to find the cause I found that the Surreys were not yet over the river. They had come under heavy mortar and small arms fire from the moment they started crossing. Many boats had been destroyed, many carried downstream by the swift current and others sunk by small arms fire. A sort of flying ferry had been fixed up, but with only two boats working in the later stages crossing was painfully slow. In the meantime casualties were being incurred from stray small arms and mortar fire both at the crossing and by the battalion waiting to cross. to add to our problems, whilst still waiting, promptly at 0141 hrs we heard the barrage, which was supposed to carry us from our start line on *BROWN* to our objective on *BLUE*, start up and rumble off into the distance. There was nothing we could do about it.

"Once the Surreys were clear 'C' Company started crossing at 0200 hrs and 'B' Company followed a few minutes later. The intention had been that the two halves of the crossing should be about one hundred yards apart but, with visibility practically nil and following the strength of enemy reaction, the two flying ferries had been set up within a few yards of each other. This inevitably led to some confusion on the far side as groups made their way forward, but security (silence) being no longer a factor, this was quickly sorted out and 'B' Company reported they were over and moving on to their first objective just before 0300 hrs, and 'C' Company similarly shortly after. 'D' Company reported over at 0345 hrs.

"'B' and 'C' Companies almost immediately ran into minefields and suffered casualties but, with great courage and determined leadership from company officers and NCOs, pressed on. Battalion

147

Headquarters had crossed and was established about five hundred yards to the left of the crossing point. Communication was established with Brigade who informed us that the artillery barrage would be repeated at 0400 hrs. They were, however, unable to give us any information about the Surreys, whose progress on clearing the ridge to our right was so vital for further advance. Neither could they give us any information about our left beyond the belief that 28 Brigade were much behind schedule. The Intelligence Officer was despatched along the river bank to the right to see if any contact could be made with the Surreys headquarters.

"Meanwhile 'B' Company after clearing some enemy forward positions near the road reported they were in position on the start line shortly before 0400 hrs. 'C' Company followed at 0430 hrs having had a bad time in the minefield. It was here that Tony Taylor, his platoon held up, with, as one member put it, mines going off all round them, rallied his platoon and, no doubt with his pipe firmly wedged in his mouth, led them through to rejoin his company in its advance. He was awarded the Military Cross.

"The barrage timed for 0400 hrs had been cancelled since nowhere on the divisional front were forward battalions in a position to take advantage of it, but by 0500 hrs 'B', 'C' and 'D' Companies were poised on the start line ready to advance, with 'A' Company in position to their rear. There was still no information either from brigade or available on the ground regarding the Surreys. Enemy shelling and mortar fire continued and returning from a survey of the position I was met by a clearly startled adjutant with the question 'Have you seen our hole, Sir?' The hole which had been my headquarters and shelter had received a direct hit and nothing remained of the equipment I had left there but a few shreds of webbing.

"It was by now becoming daylight and, summing up, the situation looked far from promising. On our right we had been unable to make any proper contact with the Surreys and Brigade could give no information about them. On our left it was clear from the guarded statements from Brigade that the 28 Brigade crossing was not going well. To our rear, bridges and rafts had made little progress under the heavy shelling during the night and as the mist cleared the river banks had come under heavy machine-gun fire from the flanks. All working parties had been withdrawn, It was clear that nothing more would be coming over the river before nightfall. 'B' Company on the left and "D" Company on the right were in fairly close contact with the enemy. Opposite 'C' Company the Germans held the high ground some three to four hundred yards ahead. 'A' Company were in reserve between the river and the forward companies.

"The situation was clarified shortly by an urgent order from brigade to dig in where we were and hold on to the bridgehead we had won at all costs. This relieved us of a difficult decision but with our bridgehead only some nine hundred yards long and about five hundred yards deep, surrounded on three sides by rising ground held by the enemy, it was, from our point of view, marginally less attractive than attempting to continue the attack. Very little movement was possible and digging in in these circumstances meant scraping holes and improving, where possible, the irrigation ditches and gullies which intersected the area.

"Before long the counter attacks started, at first on 'B' on the left. Accurate artillery fire broke the main force of the attack but the enemy continued to press forward with great determination. Private Savage set the fashion for the defence by standing up time after time, amidst a hail of bullets, to get a better shot, whilst Major Jenkins when asked by me whether some of the defensive artillery fire was not falling rather short in his sector reported, 'Yes, some rounds are actually falling inside the company area, but don't lift it. The Germans are just the other side of the ridge and if you lift it you will miss them.'

"From time to time an enemy tank poked its nose over the ridge and took a shot mostly at Battalion Headquarters, which, with our communications and those of the supporting arms, presented a small forest of aerials which could not be concealed. After the first few appearances, however, it was met with such a hail of fire from the far bank that it evidently decided 'discretion was the better part of valour' and did not reappear.

"Counter-attacks, accompanied by artillery fire of varying intensity continued along the whole battalion front all day but were repulsed with the same spirit though not without considerable loss on our part. It scarcely needs to be said that in all this testing time from the river crossing onwards such steadfastness would not have been possible without the highest standard of leadership and example from all company officers from the company commanders down to the most junior section commander. It is also most unlikely that the result would have been quite the same without the magnificent support of the artillery. There was a Forward Observing Officer with each forward company and they were able to call down defensive fire on the spot without delay. They did us proud.

"As the evening approached we had a signal from Brigade that 'the highest Sunray of all' had been watching and was very proud of the Battalion's performance. At the same time we were informed that three Field regiments and two Medium regiments of artillery would be available for defensive fire on the Battalion front during the night.

"No further ground attack took place during the night but shelling continued with 'Nebelwerfers' joining in. These seemed to be targeted on the back areas and their fiery trail overhead, together with the shelling of our area, gave quite a 'Guy Fawkes' night feeling to the moment.

"Unbeknown to us General Ward had decided that the situation could not be maintained much longer and that it was pointless to resume the slow and expensive process of ferrying more troops across the river unless supporting arms could also get across. He had therefore decided that the sappers must complete the Bailey bridge behind us at all costs. "Under cover of a thick smokescreen this was done with great gallantry but at heavy cost by 225 Field Company Royal Engineers and at about 0500 hrs on 13 May we heard the unmistakeable clank of tank tracks approaching. After an urgent setting up of Piats, preparation of grenades and such measures with which the infantry soldier, always the optimist, prepares to meet a tank attack, our relief can be imagined when, through the early morning mist appeared the leading tanks of the Lothian and Borders. Within the next hour units of 12th Brigade (2 Royal Fusiliers, 1st RWK and 6th Black Watch) came over with the intention of moving to our left and carrying out the task originally assigned to 28 Brigade. The tanks, however, could not negotiate the high bank of the Peppieto stream which ran into the Gari on our left, so the plan was rapidly changed. The Black Watch and Royal Fusiliers with tank support passed through our positions to continue the attack on our objectives on *BLUE* Line. The 1st RWK protected their left. Meanwhile a battalion of the Hampshires, which had been placed under command of 12 Brigade came over, crossed the Peppieto stream and secured the *BROWN* objective and cleared the banks of the river on the 28 Brigade sector. In the afternoon the DCLI came over and cleared up the area which had been the Surreys' on our right. They found several groups of the Surreys who, whilst they had not cleared all the area, had achieved parts of their first objective and clung gallantly on, even enduring the bombardment that preceded the DCLI.

"The Bedfords were now able to stand up and leave the waterlogged irrigation ditches and holes in which they had sheltered for the previous thirty-six hours. Relaxation was not complete, however, when we were informed we were now divisional reserve and must be prepared to counter-attack anywhere on the divisional front. Even in this capacity we lost two officers and twenty one soldiers from enemy shelling."

19

CASSINO – 11 MAY 1944

The battle as seen by other members of the Battalion. At 2100 hrs on 11 May the Battalion moved off in single file, in prearranged order, down the hill to Route 6 and then through the gun lines. The field guns were hub to hub, with huge piles of shell around them. The route turned off Route 6 down a dried-out river bed. Thousands of fireflies were sparkling as they flew around and, but for an odd shell screeching over, there was silence. Only frogs in nearby pools were making a noise. Cassino and the Monastery stood out above as the men moved to the crossing points on the Rapido.

All of a sudden hell broke loose. It was 2300 hrs and all the guns opened up. "The screaming of shells over our heads was fantastic. I had never heard such a terrific noise. Howling over us was a real curtain of rushing steel with continuous flashes coming from behind, and the crunch of the explosions in front of us" – such was the impression the barrage made upon Lieutenant Frank Sutton.

On reaching the river bank there was a delay as the Surreys had started crossing but many of their boats had been sunk. Although the Rapido was only a small river it was fast flowing. Nevertheless it looked big at night and under fire. The artillery barrage had raised huge clouds of dust which was drifting back towards the river. By this time only two boats were available for use and the Battalion proceeded to cross over. Both "C" and "B" Companies had crossed over by 0300 hrs. The whole Battalion had crossed the river by 0440 hrs.

"When I set foot on the other side I was scared stiff of mines. Soon I realized that the bank had been cleared, " said Frank Sutton. "We could not see much and we marked a safe lane with white tape from the river to the rifle companies, who by now were some eight hundred yards into enemy territory. Casualties were fairly high, mainly from mortar fire and mines.

"The enemy counter-attacked seven times during darkness, but they were beaten off each time with the help of our artillery. Our artillery Forward Observation Officer (George Smith, Royal Artillery) was just 'pulling the chain', as he said, and down came the barrage on any nominated spot."

Frank Snape picks up the story. "When our artillery opened up to cover the start of the attack it was terrific. No one there had ever witnessed such a weight of weapons firing at one time. The flashes almost turned night into day and the noise of the bangs and the roar of the echoes rolled back and forth between the hills. The advance down towards the river settled into a familiar pattern of moving twenty yards and then stopping or so it seemed to us who hadn't the slightest idea of what was happening. Eventually we arrived close to the water's edge and found the bulk of the Battalion were still on our side of the river too. We took cover in small irrigation ditches and I went to find out what was happening. I was told that all but two of the boats that were to be used to ferry us across had been destroyed due in part to enemy action, and to a greater degree, to the very fast flow of the river making the boats unmaneageable for inexperienced troops."

Sizing up the situation Captain Horace Hollick, the second-in-command of "A" Company, with the beachmasters' party, had managed to get two wires fixed across the river with the remaining two boats hitched to them. The boats were manoeuvred back and forth across the river. Only seven men could be carried at a time so the task of transporting the whole Battalion was formidable, but Hollick marshalled and instructed the troops how to get in, work the boats without capsizing and cross over all under enemy shellfire.

Sergeant Snape continues his account. " It was about four o'clock in the morning when we finally crossed the river. The situation that met us on the enemy bank was fantastic. There was utter chaos. The leading company had walked straight on to a minefield. Lieut Cox, in trying to locate his company headquarters was walking with his platoon through this minefield when a German anti-personnel mine exploded and took the heel off his boot. The odds of not being seriously wounded or killed by such an occurrence are phenomenal, but he escaped unscathed."

Sergeant Pickess endured the passage of the minefield. "I was lucky; men in front of me and behind were killed or wounded by these anti-personnel mines. Sergeant Saunders and Private Pearson were killed, both were quite near to me. We lay down in the minefield until it was light before we were able to advance."

Sergeant Snape continues the story. "Another platoon had lost its bearings and was shouting to try and locate the remainder of the Company. As it was obvious all chance of surprise was out of the question the Company Commander called out his location and rallied the Company. Mist and smoke from shells were shrouding everything and it was not possible to identify landmarks. It became clear that as soon as we were well away from the river it was sensible to dig in and send patrols forward to locate the enemy. We therefore quickly dug in and Captain John Bricknell took out a patrol. He returned later with detailed information about the enemy and also with two Germans who had surrendered to him. As a result of this information the Company moved forward two hundred yards and linked up with 'C' Company on their left and dug in again.

"The area was still blanketed in mist but before digging was completed the mist started to disperse. The corn was only about nine inches high and provided little cover. Seeing an enemy counter attack coming in I called for artillery fire, which came down bang on target just forward of our positions. Assuring myself that the attack had been broken up I crawled round the platoon visiting the sections. I found Private Bibby lying in the corn with his face streaming with blood. His steel helmet lying beside him had been shattered on the brim. He told me a stick grenade had been thrown at him and had landed on the brim of his helmet. It was too dangerous to try to get him back during daylight so I dressed his wounds and got him to a slit trench and then moved on to the sections. The first section was in good form though they were up to their knees in water. Outside one of the slit trenches of the next section I found Private Helps lying on the ground. He had left the trench to attend to the calls of nature and whilst so occupied had been killed instantly. A little further on another body was lying with a foot blown off. He had taken the full force of a shell which had landed a few feet away. The section commander, Corporal Wakeford, had been shot in the head but luckily the bullet had grazed the top of his head and done little damage. He was too shocked to carry on commanding his section so I put it in charge of a young private soldier, Private Sands, and sent Wakeford back to platoon headquarters where he could lie in a ditch and be evacuated after dark.

"Private Sands continued to command the section throughout the whole of the Cassino battle and did splendidly. The third section of the platoon was intact and it was a tonic to visit them and find them behaving as if they were on exercise. This section was being commanded by Lance Sergeant Ketland. After a chat, I crawled back to platoon headquarters just as a member of the forward sections reported that the enemy were attacking again. The platoon commander called the target position to Company Headquarters and John Bricknell said to the Forward Observation officer, Pull the chain. This brought down defensive fire and as before the attack was broken up. This was not the last counter-attack; they went on intermittently all day and in all we had twelve attacks which were repulsed either by small arms fire or by artillery. The artillery fire organized by Captain George Smith was superb.

"During the day I went round the platoon positions eight times crawling on my hands and knees. At about four o'clock in the afternoon I made my last trip, mainly to check on the ammunition state and to see how we had fared. When I came to the last section I found Sammy Ketland slumped in the bottom of his slit trench. He had been killed in the last counter-attack of the day. He had a fine voice and was forever singing 'Galway Bay' – now whenever I hear the tune I remember Sammy. Although I was deeply moved by Sammy's death I was at the moment more perturbed at an ammunition shortage, for I found that we had only seven rounds of ammunition left in the whole platoon. I went back and reported the situation and the platoon commander asked the company commander if there was any chance of more ammunition. As a result the bulk of the ammunition of company headquarters was collected in and issued to the platoon. The evening passed without incident and it was with great relief that we welcomed darkness and the ability to stand up and move freely."

As soon as it was dark Sergeant Snape organized tasks that had to be carried out at once. "The first of these was to get the wounded back to the Regimental Aid Post. Once they had been sent on their way, aided by a stretcher bearer, attention was turned to the dead. There was no indication how long the Battalion might stay in the area and the weather was warm which meant the bodies began to smell very quickly. The sight of comrades lying close to the slit trenches with flies buzzing round them is not good for morale. It was impracticable to get the bodies back at this stage of the battle with much depleted numbers so the only alternative was to bury them where they were. A party of volunteers from the platoon set about this task. Personal papers and possessions were tied in bundles with one of the identity discs. It was a grisly business going through their pockets and feeling round their necks for the identity discs. Eventually that part was done and it remained to get on with the burying. After the strain of the day the men were in no condition to start digging full size graves so the slit trenches were lengthened and the bodies buried in them under about two feet of soil. A rough wooden cross made from bits of old boxes found in the area was placed on each grave.

"There was no question of a burial service nor wrapping the body in anything. It was just a matter of getting it under ground as quickly as possible. Later the bodies would be dug up and re-interred with a proper burial service in the Cassino military cemetery. When we had finished this task I felt physically sick as though I smelled of death."

These accounts give an idea of the battle as seen from the forward sections and not unnaturally differ in one or two points of detail. The picture of the battle at battalion level enlarges the whole frame of the picture and enables a deeper understanding of events.

It will be remembered that the crossing of the river commenced at 0200 hrs and in spite of enemy fire and only having the use of two small assault boats the whole combat element of the Battalion had crossed and established a bridgehead by 0400 hrs. As soon as the mist and smoke cleared the whole Battalion came under heavy shell and mortar fire. Enemy machine guns were active from positions which could look down and enfilade the British lines. When it became clear that no further progress could be made the Colonel decided to hold the line and established his headquarters on the banks of the river (Map 15). A number of prisoners had been taken and some of them wore paratrooper uniform, while others were ordinary riflemen, which indicated that the Battalion had attacked along a boundary line between two German regiments.

As yet no tanks or anti-tank guns had been able to cross over the river so the troops in the bridgehead were in a vulnerable position. In spite of this the positions were held throughout the day. "B" Company held counter-attacks estimated at strengths of twenty to sixty enemy.

A message from General Kirkman, the Corps Commander read, "Well done Bedfords. Hold on at all costs".

Casualties were heavy; "B" Company ten killed and thirteen wounded, "C" Company nine killed and nineteen wounded. Total casualties for the Battalion on 11th/12th were seventy-four killed and wounded.

Frank Sutton remarks: "The costs were already heavy. Waller and Coumber managed to clear a path into the minefield which had caused such losses to 'C' Company. It was a frightful sight. Some of the wounded were dying and we could not shift them yet. A new mine had done this, a hollow concrete block on a stick set off by a trip wire, and lumps of concrete tore terrible wounds.

"The artillery put down a smoke screen to cover Monastery Hill with smoke shells so that it looked as though the mountain was steaming. There was the sound of a bulldozer which started to level the approaches to the river for the planned Bailey bridge, which was to be called "Amazon Bridge". The completion of "Amazon" would allow tanks, anti-tank guns and reinforcements to bolster the bridgehead positions.

"My batman, Private Fordham and I had a nice slit trench, only it was shallow and we could not dig deeper as ground water seeped in. We sat at the bottom and were fairly well protected. I now had the whole of my platoon with me, and with the personnel of Battalion Headquarters there must have been more than twenty slit trenches in a very small area. Although we were under constant fire only those who ventured above ground in daylight were hit.

"Some food and ammunition was dumped on our side of the river. A carrier party was organized to get these provisions to the front line troops, and to bring back the wounded on the return trip. Fred Christmas was in charge of this group, and I took my pioneer sections to check on our safe lane through the mined areas. We made good progress in the dark. Just before we reached 'A' Company we heard a faint voice coming from some bushes calling for help. It was one of our wounded lying in a ditch and unable to move. We promised to pick him up on the way back. We managed to get stores to all the companies and to collect most of the wounded." Fred Christmas told Frank Sutton to take them back to the river, while he made another round of the companies. "There was some sniping and mortaring going on at the time and Fred was hit in the leg shortly after I left him.

"On my way back I had a long file of stretchers and walking wounded behind me and progress was slow. We picked up the chap in the ditch and when I got back I saw Tony Taylor on one of the stretchers with an ear and side of his head in bad shape. An assault boat ferried the wounded to the other side. It was a slow job often interrupted by shelling.

"Once I slipped into Tom La Fontaine's slit trench for shelter. Tom had just rejoined from hospital. His wounds were scarcely healed. It must have been awfully hard for him to face all this, as his brother had been killed in action with the Battalion a year earlier."

"Everyone in 'A' company thought it was a good effort that food had been brought up but took little interest in it. The prime concern was in receiving ammunition. As dawn broke the men crouched in their slit trenches awaiting what fate would bring. There was little sign of activity so Frank Snape visited his sections, crawling and making use of irrigation ditches as cover. The first section he visited was up to its knees in water and although the men were cheerful they were in some discomfort. As he went round he was asked, "Where are our tanks?" as in the original plan they had been meant to cross over into the bridgehead on the first day. Answering this probing question, he replied that they had probably gone round on a flank to cut the lines of communication, which ensured morale was maintained. In truth the tenacious hold on to the small bridgehead by the Bedfords allowing the building of the bridge ensured the battle proceeded without any reverse. Had the bridgehead not held the whole picture would have changed in favour of the enemy, who knowing the thrust of the attack, could have strengthened his defences and fought an even bloodier battle.

"The noise of tanks could be heard and one loomed up in the darkness. The turret opened up and a voice said 'Are you the Bedfords?' 'Amazon' bridge had been completed and this was the first tank across, a Sherman tank of The Lothian and Border Horse.

"More tanks came over as day dawned and Jerry opened up, knocking out the squadron leader's tank. Next came infantry crossing the bridge at the double. Then the sound of bagpipes could be heard and we knew that the 6th Black Watch were coming and they were from the 12th Brigade, which had been divisional reserve. It was apparent that a fresh brigade was to pass through and enlarge the bridgehead.

"The men in 'A' Company saw the tanks cross over, followed by men of the Black Watch and had a grandstand view of a set piece attack on positions in front of them on higher ground which had overlooked them and forced them to keep down all the previous day. The attack was a success and there was the morale-raising sight of seeing the troops going in with the pipers playing the bagpipes.

"These troops were followed by officers from anti-tank and medium artillery regiments, who moved around our slit trenches at Battalion Headquarters as if they were on a nice Sunday morning outing! Naturally this brought down another shower of shells and mortar bombs with unfortunate results for the gunners".

The Battalion could now relax and recuperate from the previous forty-eight hours' activities.

This action was reported upon in Crusader, the British Forces weekly. 'All but two boats allotted to the Bedfordshire and Hertfordshire Regiment were destroyed by German fire. In these two boats the river was crossed – a long ordeal of suspense and peril.

Casualties were heavy, but the survivors formed up on the opposite bank for the attack. Smoke of battle and dust of movement by now had reduced visibility to a few yards. Somehow or other in this awful fog of war the companies were organized and moved on to their objectives. There was a minefield in the path of one of the companies. They knew that when several men were blown up in quick succession. So an officer led the company forward in single file. They went on unflinching and took their objective. They had to stay there for thirty-six hours without support. They were shelled all the time. The Germans holding the higher ground to their right rained Nebelwerfer bombs on them. Counter-attack after counter-attack came in but the Bedfords held their ground and the Gunners put down a ring of steel eighty yards in front of them. Then a bridge "Amazon" was built across the Rapido and supporting arms and reinforcements came over'.

This report written in complimentary terms by the editor of the Eighth Army newspaper helps provide a feel and deeper understanding of the courage and discipline of the individuals involved.

20

CASSINO – POINTS 50 AND 58

Colonel Whittaker continues; "The battle was now moving in our favour and on 15 May the Battalion was ordered to take over from the Royal Fusiliers on the line which they had reached, half-way between *BROWN* and *BLUE* lines. On the 16th we received orders to attack and occupy two features, Points 50 and 58, about six hundred yards apart and partly on the *RED* and *BLUE* lines which had been our original objectives. The companies were by now well below strength and "B" Company, which had suffered most, was reorganized into two platoons, one of which was allotted to "A" Company and one to "D" Company. "A" Company was to attack Point 50 on the right, and "D" Company Point 58 on the left. "C" Company was in reserve. Each forward company was supported by a troop of tanks. An artillery barrage was arranged with a Gunner Forward Observation Officer with each company.

"Companies crossed the start line at 1800 hrs. Almost immediately the enemy artillery defensive fire opened up. This became so heavy that, after some distance, Major Rayner began to fear that his company had walked into our own barrage. The Gunner representative with him was able to assure him that this could not be so, and the advance continued. Major Rayner, close behind his leading platoon, was then himself seriously wounded. A few minutes later he was carried past Battalion Headquarters sitting up on a stretcher and announcing cheerily to me 'It's going fine'. He died back at the Regimental Aid Post.

"On the left 'D' Company had scarcely left the start line when they came under very heavy machine-gun fire from their left, an area in which 12 Brigade were attacking but had themselves been held up. Major Charkham gallantly attempted to continue the attack but the fire in enfilade and from the front was too much. He and two of his platoon commanders were killed and, suffering severe casualties, 'D' Company had to dig in where it was.

"Away to the right the attack continued. Major Rayner's plan had been for two platoons to attack the farm buildings on Point 50 whilst one platoon (the one attached from 'B' Company) attacked a bridge over a stream some three hundred yards to the right and beyond the farm buildings. The artillery barrage had done little to cow the defenders, members of a machine-gun battalion of the German 1st Parachute Division. When the barrage lifted the two platoons were met by heavy machine-gun fire from several positions. This brought them to a temporary halt, but to the left there were more drainage ditches, gullies and some broken ground. With the help of covering fire from our tanks they slowly worked their way round the flank of the buildings. Both platoon commanders were severely wounded but Captain Hollick, sensing that the attack was about to falter, though wounded himself, rallied the remainder of the two platoons and, after a fierce struggle, carried the position at the point of the bayonet. He was awarded the DSO for his gallant leadership.

"On the right the platoon led by Sergeant Snape, whose platoon commander had been wounded early in the attack, had got past the farm buildings under cover of the artillery barrage when they suddenly found themselves under machine-gun fire from their rear. Sergeant Snape, 'outraged', as he put it, at being taken this way, immediately carried out a personal assault on the gun position and, miraculously escaping the fire aimed at him, leapt into the trench and shot the gun crew before they could recover from their surprise. He then gained his objective without further casualties. His courage and example gained him the DCM.

" 'A' Company had gained their objective but had suffered severe casualties including all their officers. I moved up one platoon from 'C' Company to strengthen 'A', organized the consolidation and placed the Intelligence Officer, Lieut Calvert, in temporary command until the situation on the left could be sorted out. It was by now dark. A patrol sent out from 'D' Company reported that the enemy appeared to have withdrawn from Point 50, no doubt as a result of further advances of 12 Brigade on our left. 'C' Company moved up and occupied Point 50 unopposed.

"May 17 was comparatively calm as operations continued elsewhere in an attempt to seal off the entire Monte Cassino area. At dusk a patrol went forward from 'C' Company to Route 6. The Germans appeared to have abandoned the area between the railway and the road but both this patrol and Sergeant Snape's platoon had sharp clashes with parties of Germans attempting to escape from Cassino in which some forty Germans were either captured or killed. 'C' Company then moved up astride the road but there were no further incidents.

"The following morning the Surreys and DCLI moved into Cassino. There was no further fighting. A few Germans emerged from various dugouts and holes but the bulk of the remaining garrison had got out in small parties over the hills during the night.

"The Bedfords turned their backs on the monastery and somewhat wearily, though well aware that they had given a good account of themselves, marched back to where they had started a week earlier on the reverse slopes of Monte Trocchio. The Battalion had lost, during the seven days, four officers and fifty-seven other ranks killed and eleven officers and 147 other ranks wounded; almost all from the rifle companies.

"On 20 May the Battalion moved back to Piedmonte d'Alife for a period of rest and the welcome arrival of the mobile bath unit, mobile cinema, etc. Reinforcements joined us, amongst whom were quite a number who had been wounded in previous battles whom we now welcomed back to the fold.

"The Army Commander came and congratulated the Battalion warmly on its achievements in the battle, and we prepared ourselves for the next one."

Frank Snape tells his story of this phase of the battle. "The battalion remained in reserve during the next twenty four hours suffering a further ten other rank casualties. The following day news came through that the Battalion was to attack again that afternoon. The Battalion was reduced to three rifle companies as the remainder of 'B' Company had been used to bring 'A' and 'D' Companies up to strength.

"We spent the day in comparative ease and then on the morning of 15 May we moved forward towards Cassino. By this time a considerable quantity of equipment had been brought across the river, amongst it some 4.2-inch mortars and our next job was to dig in round them to provide protection in case of ground attack by the enemy.

"As, by this time, the numbers in each platoon had been depleted by casualties and sickness the company was reformed on a two-platoon basis. Sergeant George Woodrow had gone with a burial party to collect the bodies we had buried earlier in temporary graves to re-bury them in a central cemetery. Further reorganisation took place on the 16th and the company was broken up with my platoon going to

'A' Company and the other platoon to 'D' Company.

" 'A' Company had the task of capturing Point 50, a hill which over-looked the main road out of Cassino and also a bridge which was about five hundred yards forward of the hill. The original 'A' Company platoons were to capture the hill and then support our platoon which would capture the bridge. During the two hours lull before the battle George Woodrow returned and, as he was not required as a Platoon Sergeant, the Company Commander suggested that he go back with Headquarters and not take part in the battle. George was very keen to have a crack and persuaded the Company Commander to let him go as a Section Commander in his platoon although he was senior sergeant in the company. It was an awful pity that he was allowed to do this for the next day I found the bodies of George and Cyril side by side. They had obviously been going forward together when they were both killed. We could ill afford to loose such valuable NCOs, especially when one of them need not have been there.

"At about 1800 hrs we assembled in a thick hedge at the approach to Point 50 and waited for the start. Promptly at 1830 hrs we moved forward and almost at once the platoon on the left came under heavy fire from buildings on the objective. The Company Commander, Major S.F.Rayner, affectionately known as 'Ginger' by all ranks of the Battalion, was following closely behind the leading platoon and was severely wounded almost immediately. This was a great blow which was even greater when we learned he had died as a result of his wounds. Captain Horace Hollick was second-in-command and immediately pushed on with the attack and succeeded, but with a great number of casualties, to occupy the hill. During this action Captain Hollick was wounded in the neck. He refused to be evacuated and remained in command until all objectives had been taken. Captain Hollick was awarded the DSO for this outstanding act of leadership.

"Meanwhile our platoon was pushing forward on the right but as we were in the lee of the hill we did not encounter any opposition until we were beyond Point 50 when we came into view of the buildings on the hill. A spate of machine-gun fire was the result and this caused several casualties including the platoon commander. He had been hit in the leg and, handing me his revolver, map and compass said, 'It's all yours now'. Taking command I led the men forward towards our objective. We met with very strong opposition but seemed to bear charmed lives for we moved straight through mortar and rifle positions killing Germans all round and none of my men seemed to be getting hit.

163

"Suddenly, after we had passed a heap of rubble a machine gun opened up from behind and the man walking next to me fell down, obviously dead. I turned round and there about twenty yards away was a German M.G.42 dug-in in a concealed position sited away from the front lines pointing to the rear. It had been put there to deal with the situation now arising, the overrunning of the area by an attacking force. I was absolutely livid that we should be caught in this way and in one of those fleeting moments of madness that take possession of one in such circumstances, I started to run towards the firing machine gun. Tucked into my equipment I had two No 77 phosphorous grenades that were normally used for smoke screens. I took them out and threw them as I ran and they both landed in the dugout position and exploded a second or two before I jumped in.

"The gun was manned by four Germans, my weapon was a .38 revolver. As I jumped into the weapon pit I shot at the man behind the gun and by a million to one chance killed him with the first shot. Immediately I turned to the other three and shot each in turn. It all happened in seconds and was over before I really appreciated what was happening. I rejoined the platoon and we carried on with mopping up.

"Almost immediately after this incident a bunch of Germans came towards us with their hands up and others followed from odd holes dug into banks which carried the road. Resistance in the position had ceased and a count showed that twenty-seven Germans had surrendered. We were still being fired at from buildings on the right of the positions but with the platoon in its weakened state and the encumbrance of prisoners it was not possible to make an attack on them. Another deterrent was an acute shortage of ammunition. All our rifle and Bren ammunition had been expended. I therefore decided to take up a position of all round defence in the area captured and turn the German guns round and use them on the enemy. This action had mixed effects: it was the means of silencing the enemy but it brought down fire upon us from our own tanks.

"We stopped using the guns and tried to get into wireless touch with our own troops. Unfortunately a bullet had gone through the wireless set and had effectively silenced it. I sent back prisoners with an escort of two men with details of the situation and a request for more ammunition. After about three hours as we had not any contact with Company Headquarters I sent back two walking wounded with the same details – it was now about 2230 hrs. The expected counter-attack had not developed but as the platoon was by now much depleted I did

164

not consider I should be justified in sending back more men, and, therefore, decided to hold the position with the abundance of German arms and ammunition available.

"At about midnight a small contact patrol led by Lance Corporal Day of 'A' Company arrived with ammunition and four reinforcements. He told me that the Platoon Commander, together with the prisoners, had arrived safely in Company Headquarters and passed on information of our position but that the delay in contacting us was due to the very weak strength of the Company. Horace Hollick had been wounded but had seen the attack to a successful conclusion and had been relieved by Lieut Calvert, the Battalion Intelligence Officer. "At about 0200 hrs on 17 May my forward section reported sounds of movement of tracked vehicles somewhere in front. I ordered the platoon to stand to. Shortly after this an enemy patrol was seen about twenty yards in front of our platoon positions. A two-inch mortar flare was fired and the automatic weapons opened fire. About ten minutes later a man was seen walking towards the platoon with his hands above his head. He said he was an Austrian who had been forced to serve in the German Parachute Division and was the sole survivor of the patrol on which we had fired. He told me the tracked vehicles which we had heard were German tanks withdrawing from Cassino. This information was later confirmed as being true."

The Commanding Officer visited "A" Company and directed the Company to consolidate all remaining troops on Point 50 as numbers were so depleted. Sergeant Snape received instructions to withdraw to this area at 0300 hrs. "Although I was sorry to give up such hard-won ground I was not unduly sorry to get away from the area as the German bodies were beginning to fill the air with their horrible smell. It was odd, but their dead bodies had a smell much different from ours. I did not know how many of the enemy we had killed, so the next day I went back and took a count and found thirty-one bodies so that our little band of a handful of men had attacked a position and captured twenty seven prisoners and killed thirty-one for the loss of only one killed and three wounded."

At 0900 hrs the next day 14 Platoon under Sergeant Penfold, assisted by a troop from "C" Squadron 19 NZ Armoured Regiment, went forward to clear Point 58 and Point 49. No opposition was encountered.

During the night the German Air Force bombed the Battalion positions and flares were dropped but there were no casualties. The next morning all effective members of "A", "B" and "D" companies were reorganised as one company under the command of Captain Stenning to be known as "D" Company.

Frank Sutton, looking at the prisoners, noted that they were mainly paratroopers in German Air Force uniforms. There were many sergeants and corporals who were boasting that they were the best division in the German forces. They looked a very healthy lot of young men, and they had fought well. They were of the opinion that they would win the war. If Cassino was lost, another spot would be found to hold us long enough. Then their counter-offensive would change everything.

Sergeant Snape returning with his platoon to Point 50, found, apart from the company commander, he was the senior member of the survivors. "I took command of a composite platoon made up of survivors from 'A' company and my own men and put them into an all-round defensive position of company headquarters and got them digging.

"Much of the day was spent in collecting and burying the dead in temporary graves. When all was ready Lieut Calvert came over and we stood around whilst he recited the whole funeral service from memory. I was astounded. It was very moving to stand there looking at this long row of dead faces; faces of comrades with whom we had joked and chatted but a few hours before and hear the calm strong tones of Derek's voice in the moving service."

The Commanding Officer ordered a strong two-platoon patrol out to lay up on Route 6 to ambush any Germans. The patrol leader, misreading the map, passed by the outskirts of Cassino which was mostly rubble but there was one house still standing with four walls. The patrol arrived at the designated spot and laid up facing the direction from whence they had come. Almost at once there was the sound of marching men coming along the road. The body was challenged with the password "Briar", but failed to respond with the expected reply "Pipe", rather there was a torrent of German. The patrol opened up with rapid fire accounting for the whole party killing seven and wounding two. The wounded were asked why this party had come along the road in such a casual manner. Their response was that they were to withdraw that night and were to follow the first troops withdrawing out of Cassino. They had been inside the four-walled house and seeing our patrol pass by had assumed we were the first German party and had followed along behind. They had not considered that we would have the audacity to send a patrol through the outskirts of Cassino.

The next day the Battalion was ordered to be prepared to attack

166

and capture the town of Cassino but this proved to be unnecessary. As a result the Battalion buried their dead and marched back across the River Rapido to a position near Trocchio. "As we neared the position I saw in the distance the Commanding Officer standing beside the road waiting for us to come in. I was leading the remains of 'B' Company and I turned to them and said, 'Right, look up now, keep in step, let us show the C.O bags of bull.' To a man, the weariness seemed to drop from them and they marched as proudly as if they were on the drill square. I know that I shall never have a finer lot of men under my command and it was a great honour to give the 'Eyes Left' to the C.O. and to hear him say 'Well done, Snape. Well done chaps'

"When we arrived at Trocchio I immediately ordered the men to clean their weapons, wash and shave and laid on a weapons inspection. We were all dead tired but it was much better for morale."

"A" Echelon played its part during this battle in enabling the front line companies to perform as they did. " Following the breakthrough at Cassino the method of running 'A' Echelon followed set procedures, which were adapted where necessary to meet prevailing circumstances.

"It was wisely decided by Higher Authority that 24 hr rations should be carried on the man for the assault crossing of the river. On the night 11/12 May the Battalion was established somewhat precariously on the far bank.

"'A' Echelon was established on 12 May at 'The Barracks' – a large white building standing well up on a rise just behind (or east) of the river. It was so conspicuous that the temptation to shoot at it must have been very strong for the Boche. He made little attempt to resist it, and many a fervent prayer of thanks was offered up to the unknown architect who designed its eighteen inch thick walls – even if the siting of the building left much to be desired at that time.

"On the night of 13 May the Battalion was holding its bridgehead and the Bailey bridge ('Amazon') had not as yet been built. The only link with the battalion was by a No 18 radio set and two assault boats. Hard rations were to be taken over in the boats. Unfortunately one of the boats was sunk by machine-gun fire before it left its moorings. This left only one frail boat by which rations, ammunition, water and wounded could be transported over the river. This boat was, in fact, working on the 'flying ferry' principle, and it played a very large part in the battle as a whole because, although under shell, mortar and machine-gun fire, it made many trips to and from the Battalion during the first two vital days. It was holed in many places, the cross cable which protected it from the swift current was shot away – but it never sank.

"By the evening of 14 May 'Amazon' had been completed, some armour crossed, and normal maintenance traffic was possible. A Forward Maintenance Area was established west of the river ('Too bloody forward' as one RASC Corporal was heard to remark bitterly.) Rations and ammunition were drawn nightly after dark as the area was still under observation by the Germans, split up on the spot and issued direct to companies by jeep. This hand to mouth procedure is fortunately rarely necessary; the breaking of bulk rations in complete darkness is in particular to be avoided whenever possible as identification of different commodities is all but impossible. All one could safely promise during this difficult period was that everyone would get something to eat. In point of fact 'Compo' rations came into use on 15 May and the difficulty was over.

"On 16 May at 1830 hrs the Battalion moved forward to attack Points 50 and 58, and in view of the uncertainty of the situation all supplies were drawn early and held in jeeps at Rear Battalion Headquarters until such time as they should be called forward. The tale of that most gallant but costly attack is recorded elsewhere; suffice it to say that the two companies immediately engaged reached their objectives and held them. The confusion was such that no one could say for certain where anyone was, reports filtering back to Battalion Headquarters indicated that both companies had become very split up, and one could only hope that the supplies would eventually reach their right destination. The bulk of them did, but inevitably a number of troops who had become parted from their companies during the action went hungry that night. By the morning of 17 May the situation was stabilized and exact company locations were known so the supply problem eased. On 18 May the battalion came out to rest."

The casualties suffered by the Battalion during the period 11 – 18 May were:

	Officers	Other Ranks
Killed in Action	5	57
Wounded	10	147

Capt Browning comments: "Our casualties were very heavy by present day standards, the Battalion going into action with twenty officers and 450 men, and when relieved five days later coming out with five officers and 200 men.

"When we were pulled out our spirits were right in the air. I should be foolish indeed if I did not say that the reception we received as we marched back through our own gun lines made me proud and happy to be a Bedford.

"Officers and men together were congratulated by the Army Commander, General Sir Oliver Leese, in the most glowing terms."

That then is the story of the forward troops at the Battle of Cassino as described by a few of those who took part. The accounts indicate a fighting spirit of the highest degree. Here was a battalion which only five months earlier had been far below strength, having been milked to provide reinforcements for units fighting in the line. Once it had been made up to strength the Battalion was in action inside five weeks culminating a few weeks later in the battles which resulted in the defeat of a determined enemy, aided by terrain, holding well sited and strong positions. The holding of the bridgehead over the Rapido without tank support in spite of repeated counter-attacks and in spite of heavy casualties among senior ranks was in the best traditions of all that the British Infantry is renowned for.

The leadership shown by officers and NCOs in the attack on Points 50 and 58 can only be fully appreciated now that all the noise and dust of battle is long subsided.

An indication of the *élan* of all ranks is shown by their determination to carry the fight forward in the face of losses which would have deterred lesser spirits. The forward companies lost 75% of their officers killed or wounded, and 50% of their overall strength.

The attitude of the men in marching past their C.O. after seven gruelling, hard-fought days as described by Frank Snape shows the character of all involved. The battle honour "Cassino" was well deserved.

21

ITALY – MAY/JUNE 1944

The assault against Cassino had at last been successful after a long and bloody battle in which both sides had suffered heavy casualties. The 'Gustav Line' which had held up the Allied advance through the winter months had been breached. The Germans threw reinforcements piecemeal into the battle but were unable to prevent the link up with forces operating from the Anzio bridgehead. The capture of Rome came quickly after this link-up on 4 June. North of the capital the U.S. Fifth Army continued to advance alongside the coast on the left flank. The Eighth Army advanced up the valley of the River Tiber towards Lake Trasimene. Both Armies met with increasingly dogged resistance.

The Germans had been developing a strong defensive line, The Gothic Line, which stretched from Rimini on the Adriatic Coast to La Spezia on the west. This line made use of the Apennine mountain ranges rearing up to the north and east of Florence. The German High Command managed to build up their forces to some fourteen divisions which were tasked to delay the Allies closing up on 'The Gothic Line'. The country over which the British Forces were advancing was hilly with lateral roads affording the Germans ample choice of defensive positions to suit their weapons. It was not good tank country, and the German Tiger tank with its heavy armour and superior gun favoured the defence. Demolitions, mines and booby traps all played their part.

The Allied eyes were now on France where the Normandy battle was in progress. Some seven Allied Divisions were transferred from Italy to support the invasion of Southern France. The weakened Allied Command continued to press forward against this increasingly obstinate enemy (Map 16).

On 20 May the Battalion moved to Piedmonte D'Alife, where it remained for the next two weeks. The rifle companies had sustained such losses that the survivors of "A", "B" and "D" were amalgamated together to form "D" Company under the command of Captain Stenning until such time as further reinforcements were received. The next fortnight was spent in reorganization, training, refitting and on necessary administration. The war diary lists this activity laconically as 'Battalion normal training'.

On 1st June a ceremonial burial service was held at the Brigade cemetery and the officers of the Battalion toured the battlefield. Reinforcements were drafted in and the Battalion reformed with the principle appointments held as below:

Commanding Officer	Lt Colonel W. A. Whittaker
Second in Command	Major A.G. Powell
"A" Company	Major The Lord Wynford
"B" Company	Major E.S.Jenkins
"C" Company	Major G.V.Martin
"D" Company	Major A.R.A.Wilson
"S" Company	Capt T.S.LaFontaine
"HQ"Company	Capt D.A.T.Mole
Adjutant	Capt J.E.Douglas
Quartermaster	Capt (QM) H.T.Beasley

Time was spent on training, refitting and on necessary administration. The war diary lists this activity laconically as 'Battalion normal training'.

Sergeant Snape comments, "Early in June we went forward again and spent a week in the most maddening type of warfare. We rode on tanks and then marched. We did attack after attack but each time we were too late and the enemy had gone leaving behind blown bridges and burning ammunition dumps.

"At the end of this spell of chasing we were withdrawn and carried out our longest march of the Italian campaign, about fifteen miles. It was hot and the roads were dusty. Many of the chaps were new to war and it was with great difficulty we kept them going. After this stint in the line the Battalion spent the next two weeks until 23 June carrying out further training."

Lt Colonel W.A.Whittaker, who had served with the Battalion from mobilization in September, 1939, and who had commanded the Battalion during the locust days in North Africa and through the slogging battles culminating in Cassino, relinquished command on 15

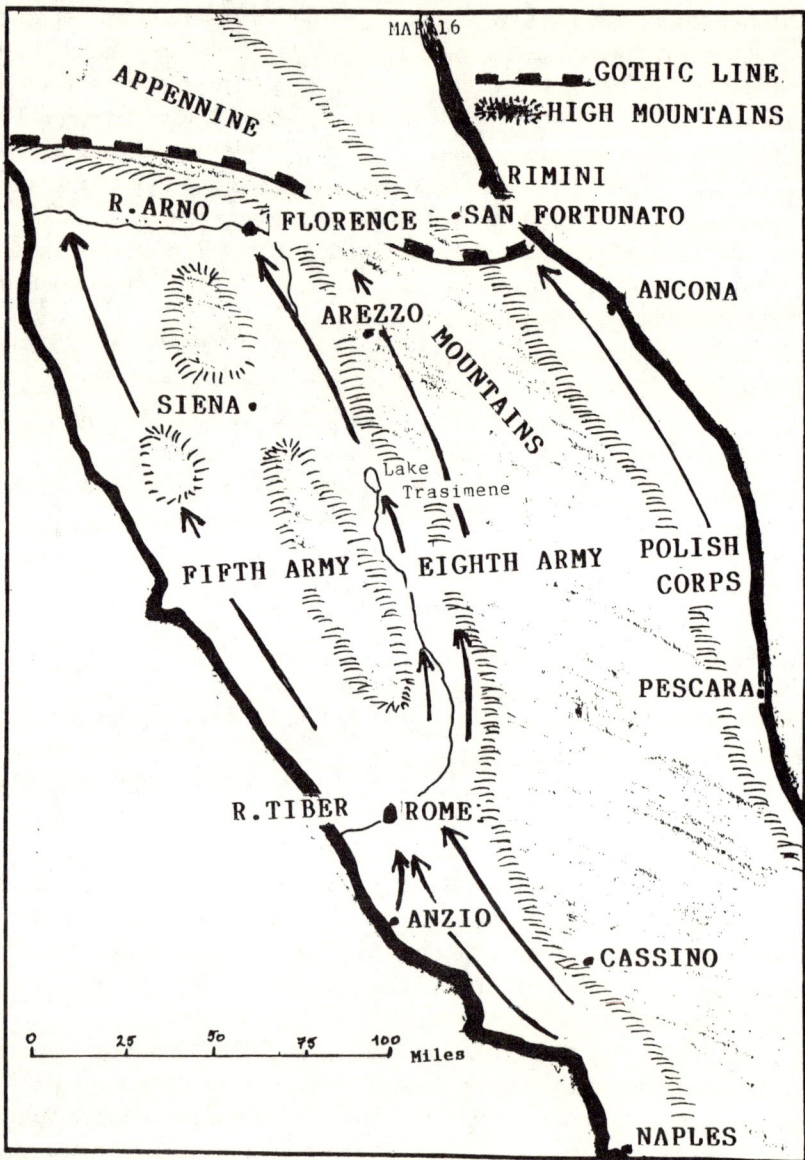

MAP 16
ITALY – ADVANCE JUNE TO AUGUST 1944

June, 1944. He had been a highly respected Commanding Officer as evidenced in the words of Corporal F Baldock "He was with his forward troops the whole time, ready to handle any situation which presented itself". Sergeant Snape writes " I believe Bill Whittaker should have been awarded the DSO for Cassino."

Command of soldiers in battle is a privilege and honour of the highest degree. No commander wishes for war but when it is unleashed seeks to ensure his soldiers are as well trained and prepared as is possible. Leadership is by example and Bill Whittaker followed the traditions of leadership passed down in the Regiment through the years earning the respect of all ranks. He had managed to retain key members of his Battalion team whenever demands were made to supply reinforcements for other units. This policy ensured that training of all reinforcement drafts was thorough and detailed and that the Battalion was able to stand up to the demands placed upon it. This is Bill Whittaker's tribute.

The second-in-command, Major Powell assumed temporary command and there was much discussion and speculation among all ranks as to who would take command. Mention is made at this time in Battalion Orders of Major W.Rickman, MBE, who had joined as a replacement, taking charge of a unit harbour party on 17 June.

An indication of the Allied air superiority at this time is shown by the Battalion bivouacking in a camp site in open fields north of Rome.

On 24 June Lt Colonel B.A.Burke assumed command of the Battalion. On 25 June Sergeant Snape was catching up on sleep in his bivouac when he was awakened by a voice saying "Who is the platoon commander?" Crawling out of his bivouac Sergeant Snape said "I am. Who wants me?" He continues " Then I saw standing there a man in thick horn-rimmed spectacles. He looked to me rather comical; as he was wearing a type of khaki drill shorts which we called 'long shorts'. They buttoned up at the knee and could be let down into semi trousers. We were all in the habit of wearing our khaki drill shorts very short and my impression of this individual was of a rather untidy man, wearing shorts that were too long and wearing a General Service cap. He was carrying a fly swatter!

We had a conversation that went like this:
  'Are you the platoon commander?'
  'Yes, I am'
  'What platoon is this?'
  '10 Platoon, B Company'

'How long have you been with the Battalion?'
'Four years plus'
'Well you probably know all the answers'
'A few'
'How many men have you in your platoon?'
'Twenty four'
'Well I shall see a lot more of you. I'm the new Battalion Commander.'

"He shook hands and said, 'Good Afternoon'. I replied 'Yes, Sir. Good afternoon, Sir.' I was absolutely staggered. Having been abrupt almost to the point of rudeness, I thought I would certainly be on the carpet for that afternoon's effort.

The next afternoon all officers and NCO'S were assembled for a talk by the Commanding Officer. We were astounded when we received a lecture in a quiet voice on fire and movement and minor tactics. This did not inspire confidence and we went away wondering what the powers that be had inflicted on us. Although at the time the talk did not inspire confidence it gave us an insight into the quiet, unruffled nature of 'Daddy Burke' as he was to become affectionately known throughout the Battalion. In a short time in battle we were to learn that Colonel Burke was anything but weak and ineffectual, for a couple of days later we were committed to a full-scale attack on enemy positions which lay to the west of Lake Trasimene."

22

ITALY – JUNE 1944

The following story of the battles near Lake Trasimene relies on accounts of survivors from "A" Company and provides a more detailed account at platoon level both from Sergeant Snape, who had been awarded an immediate DCM at Cassino and was by now an 'old hand', and Lieutenant Robson a newly-joined platoon commander. Many of the actions are therefore related to "A" Company though it is possible to appreciate the parallel actions of "B" Company, which was the other leading company. As will be seen the leading companies suffered heavy casualties with many officers killed or wounded. This has reduced the number of individuals who can tell the story.

The Battalion was to pass through the DCLI who had seized their objectives astride the road running eastwards across the front from Casamaggiore. The plan in outline was for the Battalion to advance with two companies leading. The move up to the start line on 28 June was during the hours of darkness but as light dawned the companies were caught in enemy artillery, mortar and nebelwerfer fire. In spite of this the men continued to press forward with "A" Company under Major Lord Wynford on the right and "B" Company under Major Jenkins on the left. Their objectives were two small hill features Points 340 and 386. (See Map 17). The area through which the troops were advancing contained numerous small farmhouses all garrisoned by well armed and determined Germans.

Sergeant Snape was leading a platoon in "A" Company and he tells this story. "Just about five o'clock, my platoon, which was leading, and the leading platoon of the other forward company broke cover and started across the open country. Suddenly we heard the horrible noise of nebelwerfers, enemy multi-barrelled mortars. The noise was like a number of screaming air raid sirens which had got out of control; and were all screaming together and gradually increasing in volume. There

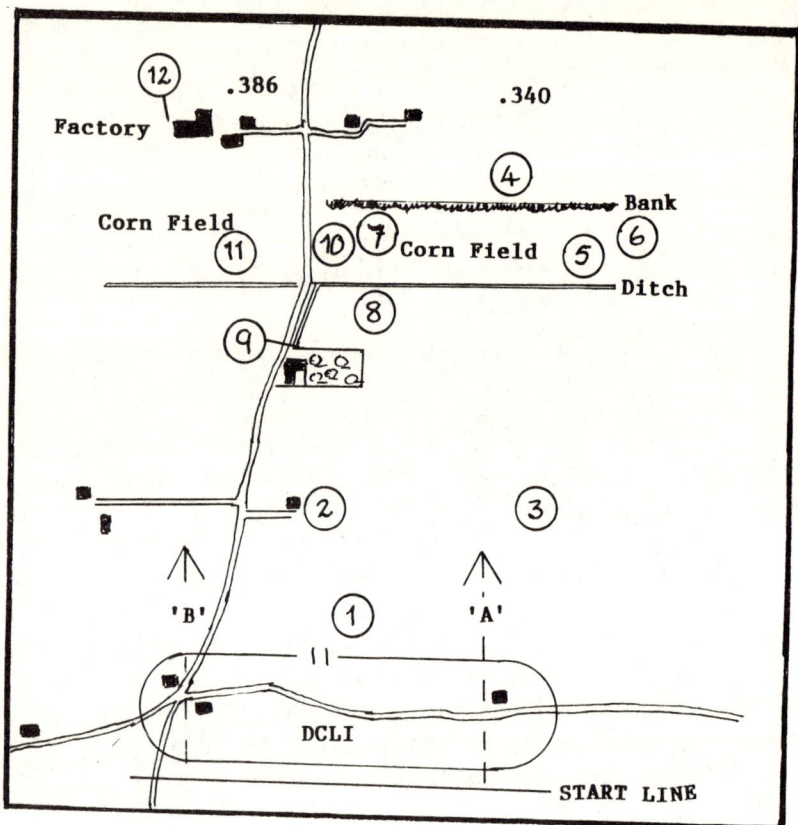

MAP 17

WEST OF LAKE TRASIMENE – 28 JUNE 1944

1. Companies shelled and mortared. Major Lord Wynford and Captain Bricknell wounded. Lieut Cox now O i.c of "A" Coy.
2. 10 Platoon "A" Company under fire from farmhouse.
3. Lieut Bailes' platoon on right of "A" Company.
4. Lieut Cox killed on bank.
5. Enemy MG on right.
6. Lieut Bailes killed.
7. Sergeant Snape reforms platoon behind bank.
8. Ditch along edge of cornfield.
9. Sergeant McHugh in slit trench.
10. German counter-attack from cornfield.
11. Enemy form up for further counter-attack.
12. Tiger tank near Factory.

13. "The Battalion dug in on the reverse slopes of Monte Trocchio on the evening of 3/4 May" (p144). (*Imperial War Museum*)

14. "I was lucky; men in front of me and behind were killed or wounded by these anti personnel mines." Sergeant Pickess visits Cassino cemetery in 1989 (p153).

15. "I believe Bill Whittaker should have been awarded the DSO for Cassino" (p173). Lt-Colonel W.A. Whittaker; Painting by T.S. LaFontaine.

16. "'A' Company was to attack Point 50 on the right, and 'D' Company Point 58 on the left" (p160); painting by Terence Cuneo. (*Ben May*)

is nothing quite like it. With artillery shells one gets used to the sounds so that one could say with reasonable certainty 'That one will go over' or 'That one will be close' and duck, but with these mortars it was impossible. As we moved forward the bombs started dropping around us. We hit the ground and pressed as close as was possible. We were caught in the open without any cover and could only hope for the best.

"When the noise of the explosions stopped I got up and yelled for 10 Platoon to get moving forward. The air was filled with dust and smoke caused by the explosions and our noses and throats were filled with the bitter sweet fumes. As the air cleared I was amazed to see that my platoon was intact and we moved on only to be shelled again a few moments later."

Lieutenant Robson, the Platoon commander of 9 Platoon takes up the story. "I had not fired a shot in anger, and was very aware of the fact that, although other reinforcements were in the same 'green' state as me, there were in the Battalion, and in my platoon many who had experienced everything that war is. I cannot remember how long it was before we were on the move – not long-but during this period I formed a high respect for Major Wynford and Lieut Cox.

"Our move forward, and my baptism of fire was the Trasimene line. It seemed to me that all hell was let loose when we were stomped by nebelwerfers, and it was early at this stage that Lieut Cox shouted to me that Major the Lord Wynford had had an arm blown off, and that he was now in command of the company." (Map 17, note 1).

Sergeant Snape continues; "In this bout of shelling Captain Bricknell was wounded; again my platoon was fortunate. Other companies were not so lucky. When we arrived at the start line Bob Cox came up to me and said, 'At last Sergeant, I've got command of a company, Major the Lord Wynford has been seriously wounded on the start line.' Bob's words were not heartless but when he joined the Battalion he was a temporary captain with high hopes of getting a company early on, but so far he had served as a platoon commander in 'B' Company, 'C' Company and now 'A' Company and had only got command of a company when the company commander was seriously wounded."

Captain Bricknell, as stated, was wounded during this strafing : "I felt a heavy blow on the chest which knocked me over. Two stretcher bearers came over and I had a wound in my chest. They put a field dressing on it and I made my way back to the road, helping a soldier who had been blinded. We managed to make the road and a Red Cross jeep picked us up and took us to the advance field hospital where the doctor found that a piece of shrapnel had gone through my ribs and out of my back. Whilst I was in hospital Major Jenkins was admitted with a wound to his leg."

Sergeant Snape continues:"We moved over the start line and went forwards towards our objective under cover of a supporting artillery barrage. Once across the start line the ground fell away sharply before rising to the ridge that was our objective. At first the ground was meadowland and then, on the lower slopes of the ridge, it was thick with corn which continued up and beyond our view. At about half way from the start line to the objective was a collection of farm buildings and then on the top of the ridge was a farmhouse complete with garden and orchard. I was walking along with one of my sections on each side of me and it was only by shouting at the top of my voice that I was able to keep the men going – but keep going they did (Map 17, note 2). As we began to ascend the ridge we started to receive attention from a section of Germans occupying the farmhouse, but although bullets were whistling over us the men went steadily on. It was absolutely splendid the way they never faltered for a moment.

"As we went towards the house my leading Bren gunners fired bursts from the standing position and as we entered the farmyard about fifteen Germans came running out with their hands up. We handed them over to Company Headquarters. The advance continued. However, we were too far to the right and Major Jenkins decided to move along a road on the left; and I was ordered to move on the left of the road and clear up to a building some two hundred yards away while another platoon under Lieut Bailes was to advance on my right." (Map 17, note 3).

Robson now takes up the story. "We advanced successfully – my platoon at one stage flushing out the enemy by setting fire to a haystack in which they were hidden, with the aid of a phosphorous grenade. It was soon after this that Lieut Rose was mortally wounded. Continuing on, 'A' Company and my platoon in particular got rather bogged down by a troublesome Tiger tank and Lieut Cox crawled forward to see for himself. I was lying in a ditch. Lieut Cox crawled over the top of this ditch and was immediately shot and killed by the tank. It must have been uncomfortably close at this point.(Map 17, note 4).

"We were pinned down in this position for a while, during which time our morale was heightened by the arrival of one of our tanks and by crawling to the rear of the tank I was able to telephone to the commander and indicate the general direction from where the trouble was

178

coming. This tank blazed away quite a bit and we were then free from immediate trouble."

Meanwhile Sergeant Snape; "About as soon as we left the shelter of the farmhouse orchard we came under enemy machine-gun fire from our right. (Map 17, note 5) Moving forward, I spotted the enemy machine gun in the corner of a field and sent one section to deal with it and to support them with the 2 inch mortar. My platoon sergeant, Tom Newnham, quickly sized up the position and range and started putting down high explosive bombs on the MG post. We were kneeling side by side with Tom directing the fire when I heard a rifle crack and a metallic ping. Turning to Tom, I was about to ask what it was when I saw he had been killed by the bullet. At the same time someone in the platoon said, 'There he is Sarge' and pointed to the corner of the field in which we were. Catching a glimpse of movement I said, 'Come on' to the mortar team and started to run towards the sniper. I had a Luger pistol with fifteen rounds and started firing as I ran when I was thirty yards from the German. I missed with every shot and finally struck him with my rifle bayonet. By this time my platoon had fallen behind Lieut Bailes and his platoon, which was moving through corn some seventy yards from the buildings that were our objective. As my platoon moved into the corn we heard the chatter of machine-gun fire and a tank engine in the area of the houses. The bullets whipped overhead and we went down in the corn in a flash. Calling to the men, we managed to crawl forward in line with the other platoon. A few yards in front was a bank and I decided to get up to it and see what were the chances of going forward beyond it. I crawled up to the bank and as I reached it Lieut Bailes called to his platoon to advance and, standing up, walked right over the bank. The enemy machine gun opened fire and he was killed instantly and several of his platoon who had advanced with him were hit also. (Map 17, note 6) The others immediately scattered in the corn and all control was lost. At intervals the enemy sprayed the cornfield and road in front of us with bullets. It was plain to go forward in isolation was madness, and I decided to contact the Company Commander to let him know the situation. During these skirmishes I had not kept my platoon intact. My platoon sergeant had been killed and a number of men had been wounded including my wireless operator. The wireless had been hit and was not working. I decided the only thing to do was to collect as many men as possible of both platoons and see what was the score. It was worse than I had thought. Of the two platoons I could only muster fifteen plus the platoon sergeant of the other platoon and me. With the other platoon wireless I attempted to make contact with Company Headquarters but although I could hear them they could not hear me.

"I decided the only sensible course was to try to rejoin the remainder of the company. Collecting the survivors together behind the bank (Map 17, note 7) I told them I intended that we crawl back to the edge of the cornfield and then, when we came to the open bit of ground where we had disposed of the sniper, I would make a plan to get back to the rest of the company. Giving instructions that all were to follow me, I told Bob Lamplough, the platoon sergeant of the other platoon, to bring up the rear and we set off. We were not able to take the wounded with us, much as I disliked leaving them. We did not know where they were in the cornfield so I had no option. After a nerve-wracking and tiring crawl we arrived at the open space. A ditch ran along the edge of the cornfield and eventually joined up with another which ran at right angles and followed the line of the road. (Map 17, note 8)

"We reached the point where I had to decide what to do next. Bob Lamplough came up beside me and said, 'I want to make a run for it'. He got up and doubled into the open, immediately bringing down a hail of bullets. He went down and I was afraid that he had been hit. However, after a pause he got up and doubled forward again to the shelter of a large olive tree. These movements again brought down a hail of fire. Whilst I hoped Bob would get away with it I did not feel justified in risking the rest of the party being shot, so decided we would crawl on. Had I known that Bob Cox had been killed while lying in the very ditch along which we were crawling I would not have felt so comfortable. That news I received later. After a very difficult crawl I saw Sergeant McHugh of "A" Company staring along the ditch with his rifle at the ready. (Map 17, note 9) With his platoon commander, Lieut Harold Robson, he had dug a slit trench in the corner of the farm garden to cover the ditch along which we had crawled and which they thought a likely enemy approach.

"I was pleased to see some more of our own men and getting up on all fours, was just moving to the side of the trench when Robbie screamed, 'Get down, get down. We are being fired on and Mr Cox has been killed just out there'. I said, 'You're being fired on, Sir. What do you think we have experienced out there in the cornfields and why do you think we have exhausted ourselves crawling along this filthy ditch?' and flopped over into his slit trench. I got my men into cover and told them to rest while Robbie told me the situation. I then went to find the Company Commander. When he saw me Jenks said,

'Thank goodness you are back. Have you brought any soldiers with you?' He was pleased when I said I had fifteen, it made the company a little more able to withstand a counter-attack.

"I related our experiences to Jenks and learned that John Barnwell was missing with some of his platoon and that the remains of 'A' and 'B' Companies had amalgamated to make one reasonable sized force. The Company Commander then sent me with the fifteen remaining men of 10 and 11 Platoons to take up positions in the area covering the flank looking towards the ground over which we had so recently travelled. We dug in on the edge of the orchard but before we had finished we saw the enemy advancing from the cornfield in which we had been caught earlier. (Map 17, note 10) Immediately we opened fire with all available weapons and the enemy counter-attack faltered and failed.

"Shortly afterwards we saw in the distance on our left a number of enemy collecting. It appeared they might be forming up for a counter-attack in some strength so I sent a message to the Company Commander who arranged for artillery fire to be brought down on the area. I observed for the gunners and after one correction the area was plastered with shells and the Germans scattered and disappeared. (Map 17, note 11) We thought we had effectively dealt with the threat of counter-attack by this action, but not a bit of it. Very soon advancing enemy infantry broke cover about seventy yards away and came towards us. I let them get well into the open before taking any overt action and then gave the order to open fire. We gave them a terrific pasting and the survivors ran for cover.

"Meanwhile the German Tiger tank which had wrought such havoc in the cornfield had now moved to the west and taken up a position by a red brick factory building from which it scored again and again against Sherman tanks which were brought up to give us support and knocked out most of them.(Map 17, note 12).

"After dark we went out and made a search of the area over which we had advanced in hope and crawled back in despair. Several of our wounded were found and brought back and these said that others of our men had been taken prisoner by the enemy earlier in the day. The dead were also brought back and buried in the farm house garden."

Lieutenant Robson went on patrol after dark and nothing much happened. Later a strange noise came from the road. Fire was held and out of the gloom came a German officer, blind drunk and driving a sheep in front of him. It was assumed that he had got fed up with the war, fortified himself with plenty of vino and set about giving himself up.

The battle had been fought against a tenacious enemy, over rolling terrain with numerous farm buildings affording the Germans choice of positions from which to delay the attacking force. They had made full use of artillery and mortar defensive fire and their armour included the powerful Tiger tanks which they used skilfully.

The story of the leading infantry as it was told may seem confusing. Once battle is joined the leader, whatever his rank, is there to ensure the immediate objective is captured. The ebb and flow of events demand a cool and confident approach to the task in hand. Shelled, mortared, fired on by automatic weapons, pinned down with casualties on either flank the situation is utterly confusing. The story tells the series of events as each individual saw them. It is a confusing picture but no attempt has been made to edit as this would destroy the feel of the battlefield.

The battle at the end of the day ended with Major Jenkins of "B" Company holding the ground won with remnants of two companies. His company second-in-command, Captain Bricknell, had been wounded early on in the advance. Lieutenant Rose had been killed, and Lieutenant Barnwell and his platoon were missing and cut off. In "A" Company the Company Commander, Major the Lord Wynford, had been seriously wounded, his successor, Lieutenant Cox, killed leading the company attack, and Lieutenant Bailes killed also. Under the leadership of Major Jenkins the remaining men of the two companies had dug in and fought off a number of determined German counter-attacks.

The next morning Sergeant Snape went out on a reconnaissance patrol to the area of the factory. The tracks of the Tiger tank were clearly visible and there was a heap of spent shell cases and cartridges, but of the Germans not a sign. The enemy had withdrawn during the night.

The advance continued in bounds from one feature to the next with companies taking it in turns to lead. "A" Company had taken the lead soon after 2030 hrs with the task of attacking the next ridge some five hundred yards ahead. The company started forward with tank support when enemy machine guns and artillery opened up and caused some confusion among the reserve platoons. Major Jenkins was forward with Company Headquarters and missed this fire and, as it was now getting dark continued to press on not realizing he had only his headquarters with him. Sergeant Snape started to move forward with his platoon when the Commanding Officer appeared and told him to hold his ground. Not long after Major Jenkins came back, having left his headquarters in possession of the objective, and led the rest of the company forward in single file straight across country and on to the objective. However, the other companies had halted on the slope where Sergeant Snape had met the Commanding Officer, so "A" Company was now out on a limb.

"A" Company set to and dug in. At about 0300 hrs footsteps were heard from the rear and this party was challenged. "It's all right, it's only the Commanding Officer bringing food." A ration party had returned to Battalion Headquarters saying they could not find "A" Company whereupon, the Commanding Officer had personally led the party forward. Sergeant Snape takes up the story. "When daylight came we found we were overlooked by snipers from all angles and while eating breakfast one lad, who was imprudent enough to stand up outside his slit trench was shot in the head and killed. We were heavily shelled in this area but fortunately I did not have any casualties in my platoon. During the afternoon the shelling and mortaring diminished and had ceased by early evening. I was sent out with a fighting patrol of a platoon strength to see if the area in front of the company was occupied and to ensure the enemy was not forming up in front of the company to put in an attack. To try and control some thirty men was well nigh impossible and I was very thankful that we did not meet anything on the way and I could report 'All clear'."

In the early hours other troops passed through and in the morning of 30 June the Battalion was withdrawn for a few days' rest.

Major Jenkins was awarded an immediate DSO for his leadership in these actions.

23

ITALY – JULY 1944

More reinforcements arrived to make up company strengths after the last battles, among them Major Horace Hollick who had been wounded at Cassino. He was posted to command "A" Company. He tells the story of his movements after he was wounded at Cassino. "Off to hospital at Bari then to Trani hospital for remedial treatment and so back to No 1 Infantry Reinforcement Training Depot (IRTD) where I met up with Slater my old batman. The plan was for me to stay at the IRTD as a training officer but my plan was to get back to the Battalion as soon as possible. (Being away from the Battalion was like being cut off from the family).

"How the Officer Commanding the Transit Camp explained my absence I don't know.

"We travelled on several convoys until we finished up at our own "B" echelon and Harry Beasley and so to the Commanding Officer, Billy Burke, who, to say the least, was surprised".

There was a Church Parade on 2 July and on the 4th the officers toured the previous battle area and visited the Battalion cemetery.

On 5 July the Battalion moved forward in troop-carrying vehicles some twenty miles to a concentration area behind 28 Brigade near Arezzo. The Commanding Officer had been told to expect that the next move forward would be along Route 69 into Florence. The Battalion had a fairly quiet time taking over in the line on 8 July. The war diary mentions shelling and mortaring of forward positions and active patrolling by the Battalion. On the 13th a harassing patrol went out to shoot up enemy positions and drew fire. On 17 July the advance continued. Opposition was light though enemy artillery harassing fire was at times heavy and the advance made steady progress with rifle companies taking turns in the lead. On the evening of 18 July Major Jenkins was wounded during an enemy bombardment and Captain Tyndale assumed command of "B" Company. At this time the Company Sergeant Major was evacuated sick and Sergeant Snape was given the job. He handed over his platoon to Sergeant Lamplough.

There follows an account of a typical day in pursuit of a retreating enemy as recounted by Lt Colonel Burke.

"The advance resumed at 0600 hrs on 19 July down the axis of the road through Pergine to Levane, a town some six miles distant. "D" Company under Major Wilson was leading and occupied Pergine without opposition consolidating preparatory to "C" Company passing through. Almost immediately the town was shelled and the enemy was reported on high ground about one thousand yards ahead.

" 'C' Company passed through Pergine and moved towards a small farmhouse on a small ridge, The approach was uneventful, but, as they cleared the crest of their objective, they came under machine gun fire from the ridge beyond and any further forward movement was checked. 'B' Company was now directed to move round the flank of 'C' Company to assault the enemy position but before the plan could be executed the enemy were seen to withdraw.'B' Company passed through to continue the advance. The country ahead was hilly, interspersed with deep steep-sided gulleys. The hills were mostly wooded, though on either side of the road were open fields. A railway line ran alongside the road on the right, whilst on the left was a large wooded knoll.

"Meanwhile 'A' Company, supported by a troop of Sherman tanks and with Captain Smith, the Artillery Forward Observation Officer, was ordered to advance down a loop road, via Montozzi to join up with the battalion just short of Levane. This advance progresses without incident until the forward troops reached a demolished bridge about five hundred yards short of the main axis. The leading platoon, under Lieutenant Robson, had just crossed the demolition when an MG opened up at close range from its right front. Sergeant McHugh, then commanding the second platoon, was ordered to move round to the right and clear a farmhouse two hundred yards away. As soon as this platoon moved a second MG opened up from the left front. Lieutenant Richardson, commanding the third platoon, moved to deal with it. The movement of both these platoons was covered by fire from Robson's platoon.

"Sergeant McHugh and his platoon occupied the farmhouse and Lieutenant Robson's platoon joined him there. Lieutenant

Richardson's platoon had worked its way up to the forward edge of a wood and consolidated there. The supporting tanks engaged suspected enemy positions with High Explosive and MG fire.

"Lieut Sutton, the Pioneer Platoon Commander, and an Assault Section now started work on repairing the demolished bridge and made it passable. Their action enabled tanks to move up and support the leading infantry. It was subsequently officially called Sutton Bridge.

" 'A' Company now consolidated in the area of the farmhouse having suffered no casualties in this small action. Meanwhile 'B', 'C' and 'D' Companies were continuing down the main axis moving off the road to the left in among the trees on the right side of the knoll. Progress was slow, owing to rough going. Practically every bridge along this main axis had been blown and it was impossible for any form of transport to follow along this route.

"After about an hour 'B' Company halted as a small party of Germans had been spotted moving in the area of a railway station on the right. Lieutenant Evans was sent to mop up this party. He returned two hours later and reported that he had followed the enemy to a house five hundred yards behind the station and when he had attempted to take the house had been repulsed by MG fire. He considered the position was fairly strongly held and two of his men were missing. Shortly after this, sounds of battle were heard from the left on the far side of the knoll and a Spandau was firing from over the north shoulder of the knoll.

"The advance was continued by 'C' Company, followed by 'B' and 'D'. As the leading platoon cleared the northern slopes of the knoll it came under close-range MG fire from a group of farm buildings immediately in front. The enemy withdrew to another house just eighty yards beyond and fired into 'C' Company area. In addition two snipers, who could not be located in long grass to the right, were causing trouble.

" 'B' and 'D' Companies passed through and linked up with 'A' Company. All companies were now out of radio range so a decision was taken by the company commanders to remain where they were until the situation could be reported to me. I arrived shortly afterwards and at 1800 hrs ordered the continuation of the advance towards Levane. The plan was for 'D' Company to consolidate on a small feature about a mile distant to the south-west of Levane, whilst 'B' Company, with the Carrier Platoon under command, was to consolidate forward of the town. 'A' and 'C' Companies were to remain where

186

they were. Both leading companies accomplished their tasks without incident, but 'B' Company was shelled shortly after its arrival.

"An Italian partisan reported at 2300 hrs that six armed Germans were holding out in a house near the railway station that had been passed earlier in the day. He further stated that a number of women had been imprisoned in the house, including his daughter, and offered to act as a guide. A strongly armed patrol under Sergeant Jackson was sent out which returned three and a half hours later to report that the approaches to the house were held with MGs. The patrol had been fired on and it was estimated the enemy numbered about twelve. The house was captured by 'C' Company the following day and fifty Italian civilians released.

"On 20 July the 2nd DCLI passed through the Battalion to continue the advance and occupy Montevarchi. The Battalion meanwhile moved out of Montozzi and dug in for the night around Levanella." On 21 July 'D' Company, mounted on tanks, set off from Levanella at 0530 hrs passing through Montevarchi and were held up short of San Giovanni. On the right of the Battalion on the far side of the River Arno units of the 6th British Armoured Division were finding the going very difficult and were some miles behind. Company Sergeant Major Snape now takes up the story.

"Our company was leading when we came in sight of the town itself. It had a main street which was quite straight and gently rising to a ridge at the further edge of the town. Bob Williams was the NCO leading the forward section of Lieut Robson's platoon. As he came over the river short of the town and was well out in the open a German machine gun opened fire and Bob was hit and went down. Alongside the road was a low wall and the rest of his section jumped over it and withdrew into a river bed leaving Bob out on the road. I went forward and looked over the edge of the wall and as he was not moving I thought he was dead. However, one of his section went along the wall and climbed over to see. Immediately he moved on to the road the machine gun again opened fire and he was hit in the back but managed to jump over the wall and get back to the ditch. He had found Bob Williams was still alive.

"I got hold of Lance Corporal Slade MM, and told him the situation and asked him to go out with one of his stretcher bearers and bring Bob in. Without a moment's hesitation he came along and I went with him. When we got to the edge of the gully he said, 'Take off your revolver, Sergeant and leave it here'. This I did and, carrying a Red Cross flag we went straight forward down the street. We stood completely in the open, picked up Bob and put him on the stretcher and walked slowly back to the gully. I don't think I've ever been so frightened in my life as I was during that time. Slade and his companions had done that sort of thing on numerous occasions and did not show the slightest fear. If ever a man earned a Military Medal and more, it was he.

"I also take my hat off to the Germans there who gave us complete freedom of movement whilst we were showing the Red Cross flag. That they were still there and watching was amply proved a few moments later when a couple of our tanks which were in support nosed forward to the edge of the bridge debris. A German tank sited part way up the street fired and knocked out both. The tanks burned and some of the crew failed to get clear. It was horrible for them. Later that day I passed by one of the tanks and there lying in the road was part of a man very burned and a quite revolting sight. I went into one of the houses and got hold of a blanket which I threw over it.

"We made several attempts to get on but the Commanding Officer told us to remain where we were whilst other troops tried to by-pass the enemy position. We stayed in these positions for two days and then moved on once more.

"We moved forward straight up the town street in the same way we had attempted a couple of days previously, but this time we did not meet any opposition at the start. At the very top of the street was a large red brick factory which was an obvious place for the enemy to be and I kept my eye on it. When we were about half way along the street we were heavily shelled and had a number of casualties, among them my faithful friend of Cassino, Private Murphy, who was so seriously wounded that he died later.

"Arriving near the top of the street we saw an enemy position on which one of the platoons attempted to fire with its two inch mortar. Unfortunately the mortar man sited his weapon under a tree and the bomb exploded overhead wounding one soldier. Having found the factory free of enemy, 'A' Company continued to press forward along the street. The leading platoon under Lieutenant Peter Evans rounded a bend and were some fifty yards up the road, but as soon as the remainder of the company started to appear round the bend and was clear of the factory the enemy opened up with 88mm guns. The fire was devastating and frightening. At the side of the road was a ditch into which we all tumbled, but in order to get on or back it was necessary to show ourselves as the ditch was too narrow to crawl along. We had a lot of casualties in the shelling and the Company Commander decided to consolidate back in the town. He gave the order to move back, but as soon as anyone showed himself a shell was fired. We were being fired at over open sights: virtually sniping by artillery guns. For the next hour, one and then another would try to work his way back to be fired on at once. The shelling was taking its toll and I considered that the only thing was to be bold and make a dash. Therefore, I called out to the men gathered around me that when I shouted 'now' all were to get up and double back to the cover of the factory. I shouted and as a man we rushed. A shower of shells landed but we got away without further casualties.

"Meanwhile the leading platoon had taken up positions by a stream and could not get back because of the shelling. We were in wireless touch with them and told them to sit and wait for darkness and then return.

"Moving back into the town, we took up positions in the brick factory and Company Headquarters settled in in what had obviously been the manager's office. It was well furnished and in a cabinet we found a bottle of extremely good Vermouth. I then set about compiling the casualty report for the company. Shortly afterwards there was a terrific crash. I opened the office door and there spinning on the floor was a German 210mm shell which had hit the roof, torn a hole through, and landed on the floor by the office door. It was a dud and did not explode! Next morning John Barnwell, who was acting in command of the company, sent it by jeep to Battalion Headquarters with my casualty report. The Company Commander and two platoon commanders were wounded; two soldiers were killed and thirteen wounded."

"A" and "B" were now amalgamated under Major Hollick. The Battalion strengthened its hold on San Giovanni over the next few days remaining in contact with the enemy. Further reorganization took place as reinforcements came forward to replace casualties and Major Rickman took over command of "A" Company with Captain Stenning as second-in-command.

Commenting on this phase Lt Colonel Burke states, "This battle for San Giovanni lasted from 20 to 27 July with the Battalion fully engaged throughout this action. It had been an anxious time for us as the axis was alongside the River Arno, which was the inter-divisional boundary. The 6th Armoured Division on the right was meeting strong opposition and the Battalion flank was often exposed.

" On 27 July the CQMS of "A" Company captured two German prisoners in San Giovanni. A feat which is documented in Battalion records.

"The Battalion was released from the line at 1400 hrs on 27 July and moved back to a rest area in Montevarchi where it enjoyed its first real rest since 24 June before Lake Trasimene."

Early in August the main advance was held up by stubborn enemy resistance around a nunnery on a hill feature which dominated the approach to Florence. This hill was called Icontro. This feature was stormed and captured by 2 DCLI. The Surreys took the next minor height, pushed ahead and reported the Germans had crossed the River Arno. The Bedfords now passed through, advancing to the final ridge overlooking the Arno and digging in on the reverse slope. Lieutenant Geoffrey Need remembers: " I missed direction slightly with my platoon and went over the ridge where we had a magnificent view over the Arno, with Florence sprawling out about two miles over to the left. Beyond the river were mountain ridges rising higher and higher towards the main range of the Apennines where they swing across Italy. Having gazed upon this sight, probably standing on the skyline in un-military fashion, I brought my platoon behind the ridge to our correct positions. That evening, 8 August, came the welcome message; 'Advance parties of the Seaforths coming to take over'. The 4th Division was being relieved by the 1st Division."

Sergeant Major Snape continues; "On the final day before we were relieved by the 1st Infantry Division our company again went into the lead and we reached the final ridge before Florence before meeting opposition where we were pinned down by enemy fire. We dug in so near to, and yet so far from, the city into which we had been going to drive at the beginning of July.

"On the next day we were relieved and taken in troop carrying vehicles away from the battle to a village near Assisi. Here everything was peaceful and normal. War had passed over and was already forgotten.

"We very quickly settled down to a semi-peacetime existence with daily drill parades and other training. Messes were opened and we got to know the many new faces who had joined the Battalion during the weeks of fighting and much good wine cemented friendships. It was with some regret that on picking up the phone in the early hours of 10 September I was informed that we were to embuss that day to go forward again."

Lt Colonel Burke comments; " Whilst at Assisi we attended a brigade parade when the Army Commander, General Sir Oliver

Leese, addressed the troops. He told me how well he thought the Battalion had done in action since arrival in Italy."

It is interesting that the 1st Battalion, The Hertfordshire Regiment, who had joined the 1st Infantry Division entered the line at Florence, continuing the battle on this sector where the 2nd Bedfords had broken off to move to another sector of the front. Both battalions took part in the battle of "The Gothic Line".

24

ITALY – AUGUST/SEPTEMBER 1944

The Allied Forces which were now lining up against the Gothic Line did not have a preponderance of strength over the Germans. General Alexander decided to strengthen the Eighth Army and develop his main thrust up the east coast. Accordingly the 4th Division was relieved from the western front and transferred to come under command of the Eighth Army operating on the east of the Apennine mountains. The country was hilly and interspersed with rivers running down to the sea across the line of advance. The aim was to break through the Gothic Line on this front and outflank the German positions with a pincer thrust towards Bologna. It was hoped that the attack by the Eighth Army in this direction would draw German forces from their strong defensive positions in the mountains east of Florence.

In the first week of September the 4th Division was placed in reserve under command of the Eighth army and the battalion was put under orders to move to the Adriatic coast. The route ran through Foligno, then up Route 3 to Fabriano, thence across to the coast through Jesi. The route then went up the coast through Senigallia, Fano and Pesaro and thence inland to the village of Tomba di Pesaro where the Battalion stayed for a week.

The Eighth Army was now facing up to the Gothic Line a series of defences sited in depth including anti tank positions across the whole front. The initial attacks on this sector had been initiated by the Polish Corps with the Canadian Corps and the British 46th and 56th Divisions. The latter had both recently returned from Egypt where they had undergone rest and training. These attacks had made steady progress but had not broken through all the defences. The 4th Division was now brought into the attack to continue the drive forward after a fierce German counter-attack had driven our front line troops off Corriano Ridge.

The country for the twenty-five miles alongside the coast between Pesaro and Rimini was ideal for defence consisting of a succession of ridges, a narrow valley with a river and a towering ridge to be stormed beyond the river, this pattern repeated again and again. The ground was flat for only about one mile inland from the coast. The Greek brigade was in this sector. It was a mountain brigade.

CSM Snape describes Corriano, which had seen fierce fighting, as being a shambles. "Disabled tanks littered the area and there were several bodies lying around. One of the bodies was a German who was lying in a ditch with one arm pointing upwards. On the wrist was a watch at which all the soldiers looked but no one would go near enough to take it off. As a rule soldiers had no compunction in removing wrist watches but this looked so obviously put there for a purpose that everyone thought the body must be booby-trapped!

"We dug slit trenches among grape vines which were ripe and very large and juicy. On the second day of our stay I went round the company and on walking out to check a position I kicked a wire which set off a booby trap. Fortunately the only damage I sustained was a cut from a piece of metal the size of a half crown which embedded in my arm. I went along to the MI room and had it pulled out and the arm dressed and then went back to duty."

The plan for 16/17 September was for the Bedfords to advance and establish a bridgehead over the River Ausa and a smaller stream, the Budrioli, and if possible to take the San Aquilino Ridge beyond. This would then allow the other battalions of the 10th Brigade to pass through to continue the advance. This involved a long night-approach march. In the event this plan was put back twenty-four hours and the Battalion set out at 2100 hrs on 17 September. The Battalion plan for the attack was "D" Company under Major Wilson on the right, "B" Company under Major Rickman on the left with "A" Company under Captain Francis in close support of "B" Company.

"B" Company was one of the leading companies and Lieutenant Need with his platoon was bringing up the rear. "To start with things went slowly but according to plan and the company crossed the Ausa at a dry spot without opposition. Artificial moonlight was being provided by searchlights which made visibility reasonably good. Having crossed over the river we proceeded up ditches to a track leading to a lateral road from Rimini to the neutral Republic of San Marino. Just then our leading platoon was fired on by a Spandau from a farmhouse straight ahead by the main road.(Map 18, note 1) The leading platoon stormed the house and, at the cost of one man killed, took the

193

whole bunch of Huns prisoner – about twenty of them. Peter Evans leading the second platoon set fire to a haystack by chucking a phosphorous grenade on it, the better to see what we were doing. This of course raised the odd sniper fire but we sheltered behind the house. The Company Commander, Bill Rickman, called up Peter and me: 'I think you might push on with your platoons now. Get over the next ditch, the Budriolo, and see what's up on the ridge.'

"We crossed the Budriolo and half way up the ridge came up against the wires protecting a complete circular mine field. (Map 18, note 2) We also started to run into our own artillery fire, which had been scheduled to stop by then. Daylight was coming up and we were ordered to draw back and dig in around our farmhouse. (Map 18, note 3) We were shelled once shortly after dawn and Peter Eames was killed. All this time we were lying up or moving about in full view of the Hun; we could pick out every detail of the church and village of San Aquilino.

"About 0830 hrs we were ordered to have another crack at San Aquilino (Map 18, note 4) – 'A' Company left and 'B' Company right of which my platoon was in the centre with a Forward Observation Officer Royal Artillery up with us to direct the artillery plastering our objectives. We made slow progress half way up the hill. I skirted the minefield by going straight up the road and deployed beyond the minefield. Then I saw 'A' Company appeared to be stuck around a small house back on my left and the platoons on my right were also well back so I dropped back into line on the road again (Map 18 note 5). Later I noticed the platoons on my right drifting back towards Company Headquarters and I was ordered to join 'A' Company round their house by Peter Francis, their Company Commander. Almost as soon as I arrived Francis was hit and wounded. I knew where I was then; prior to that with our shells and Jerry's mixed up bursting all around and the whir, whir, whir of Jerry's multi-barrelled mortars loosing off at targets further back I wondered what the bloody hell was going on. We stayed there until late afternoon supported by half a dozen Churchill and Sherman tanks which had come up. I was now ordered to 'B' Company Headquarters and found that both Bill Rickman and his sergeant major had been wounded and evacuated. Late that night the DCLI passed through and captured San Aquilino. On our right the Canadians went in to assault San Fortunato, the main feature dominating Rimini."

The story now tells how CSM Snape experienced this battle. "After a couple of false starts we eventually went forward into a night attack

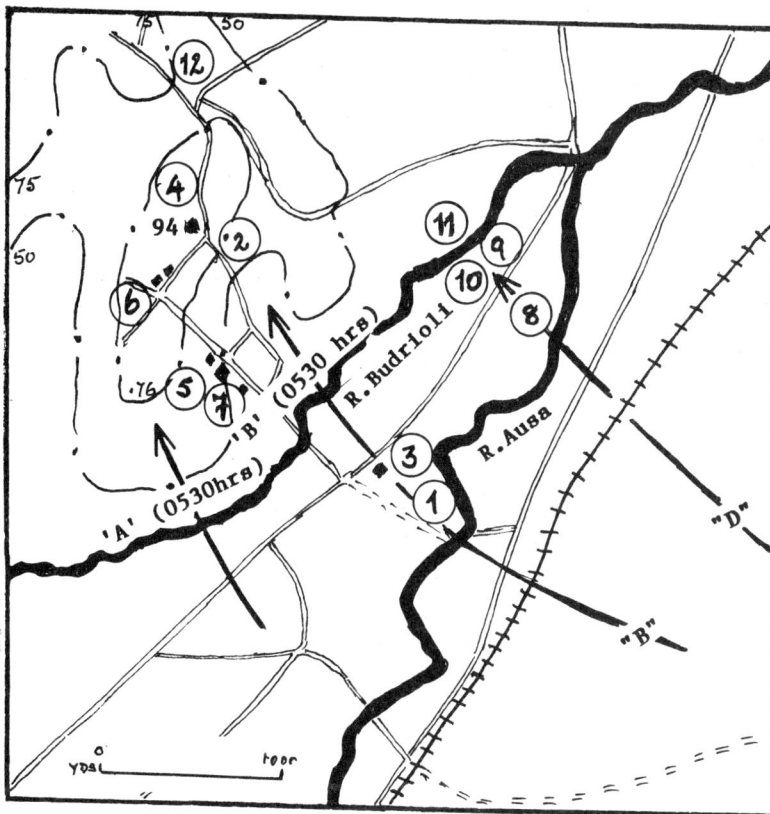

MAP 18

CORRIANO RIDGE

1. Leading platoon "B" Company fired on from farmhouse.
2. Wire round minefield.
3. "B" Company consolidates round farmhouse.
4. San Aquilino Ridge.
5. "A" Company held up.
6. Well.
7. "A" Company consolidates round farmhouse.
8. "D" Company crossing points of River Ausa and Budriolo.
9. Ditch
10. Burning haystack.
11. "D" Company Assembly Area.
12. German Headquarters in farmhouse.

using artificial moonlight. This was a system of lighting made by playing searchlights on to low cloud and the results were most weird. It was not as bright as full moon but it definitely was an asset in that one could more easily recognize landmarks and negotiate obstacles. Lieutenant Terry Quelch, a newly joined officer, was commanding my old platoon which was leading the company. Our objective was something like a mile away from the start line.

"Early on in the advance we were halted because, as it transpired, the start line which should have been held by our own troops was still in enemy hands. However, eventually we moved on and went slowly forward towards a farm on a ridge which was our intermediate objective. We were moving along in single file on a track which led up to the farm. Company headquarters, of which I was in charge, was immediately behind the leading platoon. The Company Commander was walking with me and when we were about fifty yards from the farmhouse he decided to halt the Company and send the leading platoon to see if the farmhouse was occupied. As the leading man of the platoon came abreast of the house he was fired on and returned fire, whereupon a whole band of enemy came out with hands up to surrender. Unfortunately one member of the platoon fired on these men who withdrew back into the house and started firing with everything they had. Our chaps went in and eventually took control. The Company Commander and I had watched this battle from a ditch a few yards away.

"When we saw that our men had taken command we started to move across to the building but, before we arrived, a German threw a stick grenade at us and it landed in a tree. We dived for the barn door only to find it fastened and stood pressed to the door watching while the grenade tumbled down the tree. Several hay and corn ricks in the area had been set alight and it was as bright as day. It was most disconcerting to wait for the grenade to burst knowing there was nothing we could do about it. When it hit the ground it exploded and a small piece hit my wrist and it is still embedded there. The wrist bled profusely but I clapped on a field dressing and the Company Commander tied it up for me and wanted me to go back to the R.A.P but I said nonsense and remained on duty.

"In the battle for the house Terry Quelch had had a number of casualties and the Company Commander decided to reorganize before going forward. Captain George Smith of the Gunners came up and the three of us stood by the end of the house talking of fire support to continue the advance. Just at that moment a German drove up with a motor cycle and side car and was just going to get off when he realized that something was wrong. He started to drive away and we all fired at once and whether it was my Tommy gun or the revolvers that did the trick we never knew so we agreed to claim a third each!

"It was decided to continue to advance with 12 Platoon under Lieutenant Need leading, but as soon as they crossed the road and started forward they were met with strong enemy fire and pinned to the ground. The Company Commander decided to dig in round the farmhouse and wait for daylight and gunner support before moving forward.

"18 September dawned bright and clear. Soon after 'stand down' Peter Evans was going round his platoon when there was an intensive bout of shelling. He and his platoon runner dived into a slit trench and were crouching waiting for the shelling to stop when a shell scored a direct hit on their trench and killed them both.

"Immediately after breakfast the Company Commander made a plan for an attack on the ridge ahead using both 'A' and 'B' companies with gunner support. The Forward Observation Officer was to direct fire from the farmhouse.

"The Company Commander decided that as the country was very close he stood more chance of controlling the battle if he watched the initial stages from the farmhouse. At about 0900 hrs the advance commenced and we watched from an upstairs window until it seemed that the attack was going to be unopposed. The leading platoon was about half-way up the opposite slope when Bill Rickman decided it was time to join them and this we set out to do. We were nearing the top of the ridge which was our objective when the enemy opened up with everything from heavy artillery to rifle grenade and machine guns. The Company Commander and I were caught out in the open and the only cover was a low brick wall round a well on the hillside. We threw ourselves down behind the wall and hoped for the best (Map 18, note 6). Shells were bursting with a terrific ear splitting din all round when suddenly one fell about four feet away from us to our left rear. There was a terrific roar as it exploded and I went completely deaf on that side. I felt some pricks in the neck, head and in my left leg. The Company Commander and I turned to each other and said together, 'Have you been hit?' I felt round my neck and when I took my hand away it was covered with hot sticky blood, and when I felt my leg there was a big lump and more blood. One of the company signallers, Private Horne, came up to me and bound up my wounds. The Company Commander said he had a slight wound in the body but would double back to the farmhouse. The attack by this time was a bloody shambles with many troops already at the farm and it was decided to consolidate back in that area where we already had slit trenches and fighting positions dug (Map 18, note 7).

"Before trying to get back to the farm the Company Commander contacted and ordered the remains of the two platoons back, and when going to the third platoon he collapsed. When I limped down the road supported by the wireless man he was lying by the side of the road. We stopped and checked up and he said he could go no further, I said I would send back stretcher bearers for him which I did. Eventually I managed to let the Commanding Officer know what was happening and then I found the one platoon commander who had got back and told him that the Company Commander was wounded and as he was the only officer there he should take command. My next action was to instruct the company runner to go to the remaining platoon of 'A' company and tell them to withdraw in accordance with the Company Commander's plan. I could not get anyone to go forward so I decided that I would go. Unfortunately I had lost a lot of blood from my neck wounds and before I had gone very far I passed out. When I came to I was sitting in a house with an Italian forcing some red wine between my lips. I took a good drink and felt better, and despite the advice of the Italian to stay went out again intending to push on. The gunners at this time were putting down smoke, which I later learned was to help 'C' Company to move forward to join the forward companies.

"The effects of the wine quickly wore off and I felt myself having waves of dizziness. My leg was beginning to be very painful and my vest was soaked with blood from my neck. I sat down on the track and the next thing I knew was that I was being bumped along in an ambulance of the Black Watch and on my way to the Regimental Aid Post. I was too exhausted to argue so I eventually finished up in a General Hospital."

Private Scully, who had been wounded in the bridgehead over the Garigliano at Cassino had rejoined "D" Company. His account of this action follows. "D" Company was to cross the river at the point where the Budriolo, one of its tributaries, joined it and both were crossed by bridges (Map 18, note 8). He writes "At the time I was a rifleman acting runner in 18 Platoon under command of Lieutenant Norton. After advancing cautiously through ploughed fields without any interference from the enemy the leading platoon hit a dirt road. On the far side running parallel was a high railway embankment with a four foot deep drainage ditch (Map 18, note 9). The Company advanced up this ditch. The leading section commander rose out of the ditch hearing a noise and found himself face to face with a German. The NCO and the German opened fire with Tommy gun and Schmeisser and both died instantly. Germans now ran forward towards the ditch the Company was in and supporting fire came from a weapon pit dug into a haystack. More Germans appeared converging from both flanks but the ditch provided good cover and the artificial moonlight helped the Bedfords to aim well. The attack broke up and there was a lull in the fighting. After reorganizing the Germans put in a further attack, one of them leaping into the ditch but he was knocked unconscious with a rifle butt. Our fire was now directed towards the haystack and phosphorous grenades and tracer were pumped at it(Map 18, note 10). Suddenly after what seemed a long wait there was a whoosh and the next moment there was an inferno of blazing straw. The men of 'D' Company waited but there were no more attacks. The Germans continued to fire and fell back to other positions. This firefight alerted the enemy and the defenders of the river line were now fully aware of our presence.

" 'D' Company now continued to press forward. The ditch changed direction so the company abandoned it and pressed on over ploughed fields. At about this time it was discovered that some stretcher bearers and signallers belonging to Company Headquarters were missing. It was presumed they had been left behind in the ditch and I was ordered to go back and round them up.

"The haystack was blazing away on the skyline like a torch as I set out on my mission. On reaching the dirt road there was ample and horrible evidence of the previous fighting. The leading section commander who had climbed out of the ditch to be confronted by a German Schmeisser was lying flat on his back in a grotesque attitude of death with his German counterpart. So close were they that the soles of their feet were almost touching. Propped up against a smouldering German corpse was another wounded German. Finding my bearings I crawled along the ditch and found the missing men. They had been told to stay there by CSM Kennedy who had then gone forward to join the battle. They were awaiting further orders. I now led this party back towards the Company and thought we would never catch up as the stretcher bearers slowed us down to a crawling pace. What with this and the possibility of running into a German patrol I was feeling far from happy. Eventually we came across the Company assembling near the bottom of a steep ridge under the watchful eye of the CSM in preparation for their assault on the River Ausa defences (Map 18, note 11).

"I was now hustled into the ranks of the section that was to lead the attack. With an encouraging nod from the Company Commander, the section moved towards the crest in extended order. It was pretty rugged on the top and I ended up perched on the lip of the ridge awaiting the command to attack. On receiving the order we went full pelt down the ridge. We had barely gone ten yards when the enemy reacted vigorously with small arms fire but the charge developed with good force. We returned fire with Tommy guns and rifles as best we could and things didn't seem to be going too badly until a Spandau hissed into life, quickly followed by another. Bullets were buzzing around like angry hornets and a piercing scream told us that the following section was running into difficulties. Their line wavered, then fell back and, with heavy fire coming from the front and flanks, the forward section tried to join them. The section broke off the attack and wheeled left. I was out in front and could see tracer heading my way. I felt a violent blow to the head, my knees buckled and then gave way. I tried to raise myself but when I was half-way up I fell back to the ground unconscious. I came to and it was quiet at the time when the Germans came and captured me. A medical orderly was in attendance, but they were taking no chances and a Luger was pressed into my ribs. I knew then I was a prisoner."

Lt Colonel Burke recalling this battle states, " Although the final Battalion objectives had not been gained, the main object, namely to secure a crossing over the River Ausa, had undoubtedly been achieved on the left side. On the right side, the enemy withdrew from the river after the mauling by "D" Company.

The success of the Battalion, which earned the praise of the Division and Brigade Commands, had not been achieved without fairly severe losses. The final casualties were:- Killed: one officer and twelve soldiers; wounded: five officers and forty five soldiers."

25

PRISONER OF THE GERMANS – PRIVATE SCULLY TELLS HIS STORY

"I expect there are worse things in life than having a Luger jabbed in one's ribs by a trigger-happy warrior belonging to the Third Reich whilst tottering down a bleak Italian ridge during the early hours of a September morning but at the time I couldn't think of one. Half supported by the unarmed medical orderly and with the Luger tickling my ribs I eventually reached the bottom. The rays of first light were creeping over the battlefield and I was very impressed by the outlay of the German defences. A long line of deeply dug slit trenches met my eyes manned by automatic weapons and interlocked with sandbagged machine-gun nests. The more I saw of them the more I realized what a daunting prospect 'D' Company had taken on. In the background the Ausa was plainly visible. It looked insignificant to say the least. The river had a shingle bed with only a trickle of water. Skirting past the last of the machine-gun nests, with gawking Jerries staring at me as though they had never seen an Englishman before, we were brought to a halt by a lurking sentry. behind him in a large hollow lay a cream coloured building, typical Italian, strongly built with walls of solid stone (Map 18, note 12). Sadly it showed shell-scorched gaps a testimony to the accuracy of the British Field Artillery. The sentry let us pass and I was prodded down a long flight of stone steps leading into a dimly lit cellar. Where pigs would have lain was taken over by sleeping German soldiers.

"An upturned ammunition box was placed by me and I was ordered to sit, at least that is what I presumed. I did not understand the words of my escort but his tone of voice and gesturing implied what was expected. My escort looked a rough bastard, a sturdy six foot Austrian with legs like tree trunks and with a thin mouth and penetrating eyes.

"After my ordeal I was not feeling too chirpy, my mouth was parched and I felt dizzy. I made signs I wanted a drink. I was given a mug of water which I quaffed down and felt much better. The Austrian guard now holstered his Luger, grunted a few words to the medical orderly, and then strutted up the steps shouting *Englisch Schwein* as he left. The medical orderly now started to clean my head wound when into the cellar strode a dark haired, thick set major of medium height accompanied by three senior NCOs. The major exuded friendliness giving a cynical glance at the bleeding wound. He then brought forth pen and paper. Ah I thought, just my bloody luck an interrogation in the offing. I've seen worse concussions said the major watching the medical orderly bandaging my head. He surprised me greatly by speaking to me in English with a strange pronunciation but with considerable fluency. Then he added with a twisted smile, 'Had the wound been a fraction deeper a dressing would not have been needed.'

"No sooner had my wound been dressed than a table was brought in and set before the major. I was thoroughly searched by one of the NCOs. The first object from my webbing pouch was a phosphorous grenade, its twin I had lobbed at the haystack. A flicker of interest lit up on the major's face but his sardonic smile remained. There followed the usual bric-a-brac to be found in the battle dress pockets of any normal British Tommy; clasp knife, pay book, coins, fags, matches etc; but the highlight of the search came towards the end with the arrival on the desk of a neatly tied bundle of letters each bearing my name, rank, and number and also the name of the regiment. I felt an utter twerp and could have kicked myself. With this free information the proceedings livened up a bit. The majors smile became a positive leer. In no time at all my pay book and bundle of letters vanished into his top tunic pocket. All the letters taken from me were ones which had accumulated in the orderly room awaiting my return from hospital and I had not even read them! My first night in action since leaving hospital and already I had been shot – taken prisoner and now the Germans had taken my mail.

"During my hours of captivity I was to see the major and his NCOs once more in the late afternoon of the same day 18 September. Up till then excepting for the odd popping in of the German medical orderly and a surprise visit from my over-zealous Austrian captor I was on my own most of the time. The crazy bastard had retrieved my steel helmet from the battlefield under shellfire and showed it around. There were two holes in line with each other, the entrance hole small and neat and tidy, the exit a much larger jagged affair which said much for the marksmanship, if not for my steel helmet. I thanked the good Lord for giving me a thick skull but most of all for the German machine gunner for only grooving it.

"During the late afternoon another British artillery stonk rained down on the German riverline positions, it was more accurate this time and shells bracketed the farm building. The cellar emptied except for a lone sentry and it was now that thoughts of escape crossed my mind. While I was reflecting on the pros and cons of a sudden dash the earth outside was being subjected to a bombardment. After directing fire at the weapon pits the guns now ranged in on the farmhouse the first shell exploding somewhere on the roof. More shells followed and fragments of tiles and masonry fell around the sentry. He promptly dived down the cellar steps and cowered on a blanket next to me. More figures appeared at the top of the steps amongst them the major and his NCOs. A heated discussion took place and at the same time more men came crowding into the cellar. The major seemed to be giving a pep talk just as a further salvo of incoming shells descended and another mad rush of Germans scrambled to reach the cellar floor.

"At long last, after what seemed an age, the shelling abated and cowering men crept out from their corners, amazed they were still alive. More amazing was the fact the major and his NCOs had seen fit to make good their escape – one minute they were with us the next they were gone. They just went away. There was no explanation. There were no apologies. It beggars description. A little later I spoke to the medical orderly who seemed highly agitated over the whole business and in a mixture of broken English and German swear words and fluent Italian admitted it was a poor show. He did point out that German officer casualties were much higher in proportion to those of other ranks. In turn I assured him the same applied in British front line units. I also pointed out that in no way would a British officer desert his men in time of battle. My medical orderly friend then said, 'He who fights and runs away lives to fight another day' and we both had a good laugh.

"I decided to see if I could encourage the medical orderly to assist in helping me return to our lines. Taking stock it seemed that a seasoned fighting unit of some two hundred Germans had over a short period been whittled down to about forty men, food supplies were non-existent, medical supplies were running out and now they had no leader and no senior NCOs to bolster their morale. Most of the men refused to man their posts and remained in the cellar. Their chances of survival looked pretty slim. I approached the only NCO among the crowd of Germans and suggested they surrender to me. The idea went down like a lead balloon. He gaped at me dumbfounded then laughed, though how much mirth was in the laughter was difficult to estimate. He then whispered slyly, 'The medical orderly is the man to see'. I went across to him. 'Just the man I want to see,' he said, 'I have no morphine and the condition of the wounded is getting worse.' It's not often I'm swayed by emotion but in the next few hours he was to grow on me like a brother. We understood each other perfectly. My main intention was to return to the British lines as quickly as possible, his was the welfare and safety of the German wounded. We both agreed that the only way these two aims could be achieved was by persuading the other Germans to throw in the towel.

"Night had descended and I was placed at the foot of the cellar steps as their passport should the British arrive. To ensure that no accident happened the NCO made sure that I was kept awake throughout the night. I was up at 0630 hrs. Some excitement was caused when it was discovered the machine-gun crews had left during the night taking their Spandaus with them. My captor had also gone, as had the skinny NCO from the cellar. This, to my way of thinking, left me in charge as the Germans left behind were a motley group except for the young medical orderly who now joined forces with me in persuading these men they would be better off as prisoners of war. The medical orderly was a real charmer, dropping a hint here, flashing a smile there and in no time most of them were in favour of surrendering but on the one condition they all wanted to be shipped to Canada! In no way did I dishearten them. If it was Canada they wanted to go to well so be it. Dolloping on the famous Yorkshire charm thick and heavy I said I, Private Scully, would personally escort them aboard their ship when due to sail to the chosen location. For the next twenty four-hours I was their company commander, father confessor and God himself. Now I had to solve the problem of getting them back to the British lines.

"It was agreed that unless the British advance reached us before-hand we would evacuate the cellar at first light the following morning as any move by night was out of the question. At about 1700 hrs that day sounds of a heavy battle could be heard and the medical orderly and I climbed to the third floor of the building to see what was going on. We had a panoramic view of the battleground. Two Churchill tanks were brewing up and another had been hit by an 88mm shell. I saw

British infantry seek cover and stretcher bearers scouring the battlefield. Returning to the cellar and the six German wounded, I noticed a Luger placed at the foot of one stretcher which I decided to appropriate. No one in the room protested, though they had all seen me take it. We spent the night with little if any sleep.

"On the morning of 20 September each man laid down his weapon. They said 'Good morning' and some whistled and sang, the first exhibition of pleasure that had taken place on that spot. Quickly I totted up my prisoners, twenty six including the six wounded. I experienced a delightful feeling as I led my long line of Germans out of the cellar. There was laughter as they took their assigned places, the walking wounded in front with the medical orderly in charge. I reviewed them for the last time before proudly taking my stance at their head. Setting out for the British lines I thought, 'It's a funny old war we are having' and led my party to our own lines and rejoined the Battalion."

Strange things happen in life and truth is often stranger than fiction. Private Scully's experience is further proof of this.

The River Ausa battle over a period of forty-eight hours had been a bitter one with all four company commanders being hit and out of action, and casualties being suffered quicker than reinforcements could replace them. The Battalion had secured the crossings over the River Ausa but been denied the features on the ridge beyond. The Battalion suffered one officer and twelve soldiers killed and five officers and forty-five soldiers wounded. Four of the officer casualties were company commanders which could have presented problems. Fortuitously, however, Graham Martin and Horace Hollick rejoined from hospital and took over "B" and "A" companies respectively.

The DCLI passed through and succeeded in clearing the ridge and the Canadians further to the right took San Fortunato the dominant feature on the ridge looking down on Rimini. Together with the other battalions of 10th Infantry Brigade the Bedfords reorganized on a three-rifle-company basis. The weather deteriorated and it was four weeks before the Battalion entered the fray once more. It was during this period that Robbie Robson was accidentally wounded. "We were issued with Piat the infantry anti-tank weapon, and were learning how to use it against the remains of a German tank. Part of the blessed thing came whizzing back, inches off the ground, tore through my calf and lodged in my thigh. A typical conversation followed for I was lying as close to the ground as possible near my Sergeant. 'Sarge, I think I have been hit.' The reply was, 'Don't be so bloody silly Sir, ' followed by a close inspection and 'Oh Gawd'. That was one of the occasions that have given me a lot of food for thought, for the young officer who took over my platoon was killed in the next action as were other members of the platoon, including my batman, Private Pendry, when they walked through a minefield."

26

HOSPITALIZATION

His section, platoon, company and battalion are home to the Infantry soldier. The thought of being sent down the line, sick or wounded, not knowing when he may return to his friends is a very real fear. His sense of security is lost. Lieutenant Geoffrey Need was taken ill with jaundice a few days after the battle at the River Ausa. His tale provides a good example of the experiences of evacuation and being caught up in 'the machine'.

"I was evacuated back through the Main Dressing Station, the Canadian Casualty Clearing Station at Catholic, to 5 Casualty Clearing Station at Fano where I stayed the night. I then moved on to 11 General Hospital at Porto Recanati, south of Ancona where I remained for three days. I was then shifted back by hospital ship, *The Somersetshire*, from Ancona to Bari. The quay facilities at Ancona had been blasted by our bombers and big ships could not come nearer than two hundred yards from the side. We were transferred out to the ship by flat-bottomed caiques manned by the RASC. We reached Bari in twenty-four hours and were whisked off by ambulance to various hospitals; I went to the 93rd at Barletta.

"The hospital was in an old Italian barracks which formed natural wards. I started in the main officers' ward and met several pals from the Infantry Reinforcement and Training Depot (IRTD) and other units in our division. Later they moved about twenty of us out into a marquee under the care of South African Doctors and Nurses.

"I was discharged on the 10th of October and went to a Convalescent Depot at Trani. This was located in a monastery and I stayed there a fortnight. The routine here was to do just as you pleased. The meals were good and I had to report to the medical officer weekly until discharge. I left the Convalescent Depot on 26 October and having been away from the battalion for more than three weeks I was posted to the IRTD. (If an officer or man was away from his unit for more than three weeks he was struck off strength. He now became a body at the IRTD available to be posted to any unit in need of reinforcements. He also lost any temporary rank and reverted to his substantive rank.)

"After a day and a night at the transit camp at Barletta, where the food was first class, we caught the train for Naples being dumped at Caserta at 0400hrs. Transport from the IRTD collected us. I found at the 5th Battalion IRTD, ex-hospital fellows from front line units were treated more civilly than initial trainees. 'I should put in for leave, old boy.' I did and I duly went off to Amalfi for a week.

"Three days after returning to the IRTD I left on a draft for 2 General Reinforcement Unit (GRU). The old cross country rail route again, in goods trucks this time, through Bari and down to Brindisi. This rail trip took more than twenty four hours. I got on a boat at Brindisi next morning and reached Ancona next day. After a long wait on the quay we were transported to the GRU in a big barracks at Fano. I spent a weekend there and was then authorized to move back to rejoin the Bedfords.

"We moved off in a convoy passing through Pesaro, Rimini, Sant Archangelo to 5 Corps Transit Camp at Cesena. I spent a day there and reported to the Bedfords' 'B' Echelon in Forli on 22 November. I found the Battalion advance party had already left for Palestine and the colonel did not summon me any further forward than "A" Echelon, where I stayed, taking my turn as duty officer on the phone."

This description of the way in which sick and wounded were handled helps to indicate but a part of the vast support organization required to provide back-up for the front line troops. Each IRTD, GRU, Transit Camp and Convalescent Depot not only had to be staffed but they all had to be provided with the wherewithal to perform their respective roles. There were the transport aspects, trains, vehicles and ships. The ratio of men in a supporting role was in the region of eighteen men to every one front line soldier.

17. MC team, Greece, 1946. "The battalion took part in an active training programme" (p224).

18. 1st Herts shooting team, Palestine, 1945, Sergeant Hart MM on the right (p248).

19. "Supply of ammunition and food was now carried on mules and by man pack" (p244).

27

ITALY – OCTOBER/NOVEMBER 1944

By the middle of October the Battalion was still at twenty-four hours notice to move. This restricted training, which had to be devised on a day-to-day basis. John Bricknell rejoined the Battalion after discharge from hospital and three weeks convalescent leave at Sorrento. He was greeted by the Commanding Officer and told he was improperly dressed as a Captain. Colonel Burke produced a pair of major's crowns from his pocket and gave them to John and told him he was in charge of "D" Company.

At last news came in that the 4th Division was to relieve the 46th Division, which had just captured Cesena and reached the Savio River. The German pattern of defence was to hold these river lines as these ran down from the Apennines to the coast. These rivers had become more formidable obstacles to cross due to heavy rains and mud.

The East Surreys had secured a crossing of the Savio River and established a bridgehead with a squadron of Churchill tanks. The tanks had crossed over three special bridges formed by 'Ark' tanks, a tank with its turret removed and a folding bridge placed on top which unfolded extendable ramps once the 'Ark' was in place in the obstacle. The gun tanks then used the 'Ark' as a bridge to cross over the obstacle.

Colonel Burke takes up the story. "On 26 October the Battalion had been slowly advancing behind the 1/6th Surreys, who bumped opposition in the late afternoon on the road which ran at the foot of Bertinoro Hill. This was an extremely steep feature of twin peaks rising sharply about one thousand feet and nicknamed 'The Tits', which overlooked Route "E", the main axis for the Army, and barred the way to the next river obstacle, the Ronco. It was thus of considerable tactical importance and necessary to secure, and I had been wondering who was going to be given the job. At about 1700 hrs I knew. Brigade

Headquarters ordered the Surreys to clear the opposition in front of them and for the Bedfords to pass through and take Bertinoro as soon as possible. In view of the failing light, inadequate time for reconnaissance and a proper fire plan, and the formidable task, I remonstrated with Brigade Headquarters but got no change out of them and was told to get on with the job.

"I decided the best plan was a silent night advance by two companies approaching from the far end thus the most unexpected face of the hill. This precluded any artillery support but, as the guns anyhow were not registered, any support would have been very difficult.

" 'A' and 'D' Companies, who were to make the assault, were told that if they bumped any strong opposition they were to withdraw, and another more detailed plan would have to be made.'B'Company were to clear the low ground before the assault line and form a firm base there. They set off at about 2200 hrs and by midnight reported themselves in position, having encountered no opposition. 'A' Company (Hollick) and 'D' Company (Bricknell) then passed through and were not heard of again for another four hours. For security and to facilitate the carry they closed down their wireless sets. At Tactical Headquarters one merely had to wait and hope for the best, but it was a trying time as I did not like the operation, and feared we might get a bloody nose. At about 0400 hrs it was with relief that'A' Company reported themselves on top, not having met any enemy, but having run into extensive booby traps which caused twelve casualties, including the death of Lieutenant Goosey and Sergeant Jones. A little later 'D' Company reported themselves in position, not having met any trouble. I delayed the second phase, which was to swing along the ridge and occupy the town of Bertinoro itself, until daylight when the Pioneer Platoon could deal with any further booby traps or mines. The whole area incidentally, was full of traps and mines, and in the road in front of Headquarters a tank and a Pioneer jeep went up during the morning."

That then is the battle as the Colonel saw it. The story is now taken up by other participants. Passing through the lines of the East Surreys Lieutenant Sutton, the Pioneer Platoon Commander, saw a new German anti-tank mine which had been lifted. It was made from tarred cardboard and had a glass screw top. There was no metal and this meant the electric mine detectors were incapable of picking up signals. "We had stopped using these mine detectors some time before as the enemy's wooden mines contained only a few iron nails. We were therefore relying entirely on our experience, trained eyes and prodders. We made the prodders ourselves; the iron or steel rod was about a half inch diameter and was attached to a wooden handle. We found they gave quick and safe results so this new type of mine did not cause us any additional problems to those we already had. When we reached the leading platoons we found a number of glass mines which we lifted. The Germans had created many demolitions and every crossroad was cratered. These obstacles did not stop our jeeps getting through and after some work the tanks got forward too. The enemy withdrew leaving the heaviest mined and booby-trapped area we had yet come across."

John Bricknell takes up the story. "Billy Burke briefed Major Horace Hollick ('A' Company) and myself to make a night attack. It meant moving up the main road for several miles and then forming for an attack. Horace was to take the village on the right and I was to take the left hill with a burial ground and farm. The CO told us to get as far as we could but if we were gunned down to dig in and wait for reinforcements. We would have no support from artillery or mortars. We moved down the road – Horace and company leading. I led my company most of the way and both companies were moving well and quietly. We did not encounter any patrols and arrived at the bottom of the hills. Horace and I said goodbye and I formed the company up to climb up to the cemetery – two platoons up and one in reserve. I could not contact Battalion Headquarters as the wireless proved useless. We fixed bayonets and moved forward. After about an hour we arrived at the cemetery and I went into it with a platoon commander and a section. No one there – the Germans had left the previous night. At first light a platoon commander and section went into the farmyard which had been booby trapped with 'S' mines and he and four men were killed and three others wounded. We had a difficult time getting them out as the courtyard and buildings were mined and booby-trapped. We occupied some German slit trenches until we were relieved."

Private Scully's story: "The ground was soggy and cushioned the men's footfalls as they slowly ascended the main track leading up towards the summit. Their webbing pouches bulged with ammunition and their bayonets were fixed. There was a smell of fog in the night air. On nearing the summit the air freshened and sharpened. Throughout the whole of the three hour climb there had been no hint of trouble when out of nowhere came a civilian running towards us. He informed us that the track had been laced with mines and booby traps by the retreating enemy and he was sent on his way. A runner was sent to pass on this news to 'A' Company Commander. He had

211

barely arrived back with the Company before a Schu mine blew off the foot of a man at the rear of 'A' Company and the men following were showered with gravel and stones. A flush of fear swept throughout the ranks as the dreaded word mines was passed down by word of mouth. Another explosion heavier than before shuddered the track and shouting began ahead followed by a further explosion. Men were being blown up in quick succession. I ran past the mangled remains of the recently joined young Lieutenant of 16 Platoon. He had been blown off the track and his face and limbs were as white as marble and his clothes were shredded. The men of "D" Company pressed on. Sergeant Jones was a prewar regular soldier who had fought on the North West Frontier of India. He had survived the battles on Ceresola Ridge and Cassino where he had been a section commander in 'D' Company. On promotion to the rank of Sergeant he had been posted to Headquarters Company. This posting was far too sedentary and not to his liking and he was forever seeking to return to his roots in a rifle company. His bantering and cajolery eventually paid off and he found himself in 'A' Company. He was with the leading platoon of 'A' Company when the advance faltered. When the first mines were set off he volunteered to lead six men into the village, which was shrouded in mist, to see if the enemy was still there. Fifty yards ahead, barely discernible, lay a ragged circle of stone houses. Sergeant Jones led his section forward at a slow trot heading for the nearest buildings. The man bringing up the rear set off a trip wire and was blown apart. The whole area had been wired up and the section found themselves enmeshed in a circle of mines and booby traps. Mines and booby traps exploded together and the crest of the hill erupted in a sheet of flame. Those behind could only watch and were powerless to do anything. The next day seven mangled bodies were found still surrounded by further mines and booby traps. Sergeant Jones had died at the front of his men. Twelve men died in this action."

Lieutenant Sutton continues: "A section of Royal Engineers from the 46th Infantry Division arrived at the Commanding Officer's Command Post at dawn and started to give us a hand with mines and demolitions. When I arrived there a little later I was told they had cleared the area of mines. I went into a farm and saw the Commanding Officer who looked tired. He told me that 'A' and 'D' Companies had taken the higher Bertinoro Hill but had run into booby traps which had caused fairly heavy casualties. I was to take my three jeeps forward, send one section to the top of the hill to help 'A' and 'D' with the booby traps, and with the other two sections to clear the way for

'B' Company and the tanks to take the town of Bertinoro.

The farm was in a cul-de-sac; we turned the jeeps round and drove fifty yards to the crossroads we had passed before. I was in the leading jeep, Waller was in the second and Warboys was in the third. There was about ten yards between jeeps. I had just reached the crossroads when there was a terrific bang, and a dark cloud of smoke hung over the whole scene. I saw that Waller's jeep was all right, but the third one had blown up on a mine, over which the other two must have driven moments before. All the crew of five were knocked out but luckily none were killed. The driver had a piece of metal in his back and was shellshocked. Corporal Warboys had his left ear drum burst. Private Bayliss, who had been sitting over the left rear wheel which had been torn off, had sailed fifteen yards through the air. He was picked up by Colonel Burke who had come running from the farm to help. Bayliss looked a heap of misery but he was the luckiest of the lot as nothing was broken in his body. Private Maile, who was a big chap, had been blown into the ditch. He seemed all right and volunteered to stay but I insisted he should go back with the ambulance. It turned out he had fractured a part of his spine. Private Paxton seemed to be the worst off. His left leg was broken in five places. When I saw him in Luton a year later he was just beginning to walk again. When the ambulance had taken care of the wounded we took the trailer of the third jeep and hitched it onto Private Old's jeep which was now towing two full trailers. We then took the three good tyres and spare wheel, as jeep tyres were at a premium just then. We pushed the damaged jeep into the ditch out of the way.

"I told Corporal Mann to take his section up the hill to 'A' Company to clear booby traps. Waller and I started to walk towards Bertinoro while the jeeps followed slowly with the remaining section thoroughly checking for mines on the road. Waller and I lifted mines as we progressed and we found some 'Riegel' mines for the first time. These mines had the form of a bar about 4" x 5" x 30" and they could not be disarmed. We had to yank them out and lean them against trees on the verge visible to all. At a blown bridge we left instructions for the section behind us to prepare a passage for tanks. We came to "B" Company and found Graham Martin waiting for us to clear a way into Bertinoro for his company. A few mines were in the road just there so Waller and I showed we had the situation under control and lifted the lids off the mines, extracted the detonators and threw them into the next field heaving the mines after them. 'B' Company were duly impressed.

"At this time the Company Sergeant Major came along and pointed to a big wooden box. It was standing on the verge and had obviously been left behind by the enemy. It would make a nice kit box and the Sergeant Major apparently needed one. Waller lifted the lid carefully. I could just see a piece of string underneath and I yelled. Waller held the lid and I cut the string very carefully. There were no further strings or wires so we opened the lid. The box contained about one hundred two pound demolition charges, all high explosive. One of them had a detonator and a pull switch which had been connected to the lid by the string we had cut.

"Before the entrance to Bertinoro the enemy had blown a dozen large trees across the road and I left instructions for the jeeps to tow them out of the way. We went to get 'B' Company through in single file. I was very conscious of possible trip wires in the branches of the felled trees and we walked very slowly, advancing inch by inch. Then I saw a dead dog among the branches. I thought it must have run through the trees, tripped a wire and been killed that way. I looked around and suddenly I could see a wire only a few inches away from my legs. It was difficult to see because it had been painted green and it led to a green concrete mine two feet away. I was too afraid to move and Waller reached forward slowly to cut the wire. We then disarmed the mine. There was another one and then we were through the trees. A few more mines on the road and we entered the town of Bertinoro.

"We quickly made sure all the Boche had left. 'B' Company occupied the exits of the town and I made for the town hall, a nice ancient building with a terrace from which one had a glorious view of the Northern Italian plain towards the River Po. The second of the Bertinoro hills was just above the town. It had a beautiful medieval castle on top and the Italians told me the Boche had mined the castle. I passed this information on to the Royal Engineers, and I later heard that they had found a large charge with a precious clockwork fuse.

The DCLI now passed through the Battalion and advanced into the plain of the Ronco River. In the afternoon General Ward, the Divisional Commander, came to Bertinoro with the Brigadier to hear the story of the mines and booby traps. I was hoping for a good night's sleep and the platoon had taken possession of a nice house and allotted the rooms and beds. The DCLI had already reached the banks of the Ronco River and the Battalion was ordered to keep close behind ready to pass through their bridgehead the next morning so our billet could not be used."

The contrast in the German defensive posture between the battle for the Rivers Ausa and Budrioli and the attacks on the twin peaks at Bertinoro deserves comment. At the rivers the Battalion was met by the enemy in well-prepared positions who initially fought tenaciously to hold his ground. His defensive tactics delayed the capture of high ground over the rivers for some forty-eight hours. At Bertinoro the Germans made the maximum use of natural obstacles and the extensive use of mines and booby traps. They then withdrew leaving the attacking force to be caught up in the mine fields which would cause delay and enable them to make a clean break. These tactics achieved the enemy's aim as clearing the way forward was an exhausting and time-consuming activity. Although once the route had been cleared the Brigade Commander passed another battalion, the DCLI, through to regain contact and continue to maintain the pressure upon the enemy.

The weather broke and the DCLI, who had secured a bridgehead, suffered heavy casualties fighting off an attack by German infantry supported by Tiger tanks. As a result the Bedfords were brought forward hurriedly to hold the river line. It was a very wet and miserable night and the Battalion came in for some heavy shelling. John Bricknell remembers his company second-in-command, Captain Russel Conway, driving up to company headquarters in a jeep with the rations. At that time the Company Headquarters was in a large house which had suffered several hits from a Self Propelled (SP) gun. "This SP gun had moved forward after dark and was knocking down the front part of the house. Just as Russel arrived in the yard the SP gun had a direct hit on the roof and shell splinters rained down on the yard and the jeep. The driver was not hit but Russel had a shrapnel wound in the chest. Russel was a brave and efficient officer and a personal friend. We carried him into the back room and I put a field dressing on his wound which was bleeding badly. He was very shaken and told me he would die. I tried to comfort him and showed him my scar, which was in the same area of the body as his wound. He gave me his American automatic and German binoculars and made me promise to give them to his father. I wirelessed for an ambulance which arrived very promptly driven by a 'Friend' (The Friends Ambulance Unit – Quakers from America) and we sent him back to Battalion Headquarters and to hospital where Russel died. I kept my promise after being demobbed and gave his pistol to his father – the binoculars were stolen from my kit during my journey to England. The CQMS of 'D' Company was also wounded this night."

Dennis Mole recounts the difficulties faced by "A" Echelon in meeting the challenge of bringing up the daily supplies during this part of the campaign. The Battalion was static on the near bank of the River Ronco for about a week by which time the floods had subsided sufficiently for a pontoon bridge to be put across the river. The Battalion crossed and established themselves near to Forli aerodrome. A battalion supply column got over on the first evening. With the pontoon bridge in place tanks and anti-tank guns were also brought into the bridgehead. Brigade managed to dump three days supplies of food and ammunition forward during the night. This was just as well as the rains came again and the pontoon bridge was submerged and the bridgehead cut off. During the next few days supplies were ferried over the river by boat. Later Bailey bridges were built and the Ronco was beaten."

Colonel Burke continues: "With better weather on 4 November I decided to improve the tactical layout of the Battalion, which consisted of companies one behind the other on a very narrow front. 'B' Company were ordered to seize and capture a large country house called Casa Bordi, which lay on a feature some four hundred yards left of 'A' Company. 'A' Company of the 1/6th Surreys were placed under my command and took over the positions vacated by 'B' Company. The attack was well planned and carried out by Major Martin and his company, and, although it produced violent artillery reaction and resistance from Casa Bordi itself, it was entirely successful with very few casualties. They had their anxious moments, however, particularly during consolidation on arrival, when a cluster of Tiger tanks were observed about three hundred or four hundred yards away heading their way. 'B' Company's supporting troop of tanks, however, reached Casa Bordi with some difficulty owing to the heavy ground. These tanks together with a very heavy artillery barrage directed at the Tigers stopped any counter-attack from them.

" 'A' Company was holding on doggedly to their positions under constant shelling. A chance shell killed Lieutenant Trevett, a particularly brave and good Platoon Commander.

"The Battalion was relieved on 8 November having been in the front line for fourteen days without respite."

On about 15 November the Battalion moved forward to Forli where it was billeted. The Battalion now provided night patrols along the River Montone.

Captain Glyn Lloyd was commanding the mortar platoon at this time. He recalls an incident which remains vividly in his mind. He had deployed the mortars in a courtyard of a large building. Looking for a suitable observation post he climbed to the top floor and out onto the roof. Glyn is of short stature and he had to be assisted up to the ridge of the roof where he retained his position by placing his elbows over the ridge. He was joined by the observation post party.

Captain Lloyd gave the order and one round of smoke was promptly loaded and fired. The German response was an immediate artillery stonk. The observation party, with the exception of Captain Lloyd, left their exposed position and took cover in the cellars. Glyn, who had been helped up to his position now had no one to help him down. Such was the pitch of the roof he had no wish to slip over the edge. He called for help but none was forthcoming. the noise of the bombardment drowning his cries. He remained on the ridge of the roof held up by his elbows and with his legs dangling until the firing ceased. He was rescued by Sergeant Norris when he returned to the observation post!

The task of assaulting across the river was given to the other battalions in the brigade, but "D" Company and the Carrier Platoon were part of the attacking force. The initial plan was for 16 Platoon of "D" Company to cross the Corsina Canal on the right flank, to draw the enemy from their canal defences, and to enable other platoons to break through. The plan did not quite work out as intended. 16 Platoon crossed the canal and ran into a hornets' nest coming under fire from a house on their flank. The Germans then counter-attacked and forced 16 Platoon back over the canal. The Germans followed this success by crossing the canal and penetrating between the "D" Company posts on the near bank, and encircling round behind the rear of 16 Platoon. This caused 16 Platoon to fall back onto the positions of the other two platoons. A confused battle then took place with many hand to hand engagements. Eventually, the Company pulled back with the platoon commander of 18 Platoon, Lieutenant Norton, being wounded in the last salvo fired: and Private Rance of No 3 Section, 16 Platoon being killed.

The positions were recaptured later and the Battalion then withdrew from the line to go to Palestine to rest and retrain with the rest of 4th Division.

28

GREECE AND EGYPT

A Battalion Advance Party had set off for Palestine under Major Bricknell but before the Battalion followed a change of orders directed the Battalion to move to Greece where a state of civil war had broken out. Since 1941 two groups of partisans had harassed the German occupation forces. These groups were the ELAS, the National Population Liberation Army which was communist controlled, and the EDES, the National Republic Greek Association. ELAS was the larger of the two groups.

The liberation of Greece by the Allies began in October, 1944 when British Commandos were sent into Southern Greece. They were followed by paratroops who landed about eight miles from the capital. Greece was in ruins as the Germans destroyed roads and railways as they withdrew northwards. Guerilla forces from the country regions moved down towards Athens. Attempts were made politically to try to find a working solution to the differences between the Government, which had returned from exile in Egypt, and the armed and hostile civilians forming armed ELAS bands. On 3 December communist supporters took part in a banned demonstration in Athens and resorted to armed insurrection. ELAS quickly gained control by force of the greater part of Athens and British forces found themselves caught up in a state of civil war. It was evident if law and order was to be re-established that major reinforcements would be needed. The British Government directed General Alexander accordingly and the 4th Infantry Division was diverted from Palestine and despatched to Greece.

The 2nd Bedfords disembarked in Piraeus on 17 December, 1944. Robbie Robson, who had been wounded by a Piat and hospitalized, rejoined the Battalion. "I rejoined in the belief that we were to go to Palestine. I think we did in fact send an advance party; we certainly had handed over just about all our transport and equipment – and then along came Greece. I don't think anyone at my level really understood what was going on. We knew that the Greek Resistance had turned on us and that the Red Berets were besieged on the Acropolis. We landed on a beach and moved to an airfield which we secured. My platoon was then part of a flying column which went up to Kiffisos to liberate the RAF Regiment who were surrounded by ELAS It was so strange driving through the hamlets in an assortment of vehicles and armoured carriers being welcomed by villagers. On arriving at Kiffisos we were sniped at and Private Rudd was killed in a troop carrier. We rushed into the main building and Corporal Cooke killed an ELAS man in a doorway in the nick of time as he was about to fire at us. We found the RAF men and got them out. We then put grenades into the engines of all the trucks there to make them useless and, having seized a jeep, returned to base. After this we took part in house-to-house fighting in Athens an experience which I did not enjoy as it was difficult to distinguish friend from foe."

Lieutenant Need, who had been sent to hospital, rejoined "B" Echelon at Forli on 22 November. "On 15 December we approached the Peloponnese coast and the scenery was grand, not unlike Scotland. We anchored off the Piraeus peninsula. Two destroyers were patrolling up and down controlled by the cruiser *Orion* flying the Vice Admiral's flag, and signalling fussily all the time.

"We began our clearing job, street by street, working towards the centre of Athens. The job had to be done in 'kid glove' style to cause least inconvenience to innocent civilians. We had Sherman tanks working with us, three to an infantry battalion, and they would pump lead into any building to which sniper fire could be traced. We had a fairly uneventful bit of clearing in the opening stages doing a few streets each day and then consolidating. We had a two day break at Christmas and when we went forward again had a gruelling time around the suburb of Kathsipodi. On 27 December when engaged in a clearing operation I lost four men wounded when a 2" mortar bomb dropped on them out of the blue as they were crouched behind a wall. The following night a billet occupied by two sections of 'A' Company was attacked and all were put in the bag. As a result Brigadier B.A. Burke directed that billets would not be occupied by less than platoon strength, and that half the platoon would be alert and on sentry all night. (Brigadier Burke had assumed command of the Brigade after his predecessor was wounded whilst flying over Athens in an observation plane. Lt Colonel W. Rickman was now commanding the

Bedfords). This ruling made us very tired but effectively checked any further trouble. The ELAS never dared to do more than snipe by day, but made bold sorties by night. Two days later we cleared through a large factory on the eastern outskirts where we stayed for a few days. The same day Athens was declared clear except for the northern suburbs and these were cleared a few days later by the 28th Infantry Brigade.

"The policy now was to chase the ELAS away north and the Battalion headed up the main route. Short of Thebes there was a pass which the ELAS had fortified and were defending in some strength on the heights at the entrance. There was insufficient daylight to organize and carry out an infantry assault, so all heavy weapons pounded away at their positions until dark. Next morning it was found that ELAS had pulled out and we pushed on to Thebes which we found clear after a rapid house-to-house search. We settled in for the night and stayed there quite a while. A few days later a truce was declared and individual ELAS members were allowed to return to their own homes retaining their weapons."

Lt Colonel Burke takes up the story. "I rejoined the Battalion in Thebes and on 5 February we had our postponed Christmas celebrations, which had not been possible on the correct date. Everyone enjoyed themselves but it was a sad day for me, for I heard I was to leave the Battalion and return to Italy to take up a staff job. It would be invidious to mention any individuals, for everyone from the top to the bottom in the Battalion had given me such grand support during my eight months in command, which had been spent almost entirely in action.

"No Battalion could have had a finer spirit nor fought better."

Lieutenant Need continues, "On 21 February we returned to Athens just getting through the pass near Thebes before it was blocked by snow, and whilst here I was transferred to 'S' Company. Some ten days later the Battalion moved north through Larissa to Trikkala and Kalabaka where the ELAS handed in their arms. There was a Nazi cemetery at Larissa."

Frank Sutton tells his story. "My Pioneer Platoon was organized as a rifle platoon under command of 'A' Company. It was a different type of fighting from the sort we had got used to in Italy. We had a few tanks against which the ELAS could do nothing in daylight. With the tanks we cleared street by street. When an area was cleared it was taken over by the gunners of the 4th Division who had come to Greece without their guns, and who were organized as infantry battalions. Whenever

220

they took over an area from our chaps we could not resist asking them how they liked marching!

"During the night we protected our company positions with a net of booby traps on trip wires. I had made them up with explosives I found on Kalamaki airfield.

"One never knew in this type of warfare whether the Greek who had treated one to a glass of local wine in a pub during the day would come out and slit one's throat by night. Hospitality in Greece is an old oriental custom. We were offered meals, again and again, even in the poorest quarters, although it was obvious the Greeks had not had enough themselves. We made many friends and soon picked up a smattering of the language.

"Our enemy, the ELAS, were a very rough lot judging by the unkempt sight of the prisoners we made. Many of them had come from central Greece and the majority had never been in a big town like Athens. The people of Athens regarded them as worse intruders than us who they saw as guarantors of food and order. We had units of the Greek National Guard working with us. They had just been raised and were equipped with rifles and uniforms. They were certainly not Fascists in disguise, rather they were more like a flock of lost sheep, yearning for peace and very proud of their British army boots and battle dress. They did their job which was maintaining law and order in the areas just liberated from the ELAS.

"The clearing of Athens proceeded according to plan. There was one exciting night. It started with an advance to take a large factory which made war material for the ELAS During the afternoon Battalion Headquarters occupied a large modern building; the rifle companies consolidated in houses around this building. At dusk some men in British battle dress approached the house of a forward section of 'A' Company. Foolishly the sentry let them get near and was overpowered; the ELAS then rushed the house before the section could make use of their weapons. This enabled the ELAS to get near to battalion headquarters in the darkness. We could hear them surge all around the house. Then grenades and machine-gun bullets came through the windows. It was too dangerous to use the tanks during the night and we had a few anxious hours. Our machine gunners got two of their Vickers machine guns into position; they kept both sides of the house under protective fire all night. Although their fixed lines were too high such a row was created that the enemy retreated before dawn. That was the ELAS's last fling in Athens as far as we were concerned."

221

Horace Hollick comments: " Greece was a nasty kind of war with civilians using all the dirty tricks such as driving up to a cemetery in ambulances as if to bury the dead and loading them up with arms and ammunition; women pushing prams with babies laying on weapons and ammunition. At dusk it was wise to get off the streets. One day Captain Calvert, who was the officer I handed over to when I left the Battalion at Cassino, was gunned down after dark."

Lt Colonel W. Rickman had handed over to Lt Colonel W. A. Salmon of the HLI who remained in command until June 1946 when he handed over to Lt Colonel A. C. Young.

Captain Robson remarks on the standard of reinforcements being sent to replace the drafts of men returning to the UK for discharge after war service. "We were at Athens prior to our move to Edhessa and our move involved three of four of a new draft going under 'close arrest' and I think in hand-cuffs. The Regimental Police Sergeant was a tough character, a disciplinarian and a good soldier in action, yet he requested an interview with me and confessed to being frightened. I think we got them 'put away' fairly quickly and life became more pleasant again.

"Whilst in Athens during my period as Adjutant I remember a convivial evening spent with one or two others and somehow or other we got involved with some men of the Royal Navy. We were all in the sort of state when we were not terribly sure of the 'pecking order' of ranks in the different Services. It turned out that the senior naval man was a Petty Officer who was with a destroyer visiting Athens. He very warmly and somewhat inebriatedly invited us to visit 'his ship'. This we did next day and were piped aboard. Although this had started off by an invitation from a Petty Officer who had no right to take such a step, and probably would not have if he had been sober, it had very pleasing results. Some of us, including Lt Colonel Salmon, were invited to dinner in the wardroom and a party of all ranks were invited to sail with them for a couple of days during which they gave us a demonstration of smoke laying. We returned their hospitality with dinner in the mess, and with a firing exercise and competition. All very good fun at a time when life was a little unreal.

"Throughout the whole time in Italy and Greece I found in The Bedfordshire and Hertfordshire Regiment a tremendous Esprit de Corps, and will always remember and value serving under such incomparable people as Lt Colonel Burke and Lt Colonel Salmon.

"I found the action in Greece unpleasant in the extreme. I had always felt confident in Italy but the house-to-house stuff in Athens was totally alien. We had not been trained for it. In retrospect the nighttime positions we took up when we were attacked were quite stupid, and of course we, like everyone else, did not really know friend from foe." This comment emphasizes the hazards of inserting troops into a terrorist scenario straight from active operations against a known enemy. Captain Robson found his appointment as Adjutant thoroughly satisfying, particularly under Lt Colonel Salmon. "The hand over to Lt Colonel Young was a bit traumatic. I think as a regular soldier of the old sort he found it difficult to accept me as a wartime adjutant, and the feeling was mutual".

Once the general situation became stabilized the British Forces in Greece were deployed to key towns throughout the country. The 2nd Battalion was sent to Edhessa, a small town in the north not far from the Macedonia border in the Monastir Gap. Companies of the Battalion were each located in other towns in the area with the task of showing the flag and keeping the peace. Captain Robson continues his reminiscences:

"At Edhessa we formed quite a liaison with the local community and were invited to local civic functions. At the same time we maintained patrols in areas which were not at all friendly towards us."

Company Sergeant Major Snape, who had been wounded at the crossing of the River Ausa during the assault on the ridge now rejoined the Battalion. Shortly after this he was granted an immediate commission in the Battalion. Frank Snape had joined the 2nd Battalion in France in April, 1940, and had risen through the ranks. At each level he had continuously shown exceptional leadership skills. To those who served with him this award of an immediate commission was well deserved. Homegoing drafts of men continued to drain the Battalion strength, yet the presence of the Battalion at Edhessa was the sole guarantee of peace, as the communists in the mountains were flexing their muscles. A truck driver travelling from a company outpost to Battalion Headquarters after dark was ambushed and killed.

As it was a regular battalion, the staff sought to bring it up to strength, and apart from drafts, individual officers and senior NCOs were returning to the fold. In particular a strong draft arrived from the 1st Battalion the Hertfordshire Regiment which had been disbanded in Egypt. The more senior officers all had war service and they filled the key vacancies. The men had all volunteered to transfer under officers whom they had come to know, and were all specially picked. Among this draft were Major 'Hippo' Phipps, who had been acting Commanding Officer of the Hertfords and joined the Battalion as second-in-command, and Major Ian Ross, both originally 1st Bedfords. Major Robin Medley and Captain Stan Chandler, who had been platoon commander and platoon sergeant in 13 Platoon together in "C" Company of the 2nd Battalion at Dunkirk, and Captain Jack Richardson, an ex Prisoner of War, who took over from Captain Robson as Adjutant also joined at this time.

Arriving by ship at Piraeus the draft disembarked and spent twenty four hours in a transit camp. This allowed time to visit Athens and see the Acropolis.

The journey north was in an old cargo ship which steamed slowly up a cleared channel along the coastline. The journey from Salonika to Edhessa was by roads which were in a bad state. There were burnt out railway engines and much damaged rolling stock at the wayside stations. The whole country showed signs of devastation. It was evident much needed to be done to recover from the war.

These months in Greece in the winter of 1945/46 were spent actively reorganizing so as to be ready to fulfil whatever peacetime role was placed upon the Battalion. Officers were instructed in the requirements of peacetime administration and man management. They were also brought back to the niceties of mess etiquette. Formal mess nights became part of the pattern of life.

The British Army, which at this time had two infantry divisions deployed in Greece, was contracting its forces in preparation for handing over to the newly reformed Greek Army. The Battalion moved out of Edhessa and with the outlying companies concentrated back at Salonika. The move from Edhessa caused great dismay among the local population who were sure the communists would occupy the town once the Battalion left.

Arriving at Salonika the Battalion continued with an active training programme and took part in battalion exercises. Off duty a party of officers led by Major Phipps went out at weekends to shoot geese which flew in over the river estuary in their thousands. At first the shoot did not have much success as the birds seemed unaffected by the shot. As a result spare time was spent in the evenings in the mess manufacturing heavier shot. Subsequent forays were so successful that not only did the Officers' and Sergeants' Mess enjoy the results of this shoot but there was enough to feed the whole Battalion.

The Regimental Band joined the Battalion over Christmas and apart, from adding to the pleasures of the festive season with their band concerts, they also played on formal parades. A highlight was their support for a Guard of Honour for General Sir Miles Dempsey, the Commander-in-Chief Middle East.

Then the bombshell struck. The Battalion was to be placed in 'Suspended Animation' and was to move to Egypt to break up. A sad farewell was said to Greece and the Battalion sailed from Salonika aboard the S.S *Orbita*. The ship put in at Piraeus en route and the Battalion enjoyed listening to a concert by the Regimental Band, which had returned to Athens earlier. Mr Elloway, the bandmaster, had managed to organize a landing craft which circled the ship while the band gave a spirited concert. This performance was greatly appreciated by all ranks.

Arriving at Port Said the battalion was placed in a camp near the Great Bitter Lakes near General Headquarters Middle East Land Forces at Fayid. Amongst its duties was the provision of a guard for the C-in-C and the ATS Camp. The Battalion camp was sited on the edge of the desert with a single strand wire fence as its boundary. The officers' tents were near to the camp perimeter and the first morning after arrival a young officer woke up to find every stitch of clothing and all his possessions had been removed overnight. Accordingly the next evening after dark Bren gun teams laid in wait near the wire. During the night figures were seen crawling towards the sleeping quarters. There were rapid bursts of fire and the Battalion was not troubled again.

One aspect of these guard duties was the concern of the ATS that soldiers would enter their camp illegally at night. The Bedfords' Field Officer on duty would be called to the phone to receive an urgent message – "there's a man in our camp" – and he had to ensure the guard reacted as required. This call seemed to be a fairly frequent one. At a farewell drinks party a call was put through to the ATS Officers' Mess and their duty officer was told that the Bedfords "had a woman in the camp".

The life of the Battalion was drawing to a close. It had fought with distinction in the Second World War at Dunkirk, in North Africa and in Italy and latterly in a new role in Greece. Honours and awards were won in all the campaigns.

A formal parade was held at Fayid in May, 1947, in the prescence of Lieut General Sir Charles Allfrey KBE, CB, DSO, MC. the General Officer Commanding Egypt to mark the disbandment of the Battalion. This parade was witnessed by many Bedford officers serving in Egypt at that time. The men on parade exemplified all the best traditions of The Bedfords. A page in history had been turned.

A cadre of officers and men escorted The Colours to the Depot at Bedford where they remained until returned to Greece for the amalgamation parade at Salonika with the 1st Battalion The Bedfordshire and Hertfordshire Regiment in October, 1948.

II

THE 1st BATTALION
THE HERTFORDSHIRE
REGIMENT (TA)

29

DEPLOYMENTS 1939–1944

An outline of the actions of the 1st Battalion The Hertfordshire Regiment is set out in Chapter 29 of Volume II *The Story of The Bedfordshire and Hertfordshire Regiment.* The following chapters make use of some of the original material as a lead in to this more detailed account of events.

The pace of life in the Territorial Army changed markedly during the summer and autumn of 1938. In March, 1939, the Battalion received instructions to recruit beyond its full war establishment and be ready to split into two battalions. Success in recruiting was such that Lt Colonel J. Longmore, the Commanding Officer was able to report the required strength had been reached in April.

The Battalion went to Annual Camp at Shorncliffe with forty officers and over 1200 men, well above its normal war time establishment, of whom over half had enlisted since the previous year's camp. At the end of camp the Battalion split into two, the two Hertfordshire battalions joining 162 Infantry Brigade with the 6th Battalion of the Bedfordshire and Hertfordshire Regiment. At the end of October, 1939, the Battalion deployed in a coast defence role in the Dovercourt/Harwich area and supplied Lewis gun crews on ships ferrying equipment and supplies from Harwich to Calais. Many floating mines were sighted and provided the mine was five hundred yards away permission was given to engage with fire. Sergeant Crase is the only member of the Battalion known to have exploded a mine.

In December Lieutenant Michael Lofts was posted to the 2nd Battalion of the Bedfordshire and Hertfordshire Regiment in France in exchange for 2nd Lieutenant John Kitto. The Battalion moved to Northumberland in April 1940.

After Dunkirk there was an exchange of drafts of men with the 2nd Battalion The Bedfordshire and Hertfordshire Regiment. In May 1941 Lt Colonel A.C. Young took over command handing over to

Lt Colonel G.W.H. Peters, MC, in November, 1942, who remained in command for the rest of the war.

This coastal defence role continued until 1943 when the Battalion was moved to Brigg to mobilize for overseas service. In March, 1943, it was confirmed, to the general disappointment of all ranks, who had hoped the Battalion would at least take part in active operations, that they were in fact to join the Fortress Garrison in Gibraltar. At this time German forces were still fighting in North Africa, though they were being pressed back towards Tunis. There was still a possibility that Hitler might try to persuade Franco to allow his troops through Spain in an attempt to seize Gibraltar in an effort to seal the Mediterranean. The fortress at Gibraltar remained vital to Allied interests.

The advance party left by air on 31 March and the Battalion followed by ship sailing from Glasgow on 13 April and arriving in Gibraltar on 22 April. The Battalion shared a troopship with the 2nd Battalion The Royal Scots alongside whom they were to work, and later fight, for the next two years.

On arrival the Battalion was directed to send Captain Tasker Evans, two other officers and fifty soldiers to join an "independent company" trained on commando lines and reporting to the other brigade on the Rock.

Captain John Evans recounts " I well remember the disappointment we all felt when the Battalion arrived on the confined space of the Rock instead of going on active service. It seemed a real let down, yet our Commanding Officer was never phased, he immediately set about making sure that we were the smartest troops when providing ceremonial duties, that we became the best 'diggers' in the tunnels, and that the officers and NCOs did their share of digging with the men. With such a small area to operate in, route marches seemed out of the question, but the Commanding Officer devised ways in which we could go round and over then back along the outward route so that in marching 20 odd miles, we appeared not to have traversed the same route twice so we wouldn't get bored.

"Techniques which were innovative at that time, such as abseiling down the side of the Rock, became normal training which proved to be useful hardening for when we reached Italy."

A "battle school" had been set up in Morocco where live firing exercises could be carried out and companies were sent over in turn. This training was very welcome after the confines of the Rock. Eventually after this period of "drudgery, disillusion, boredom and frustration", as Colonel Peters later described it the Battalion was relieved by the

30th Battalion of the Dorset Regiment and sailed for Italy, arriving at Naples on 29th July.

At this time Allied Forces had invaded Southern France whilst in Italy Rome had been captured and Arezzo, Ancona and Leghorn occupied and leading elements were heading for Florence. (Ed: The 2nd Bedfords were among these troops.) On 4 August the Battalion came under the command of 66 Infantry Brigade together with the 2nd Battalion of the Royal Scots and the 11th Battalion of the Lancashire Fusiliers, who had come from Malta.

The Battalion disembarked at Naples on 29 July, 1944, and moved to a camp in vineyards in sweltering weather and proceeded to draw up stores, vehicles and equipment. There then followed a short period of intensive training. Water was rationed to one pint per day per man, and there was a weekly NAAFI issue of 100 cigarettes or tobacco in lieu, a half bar of soap, some sweets and chewing gum.

On 15 August the Battalion entrained at Caserta and passing through Cassino and Rome, moved into a camp some fifteen miles from Florence after three days on the train. The next day the Battalion took over from an Indian battalion.

Captain Evans, who was in charge of the Carrier Platoon, recalls being met by an Indian guide and taken right through Florence to the north-east and being directed into an expensive residential area consisting mainly of large flats two to three levels with very large rooms and with beautiful furniture inside.

"When we moved in the Indians had already moved out but there was plenty of evidence of their having been there as there were chapatis and curry and hot rotis left all over the place. Everything was quiet. Our task was to cover the road and we set about finding the best spots from which we could do this, passing through the rooms to examine possible fields of fire and best observation posts.

"We sited our positions and watched for any enemy movement. We had been told they were to the north but not in contact. We were all a bit on tenterhooks, it being our first night in the line and there was nothing between us and the enemy. Nothing happened that night and it gave us a chance to establish a routine and a feel for this new need of constant alertness.

"The next morning we moved on, but as we left, we could see coming up the road behind us, many kids wheeling prams or homemade barrows with ladies in peasant dress collecting any food and any other items from the houses. A group of Italian men, sporting the red neckerchiefs of the partisans, were giving them a hand. There was no sign of any Italian Police to control what was obvious looting. I trust that the poor old British Tommy wasn't blamed for any missing items when the owners returned!

"The takeover of positions from the Indians went smoothly despite difficulty in communication. The positions were overlooked by the enemy, who occupied higher ground some 1200 yards away."

The axis of advance was generally north from Florence heading towards Fiesole in the direction of Bologna which was on the far side of the Apennine Mountains (Map 19). The terrain ahead was rugged and hilly rising from the river valley in which Florence nestled. With the Battalion in position, early patrols indicated that the enemy infantry was neither close nor very strong. The Commanding Officer therefore decided to advance to secure a base from which to mount deeper patrols into the hills ahead. The Battalion advanced some one thousand yards without opposition and dug in. It then sent out patrols reaching deeper into enemy territory every day pinpointing enemy positions which were then harassed by friendly artillery and mortars. These early activities earned well merited praise from senior commanders.

Captain Scales took out a fighting patrol on 24 August made up of twenty men from "2" Company. The patrol advanced two miles in front of the forward lines to Castel Vincigliato spotting enemy positions without being seen. It was noteworthy that even at this range the patrol maintained radio contact with Battalion Headquarters throughout the operation.

As a result of this "2" Company was given the task of attacking Castel Vincigliato. Arriving in front of the castle it was found it was defended from the front by Spandaus in the moat and on the walls. Reconnaissance round the flanks by the Company Commander and Lieutenant Firth drew fire which shot off the seat of the latter's denim trousers. This probing attack showed that the position was too strongly defended for a company assault and that a planned attack with artillery and engineer support was needed. Higher command decided to try and bluff the enemy out of the position by a show of force elsewhere. This and other actions on the flanks proved abortive.

The Battalion consolidated its positions, with "1" Company on the Right. Lieutenant Eames led a patrol which penetrated in great depth. "3" Company carried out a number of patrols locating enemy positions with Lieutenant Sutton clashing with enemy fighting patrols on two occasions.

The Vickers machine guns of the Carrier Platoon moved up to take

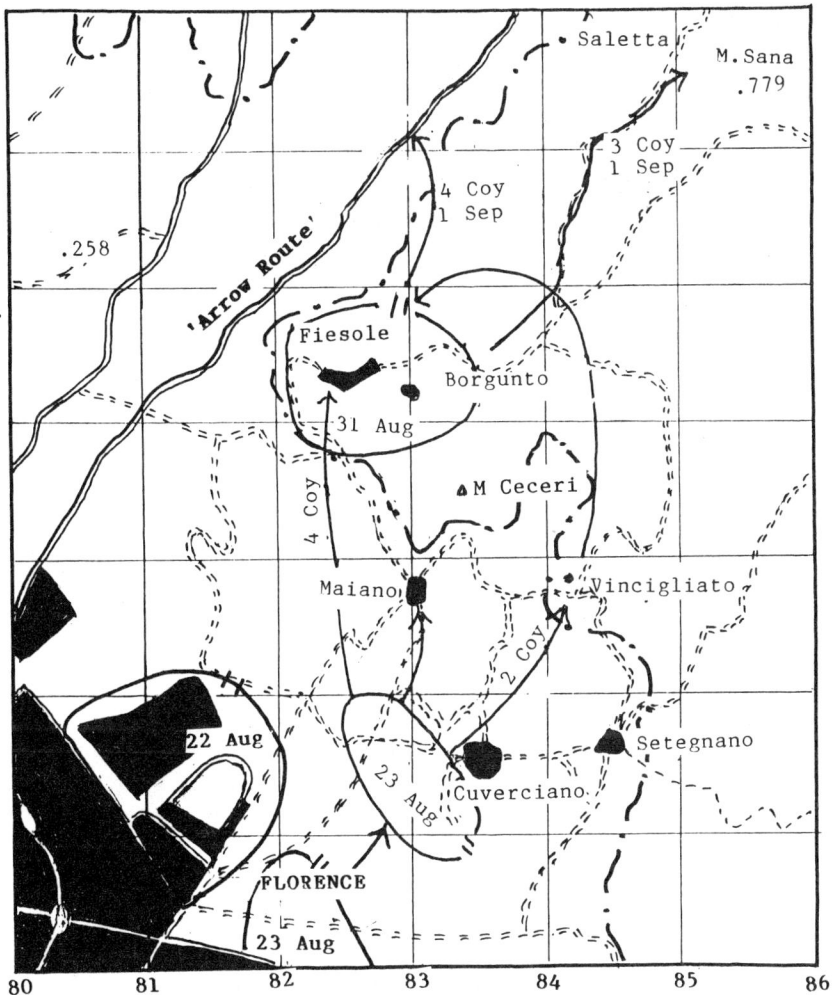

Saletta

M.Sana
.779

3 Coy
1 Sep

4 Coy
1 Sep

.258

'Arrow Route'

Fiesole

Borgunto

31 Aug

▲ M Ceceri

4 Coy

Maiano

Vincigliato

2 Coy

22 Aug

Setegnano

23 Aug

Cuverciano

FLORENCE

23 Aug

80   81   82   83   84   85   86

Scale   1:50000

MAP 19

ADVANCE TO FIESOLE 23/31 AUGUST 1994

233

on specific harassing tasks against enemy positions as they were identified by patrols. After a suitable period of fire the Carriers disengaged and moved out. It was noticeable that the Carriers were given a cool reception when they began to set up their machine guns in a company area, as not long after they had left the Germans would bring down artillery and mortar fire against the deserted fire position and the rifle company caught the retribution. Appreciating this it was not long before the Carriers were careful to set up fire positions well away from company positions before engaging the enemy.

"4" Company moved up into the line some two days after the other rifle companies and moved forward in close contact with identified enemy positions. Lieutenant North managed to get within eight yards of an enemy radio operator in daylight.

All enemy posts located by patrols were engaged by the mortar and machine-gun platoons.

Commenting on these first encounters the Colonel stated: "Communications were excellent."

Colonel Peters decided that his men would respond to the demands being placed upon them even better if they were kept informed of activities affecting the Battalion front and actions of their own companies. He therefore issued a periodic newsletter which was circulated to all troops. This told of successes and difficulties and listed casualties. It ensured that rumours, which can very rapidly affect morale were scotched before they even started. This newsletter continued to be published until the Battalion disbanded in Egypt in October, 1946.

On 31 August a mixed force of carriers and tanks and a platoon from "3" Company went forward on the right flank through the castle of Vincigliato where "2" Company had had its first encounter with the enemy and gained two miles without meeting opposition. At the same time "2" Company advanced getting round to the rear of Monte Ceceri. "4" Company, meanwhile, had been approaching Monte Ceceri frontally, clambering up the face of the mountain. The Germans had booby-trapped the fences round the woods but opposition was slight with two enemy killed and six more taken prisoner. Colonel Peters remarks these men were poor specimens, they had had no food for twenty-four hours and stated the shelling and mortaring which had been directed at them for the previous two days had shattered their morale. Seeing that the enemy were in poor shape "1" Company was ordered to move up to take Fiesole. Mines and close country made it difficult for the company to get to grips with the enemy rearguards. The Carrier Platoon were providing support and

Captain Evans remembers, "On our journey forward we only came across one German who had no weapon and looked so pathetic that I told him in German to follow down the road with his hands kept above his head. He was more than happy to do that and I was pleased to have used my german to some effect!

"We established ourselves in some houses after settling our fields of fire and guards and I went with some NCOs to see if any Germans were left in the area, (the houses were all empty). We found a Catholic Church close by and went in. It looked as if the whole population from the village were there, all quiet as mice, including the children and well in the care of the Father, who blessed us and told us that he would keep everyone there out of our way until the fighting was over. We all felt his promise was genuine so we left them there. He did keep his word too.

"We then went back to platoon headquarters where Private Allbrow, my batman, told me there was an old truckle bed upstairs and he had found a blanket so that I could have a snooze until going out to visit the sentries. Later whilst on my rounds we got quite a heavy pasting with mortar fire mainly aimed at the village but our fire positions were outside so we didn't suffer any casualties. On returning to my headquarters I found the roof had been hit several times and the blanket and truckle bed was full of shrapnel!"

A platoon from "2" Company managed to come in to Fiesole from the rear and after some brisk fighting lasting about one hour with casualties on both sides the village was clear by midnight.

There was not much sleep for the forward companies as the Battalion had become very scattered and it was necessary to concentrate and consolidate their positions before continuing the advance.

The next morning the Carrier Platoon with "4" Company in transport set off in an attempt to regain the main axis a few miles north of Fiesole. Demolitions and enemy shellfire prevented progress during daylight but the main axis was reached after dark, the Company having moved across country on foot. During this advance they came under shellfire from both sides. Next morning the Company found itself isolated some four miles ahead of the Battalion in a poor tactical position on low ground.

30

ITALY – SEPTEMBER 1944

On 2 September the Battalion was relieved and pulled back through Florence and began to advance up the main axis – "Arrow Route". This was a two-lane tarmac road which wound along the valley. On the right there were steep rocky wooded slopes whilst on the left fields and a winding stream. The width of the fields depended on the spurs and re-entrants of the wooded slopes on the left of the stream. The spurs on the right allowed movement by bounds by the carriers giving perfect cover and good observation. The advance was led by the carriers who had orders to return fire once they came under fire. Pte Corbett was driving the leading carrier and after about one hour the column came under desultory artillery fire from enemy 88mm guns. As the enemy fire was returned Captain Foljambe was seen on foot close to this carrier leading a section of troops on foot. As he questioned Cpl Bully in the carrier on the situation a mortar bomb landed close by killing Captain Foljambe and Pte Starling in the carrier outright. The carriers moved swiftly along the route covering each other but one carrier swerving to avoid a salvo of 88mm shells went off the road into a field on the left and became bogged down. The crew debussed and joined the leading vehicles which had taken cover in some outbuildings, coming under fire from the Germans in nearby buildings. In no time flat our gunners were ranging on the enemy positions, and shortly after they opened up the enemy started running from the buildings. The Battalion debussed and continued to advance on foot and "4" Company reported the route cratered. "2" Company passed through and pressed on with elan, outpacing their communications and supporting fire. The Forward Observation Officer humping his radio set followed as best he could. Coming under fire "2" Company advanced using fire and movement and attacked the enemy position. The enemy abandoned their trenches and were pursued by fire. A stray mortar bomb killed Lieutenant Firth. Captain Evans speaking of this advance said, "He was amazed how quickly '2' Company moved and completed the job. They must have doubled all the way. As the road was damaged beyond the buildings the Carrier Platoon stayed put and I returned to Battalion Headquarters where I noticed two stretchers with bodies covered waiting to be evacuated and was told it was Capt Foljambe and his driver Private Starling. These were the first casualties from the Battalion that I had seen and it was a great shock to me as I had been talking to Peter Foljambe only a short time before."

It was evident that "2" Company had penetrated the enemy out-post positions and, as they were out of touch with their supporting arms and were out on a limb, orders were despatched for them to withdraw. There was difficulty in getting these orders to "2" Company; eventually they were delivered by a patrol from "4" Company led by Captain Hopper. This patrol had an adventurous journey coming into contact with a rather scared enemy Spandau team which was withdrawing. Meanwhile Major Sheppard, commanding "2" Company, had consolidated where he was, deciding to wait till dark. He sent a message to Battalion Headquarters at 1315 hrs giving the route by which he intended to withdraw and asking for an artillery fire pro-gramme on identified enemy positions. 19 Field Regiment Royal Artillery carried out the shoot with great accuracy and the Battalion machine guns thickened up the fire. "2" Company withdrew without difficulty, joining the Battalion in positions astride the main axis.

During the evening of 2 September "3" Company edged forward along a prominent ridge and ran into enemy, having a fight in moonlight with an enemy fighting patrol after which the enemy withdrew leaving seven dead. This fight began shortly after last light and the brunt of the fighting was against 15 Platoon which had dug itself in as darkness fell. The platoon was dispersed with 7 Section on the left occupying weapon pits and the remains of an old outhouse, 8 Section in the centre dug in in front of another outhouse, 9 Section forward covering the road and right flank with Platoon Headquarters in the most forward building covering the gap to the right and rear (Map 20). A hatless person walking up the path was challenged by the sentry and fired upon as he failed to answer the challenge correctly. The man responded by firing back with a machine pistol. Neither party was hit. The Boche ran off yelling "Kamerad". A short while later the man returned this time calling out "Hi Johnny" and this call was ignored. At 2210 hrs the sentry with 7 Section spotted a Boche prowling towards his post and held his fire until the enemy was only five yards away, then fired and killed him. The enemy was a paratrooper who had a stick grenade in one hand and a machine pistol in the other (Map 20, Note 1).

The company jeep chose to arrive in the position at this moment and drew small mortar fire. The bombs landed in the centre of the yard but did no damage. At 2240 hrs five Boche approached and fired bursts of automatic fire at L/Cpl Fensome's section and although there were no casualties the section responded and gave away their positions (Map 20, Note 2). After a short pause the enemy opened fire again and pushed men with grenades forward to try to blast the covering section. LMG fire kept these men outside throwing distance and this small assault failed (Map 20, Note 3). A Spandau then opened upon the left flank firing towards 7 Section's positions. The fire was returned by Private Murray and after five minutes the enemy moved away.

At 2300 hrs another small attack was made on 9 Section position. The Boche sent three men crawling forward trying to sneak up and grenade the position. These were scattered by Private Melia with LMG fire and everything went quiet (Map 20, Note 4).

At about 2335 hrs approximately ten men approached again up the road covered by a Spandau firing bursts everywhere, assisted by machine pistols. They succeeded in bypassing 9 Section but bumped into 8 Section who were waiting a few yards back. 8 Section opened fire and were themselves showered with grenades but drove the Boche back, two of whom were seen to fall but were dragged away by others who scattered among the vines. The enemy continued to fire at all likely positions aiming to draw fire; fire was not returned. The next resort was firing mortar bombs against 8 Section and these caused two casualties (Map 20, Note 5).

Food arrived and men withdrew in roster from forward positions for their meal. Half way through this session the enemy attacked once more with approximately 12 men and one Spandau. They went straight for 9 Section and a brisk scrap ensued one NCO and four men holding them off. After five minutes the enemy withdrew but immediately attacked again putting down a curtain of grenades which burst in the tree tops as well as on the ground(Map 20, Note 6). Things quietened down for a few minutes and feeding resumed. The moon was now up and the area was quite visible. It appeared the enemy had withdrawn to a building some fifty yards away along the road.

Approximately half the platoon had been fed when the Boche attacked again. This time he placed his Spandau much nearer our

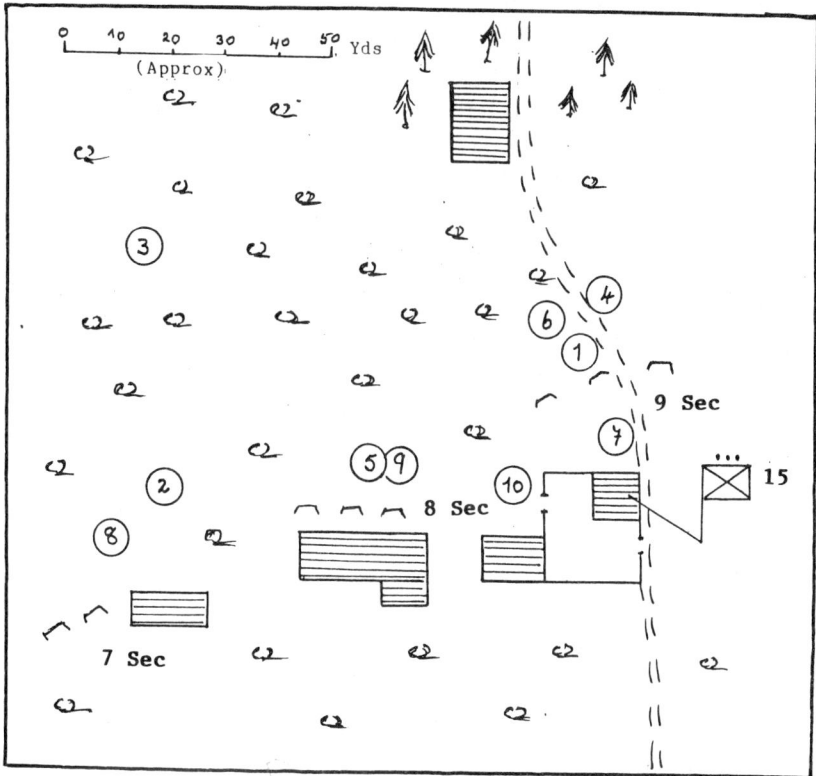

MAP 20

NIGHT ACTION BY 15 PLATOON – POINT 317 2/3 SEP 1944

1. 2210 hrs German killed in front of No. 9 Section
2. 2240 hrs Five Germans assault 7 Section.
3. 2250 hrs Spandau fires on 7 Section.
4. 2300 hrs Small assault against 9 Section.
5. 2335 hrs Ten men attack 8 Section and fire mortar.
6. 0010 hrs Twelve men attack 9 Section.
7. 0035 hrs Assault forces withdrawal of 9 Section.
8. 0100 hrs Assault against 7 Section.
9. 0120 hrs Small attack against 8 Section.
10. 0140 hrs Final assault against platoon position.

239

positions attacking astride the road and blew the LMG out of its weapon slit with grenades. This forced L/Cpl Fensome to withdraw to the house with himself and all his section wounded apart from two men who were at platoon headquarters at the time enjoying their hot meal (Map 20, Note 7). The enemy now attacked 8 Section who held them off. The Boche were now running short of ammunition and withdrew, apparently picking up everything they could find from the now unoccupied 9 Section position. A patrol sent out to try and find the LMG failed but retrieved three LMG magazines and two bandoliers of ammunition.

The ammunition situation was by this time getting poor and a runner was despatched to Company Headquarters. Meantime the platoon had a half hour's respite during which time the forward house was manned and 8 Section withdrew from the now well known slit trenches and manned the outhouse.

At 0100 hrs the Boche attempted to attack 7 Section on the left flank firing machine pistols and seeking to creep forward to throw grenades (Map 20, Note 8). Two casualties were caused by grenade splinters but the section held firm. About this time ammunition arrived and a section from 14 Platoon to reinforce the depleted sections. The ammunition party failed to get back as another small attack was initiated against 8 Section with their Spandau firing at the house and yard. This party were used to man the rear house (Map 20, Note 9).

The position was now 7 Section on the left still manning two weapon slits and a small outhouse, 8 Section manning the larger outhouse, the remainder in the two houses using windows as observation posts.

The enemy launched what was to be his main attack at 0140 hrs. It started with fire being directed at all windows and slits from the front. This continued for five minutes. The Boche came edging through the trees throwing grenades at the windows. His Spandau was suddenly whipped up the road and mounted barely fifteen yards from the house. Private Doidge spotting it from the side of the road threw a 36 hand grenade which bowled two of the crew over; the third man, grabbing his weapon, withdrew. This particular weapon did not open fire again during the night, apparently being damaged. The Boche continued to throw grenades at the windows, but, making no impression, turned his attention to the left flank again, leaving about five men firing at the house(Map 20, Note 10).

The Boche charged around the yard yelling their heads off.

20. "Major Bone ordered Captain Evans to press on with the ammunition party." Captain Evans, Lieutenants Miles and Hill (p255).

21. 2nd Herts were in the fourth assault wave landing at H plus 60 minutes (p271).

22. "Lt Colonel G.W.H. Peters, DSO, MC had been in command for over two years" (p262).

23. Lt Colonel J.R. Harper, CO 2nd Herts (p269).

24. Brigadier Peter Young, DSO, MC★★ (p294).

25. L/Cpl H. Smith, MM, 1st Herts (p322).

Meantime 7 and 8 Sections, choosing their time, picked off their targets, disposing of three men in no uncertain manner. The Boche leader was apparently among those killed as the remainder pulled back leaving six dead. Sgt Collins killed another at five yards range who attempted to creep up on the house. No more was seen of the enemy for the remainder of the night, possibly because a heavy storm broke and 15 Platoon withdrew in the early morning to new positions.

A patrol went back to the position at 0830 hrs and discovered that the enemy belonged to 12 Parachute Regiment of 4 Parachute Division. They were far finer specimens of manhood than any enemy previously encountered; they were also well clothed and well equipped. One had an Iron Cross which is now the property of the Bren gunner who shot him. The Colonel decided to occupy the feature upon which this engagement had taken place – Point 317 – as it was of obvious tactical importance and the only feature the enemy had attempted to re-occupy after being driven off. "1" Company were ordered to occupy and consolidate the position with one platoon in some old trenches which had been dug overnight by "3" Company , and the other two platoons were to dig in in the wood.

In spite of the fact that there was a morning mist, "1" Company were spotted by the enemy while reconnoitring and while waiting to dig in, and came under fire from mortars and 88mm guns. The two platoons in the wood and Company Headquarters paid for their mistake. Major Kenyon, Lieutenant Eames and the CSM were wounded very quickly. Captain Mathews who went forward from "3" Company to assume command, was killed and with the loss of so many commanders "1" Company became disorganized. A withdrawal was ordered and this was carried out successfully under cover of artillery smoke and MMG fire. "1" Company had eighteen casualties, of whom three were killed. "3" Company and the platoon of "1" Company which had taken over dug trenches had only one casualty between them, Sgt Northwood.

On the rest of the battalion front there was some good patrolling which gathered useful information with several enemy positions being pinpointed. Lieutenant Young went out on reconnaissance and, bypassing a forward enemy post, was later fired on from the same position in his rear.

There was no advance on 4 September but active patrolling took place, each of the forward companies sending out patrols under the leadership of Cpl William "2" Company; Capt Hopper "4" Company and Lieutenant Sutton "3" Company respectively. Sutton was out nearly ten hours with Private Eldridge lying up within one hundred and fifty yards of an enemy paratroop position and later returning in daylight over very difficult country. This patrol was almost certainly not spotted. The enemy was not very active on this day; his shelling was considerably reduced and casualties to own troops were due to mines which had been laid fairly thickly in front of "2" and "4" Companies which were relieved during the night by 2nd Foresters.

The Battalion now moved back to Florence in reserve and had a period of rest and recuperation. The Battalion Padre, the Rev Marcus Davies, held a short service on 7 September in memory of those who had died during the days in the line.

31

THE GOTHIC LINE

The Battalion returned to the line on 12 September as the left flank unit of the 1st Infantry Division, with American troops on their left flank. Arrival in the line was uneventful as the unit being relieved was not in close contact with the enemy. The terrain was now more mountainous as opposed to hilly and the Battalion deployed two companies on wooded forward slopes looking across a precipitous, rocky valley. Towering some two thousand feet above the Battalion positions was the Gothic Line the next main German defensive positions. This had been prepared with wire and mines and well sited lines of fire. The main assault against this line had been planned for the 14th so the Battalion had little time to prepare.

On taking over, the Battalion advanced some thousand yards to the next dominant feature. The advance, led by "1" Company, was unopposed. It was, however, a stiff climb. The Company moved well dispersed and achieved their objective and started to dig in without being seen. During the night they edged forward with "3" Company in support.

The Battalion was now facing an extremely formidable hill feature with a steep and difficult wadi at the foot. Wireless intercepts had established the fact that the enemy had been ordered to hold this position at all costs, and this order was later confirmed by captured prisoners. A patrol led by Lieutenant Sutton provided confirmation that there were enemy on the lower slopes of the feature and was able to accurately pin point one enemy position.

Colonel Peters decided to put in a battalion attack supported by fire from one Heavy Artillery Regiment, one Medium Regiment, three Field Regiments and two 3" Mortars. Success depended upon the accuracy and weight of the artillery fire on known enemy positions and on dominating ground, and on the crossing of the wadi by the lead company without bringing down enemy defensive fire.

The attack started at 1630 hrs with the aim of getting all troops on to their objectives as soon after dark as possible. The artillery fire plan allowed for forty-five minutes' pounding of identified enemy positions, followed by two and a half hours' softening up fire on the high ground.

The advance was led by "3" Company whose task it was to mop up the identified enemy positions. Making use of cover, "3" Company were able to cross over the wadi undetected and, moving round behind, took the enemy by surprise and caused him to bring down his defensive fire in the wrong place. This threat to his rear, coupled with the heavy artillery barrage, was more than enough and he surrendered, leaving desultory sniper fire from the left. The Company then went on under cover of woods up to their objective, an extremely steep razor backed ridge, which they reached by 1805 hrs, thirty minutes ahead of schedule.

"2" Company followed rapidly behind and went through "3" Company to reach their final objective by dusk. "1" Company now advanced on the right over rugged and steep terrain and were unopposed. All three companies had displayed a remarkably fine show of physical endurance and determination.

American units advancing on the left seized a neighbouring crest and made further inroads with another attack. The Battalion had played its part in the initial break into the Gothic Line. The companies now held these positions whilst other troops moved through.

On 19 September the Battalion continued the advance taking to the hills and leaving the mechanical transport behind. Supply of ammunition and food was now carried on mules and by man pack. The Battalion was given the task of making a long flank march round the enemy's right. It was hoped to gain surprise by using a narrow path through thick forest and the whole party was in single file. After three hours "1" Company came upon a difficult wadi, and suspecting enemy sent forward patrols, capturing two somewhat surprised stretcher bearers and some six stragglers. Determining the wadi, was not covered "1" and "4" Companies were ordered across to the final objective, which was 2000 yards ahead. Thick fog came down and reduced visibility to about thirty yards and to complicate matters the wadi crossing was found to be too difficult for the mules.

Meanwhile just at dusk "1" Company, leading, encountered a party of between thirty five and forty enemy who were probably moving forward to occupy outpost positions for the night. "1" Company saw them first and deployed to catch them from the front and flank.

244

Holding their fire until the enemy were twelve yards away a spirited fight took place lasting an hour after which "1" Company withdrew to consolidate for the night. Next morning the company found nine dead, five wounded and took seven prisoners at a cost of three killed. Sergeant Renwick of 7 Platoon gives the account of this action. " As we advanced in single file upwards along the narrow track in the mist, German voices could be heard. The column came to a halt and Major Andrews appeared and told Lieutenant Walton to get the platoon to the top of the hill on the left of the track. As we scrambled upwards, on all fours in some cases because of the steepness, we came across the enemy digging in. We immediately opened fire and they withdrew back through the mist which gave us a little time to organize some defence. Lieutenant Walton and I went forward and collected a Spandau and belts of ammunition which had been abandoned with the idea of using it. Somehow it would only fire single rounds so we took out the breech mechanism and threw it away. The enemy made three attempts to drive us off the position but were beaten back each time. After about an hour we were ordered back to where Major Andrews and the rest of the company were digging in. The Platoon lost a Bren gun section of Cpl Crouch, Pte Slough and Pte Price.

"Next morning we were ordered back up the hill where we found the dead and wounded and prisoners. Then we dug in again. When the mist eventually cleared we found we were looking down the valley towards Palazzuolo and the track downwards became part of the famous Bullock Track. The Platoon was fortunate to have so few casualties which I'm sure was due to the fact the enemy fire was directed over our heads as we lay below."

Meanwhile "2" and "3" Companies had come up but the mules were still stuck in the mud. Another mule convoy led by the Adjutant followed a different route and arrived on the final objective where they took up an all round defence position in thick mist and rain. When the mist cleared the Battalion moved up and joined the mule party. It was realized that the feature where "1" Company had had its battle was the most important tactical feature of the left sector of the Divisional Front, Poggio del'Altello, and well up on the shoulder of Monte Carzolano. The surprise and defeat of the enemy here turned the whole position and caused a hurried enemy evacuation of very important high ground. The next day was fine and the Battalion looked down on the enemy.

Shortly after midday on 22 September a fighting patrol was sent forward to make contact with the enemy. Visibility was good and the rough ground made it difficult for the patrol to get off the track, and its progress was watched by the Company Commander and Artillery Fire Controller from the heights above. Paluzzuolo, which was an enemy headquarters and communications centre could be seen and was engaged with harassing fire. Meanwhile the patrol made steady progress for about a mile and a half, maintaining radio contact moving by bounds and making full use of the ground, so when contact was made and the patrol came under fire, Private Sharpe was the only casualty. The patrol took cover and reported on the action. L/Cpl McGinnis and Private Howard who were leading the patrol found themselves behind the enemy when fire broke out and they were cut off. L/Cpl McGinnis threw a grenade at a suspected enemy post and then stalked and entered a house, which showed signs of occupation. He remained in the house until dark waiting for the enemy to return and when they did shot the first man at the entrance to the door and the remainder fled. Meanwhile the German, who had been badly wounded in the stomach, killed himself. L/Cpl McGinnis now left the house, found Private Howard who had laid low in his position and went back to report. Lieutenant Owen returned with his patrol after dark. During the night "2" Company went forward and occupied the positions identified by the patrol.

It was now 23 September and the Germans were in retreat in full view of our own troops who held the high ground. Observation Posts reported heavy casualties being inflicted upon the enemy by artillery and machine-gun fire; and this was confirmed by a German Sergeant captured next day, who stated that his Company had been demoralized by the weight and accuracy of the fire directed against them. Meanwhile the advance continued with "3" and "4" Companies taking the lead mopping up isolated posts.

On 24 September the Lancashire Fusiliers passed through and the Battalion rested for the day. On the 25th the Battalion advanced some two thousand yards and entered Palazzuolo. This advance was unopposed and "3" Company found themselves in a commanding position looking north along "Arrow Route". They were frustrated that the advance had progressed so far that the masses of retreating German vehicles were out of range of a large proportion of our guns which were unable to do much damage. The Brigade itself was also considerably in advance of the remainder of the Division to the right, so it was decided the Battalion would leave the main axis and swing to the right (north east), to try to get round the flank of the enemy whilst remaining within range of our guns.

Over the last ten days the Battalion had been operating across mountainous terrain away from roads, man packing all supplies aided by mules. This meant that the artillery were restricted in the positions from which they could deploy to provide supporting fire.

The move on the new axis began on the night 26/27 September with "1" Company leading the advance on to Il Monte. The enemy position, occupied by a strong section, was outflanked and the enemy fled leaving one dead, one prisoner and a Spandau machine gun. This success was followed up by "4" Company moving round on the right flank and outflanking an enemy strongpoint on Gamberaldi which was holding up our own troops on the right. An attack was planned but later cancelled due to thick fog and heavy rain, which made the going extremely difficult. Reconnaissance the next morning found the enemy had pulled out during the night.

On 28 September the pursuit of the enemy continued amid appalling weather conditions as a gale was blowing on top of the mist and rain. "3" Company outflanked a further enemy position forcing the enemy to withdraw. A patrol under Lieutenant Hill surprised and captured three Germans but were in turn ambushed themselves. The Company was now facing a tactical feature known as Hill 711.

Intelligence reports indicated this feature was strongly held so the company consolidated for the night and were reinforced by a company of the Royal Scots.

On 29 September visibility improved and it was possible to see several enemy posts on the hill and Major Bone engaged them with artillery fire. The Royal Scots moved off to the right and "3" Company sent out two fighting patrols of ten men each under Lieutenant Sutton and Sergeant Collins to create a diversion. The patrols found the going tough as the enemy were stronger than anticipated with several well sited automatics. Sutton and his patrol moved to the house which had been the scene of Hill's action the day before and found the house covered by fire from rear and flank and were unable to progress further. The patrol lay quiet near the house for two hours and withdrew after dark. Sergeant Collins and his patrol crept up on a house to the left, remaining in it until after dark, and dealing determinedly with a number of attempts by the enemy to dislodge them. The patrol captured two prisoners and Sergeant Collins, although wounded himself, extricated them and brought them all back in bright moonlight.

The Battalion was now relieved and trudged back wearily to the nearest transport point. The relief of "3" Company was not simple as they had four stretcher cases to get back from the most forward positions along a very poor mule track. The moonlight enabled the troops to get themselves back to a forward rendezvous and the move was completed successfully. It was later learnt that the diversion against Hill 711 had greatly assisted the Royal Scots in attaining their objective; it was also heard that the enemy evacuated Hill 711 on the same night leaving thirteen dead on the field of battle.

The Battalion had fought for eighteen days over rugged mountainous terrain moving along tracks often on knife edges. During this period the nearest road was ten to twenty miles away and food, equipment and ammunition had to be ferried forward from vehicle-head. The Battalion had to find carrying parties, guides, loading and guard parties as well as jeep drivers, and these parties were provided by the Carrier and Anti-tank platoons. The responsibility for organizing the complete supply of the forward companies was given to Captain Miles who placed Cpl Butler, later relieved by Cpl Bulley, in charge of loading.

Sergeant Hart was responsible for the guide party, whose team worked day and night with little rest for the first seven days going forward either as load carriers or as mule train guides. They travelled for miles in rain and mist over appalling terrain completely unguarded for over twelve hours at a stretch. Often they had to find their way across unknown ground hoping that they were on the right track!

Sergeant Hart kept a diary and he expanded on his reminiscences: "What I can remember of 14 September is that we had carried rations on our backs across a wadi and up a mountain to where our troops were. On my return to 'B' Echelon I found Captain Miles had taken over so I told him about the wounded and we went over to the Indians and got three ambulance mules. I was going forward with these when I met the Colonel who wanted to know where I was going and he said you can take these boxes of .303 ammunition to '3' Company who had run short. The Indians protested but the Colonel spoke to them in their own language and there were no further protests. We tied the boxes to the mules and set off and delivered the ammunition and collected the wounded. I realized that we would have to find an alternative route back as the track we had come up was cut into the side of the hill and there would be no room with the stretchers unfolded on either side. One of the wounded sticks in my memory, Private Massey, who was a tall, very heavy lad with size 13 boots. On the other side of the mule was Private Martin, who was dead. We also took two Spandau machine guns to balance the load. We set off down the mountain and where the track forked took the route to the right.

The track became a lane and as we went on down we came to a gate with a notice 'Achtung Minen'. I led down the centre of the track and told the Indians to follow me. I looked out for disturbed earth and went around any such places – mines or mole hills I don't know. Further down the lane was blocked by trees which had been felled. We got the wounded off the mules and carried them to the other side of the obstacle and found ourselves on a river bank. Across a field on the far side was a farm building. I saw soldiers there and thought they were Germans but I got my glasses on them and saw they were Americans. I got the two ambulance mules loaded and was just ready to cross the river when we were fired on and Private Massey got hit in the ankle. The Americans put their helmets on the river bank but these were used as a target. It was getting dark and I then spotted flashes from a Spandau. It took me two hours to get to the farmhouse where the Americans took care of the wounded. After two or three miles on down the road we came across our carriers and left the Spandaus with them."

Sergeant Hart's report is very modest. He had been in action continuously for thirty hours and had never hesitated to accept responsibility, and exceeded his duty under conditions which were exhausting and exacting in the extreme. This action earned Sergeant Hart the award of the Military Medal.

The task of the jeep drivers was to carry supplies from the nearest point to which the 15cwt trucks could get – vehicle head – as far forward as possible. The tracks were not designed for vehicles. They had rocks at awkward places. They were several inches deep in mud and at times the route was along a knife edge with precipitous drops of hundreds of feet on either side. During the first week the drivers drove continuously for eighteen to nineteen hours each day in all weather. On many occasions the jeep had to be unloaded by the driver to allow an obstacle to be negotiated and then reloaded again. The drivers who performed these tasks were Privates Wright, Little, Wood and Barker.

Cpl Faulkner was in charge of guarding all the dumps and his party often assisted as guides and carriers as well.

The following is an example of a 24 hour supply run. It gives an idea of the back up provided by these teams. At 1800 hrs a mule train left jeep-head with rations, ammunition and water pursuing the Battalion which had made a long advance during the day. It was twenty hours before this party, wet, tired and hungry returned to base with the job completed.

The administrative support never failed, encouraged by the example set by the Quartermaster, Captain Sandys, RSM Robinson and

RQMS Crane among others. On the night of the relief of the Battalion twelve men had gone forward to act as stretcher bearers, having already done a full day's carrying and guiding. This party returned thirteen hours later trudging around with stretchers to find they had not missed their dinner of turkey, quail, chicken and bully beef.

Initially Indian sepoys were the mule drivers but after a few days the Indians were withdrawn and the Battalion had to find the muleteers. Sergeant Flynn and L/Cpl Woods, with seven men, were allotted this task and they learnt how to handle the obstinacy of their charges delivering supplies daily to the forward companies. During these operations jeep-head moved from Grazziano round to *Arrow Route* at Fontana, and *Bullock* route was opened to jeep and mule parties.

The Pioneer Platoon under Sergeant Wells were fully occupied in helping to make the routes passable in the early stages.

The story of the supporting elements would not be complete without mention of the Padre – the Rev Marcus Davies. "No matter the weather or the steepness of the climb he visits the furthermost company in the line. Stopping for a breather and removing his steel helmet to wipe his forehead, he displays a white head to all the world. There are times when his visits are not conducive to vicar's chats but his presence is noticed and appreciated. He has taken great care over the graves of fallen comrades and written numerous letters to relatives of those who have given their lives, or are wounded or missing. He has provided solace and comfort."

The Padre was a much loved man and he told the story of a mule train that got lost in the mountains during an advance and arrived twenty-four hours late for some hungry soldiers. The password had by then been changed to challenge "Tokyo", answer "Bound". The mule train Sergeant did not of course know this and when, exhausted and weary, he led his mules into the 1st Herts positions the sentry called, in the pitch dark, 'Halt – Tokyo'. The reply came, 'Fucking hell! I knew we'd reach the place eventually.' Fortunately the sentry recognises the Sergeant's voice.

32

ITALY OCTOBER–DECEMBER 1944

The Battalion returned to the line on 10 October to find that Banzuole Ridge had been recaptured by the enemy. Whilst out of the line the Battalion, along with all other infantry battalions in the Division, had been ordered to reorganize onto a three rifle company basis. The Colonel therefore decided to disband No "4" Company which accepted the bitter pill and joined their new companies determined to give of their best. It was apparent during the night move up to the line that the enemy had increased artillery support which inflicted a few casualties. A patrol from "2" Company reported the enemy were firm on the ridge. Meantime a patrol from "1" Company on the left flank reported no opposition. During the day the enemy were active, firing at any signs of movement, and to create confusion the sound of a Bren LMG and a Thomson sub machine gun (TMC) fire was heard on the left front which could not be attributed to known friendly forces.

"1" Company started off on a night advance to recapture Banzuole Ridge supported by an artillery fire plan and with covering fire from the whole carrier platoon. Leading the attack was Lieutenant Clibbery with a strong fighting patrol. Initially all went well but then the enemy opened up with Spandau and mortar fire from positions in two houses near Point 528. The enemy called for their defensive fire by Very light but the leading troops were so close to the enemy by this time that it fell behind them and caused no casualties. Major Andrews brought artillery support fire on the suspected enemy position and on Point 528 itself. This fire was very effective and Lieutenant Clibbery attacked from the front whilst Sergeant Branch moved round to take the enemy in the right rear, setting one of the houses on fire with a phosphorous grenade. The enemy put up Very lights and, sighting this enveloping movement, beat a retreat leaving three dead. Lieutenant Clibbery and two soldiers, one of whom was Lance Sergeant

F.H. Dungey, were killed in this action. The Company now dug in and consolidated for the night. Next morning a platoon of "3" company now moved round to the left, whilst "1" Company sent a patrol onto the final objective, Banzuole Ridge, which was found to be clear of the enemy. It was found that each enemy position had been held by about fifteen men, and that the second post withdrew shortly after the first position had been defeated. Two Bren LMGs and one TMC which had been lost when the position had been retaken by the enemy were retrieved. These had been used which accounted for the mysterious firing reported the previous day.

The capture of Banzuole Ridge on 12 October provided good observation forward overlooking the enemy on the next ridge which was narrow and bare.

Monte Ceco was the next dominant feature. Mortar and artillery fire was directed against any enemy movement and the enemy were observed moving four stretcher cases to their rear. Monte Ceco was the dominant peak overlooking the valley and towering above "Arrow Route". Banzuole Ridge, Points 528, 734 and 677 and the Della Valle Ridge were smaller features linked to Monte Ceco (Map 21).

On 15 October patrols led by Major Bone and Lieutenant Jackson went forward onto the Della Valle Ridge to discover suitable routes for a night advance. Jackson pinpointed an enemy position on Point 428, lying up for an hour and locating eleven enemy. Although Monte Ceco had been captured the Germans remained in strength on the reverse slope on a knob, Point 734, from whence they could observe and bring accurate harassing fire down on to our troops. This feature was attacked and captured on 16 October by the Lancashire Fusiliers. "2" Company provided support in carrying forward ammunition and bringing out casualties and escorting prisoners throughout the night. On 18 October on a pitch dark night in driving rain Jackson and his platoon advanced and captured Point 677 taking the enemy by surprise and capturing fifteen enemy. The next day Jackson had been reinforced by a further section and was in touch with Battalion Headquarters by radio from first light. Initially the Germans seemed uncertain as to the situation at Point 677 and sent forward a patrol which was engaged by L/Cpl Baxter which lost five men killed and one wounded. The next enemy patrol was at 1400 hrs. It was more skilful and the first thing the defenders knew was when a grenade landed in platoon headquarters wounding Jackson. This patrol, having gleaned information on the platoon positions, went back to its own lines. Jackson did not divulge the fact that he was wounded and remained

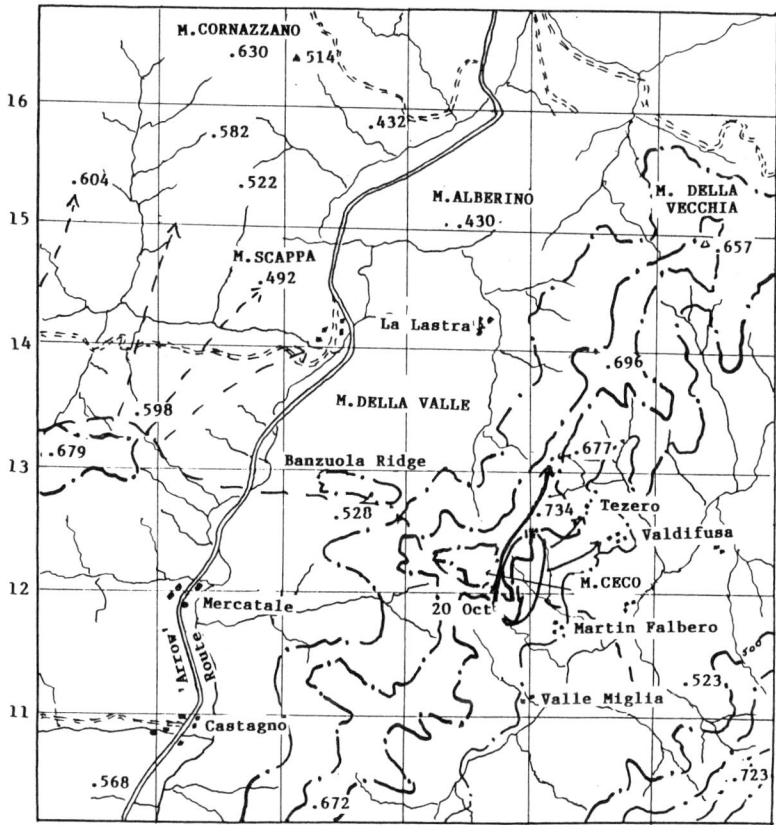

Scale 1:25,000

MAP 21

MONTE CECO AND POINT 677

253

in action. At about 1730 hrs the platoon position was subjected to heavy and accurate mortar fire and Jackson reported one man killed and six wounded. Some of the prisoners were also wounded. About an hour later at dusk two guides were sent back to report to the relief and ration party.

Major Bone and Captain Evans assembled the relief party at dusk. This group consisted of half fully armed men and the other half of ration carriers and stretcher bearers. As this party set off they came under artillery fire from our own guns which had failed to clear the crest of Monte Ceco. Sergeant Whiting was killed as he tried to tap into the telephone line to adjust fire and two others were wounded. This episode caused some confusion as the soldiers had scattered under this fire and it took time for them to reassemble. Proceeding forward once more, the same unfortunate incident happened again. Major Bone gathered up some of his party and went forward to contact Jackson.

Meanwhile after the guides had left his platoon to go to the rear, Jackson became exhausted and told his runner he was going to lie down and rest. It was only then that the runner realized that Jackson was wounded. At about 2000 hrs the Germans attacked and overran the position and opened fire on the relief force as they approached, wounding Major Bone who ordered Captain Evans to press on with the armed party with the aim of getting through the enemy and assisting Jackson. Meanwhile Major Bone collected what remained of the unarmed party and began to move back. On reaching the forward troops he fainted from the effect of his wounds, but, recovering, refused the offer of a stretcher and led his party back to Battalion Headquarters. He made his report to the Colonel, concealing the fact he was wounded until his report was made. It was discovered that Major Bone had been hit seven times. Ironically as he was being carried back on a stretcher a stray shell landed on him and the stretcher party and all were killed.

The story is now taken up by Captain Evans who has vivid recollections of the episodes of that fateful night. "I think it was about 18 October when Lieutenant Jackson and his platoon from '3' Company moved forward by night to Point 677, which they secured and, taking the enemy by surprise, took several prisoners. I followed them up with a small party carrying supplies, and brought back some of the prisoners whilst they did what they could to form a defensive position before dawn. It was almost impossible to dig in that area because of the rock, the best one could do was to dig a shallow slit and then use

254

rocks to give some protection without making the position obvious. The absolute pitch darkness added to the problems of siting the positions to get the best fields of fire or to enable one to see any covered lines of approach into the position before first light. Although Lieutenant Jackson had been given some extra men we believed that they would have a hard day on the 19th because the enemy wanted that position.

"Battalion headquarters was in contact with the platoon during the day by wireless, and the balance of '3' Company had been given orders to collect stores and ammunition and be ready to move up to support and strengthen the position that night.

"I was ordered to go ahead with a protective armed party (I already knew the way) and Major Bone would follow with men carrying ammunition and stores and stretcher bearers whilst signals would lay a land line to the position. Whilst collecting stores we heard that Jackson's platoon had been mortared and we believed they had beaten off several fighting patrols.

"Major Bone wanted to see for himself how the defensive positions were sited and he told me that I would take over with the extra armed men and relieve Lieutenant Jackson once we were there. I moved off with the armed party and again the night was absolutely pitch black which made movement very difficult. We got about half way to Point 677 when we were caught in a barrage from our own 25 pounders, which were obviously failing to clear the hill. My party scattered in pitch blackness and we all hit the dirt. When the shelling eventually stopped I checked my party and found only three men. We searched and listened to see if anyone was hit but it was impossible in the pitch darkness to move far from the track. I assumed that the others, after scattering had gone back to join the carrying party and as progress had been delayed too long already we prepared to move on.

"A runner caught up with us from the carrying party with a message from Major Bone explaining that the carriers had also been scattered by the shelling and dropped their loads, many of which had fallen down the hillside, had to be found and picked up and it would take some time to get them all re-assembled. They had also had several casualties. Because of the delay he wanted me to go forward as quickly as possible to let Lieut Jackson know what the situation was and to expect the stores and stretcher bearers to arrive there shortly.

"I collected my party together and started to go on. We had only gone a few hundred yards when our 25 pounders started another barrage which landed right amongst us. When this shelling stopped I searched around the area and couldn't find or hear any of my small party either wounded or alive.

"I decided that I should go on as quickly as possible to warn Lieutenant Jackson to expect the party or what was left of it, and to see what I could do to relieve him, especially as I expected that they had received casualties not only from their daylight activities but possibly that they also had been caught up in our own barrages. I followed the track to Point 677. Our positions were above the track, and when I was level with where our positions were, I saw and heard movement only about ten yards away and the vague silhouettes that I saw were definitely German. I decided to go on and round the back where I knew platoon headquarters had been established. I moved up as silently as I could and called out to Jackson to let him know it was me, and in return I got an egg grenade which exploded at my feet. As I was in a crouching position it knocked me off balance and I landed well down the gully.

"I was dazed by the explosion, and felt blood down my neck so I thought I had been hit, but couldn't feel any wound. I was in fact very lucky. The grenade had only nicked a lobe of my ear which bled like a stuck pig for a short while and that was the cause of my wet and warm neck.

"I realized that Point 677 was no longer in our hands, and being alone, I decided that I had to get back to the carrying party as soon as possible to stop them walking into the enemy positions without warning, particularly as they were no longer protected by an armed party, and as carriers they would be severely disadvantaged in not being able to use their weapons properly when moving. I thought too that they could have picked up what was left of the armed party, so that we could return to retake the position if we had enough armed men, as I now knew the way into the rear of their defence.

"I got back on the track and had gone about six hundred yards along the ridge on our side of Point 677 when a Spandau opened up in my direction. They obviously could not see me and I believe that they had sent out a patrol expecting to surprise any relief party coming up to Point 677 either along the track or the razor back. I moved back along the track towards our lines expecting to meet up with the others, but I met no one until I arrived back in '3' Company lines. I then heard what had happened to the others.

"Although there was a great disparity in our ages I had become very close to Major Bone and his death was a very great shock and I was not in very good shape when I went on to Battalion Headquarters to get debriefed on the information that I had gained that night. I remember the Colonel talked to me about what had happened and that we had been most unlucky and could not be blamed for the accidental shelling or the resultant problems that had come from the confusion in the darkness and that the Company had to gather itself together and emulate Major Bone's example. He said the same to the company so we quickly regained our morale and were ready to fight back.

"The next two nights I and other officers and NCOs took out patrols to find out if the nearest Spandau position this side of Point 677 was held or whether it was a fighting patrol. We found they were definitely there by night: then, I think at dawn on 21st the whole of the ridge was shrouded in a thick mountain mist and I was called to take out a daylight reconnaissance patrol to find out if the position was occupied by day. We got into a perfect position to observe their post and by luck the mist rose and we could clearly see the Spandau position with at least four men with their weapons beautifully sited along the ridge and fully covering the track which we used. They were also supported from Point 677. They did have the same problems we had encountered earlier as they had only been able to dig shallow pits before reaching bed rock and had built up extra cover with rocks to form a sangar so they could occupy the position by day. We pinpointed the spot and I believe that the accuracy of our mortar and shellfire which followed caused as many casualties from flying pieces of rock as did the shrapnel. This was the picture from No '3' Company's view point."

Reverting to the 20th the orders to the Battalion were to hold their lines while other units on the flanks pressed on. The foremost positions on Point 734 were taken over by the carrier platoon and "2" Company from the Lancashire Fusiliers. The weather on the night of 21/22 was particularly bad and the soldiers wondered whether they would ever be warm again. On the 23rd the sun shone and, apart from activity on Point 677, there was little evidence of the enemy. Patrols found the enemy was laying mines and setting booby traps, and Captain Hopper got right up onto Point 677. They could be seen from an observation post by the Colonel and his Company Commander who were horrified to see the patrol being stalked by a dozen Germans. Artillery fire was called for which came down close to the patrol and they were able to return without casualties. The Battalion came out of the line on the night of 27/28 October on being relieved by the Royal Scots.

With the approach of winter the weather and terrain aided the

257

defence and no major breakthrough of the enemy defensive lines was achieved. The Battalion now took part in a series of moves, occupying numerous different positions and engaged itself in active patrolling. After a rest period outside Florence the Battalion moved back into the line on 7 November(Map 22). Their task was to take over from the Americans in a sector which was the furthest point north held by any Allied troops in Italy. The move forward came under enemy harassing fire but march discipline and practised dispersion saved heavier casualties.

The enemy belonged to the 1st German Para Division which fought so stubbornly at Cassino and which had a reputation for patrolling. The first snow fell on the night 9/10 November which allowed tracks to be identified. Artillery and mortar fire, including American "Long Toms", were called down on houses the enemy was seen to occupy, which were hit and the enemy was seen evacuating one house. Sergeant Norman took out a patrol which failed to return.

On 17/18 November 2nd Lieutenant Crosland with Privates Sullivan and Trevaskis went out on his first reconnaissance patrol to find out whether the enemy were occupying a position at Raggi. The going was across difficult terrain, steep gullies and thick undergrowth in woods. Some one hundred and fifty yards short of the objective the patrol located a small enemy outpost and lay up for an hour listening to and watching movement before returning to our lines. During the move back the patrol heard sounds of movement as though they were being followed. Each time the patrol halted the sounds ceased. Finally 2nd Lieutenant Crosland left his two men to provide covering fire and went back to investigate and found the pursuing enemy were three goats.

The next night a patrol from "3" Company under Lieutenant Taylor patrolling forward in the wadi saw several groups of the enemy moving around. An attempt to seize a prisoner the following night was unsuccessful as an enthusiastic soldier threw a grenade which allowed the enemy to disperse.

Throughout this period the Battalion was deployed on mountain ridges, having all its supplies ferried forward from jeep-head by mules and carrying parties. The experience gained earlier in coping with these administrative arrangements paid off and it was a case of all hands to the pumps as even the postal orderlies and clerks from Battalion Headquarters joined the working parties. The Battalion was relieved on the night 23/24 November after a period of active patrolling and a time of learning to live in the wet and cold.

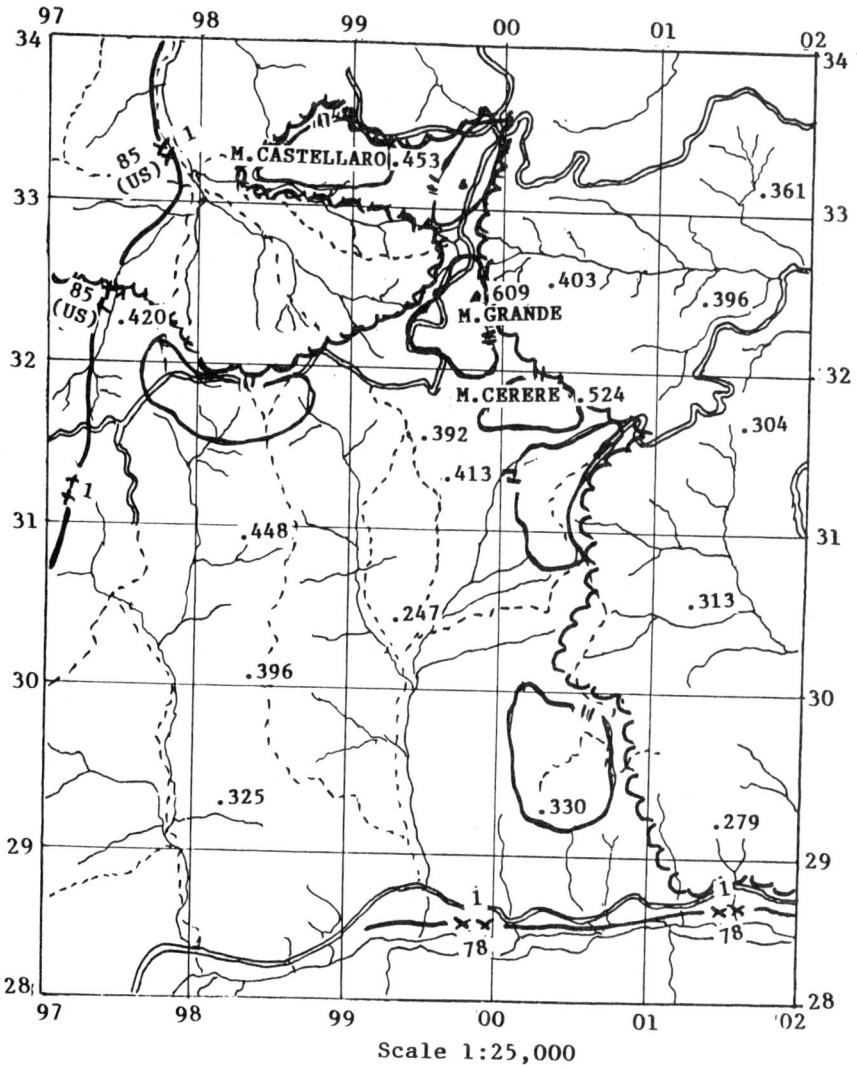

Scale 1:25,000

MAP 22

THE WINTER CAMPAIGN – MONTE CERERE

The Germans fought determinedly to deny M. Cerere, which was the key feature of the "Gothic Line" defences in this Sector. Aided by the terrain and the Winter weather they succeeded in holding up the Allied advance. The Hertfords occupied a series of positions around the mountain.

On 28/29 November the Battalion took over as the divisional reserve battalion and only the carrier and mortar platoons were forward. However, the situation changed radically as a German counter-attack had regained ground on Monte Castellaro which gave them observation onto friendly positions and supply routes. As a result the Battalion was ordered to occupy defensive positions on the Rigano feature which overlooked the rear slopes of Cecere. The counter-attack to regain the Monte Castellaro failed and this meant another rapid change of plan as far as the Hertfords were concerned. The Battalion was now ordered to occupy a new line based on the Farneto feature. Moving forward, company commanders found that visibility due to a thick mist was no more than thirty yards which made reconnaissance and tying in of fields of fire difficult to say the least. In spite of this new trenches were dug during the night. On 1 December the Battalion moved again to relieve the 2nd Royal Scots. The relief in the line went smoothly and although it was only possible to use a single narrow track between 0100 hrs and 0400 hrs no casualties were suffered in spite of the fact that the enemy put down some three hundred mortar bombs and one hundred shells in the area of the track during this relief in the line.

In both these moves the Signal Platoon established line links to forward companies and repaired them when damaged by enemy shellfire. In thirty six hours the Battalion carried out three reliefs, had to dig in and yet received no casualties. The soldier at the sharp end not having much idea for all the chopping and changing, yet at all times morale remained high.

The policy of active patrolling continued and Lieutenants Sutton and Wilson, Sergeant Meachen and Cpl Vinten all brought back useful information. On the night of 4/5 December the Battalion stood to all night as Intelligence reported the enemy were lifting a minefield on the front and an attack was expected. However, nothing happened. The enemy may have been deterred by friendly mortar and artillery fire.

On 15 December the Battalion took over as Divisional Reserve battalion in the south sector with tasks of aggressive patrolling. On 18/19 December Captain Miles took out a reconnaissance patrol from "2" Company consisting of Cpl Jones and Private Raynor to investigate suspected enemy positions in front of Monte Cerere and found two empty slit trenches at a position that the same patrol had found occupied the night before. Leaving Private Raynor at the trenches, the patrol pressed on down the track and came across a teller mine wedged in a cleft in a tree trunk with a trip wire attached and running across the track. A few yards further on there was another trip wire with a trip flare attached. Captain Miles was negotiating this obstacle when he heard sounds on the bank above him and a loud shout so he hastily took cover behind a tree. Cpl Jones was also off the track by now and Captain Miles fired his TMC in the direction of the shout whereupon the German opened up with his Spandau. This exchange of fire continued for a moment or two with neither scoring a hit. The German now threw a grenade without effect and Captain Miles and Cpl Jones were able to make their escape.

There was another move by the Battalion on 23 December into the Monte Calderaro Sector. The move took place in a snowstorm. The enemy could oversee the whole of the battalion position which restricted any daylight movement. Many of the trenches taken over had not been developed very well, so conditions were cramped to say the least. White suits were issued which provided good camouflage and which enabled the Battalion to institute an active patrolling programme. No enemy were seen wearing white clothing and their sentries in posts at Bertocchi and Dei Sarti were clearly visible in the snow. On Christmas Eve "3" Company suffered casualties from an enemy mortar concentration; Lieutenant Sutton was wounded and Private Lee was killed at the same time.

There was little activity until the evening of Christmas Day when the enemy put down their evening mortar shoot. The Battalion mortars responded with eighty four rounds of High Explosive and some airbursts over the enemy mortar positions. The Colonel commented that the enemy did not fire again that evening.

The white winter warfare clothing again proved its worth when Lieutenant Wilson and Cpl Postans were able to approach within twenty yards of an enemy occupied house without being seen. Next day this house was engaged with medium artillery and some enemy were seen to run away. The Germans retaliated about an hour later with medium shellfire but caused no damage.

On 28 December the Battalion moved back into a reserve position on Rignano ridge and enjoyed a hot meal and a dry sleep in Alpine bedrolls.

On 30 December the Battalion was in the line again on the Cerere feature and continued active patrolling. Cpl Adams and Private Dickinson were the victims of a Nebelwerfer team which brought down fire onto their listening post and two other soldiers were wounded. On 7 January the Battalion was relieved by 1st KSLI after twenty-four days in the line, little realising as they marched out that they were bound for Palestine and Syria.

The Battalion moved by easy stages to Taranto where they met up with Captain (QM) Beasley and the rear Echelon of the 2nd Battalion, the Bedfordshire and Hertfordshire Regiment which was now deployed in Greece. The Bedfords were able to loan transport to take soldiers into Taranto from the transit camp, a friendly act which was much appreciated.

The Battalion had acquitted itself well and had earned a reputation for aggressive patrolling. It had perhaps been fortunate as the Commanding Officer, Lt Colonel G.W.H. Peters, DSO, MC, had been in command for over two years and had been able to ensure that the battalion was as fully prepared for operations as possible. The Battalion itself had benefited from active training and was anxious to engage the enemy. The *Hertfordshire Field Gazette* presents a picture of a well-organized battalion with all members, whether they were in the rifle companies or providing mortar and machine-gun support, or the vital necessities of food, water and ammunition working together as a well-knit team. The activities of the support and administrative elements in moving and humping stores and kit up and down tortuous mountain trails has been fully described. Mention has not been made of the vital role played by the Signals Platoon in not only laying line to forward companies but in the equally dangerous and important task of repairing lines broken by artillery fire or torn asunder unwittingly by mule hooves. Often no sooner would a link be established than contact would be lost and a repair party would set out to find the break. At times it seemed the demands on the Signal Platoon were endless, yet they carried on no matter the weather and no matter what the enemy threw at them. There were also the medical orderlies who helped to retrieve the wounded and hasten their passage to the rear for treatment. Each and every one had contributed to the whole as part of the battalion team.

The Battalion had suffered numerous casualties. Eight officers and seventy-five soldiers were killed or died of wounds. Seven officers and two hundred and nine soldiers were wounded and another three officers and thirty-six soldiers were reported missing.

The Battalion was now to play its part in the less rewarding role of combating terrorism.

33

SYRIA AND PALESTINE

The Battalion arrived at Haifa on 31 January, 1945 and moved to a brigade concentration area at Pardes Hanna where they enjoyed a period of rest, rehabilitation and training. Training in infantry/armour co-operation was carried out in Syria during May and long service soldiers began to return home to England for discharge to be replaced by younger draftees.

Lt Colonel G.W.H.Peters, DSO, MC, left the Battalion at the end of September and Major A.Andrews, DSO, assumed command until Lt Colonel H.C.R.Hose, DSO, took over in late November.

One of the effects of the war in Europe had been the persecution of the Jews in all the territories occupied by the Germans, and this had resulted in large numbers of homeless and refugees. Palestine became the beacon which drew these unfortunate peoples in their thousands from all over Europe. The British authorities, anxious to avoid further confrontation with the Arabs, restricted the number of authorized immigrants. As a result the Jewish Agency turned a blind eye to highly organized batches of illegal immigrants, who attempted to come ashore off ships and escape inland to become lost among the members of the new "kibbutzim". Those who were caught coming ashore on open beaches were moved to camps to be processed. Those caught by the navy at sea were turned back and sent to camps in Cyprus. Thus, quite apart from the requirement for "Cordon and Search" operations to find illegal immigrants who had escaped the net, there was also the need to protect key installations from attacks by the Jewish terrorist groups, who were becoming more aggressive. This then was the background to the life of the Battalion in Palestine.

During the period 10 to 20 October, 1945 the Commanding Officer received orders to prepare for five separate Internal Security (IS) tasks – none of which were implemented. Later that month the Battalion provided two groups to work from bases in North Palestine at Rosh Pinna and Tiberias. Settlements were visited and initially the reception was cool but the calm behaviour of the troops ensured that friendly relationships were built up. The Regimental Band beat "Retreat" in many locations.

In early November there was an outbreak of widespread sabotage throughout Palestine and a major effort was directed against Lydda Station. A platoon of "3" Company and two armoured cars were called out to escort a police patrol to Beisan where damage to the railway line was discovered. This led to the introduction of night road curfews with the manning of road blocks to check night movement. On 12 November the Battalion took over the task of guarding the railway communications with companies at Lydda and Tulkarm, with responsibility for patrolling the line and keeping it open. On 18 November the Battalion bade farewell to the 1st Infantry Division and came under command of the 6th Airborne Division. The Battalion did not change their berets!

The tempo of illegal terrorist activities built up over the months and the Battalion assisted in rescue operations after the bomb outrage at the King David Hotel in Jerusalem, which was being used as Government offices and the Army Headquarters for Palestine and Transjordan, in July, 1946. The Battalion also provided the firing party and buglers for the mass funeral of the military casualties.

About this time it was expected that infantry regiments in the British Army would consist of three peacetime battalions rather than two as was the case before the war. It was thought that the 1st Hertfords would become this third battalion. The Colonel (Sox Hose) had earned a reputation as a result of his leadership in the Desert in 1942. During a visit to Headquarters in Jerusalem he invited Captain Medley, who was serving on the staff, to join the Battalion. This offer was quickly accepted and with the help of Colonel Peters at General Headquarters in Cairo a posting was effected. Other regular officers were returning to fill the vacancies caused by the discharge of the volunteers, among them Major "Hippo" Phipps, Major Ian Ross and Captain Stan Chandler, all of whom had served with the 1st Bedfordshire and Hertfordshire Battalion in Burma.

The Battalion was losing large numbers of men as wartime soldiers became due for release and two companies of Black Watch joined to make up strength. The jocks continued to wear their "Tam-o-shanters" with their red hackle and such was the camaraderie that the Battalion unofficially became "The Hertfordshire Watch".

Major Medley remembers vividly the conditions imposed by the deteriorating Internal Security situation. Life continued to follow a normal pattern and, when invited to dine at another battalion, officers dressed for the evening and repaired to the venue some fifteen miles away travelling in open jeeps. There were two officers in each jeep armed with loaded sub-machine guns. The jeeps travelled with a gap of one hundred yards between them with one officer looking forward and the other looking back ready to provide fire support should it be needed.

"3" Company was ordered to take over responsibility for guarding Jaffa railway station and the railway engineering workshops from the Arab Legion. A day or so earlier the Jewish terrorists had bombed Haifa station. The Company settled in, manning three section posts each of which was linked by telephone to the Company Office, the Officers' Mess and the Company Commander's bedside. The section sentries were armed with loaded Bren guns. While one platoon manned these posts a second platoon in camp was on stand-by, ready to turn out in the event of trouble to reinforce the duty platoon. The third platoon rested and had twenty-four hours off before starting the duty cycle once more. To ensure alertness and efficiency the stand-by platoon answered a practice call-out during its period on call. Finding the railway workshops unprotected a request was put in for wire, which was released from reserve stocks. At this time of the year there was an abnormal crush of Arabs demanding tickets to travel on their pilgrimage to Mecca, and the sentry at the station finding himself unheeded fired a warning shot. This had the desired effect but caused initial qualms at Company Headquarters.

Major Phipps was now commanding as Colonel Hose had left on promotion and he authorized the firing of live rounds after dark should any suspicious movement be suspected. As company commander Major Medley remembers calling up the sections and controlling the timing of this protective fire. He also recalls that his nightly visit round section posts never took place at the same time and that a different route was followed each time. After handing over this task to another unit these principles were not copied and the relieving company commander was shot and wounded on his rounds.

In spite of the tempo of the guard duties the on-call platoon carried out routine training and took part with the third platoon in sports against the railway police and other local units. A lively inter-section five-a-side hockey competition encouraged platoon rivalry.

"4" Company, commanded by Major Ross, had different responsibilities. Their task was to provide the guards and to run an internment camp for female prisoners at Latrun.

The Battalion continued to see a continuous exodus of drafts for release and such was the pace that there was soon a dire shortage of experienced NCOs. There were already recent arrivals in the Sergeants' Mess and the day came when the RSM departed and his post was assumed by a young man Sergeant Durham, who had joined in Palestine and who accepted his responsibilities willingly.

The inevitable orders came through in October that the Battalion was to move to Egypt to disband. Majors Phipps, Ross and Medley and Captain Chandler were summoned to Headquarters in Jerusalem and invited to volunteer for staff appointments. Much to the dismay of the Deputy Assistant Military Secretary a solid front was presented and all requested to be posted to the 2nd Bedfords in Greece. This request was acceded to. The Battalion moved to a transit camp outside Cairo and dispersed as drafts to other battalions in the Middle East. Seven officers and one hundred and eighty men shipped to Greece to join the 2nd Bedfords at Edhessa. The war service of the 1st Hertfords was now formally ended and *The Wasp* records "Those who have served with the Regiment during this period will never forget the bonds of comradeship which have united us at all times".

The Battalion reformed in 1947 with Headquarters in Hertford.

III

THE 2nd BATTALION
THE HERTFORDSHIRE
REGIMENT (TA)

34

A BEACH GROUP BATTALION

The 2nd Battalion of the Hertfordshire Regiment was formed on the expansion of the Territorial Army in 1939. The core of the new Battalion came from Numbers "1" and "2" Companies of the 1st Battalion which were located at St Albans, Watford and Hemel Hempstead. The Battalion was part of the 162nd Infantry Brigade in the 54th Division. It was deployed in an anti-invasion role until the end of 1942. Then in 1943 the Battalion was re-roled. It was to form the core unit around which a 'Beach Group' was to be assembled. The task of a Beach Group in broad terms was the provision of local defence and communications for one of the landing beaches in support of the Allied invasion of Europe.

The story is now taken up by Lt Colonel J.R.Harper, the Commanding Officer. "During, July, 1943 the 2nd Battalion The Hertfordshire Regiment was busily engaged in training with 79 Armoured Division practising the action of the infantry in close support of all the new armour such as 'Flails' and 'Crocodile' tanks. A certain amount of time was devoted to combined operations and assault landings.

"Towards the end of July the Battalion was ordered to mobilize for a combined operations beach maintenance course. It became apparent that the Battalion was going to form the infantry element of a Beach Group and all the commanders of the various elements met at Troon for the first time.

2nd Herts moved to Scotland in August and spent the next three months welding the many units forming 9 Beach Group together, carrying out beach maintenance exercises with a major exercise in January, 1944, at Gullane in the Firth of Forth.

"The beach group was made up of a headquarters, an infantry element, five specialist elements and initially eighteen technical elements. The specialist element contained Light and Heavy Anti-

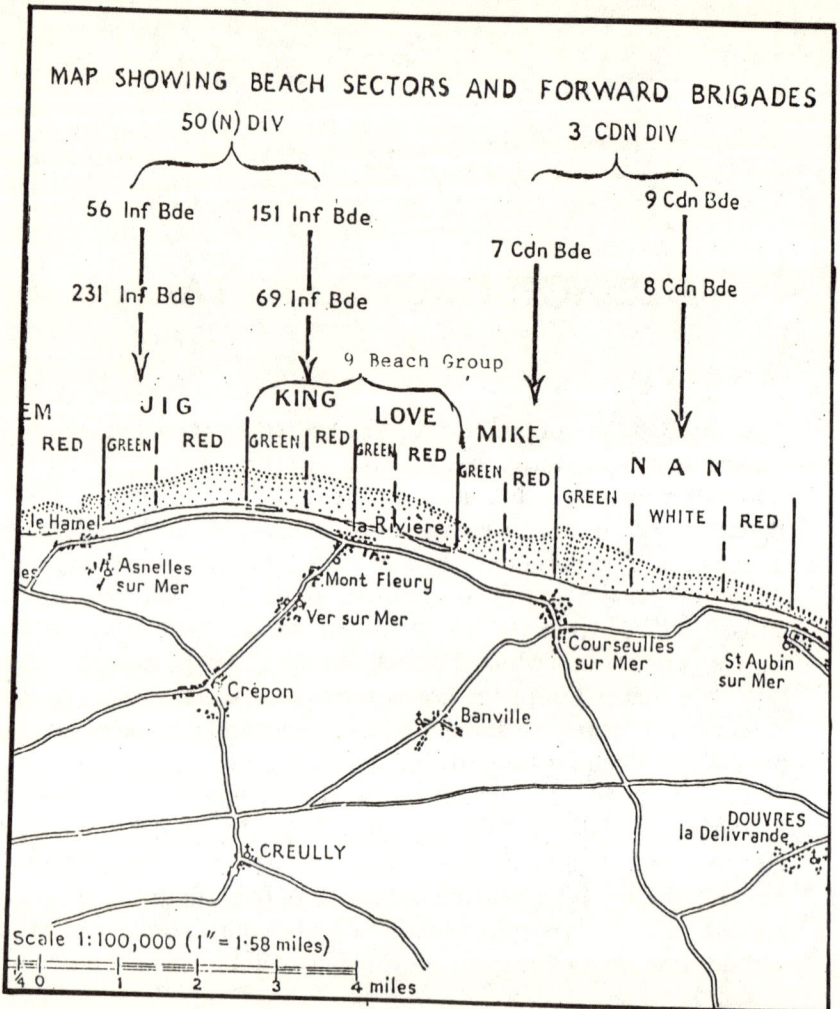

MAP SHOWING BEACH SECTORS AND FORWARD BRIGADES

50 (N) DIV   3 CDN DIV

56 Inf Bde   151 Inf Bde   9 Cdn Bde

231 Inf Bde   69 Inf Bde   7 Cdn Bde   8 Cdn Bde

9 Beach Group

EM   J I G   KING   LOVE   MIKE   N A N

RED | GREEN | RED   GREEN | RED | GREEN | RED | GREEN | RED | GREEN   WHITE | RED

le Hamel   la Rivière

Asnelles sur Mer   Mont Fleury   Courseulles sur Mer   St Aubin sur Mer

Ver sur Mer

Crépon

Banville

DOUVRES la Delivrande

CREULLY

Scale 1:100,000 (1" = 1·58 miles)

4 0   1   2   3   4 miles

MAP 23

2nd HERTS – NORMANDY 6 JUNE 1944

Aircraft artillery, Signals and an RAF balloon squadron. The technical element comprised medical, ordnance, RASC, REME, Provost and Pioneers. The commanding officer of the infantry, Lt Colonel J.R.Harper, was in command of this conglomerate which totalled almost five thousand men.

"The plan was for the Beach Group to land with 50 (Northumbrian) Division, which consisted of four infantry brigades two of which would land through 9 Beach Group.

"Rehearsals were carried out behind smoke screens at Studland Bay with a final full dress rehearsal at Hayling Island. The soldiers travelled in the actual craft they would be in on 'D' Day and all Services got to know each other well. Many lessons were learned as a result of the trials, and landing and loading tables had to be scrapped and done again. During May the Beach Group concentrated near Winchester and was gradually broken down into craft loads among the many camps in the Southampton area. From this time on men lived in 'Craft loads' and came under control of the embarkation staff. From the beach group commanders point of view this period was probably the most difficult of all. Embarkation started on 2 June starting with Landing Craft Tanks (LCTs) and Landing Ship Tanks (LSTs) on the hards at Southampton. Morale was very high and everyone was full of confidence.

"On the afternoon of 4 June the convoys started to sail, but owing to the very bad weather many of the smaller craft had to turn back and cancellation orders were received. Next day the convoys moved off and by 2000 hrs were ploughing through a very rough sea. Many of the LCTs (A) broke down and became a menace to shipping on the way over.

"At dawn on 6 June waves of aircraft passed overhead on their way to start the bombardment. A few ships were sunk by mines, but on the whole the crossing was uneventful though unpleasant. Owing to the rough sea and an onshore breeze, the fifty yards of sand we expected was covered with water and the high tide water mark was up to the second row of obstacles. The assault field company landed at H minus ten minutes and gallantly attacked the obstacles without any close fire support owing to the Duplex Drive tanks being late. Two narrow lanes were made, but many craft landing at the height of the tide failed to see these lanes and were blown up on the obstacles. In all over seventy craft were lost on 'D' Day alone on this one beach – a much higher loss than was expected. 2nd Herts were in the fourth assault wave landing at H hour plus sixty minutes and during the landing sustained only one casualty a soldier being drowned while trying to reach shore from a Landing Craft Infantry (LCI) (Map 23).

" 'A' company under Major W.R.Nichols landed on KING Red beach and although mortared sustained no casualties. 'C' Company under Major D.C.Slemeck landed on KING Green beach and were immediately involved in street fighting in the village of La Rivière and in the many dugouts round the enemy concrete defences. "B" Company, Major H.Allan and 'D' Company, Major A.G.Scott-Joynt also landed on Green beach.

"Up till 1100 hrs the fighting was local against enemy positions on the beaches in the village round the lighthouse. The gun positions at Mont Fleury and Ver sur Mer fought stubbornly and had to be winkled out. After midday the only enemy activity in our beach area was from snipers, who proved a nuisance for a day or two. During the afternoon it became clear that a strong enemy position at Vaux had been bypassed by both the 50th Division and the 3rd Canadian Division on our left. This position was harassing transport moving on the lateral road between King and Mike sectors and contained ant-tank guns which had knocked out one armoured car. I decided to attack this position with 'B' Company after it had been softened up by fire from a destroyer. Unfortunately the Naval fire failed to materialize at the time required and 'B' Company attempted to assault the position without support. They came under heavy mortar fire and were pinned down in the village of Vaux and on the road leading south, receiving twelve casualties. It was here that Lieut F.A.E.Bonney and Corporal Church performed their gallant act in retrieving the wounded under heavy mortar and machine-gun fire, for which they were awarded an immediate MC and MM. "By now it was getting dark and, as I was unable to get any gun or tank support, I decided to withdraw from the village via the beach and occupy a wood which commanded the position. During the move Lieut Eyres was wounded on a beach mine. During the night I arranged with my anti-aircraft commander for him to move up a Bofors gun . This gun moved into position and soon after dawn opened up on the enemy with one hundred and fifty rounds of 40mm tracer. 'B' Company with one platoon of 'D' Company assaulted under covering fire from the remainder of 'D' Company and took the position, leaving thirty-seven dead, taking over one hundred prisoners and liberating the village of Vaux without suffering any casualties.

"During the next two days we were occasionally bothered by snipers and everyone became sniper conscious. Prisoners were coming back in ever increasing numbers and caused quite a problem on the beaches until a cage was set up near Ver sur Mer, after which they were evacuated in batches of eight hundred.

"The obstacles in our area were more formidable than we had expected. There were five rows of beach obstacles consisting of floating logs with teller mines attached, steel hedgehogs with teller mines, and wooden stakes with 75mm shells attached. It took some days to clear the beaches of these obstacles and make safe the landing of craft. The beaches were bombed nightly with little effect but day bombers and fighters were only seen on three occasions.

"All pillboxes, gun positions, slit trenches and even sleeping quarters were most elaborately constructed of reinforced concrete. Guns were sited to enfilade the beaches and all concrete surfaces facing seaward were from eight to ten feet thick reinforced with steel plate. Overhead cover for gun positions was never less than six feet. The results of our bombing were disappointing in that not one position got a direct hit and no guns were knocked out. However, the intensity of shelling from cruisers and destroyers caused the Germans to go to ground which enabled us to get ashore. The whole area was extensively mined. It has been estimated that there were two hundred and fifty thousand mines in King sector alone, of these we lifted and cleared over one hundred and twenty thousand during the period we worked on the beaches. 2nd Herts lost the Pioneer Platoon sergeant and one pioneer during these mine lifting operations and the RE field company had several more casualties. All minefields were marked with boards until the American sailors removed them as souvenirs and from then on casualties to men and vehicles increased.

"The Battalion settled down to its role of working the beach and moved an average fifteen hundred tons a day with two thousand tons on our best day. On 15 July I received a letter from General Montgomery informing me that he would have to use the Battalion as infantry reinforcements. We came off the beach and carried on with intensive infantry training hoping that we would be used as a complete battalion. On 17 August the Battalion was placed in suspended animation and drafts were then despatched daily until by 31 August only the adjutant and I remained. We shook hands and went our different ways."

IV

THE 5th BATTALION
THE BEDFORDSHIRE
AND HERTFORDSHIRE
REGIMENT (TA)

35

MOBILIZATION, TRAINING
AND DEPLOYMENT

The 5th Battalion of The Bedfordshire and Hertfordshire Regiment, commanded by Lt Colonel A.D.Gaye was embodied on 25 August, 1939. The Battalion was in the 55th Infantry Brigade of the 18th Division. Its first task was to transfer two rifle companies "C" and "D", from Luton and Dunstable en bloc to form the new 6th Battalion.

The story of events is taken from an account written by Captain H.E.I.Phillips, the Adjutant, which appeared in *The Wasp*.

"The first few months of the war were spent in guarding aerodromes and other key points so there was but little opportunity for unit level training. After May, 1940, the Battalion was given an anti-invasion role and by the end of the year was confidently expecting to be mobilized for overseas service. This call did not come until September, 1941, when the Battalion was made up to strength from the 2nd and 9th Battalions. Lt Col D. Rhys-Thomas, OBE, MC had assumed command in December, 1940.

"The Battalion embarked on the *SS Reina Del Pacifico* at Liverpool on 27 October. The transport had been loaded a week before on the SS *Bonikom*. At the time the Battalion as part of the 18th Division had set sail its intended destination was the Middle East. However, with the entry of Japan into the war the Division was diverted to the Far East. The voyage took the Battalion via Halifax, Newfoundland, where it transshipped to the USS *West Point*, continuing the voyage on 9 November. The convoy put in at Cape Town on 6 December, moving off once more on 13 December. The convoy now sailed to Bombay, where the Battalion disembarked and moved by rail to Ahmednagar arriving there on 31 December two months after setting out from Liverpool.

"The Battalion was destined to remain but three weeks at Ahmednagar before returning to Bombay to board the USS *West Point* again sailing on 19 January. The three weeks in India had been gainfully spent in acclimatisation, route marches and training.

"Our thoughts turned to jungle warfare. No one aboard had ever seen jungle; no one had the least idea what a Japanese soldier looked like, nor were there any books or pamphlets which might enlighten us. Thus our imaginary schemes and lectures had to be based largely on guesswork, and they were not very good guesses either. As we progressed the news from Malaya was so bad that it was considered quite possible that we should be turned round into Batavia, Java's capital. However, on 29 January we found ourselves sailing into Keppel Harbour, Singapore at dawn.

"We disembarked and were sent to Birdwood Camp. On 31 January the Battalion received orders to assume the defence of an area of the north coast of Singapore Island. With our experience of 1940 Norfolk behind us, we were full of confidence and thought it easy meat. But now occurred the first tragedy, the first split in the Battalion. 'C' Company and the Carrier Platoon were ordered on to an aerodrome to reinforce the local defences and were placed under command of the OC Ground Defences there. The Battalion, besides being tasked with watching the approaches from the aerodrome and defending a main road, had a counter-attack role in the event of enemy penetration of the forward sector. We had an allocation of transport, not our own of course, for that had been loaded on a separate ship and nothing more had been heard or seen of it.

"We were never to know how we might have fared had the enemy tried to cross the Straits in our sector as news came in on 9 February that the Japanese had secured a landing on the north-western side of the island. Then came the second tragedy. Malaya Command pursued a policy of switching individual units and sub units from one sector to another and from one formation to another, often creating artificial formations in a despairing effort to stem the tide. Unfortunately, this seemed to have no regard to the chaos which must inevitably result from tearing apart coherent bodies.

"The Battalion received orders on 10 February to leave the command of 55th Brigade and go into Malaya Command reserve, but it was not allowed to proceed as an entity. The aerodrome defence sub units had to be left intact, while the bulk of Headquarters Company were required to remain behind to defend the main road. Our reinforcement company was ordered to assist in this sector, and the whole force thus constituted became known as 'Wells Force', after Major Tom Wells, who commanded 'HQ' Company.

"Meanwhile the remainder of the Battalion, 'A', 'B', and 'D' Companies and a skeleton Headquarters staff, accompanied the Colonel to the new area. Of course we were promised that we should all join up again as soon as 'Wells Force' could be spared, but it never happened in action. In outline operations lasted five more days and consisted for the most part of a series of ordered withdrawals.

" 'Wells Force' suffered badly, losing Tom Wells, Lieutenant Bill Thewles and 2nd Lieutenant Glyn Star, who were killed, and 2nd Lieutenant Frank Hall, who was very seriously wounded and died later. Moreover on 13 February Major Richard Thompson, Captain Freddie Sladen, 2nd Lieutenant Andy West, CSM Colbert and four others were suddenly called away without warning and ordered to report to Brigade. So this little force lost three senior officers and did not have a pleasant time suffering the bulk of the operational casualties between 13 and 15 February.

"The bulk of the Battalion was now under command of the 1st Malaya Infantry Brigade and fought alongside the 2nd Loyals. The action consisted of three withdrawals. It was impossible to cope with the fact that the left flank was being constantly turned as the enemy exerted all their pressure down the west and south-west coast by road and by sea. 'A' and 'D' Companies both found themselves involved, the former having a bad time from a small force of enemy who crept up unseen through the jungle country and picked off Captain S.H. Thrussell, the Company Commander, and Lieutenant D.H. Jackson, while Lieutenant A.R.Bennett was wounded and had to be evacuated. 'D' Company, however, had a rather better time before taking part in the general withdrawal, and from a commanding position covering a road mowed down a force of Japanese who impudently tried to march down it. But, generally speaking, the Battalion never had a chance to fight. Orders to withdraw were given by higher command before our own men were really in contact with the enemy.

"The order to cease fire was received by the Battalion at 8.25pm on 15 February. The battle casualties were small, although the proportion of officers was high. Six officers and twenty six men were killed; the exact number of wounded was never known.

"As the escape party left Battalion Headquarters they were shot at by the Japs from several directions. They jumped on a carrier and found Brigade Headquarters where they were told they were to be evacuated from the island with parties from every unit. They were to report to the docks at 0200 hrs on the 14th. The party consisted of Major R.J.B. Thompson, Captain Sladen, 2nd Lieutenant West, CSM Colbert, Sergeant Templeman, L/Cpl Harris, Privates Curzon and Paul of the Bedfords and Captains Price and Morgan, CSM Maddocks and Sergeant Barracliffe of the Foresters.

"This party set sail from Singapore on 15 February and progressed by stages through the local islands, rowing and sailing by night to avoid detection by Japanese aircraft and patrol craft, eventually reaching the coast of Sumatra by 22 February at Prige Rajah. Two more days travelling down the coast before heading inland and by road across the mountain range to the Western coast. On 2 March the party was loaded onto a destroyer which took them out to sea about thirty miles where they transferred on to the Australian cruiser HMAS *Hobart*. Colombo was reached by 5 March and from there to Bombay. Major Thompson and Andy West were posted to the 1st Bedfords. Freddie Sladen went to the staff at GHQ India and travelled round India and Ceylon lecturing on the events at Singapore. He later joined a special force returning to the Dutch East Indies and was not seen again."

36

CAPTIVITY – PRISONERS OF THE JAPANESE

The story now goes back to the Battalion on Singapore Island and Captain Phillips continues his story. "We were prisoners for forty two months and during the whole of this time we were subjected to hardships, ill-treatment and unpleasantness of every description. When we reassembled after the end of the battle of Singapore, we found that, including those of us at Divisional and Brigade Headquarters, we were some nine hundred and forty all ranks. Our first home was in a barracks at Changi, in the north-east corner of Singapore island. Here the whole unit was accommodated in a block which in normal times would have housed one company. A few weeks later we moved out and camped in a sand pit where we experienced our first taste of real overcrowding. this did not last for long as groups of the Battalion were sent off for work parties. First a group of one hundred from 'C' Company to a camp at River Valley Road in Singapore for the purpose of assisting in the reconstruction of the town. Then the bulk of the unit, some five hundred and fifty, moved to Bukit Timah village in the corner of the island, where they set to work to build a shrine to commemorate the Japanese victory. The details remaining at Changi consisted of the Orderly Room, the sick and certain officers and men required for special duty. Further small parties were sent to Keppel Harbour and to Havelock Road. The Colonel went with the latter group and found himself the commander of a very mixed camp.

"What work there was at Changi was in the interests of everybody – wood-cutting, ration collecting, latrine digging and the like. For a time even a school and university flourished which many a man found helpful and interesting but this did not last long. Food of course, had very soon come to be based on rice, and at Changi there was never a lot to supplement this staple diet.

"In May the Japanese began to issue a little pay, the sum for soldiers varying according to the work being undertaken between two and four old pence a day. Officers received about thirty-five shillings (£1.75 current money) a month, of which one third was appropriated to a central camp fund to help support the hospital and the sick who were not actually in hospital. The 5th Battalion was lucky in having a fair sum of money left after the fall of Singapore and all detachments took a proportionate share when they moved. As these funds were expended they were augmented a little by camp canteen profits. This meant that for nearly all our time in captivity a little regimental money was available to assist the very needy.

"The Japanese required us to sign a parole form promising not to escape, and this all men naturally refused to do. By way of reprisal all men at Changi, some fifteen thousand, were ordered to proceed to Selarang barracks, which had been built in peacetime to provide adequate accommodation for one battalion. No one who was not actually there can possibly imagine what it was like. There were about two hundred Bedfords and the living space available was about one hundred and fifty square yards. Yet everyone remained in high spirits. CSM Bennett by an ingenious arrangement of trestles and stretchers was able to introduce a double bunking scheme which relieved pressure considerably. Obviously this state of affairs could not go on for long. On the fourth day Captain Hoppe, our senior officer there, explained that epidemics were already starting and that our authorities had had to treat with the Japanese. The result was a compromise. We agreed to sign the parole by order of the Japanese under duress. We were then allowed to return to our old areas.

"In October, 1942, the great trek northwards began. The Battalion sent its men up in various parties; about three hundred and sixty from Bukit Timah split into two sections, two hundred from Changi and smaller parties from other camps. We spent five days and nights in cattle trucks, thirty men to a truck with a floor space of seventy five square feet. It was so crowded it was not possible to lie down except by arrangement with one's neighbours. Rations were poor and sanitary arrangements worse. A dishevelled party eventually arrived at Banpong in Thailand. We were now faced with a march of some one hundred kilometres which had to be undertaken for the most part through virgin jungle and all our kit was on our backs. To make matters worse it was the tail end of the rainy season, the going was appallingly difficult, and our sodden kit weighed heavily upon us.

"The Japanese plan for the construction of a railway in Thailand was broadly as follows. They had made a survey along the east bank of the River Kwa Noi north-westwards through the Three Pagoda Pass into Burma (Map 24) and thence to the railway line from Moulmein to Ye on the sea coast of Burma. The total distance to be covered was four hundred and ten kilometres starting at Non Pladoc a few miles outside Banpong the railhead at which the parties arrived from Singapore.

"The four hundred and ten kilometres was divided into sections and a group of camps was allotted to each section. The first fifty-five kilometres was the responsibility of No 1 Group which had very few of the Battalion. Next came No 2 Group based on Chungkai camp fifty-nine kilometres up the line. The conditions of those in this group were initially better than others but deteriorated when the Group moved further north. In No 2 Group were about two hundred and sixty members of the Battalion led by Major Robinson, who had seven other officers and four warrant officers, including RQMS Brown.

"No 3 Group was across the border in Burma working from the other end of the railway. It was made up in the main of Australians, Americans and Dutch but Lieutenant Spriggs and Private Hinks were in this Group. They had escaped from Singapore after capitulation and made their way across to Sumatra, only to fall into the hands of the Japanese when they captured that island.

"No 4 Group had its headquarters at Tarsao. This group had the worst of things to start, but once No 2 Group had brought the railway into No 4 area, in May 1943, things started to improve. Eventually there were four hundred and thirty Bedfords in No 4 Group. The camps in this group were arranged at intervals over the whole area. The Colonel was at Tarsao with several other officers. Bill Kendrick had a small party about ten miles south at Wampo, while 'Happy' Mills was in charge of another detachment at Tonchan about ten miles North. With him was RSM Dunham.

"The only other parties which must be mentioned are 'F' and 'H' Forces. These were large parties drawn from those who had remained behind at Singapore when the great trek started in October 1942. They came up in May, 1943, under their own Japanese administration. As a result the existing P.W. administration in Thailand, out of pique, would have nothing to do with them and would give them no assistance. Hence, these parties, which contained many sick men arrived at Banpong to find no transport whatsoever available to take them to their allotted area, which lay some three hundred kilometres away inside the Thai Burma frontier. 'F' Force had to march the whole

MAP 24

THE BURMA–THAILAND
RAILWAY

The camp sites along the railway
line, which are used in the text, are
shown.

Notes: Numbers indicate working
groups, eg; Tarsau 4
Cemeteries are shown as
follows, eg; Sonkrai ++
Hospitals with the Red
Cross symbol; +

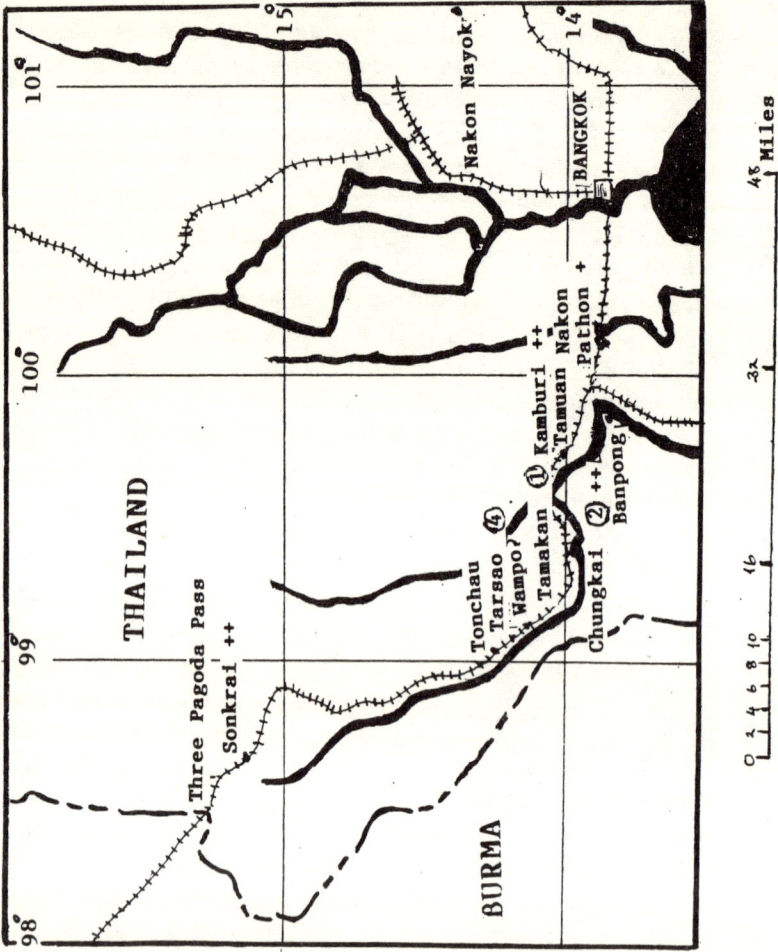

distance and the journey lasted seventeen days. Captain Fitt was the senior Bedford officer in this group with sixty two all ranks. There was a small Bedford party under Captain Hopper with 'H' Group. This party had the misfortune to run into a cholera epidemic.

"The conditions in all the camps varied only in degree. In all of them solid hard work was necessary for about twelve months clearing the jungle, preparing the ground for the rail track, building bridges and laying the railway. None of us in the early days ever imagined that trains would pass along the new railway line. But they did; and the line was finally completed by 23 October, 1943. The work took its toll. The Japanese were great believers in working to schedule, and if work fell behind, there was an immediate 'speedo' to catch up again. The men often left camp before dawn and returned after dark and sometimes there was shift work over the whole twenty four hours. They worked in all weathers. no one had any clothes that had any right to a name. A loin cloth usually was the only article of apparel and to this lucky ones added a hat and the very lucky ones a pair of old boots or shoes. Mosquitoes bit at night and the men slept on bamboo platforms shoulder to shoulder. Sanitary arrangements were usually bad even judged by Eastern standards.

"It is therefore not surprising that men soon began to go down with a variety of unpleasant diseases. Malaria and dysentery became very common, whilst sheer under-nourishment accounted for many. All our doctors accomplished wonders in keeping the death rate to a low level and a special word must also go to the medical orderlies. Many a man owes a great debt of gratitude to the little regimental team of which Sergeant Pyke and Windsor, Moran, Maddams and Rix were prominent members. Drugs and other forms of medical supplies were appallingly scarce, and the doctors had to rely on dietetic forms of treatment.

"In No 2 Group we lost about seventy men during the railway building period. In No 4 Group we lost about one hundred, twenty of whom died in a cholera epidemic. 'F' Force fared worse relatively; of sixty-two men who went north with this party only sixteen survived. Officers worked alongside the men. There was always the threat the Japanese would turn sick men out to work to make numbers up. They did so anyhow. Some men are known to have been carried to work and some to have died at the side of the railway, but if an officer could save a sick man from being dragged to work it was well worth while.

"There was another side to this gloomy picture. Whatever the circumstances the morale of the men remained high. It never seemed difficult to get an impromptu singsong going, never difficult to raise a smile. That wonderful English heritage, a sense of humour, never seemed to be lacking, and with it went a sense of decency and discipline which engendered optimism and kept tempers equitable.

"After the railway had been completed, the Japanese relaxed a little and concentrated on getting the survivors away from the jungle. New camps were built and almost everyone was concentrated within a few miles of Banpong. Food tended to improve but there were still not many other amenities. The camps were more spacious and the cookhouses were models of cleanliness and efficiency and the atmosphere was altogether brighter out of the jungle. The holding of church services was not a foregone conclusion and permission was usually required every time. This period of relaxation was brought to an abrupt end in May, 1944, when the order went about that as many fit men as possible were to be shipped to Japan.

"Selection was by P.W. number and this arbitrary division made it difficult for friends to travel together. For example eighty-nine Bedfords in No 4 Group were selected to go and these were divided across six parties of one hundred and fifty. The Japan parties from No 2 Group left Chungkai in two sections. The first containing thirty-eight Bedfords with CSM Pithers the senior left by train for Singapore on 9 June where they embarked on the *Osaka Maru*. Sixty three Bedfords in the second section embarked on the *Hofoko Maru*.

"Both ships left Singapore early in July and proceeded in convoy to Manila where they parted company. The *Osaka Maru* went on after three weeks' stop and ran into a hurricane which broke its back and it grounded on a small island. The men were picked up by two Japanese destroyers, eventually arriving in Japan on 23 August. Meanwhile *Hofoku Maru* remained in Manila with engine trouble until 20 September, when it, too, set sail. On the following morning the convoy it had joined was attacked by American planes. The ship went down quickly and the majority of men with it. Those who survived were eventually picked up by the Japanese, who, of course, dealt first with their own people. The survivors returned to Manila, undergoing another machine-gunning attack on the way. In Manila they embarked on another ship which was chased by the Allies and had to go to Hong Kong to elude its pursuers. The prisoners were eventually disembarked on the island of Formosa where to their surprise and pleasure they met up with the Battalion padre, Rev F.H. Stallard, who had left Changi in August, 1942. In all there were ten survivors of the Regiment, including Sergeants Burgess and Winstanley. After a stay of three months in Formosa they were taken on to Japan. One survivor of this party, Private Jackman, was lucky enough to reach the Filipino coast, where he joined forces with some guerrillas and remained with them until the Americans recaptured Luzon.

"Meanwhile the No 4 Group parties had left Thailand between 21 and 24 June, 1944. The first section had about thirty-three Bedfords and sailed direct to Japan. The second section embarked on two transports, the *Kachidochi Maru* and the *Rakuyu Maru* sailing on 6 September. American submarines found the convoy on the 10th and attacked it for two successive days, sinking both ships. Those who did not go down with the ships remained in the water for periods varying between two and five days before Japanese rescue ships would take any notice of them. Some were picked up and taken via Formosa to Japan. A few who managed to hold on for a little longer were found by an American submarine and taken to Saipan. Among this party were four Bedfords, who arrived home early in 1945, bringing with them an enormous amount of Regimental news about those still in captivity. Twelve of the Regiment survived this sinking and were taken on to Japan, among them Lieutenant Evans.

"Conditions aboard these troop ships were uniformly bad. The men were quartered in holds often battened down. Food and water were scarce. Sanitary conditions were indescribable, and the few doctors had to carry out their work, including surgical operations, in thoroughly unhygienic conditions and with next to no medical supplies. Several men died on board, five of ours among them. Those who did eventually reach Japan were sent to different camps some to Fukuoka, others near Nagasaki and more to Osaka. Some were set to work in shipyards, riveting, drilling and navvying. Others were sent down coal mines. Their taskmasters were unrelenting and there were many unpleasant incidents. The last few months of the war gave all prisoners in Japan a first-rate opportunity of seeing the American Air Force in full cry, and all would agree it was a frightening if inspiring experience. Some of our men actually witnessed the dropping of the atomic bomb.

"A party of thirty Bedfords from No 1 Group under Lieutenant Kimsey were part of a detachment detailed to go to Japan in July, 1944. Initially they worked on building a new dock at Singapore and only sailed in January, 1945 after witnessing several heavy Allied air raids. They were crammed on board a transport and sailed in the usual appalling conditions. They were attacked by several allied submarines but escaped into Saigon. Here they disembarked and were told the voyage to Japan was off. The men were set to work in the docks, on defences and road building. They found the French speaking local population were both sympathetic and confident. Food was perhaps a little better, but working and living conditions were as bad as ever.

"In Japan, too, there was an earlier party containing a few of the Regiment. These had left Singapore in the spring of 1943 and had an uninterrupted journey to Japan. They were employed mainly at the Syno cement works near Hakodate. Conditions were bad and the Japanese workmen very hostile. Medical treatment was quite inadequate. In the last few months of the war it seemed as though the Japanese were deliberately trying to break down the physique and morale of their prisoners.

"There were still large numbers of prisoners left in Thailand. Major Robinson had one hundred and thirty men in No 2 Group based at Chungkai and Tamakan. Major Ditton was at Tamaun, thirty six miles west of Tamuan with about one hundred and eighty men of No 4 Group. The Colonel was at Nakon Pathom, about half way between Banpong and Bangkok with another sixty Bedfords. Work during these months was mainly domestic. The big camps were always requiring maintenance, and the large numbers congregated in them made the number of essential duties enormous. Working parties still went outside the camp on defence works. The restrictions on sport and entertainment remained. Discipline, on the whole, was quite good and a tribute must be paid to CSM A. Sewell of the Battalion, who was appointed No 4 Group Camp Sergeant Major, and who thoroughly merited his acting rank of WO I.

"There were still a few parties up country. A handful of No 4 Group under Captain Teddy Corner was reinforced with further parties from No 2 and 4 groups when the Japanese started to send parties back up the railway for maintenance work and for cutting wood for locomotive fuel. So sickness which had been remarkably well held in check during the preceding months, began all over again, and it was not long after the parties went up that we saw the old familiar sight of sick men pouring back into our base hospitals. Then in December 1944 the Japanese brought everyone back into the base camps. This was directly attributable to the start of the Allied strafing of the new railway on the 7th December, which caused some unavoidable but none the less unfortunate deaths amongst prisoners, two Bedfords among them.

"During the early months of 1945 the officers with the exception of doctors and padres were taken away from the men. Of course, by international law this step should have been taken at the start of our

288

captivity. Now there was very much sorrow at parting. The long association of officers and men in the difficult conditions of our imprisonment had resulted in an excellent understanding of each other's problems and had been beneficial to all concerned. It is good to know that the camps were handed over to warrant officers and N.C.O.s who administered them most ably for the remaining months of captivity. It was a difficult enough period for now the Japanese had decided to use prisoners to repair bomb damage which was becoming far more common in Thailand especially on the Bangkok – Singapore railway. New lateral roads were also required to bolster up their greatly attenuated lines of communication. One party with only partially fit men went to Prachnabkhirikun in the Kra Peninsula and thence struck Westwards through jungle to the Burma border. Their task was road building. Within three months nearly a quarter of this party had died in 'Death Valley'. Another party, led by CSM Bennett, walked six hundred kilometres between May and August, and was still walking when the war ended. It is nothing short of a miracle that so few lives were lost. Right to the end the Japanese persisted in their utter disregard of human life.

"A few of the Battalion who managed to escape to Sumatra after the capture of Singapore were eventually recaptured. They spent two years jungle clearing and road making in Sumatra before being trans-shipped to Singapore. Their ship was torpedoed and sunk and the party were returned to Sumatra where they remained for the rest of the war.

"Some fifty Bedfords remained at Changi on Singapore island throughout internment. They had the advantage of better accommodation and electric light.

"When the war ended there were scenes common to all camps. The first was invariably the hoisting of the flag and the singing of 'The King', both of which had been denied us during captivity. Everyone will agree that the efforts of the Allies to relieve us quickly and efficiently was magnificent. Within four weeks of the official close of hostilities practically everyone was on his way home, and those who were not were being looked after in the hospitals of India and the Dominions. It was remarkable how fit everyone looked on arrival in England. The capacity of the human frame to recover from its hardships as a result of kind and sympathetic ministration has never been more clearly demonstrated.

"We paid our price. Of the original one thousand all ranks who had left Liverpool in 1941, nine hundred and forty had been taken prisoner, the rest dead. Of the nine hundred and forty who were taken prisoner three hundred and twenty six died. No officers were lost, but the Sergeant's Mess lost seventeen of its members. All who died received a Christian burial with military honours in the presence of their comrades, and their graves were looked after and carefully charted."

The Commanding Officer, Lt Colonel D. Rhys-Thomas, and a small detachment which included RSM L.S.Dunham, returned to the UK on the SS *Ormonde* arriving at Southampton in October where they were met by General Sir Henry Jackson, the Colonel of the Regiment.

So ends the account of events written by Captain H.E.I.Phillips. It shows how the officers and men of the 5th Battalion were called to meet a different challenge. A challenge which demanded strength of will and tenacity in the face of conditions the like of which none of them could have possibly envisaged. Singapore, historically, is the greatest disaster to befall the British Army. The Bedfords, like many men of other regiments, behaved in a manner in which we may feel justly proud.

V
STAFF AND EXTRA-REGIMENTALLY EMPLOYED

37

BEDFORDS WITH THE STAFF AND EXTRA-REGIMENTALLY EMPLOYED

The demands made upon the 2nd Bedfords to find drafts for other units have been detailed in earlier chapters. Suffice it to say as a result of this mixing and leavening, the cap badge was present in all major actions of the war.

Many officers and men who had been serving with battalions early in the war found themselves posted to staff or extra regimental appointments to meet the demands of a vastly expanding army. Extra regimental duties covered amongst others providing instructors and administrative staff at training establishments, running transit camps and helping the 'Q' Movements organisation. In war there are so many different tasks which need to be done, some challenging, others mundane but all playing a role in a much bigger picture. Major Scales kept a list of comrades who had served with him in the 2nd Bedfords at the outbreak of war. Perhaps the most interesting part of this record is of Bandsmen F.Bryant and P.King who sailed as Maritime Gunners on Merchant ships.

Privates R.Carter and R.Snuggs and Lance Corporal H.Toyer from the 6th Bedfords, and Privates W.Fox and F.Spicer from the 1st Hertfords found themselves posted to the Camouflage and Deception centre and were posted to the Middle East and Burma.

Officers and NCOs were posted on attachment to Colonial Forces. These attachments were much sought after in peace time as a means of gaining wider experience. The Kings African Rifles and the Royal West African Frontier Force were two examples of these.

Second Lieutenants Fawsset and Medley of the 2nd Bedfords volunteered for service in East Africa and found themselves posted to the 1st Battalion The Northern Rhodesia regiment, which they joined in November 1940 serving in the Abyssinian and Burma Campaigns.

Other Bedfords in East Africa at the time were Captain Adrian Harris-Rivett, who was serving with the Somaliland Camel Corps, and Captain Geoffrey Warland serving with the KAR. Major Dennis Rossiter MBE, who left the 2nd Battalion from France in December 1939 to attend a course at the Staff College, was on the 'Operations' staff at Headquarters East Africa Command. Colonel Gerry Steele, who before the war had been the regular adjutant with the 1st Battalion The Hertfordshire Regiment was also serving on the staff.

Following the collapse of the Allied Military Forces in Europe in May and June 1940 and their withdrawal to the U.K. the concept of seaborne raiding was seen by Winston Churchill, and others, as a way of harassing the enemy and gathering intelligence.

This led to the formation of the Army Commandos. Twelve were to be raised each of five hundred all ranks. Number 10 Commando was to be formed from Allied troops. Each man was a volunteer, and NCOs reverted to the rank of Private on joining, and in some cases officers decided to drop rank in order to be accepted.

Unlike other units on 'Special Service' such as Airborne Forces, Commandos retained their parental connections, wore their own Regimental cap badge, and returned to their parent units when the Army Commandos were disbanded in 1946.

Recruiting started in June 1940 and those chosen from the 2nd Bedfords were posted to either Number 3 or Number 4 Commando. Later reinforcements came from the 70th Young Soldiers Battalion, The Hertfordshire Regiment and the Regimental Depot. When the Middle East Commandos were formed a few men joined from the 1st Bedfords. In all nearly three hundred 'Bedfords' volunteered for service with the Commandos. The story of some of them follows.

Brigadier Peter Young, DSO, MC**

Second Lieutenant Peter Young joined the Commandos in June 1940 after Dunkirk, taking part in his first raid on Guernsey in June 1940. He took part in further raids at Lofoten and Vassgo in 1941 and was awarded a bar to his MC. His action in harassing enemy coastal defence guns at Dieppe as a Captain earned the DSO. In 1943 as an acting major, second-in-command of Number 3 Commando, he was awarded a second bar to his MC for his part in the Sicily landings and actions in Italy. He took part in the battle to secure the Ponte dei Malati bridge where he led elements of No 1 Commando seizing the bridge in a rush from the surprised defenders. As the commanding officer of Number 3 Commando, he took part in the 'D' Day landings. He was posted to the Far East as a Colonel taking part in operations at Myebon and Akyab. He returned to the U.K in March 1945 to take command of Number 1 Commando Brigade.

Captain Paul Davies.
Served in Number 6 Commando as Adjutant.

Lieut J.Wilkinson. MM
Lieutenant Wilkinson joined Number 3 Commando from the 70th Young soldiers Battalion. He was awarded the MM for services in Italy as a Sergeant.

Sergeant T.Beckett.MM
Sergeant Beckett was a pre-war P.T.instructor in the 2nd Battalion who was recalled from the Reserve at the outbreak of war rejoining at the Depot. He volunteered for Commandos in late 1940 going to the Middle East with Number 7 Commando. He was in Crete when the island was overrun by the Germans and went into hiding in the hills. He helped the evacuation of many allied personnel, collecting them from scattered hide-outs and guiding them to prearranged rendezvous. He performed this role for a number of months and was awarded the MM. Once it was too dangerous for him to remain on the island because his Cretan helpers had been penetrated by the Germans, he was evacuated to Egypt.

Private F.Drain.
Private Drain was with the 2nd Bedfords at Dunkirk and volunteered for the Commandos in June 1940. He was one of the first casualties being taken prisoner on Guernsey on 14th July 1940. He survived the war and served as a Sergeant instructor at the Depot for some years until demobilization.

Lance Corporal P.Quinne
Lance Corporal Quinne was taken prisoner during a raid on Sicily but managed to escape and returned to Number 3 Commando. He was killed on 'D' Day when a shell hit his landing craft as it approached the beach. Another Bedford Archie Guest was killed at the same time, but Sergeant Leech who was in the same hold survived.

Lance Corporal B. Magnoni
Lance Corporal Magnoni served in Number 3 Commando and after the war changed his name to Max Diamond and formed the British Jousting Association. He is still jousting in his late sixties. A man larger than life who has dabbled in "Show Business" promoting Records, Pop Groups, and doubling for many well known stars as a stunt man. He wrote Charlie Drake's hit number 'My Boomerang won't come back'.

Sergeant R. Christopher, MM
Sergeant Christopher was batman/bodyguard to Peter Young in North Africa, Sicily, Italy, Normandy and the Far East. A first class athlete he played football for St Albans before the war.

Sergeant F. Darts. DCM
Sergeant Darts was the Bass Drum player in the 2nd Battalion Corps of Drums prior to the outbreak of war. One of the very few men of Number 3 Commando who reached land on the Dieppe Raid. Number 3 Commando was attacked afloat by German 'E' boats as they approached the coast. Sergeant Darts was in the boat commanded by Peter Young which made land. The men were able to harass the crew of a German Gun Battery by sniping and thus prevented them from firing unhindered on Canadian troops. He was awarded the DCM for bravery in action in Sicily.

Corporal M. McConville.
Corporal McConville was taken prisoner on his first raid. He transferred from Number 4 Commando to Number 7 Commando to go to the Middle East. He was captured in a raid on Bardia, when although the raiding party were put ashore on the wrong beach they reached their target which was an Italian barracks. The Italians made a hasty exit leaving the remains of a meal partly eaten in their dining room. The troop set fire to the barracks and a huge tyre dump. On returning to the beach there were no boats so McConville signalled to a passing boat. Landing craft are designed to carry thirty six men and this boat was already half full. The officer in charge would not bring the boat in close as another boat had already become beached. The men swam out to it. Leech got aboard and took McConville's tommy gun so he could climb aboard. By this time the boat was overloaded the officer refused to take any more men on. Those who were left behind were captured by the Germans the following day. After the war

McConville served as an officer in the Merchant Navy.

Company Sergeant Major J. Leech. MM*

Company Sergeant Major Leech was an original member of Number 4 Commando. He went out to the Middle East with Number 7 Commando and after service in Egypt, Palestine and Syria and the Desert rejoined Number 3 Commando in Tripoli. He took part with Number 3 Commando in the invasion of Sicily and Italy being awarded the MM for heroism in Italy prior to the invasion. On 'D' Day as a Sergeant he was left to command a platoon when his officer was wounded. Two days later he was wounded in the arm, but continued leading his men when all the other officers were killed or wounded. He was awarded a bar to the MM for this action. He was Company Sergeant Major at Number 1 Commando Brigade Headquarters at the time of disbandment of the Army Commandos.

The Higher Command decided that extra troops could be inserted at selected areas behind enemy lines by using gliders. Accordingly an Army Council Instruction in 1943 called for volunteers to be trained as glider pilots for this new form of transport. Once the glider had landed its cargo in enemy territory it was abandoned. The glider pilot himself became a part of the landing force and took an active role in the ground battle. This means of carrying large numbers of men was used in the invasion of Sicily, in North West Europe and in Burma. The airborne assault on Sicily has been written up in detail by Charles Whiting in *Slaughter over Sicily*. A pilot's description is provided by Tom McMillen, who had been with the Bedford anti-tank platoon in the 10th Infantry Brigade at Dunkirk, who now takes up the story.

" I was bored and frustrated as an instructor at 162 Officer Cadet Training Unit and volunteered immediately and was accepted as one of the first officers of the Glider Pilot Regiment. After training for one hundred hours on powered aircraft, Tiger Moths and Miles Magisters and subsequently on Hotspur and Horsa gliders I joined 2 Squadron of the Glider Pilot Regiment. The squadron went with 1 Parachute Brigade to North Africa to prepare for the invasion of Sicily. We started training on the American Hadrian gliders at Relizane in Algeria and then flew across the Atlas mountains to Sousse in Tunisia.

"The regiment took off for Sicily carrying elements of the Air Landing Brigade. The whole operation was a fiasco only being saved by the efforts of individual glider pilots and their passengers who landed, if they were lucky, indiscriminately all over Eastern Sicily. The American tug pilots had, until recently, been civil airline pilots and were reluctant to face enemy flak. They cast off many gliders way out to sea without their having a hope of reaching land. Out of my squadron of seventy seven gliders only eleven arrived in Sicily.

"I was lucky as my tug pilot, Captain Smith USAF, was brave, skilful and cooperative. Our communication consisted of a D3 cranked telephone set connected to the tug by a cable looped along the tow rope. By a miracle it continued to work throughout. When it got dark I asked Captain Smith to switch on his small station-keeping lights only to be told that they were already on. I used the occasional glimpse of the USAF star on the starboard wing to station-keep and cut out my windscreen front panel the better to see it. My tug pilot had no navigator but knew roughly the direction for Sicily. We were greatly relieved to see fountains of flak rising in the distance so we headed for it. It was a very dark night so Captain Smith took us up the coast to look for my Landing Zone (LZ) We flew through one flak barrage and then another one. Captain Smith said he thought the first was Syracuse and the second Catania but to make sure he flew back through them again. We still could not locate my LZ so Captain Smith said he should take me back to Malta. As there was a large fire burning on the ground I assumed that I had friends down there so I released the tow line and went to join them.

"My second pilot, Captain Bernard Hasall foolishly undid his safety harness to be able to lean forward to read the instruments. I remember him saying, 'Nought feet, eighty miles an hour', as our wheels tumbled to the ground and then we all blacked out. Fortunately I was flying a Hadrian which had a tubular steel frame so when we hit a tree head on the nose crumpled crushing my legs. When I came to, having found out Hasall had survived, I extricated my legs and hopped out on one leg. Captain Alec Dale, on to whose burning glider I had homed, dodged behind a tree when I came in which happened to be the one I struck.

"I was put on a folding bicycle propelled by a young RAMC private. Every time a mortar bomb landed he dived for the ditch leaving me to fall in a little further on! Eventually I found a forward regimental aid post from where I pointed my small command to their rendezvous and reluctantly left them. After repelling a couple of spirited Italian attacks against the Red Cross flag of the aid post I was eventually back loaded to a South African hospital in Tripoli.

"I was proudly one of the first Allied soldiers to set foot on the continent of Europe on the Second Front, and also one of the first glider pilot officers to be decorated. Bernard Hasall also got an MC for his action at the Syracuse bridge.

"Subsequently I also took part as a glider pilot in the invasions of Southern France and Greece without major incident. Finally I took part on the Rhine crossing. On this occasion I was flying a Horsa and was struck by enemy flak on the way down. This destroyed my starboard undercarriage and consequentially I lost my supply of compressed air which operated the flaps. I had built up considerable speed but could not slow down so had no option but to fly on past my LZ. Fortunately I had enough speed to lift us over a belt of trees and found a small clearing. I dived in to this, dug my starboard wing in to the ground thus swivelling us round and coming to a halt without casualty. As we were behind enemy lines we had to conduct a fighting withdrawal during which my second pilot, Sergeant Stephens, was killed."

So this story draws to an end. It is a tribute to every man who wore the Cap Badge of the Bedfordshire and Hertfordshire Regiment and the Hertfordshire Regiment. Not only those whose name has figured in the text but also the many others who remain anonymous. It is a tribute to their endurance.

The Bedfordshire and Hertfordshire Regiment amalgamated with The Essex Regiment in 1958 to become the 3rd East Anglian Regiment, later the 3rd Battalion The Royal Anglian Regiment.

The Royal Anglian Regiment has, since its formation served in a peace keeping role in Aden, Belize, Cyprus, Northern Ireland and presently in Bosnia. It has upheld NATO in Western Germany, and in Berlin, performing all the tasks required in an exemplary manner. The ties with the Counties and Old Comrades Associations hold firm. Old Comrades Branches remain active and there is strong support for 'Regimental' gatherings, and 'Remembrance Day' reunions.

The Royal Anglian Regiment Museum, to be opened at Duxford in 1995, depicts the links with the past. These links are the more important since the 3rd Battalion, which had close links with Bedfordshire, Hertfordshire and Essex, was disbanded in 1992 after three hundred and four years service to "The Crown".

The traditions founded on hundreds of years service, so proudly upheld in the years 1939 to 1946, are in good hands. The volunteer element is maintained through Territorial Battalions.

It is perhaps appropriate to end with a quotation.

"The British Infantryman's fame rests more on physical endurance, than on valour; aggressive attack on impulse and with dash is somehow alien to him"

Extracted from a German Intelligence Summary of Army Group 'C' in Italy.

The tales of valour in this story show, that as well as physical and moral endurance, the soldiers of the 16th Foot were by no means lacking in those attributes of aggressive attack on impulse and with dash. In the words of the Regimental Collect they were Truly Valiant.

GOD SAVE THE QUEEN

APPENDIX I

LIST OF MEN IN NO 3 SECTION,
16 PLATOON, "D" COMPANY

Private Scully recorded the names of soldiers he fought alongside during the Italian campaign, some of whom have been mentioned in the text. This personal list names soldiers in his section.

KILLED IN ACTION

Sergeant	LeFanu.	M.G. Fire	March 1944
		Cerasola Ridge	Buried – Naples
Corporal	Cox	M.G. Fire	March 1944
		Cerasola Ridge	Buried – Naples
Private	Filby	Mortar Bomb	May 1944
		Liri valley	Buried – Cassino
Private	Pendon	Schmeisser fire	May 1944
		Liri Valley	Buried – Cassino
Private	Henderson	Shell fire	July 1944
		Florence	Buried – Florence
Private	Vine	Stray bullet	July 1944
		Florence	Buried – Florence
Sergeant	Jones	Booby Traps	Oct 1944
		Bertinoro	Buried – Meldola
Private	Rance	Hand Grenade	Nov 1944
		Corsina Canal	Buried – Meldola

WOUNDED

Corporal	Punch	Cassino	May	1944
Private	Scully	Cassino	May	1944
		River Ausa	Sept	1944

SURVIVORS

Corporal Cyril Slater (Attained rank of Sergeant)
Private Evans (Old Bob) Demobbed 1946
Private Charlie Fright settled in Islington.
Of the men of Number 3 section six were killed and two wounded. This provides a grim reminder of what was happening throughout the Battalion.

APPENDIX II

CASUALTIES 1st BATTALION THE HERTFORDSHIRE REGIMENT (TA)

Killed in action and Died of wounds:

5961446	L/Cpl	Lucas, E.S.	6019241	Pte	Millar, J.F.
5989417	Cpl	Logsdail, T.G.	5952941	Cpl	Wiggins, H.J.
	Capt	Matthews, E.L.	14272865	Pte	Greensides, A.
5988740	Sgt	Bygraves, D.G.		Lieut	Firth, S.
1421387	Pte	Eldridge, R.	59896502	Pte	Butler, W.P
5956502	Pte	Starling, H.		Lieut	Atkinson, R.T.
	Capt	Foljambe, P.G.W.S.	5961151	Pte	Cockcroft, W.
14369105	Pte	Martin, R.W.	10600889	Pte	Giles, E.S.
5961372	Pte	Slough, L.	5118720	Cpl	Crouch, C.W.
5961066	Pte	Price, H.G.	5118765	Pte	Fisher, A.
5962218	Pte	Clarke, E.E	5989864	Pte	Davison, S.J.
5988740	Sgt	Bygraves, D.G.	583 7057	Pte	Bailey, J.
5958512	Pte	Davis, W.B.	5118750	L/Sgt	Dungey, F.H.
5956164	Pte	Thompson, R.E.	303258	Lieut	Clibbery, P.
5989688	Pte	Barton, A.A.	5955335	Cpl	Smith, G.J.
14262232	Pte	Boden, M.H.S.		Lieut	Hill, R.D.
5961556	Pte	Currie, J.	4346733	Pte	Jesney. T.
5837073	Pte	Johnstone, W.T.	5837403	Pte	Norton, G.F.
5989547	Pte	Simpson, G.W.	5837444	Pte	Unwin, J.W.
3965466	Pte	Harris, T.	5958417	A/Sgt	Averillo, E.W.
5962228	Pte	Rolph, E.J.		Major	Bone, G.
5988962	Pte	Haines, A.	5118787	Pte	Gaston, F.D.
5989709	L/Sgt	Whiting, L.B.	14288276	Pte	Keys, F.C.
5989105	Pte	Wallace, G.	5952778	Pte	Gray, R.F.
5949791	Cpl	Walsh, P.T.	5961595	Pte	Grindley, R.
5951234	Pte	Gardiner, A.W.	5192886	L/Cpl	Griffith, J.F.
5960370	A/Sgt	Branch, A.J.	5953468	Sgt	Allwright, C.J.
1766628	Pte	Hudspith, H.	5955782	L/Cpl	Crane, G.C.
5341979	Pte	Selby, A.E.	5955204	Pte	Baylis, R.L.C.
5951167	Pte	Jefford, C.J.	5341885	Cpl	Surridge, G.P.
5734161	Pte	March, R.	1077531	Pte	Brown, T.
5734362	Cpl	Cundy, J.L.	5952344	Cpl	Munro, T.H.
1719969	Pte	Griffiths, M.	5989228	Pte	Lee, W.J.
14214760	Cpl	Coles, F.	5989686	Cpl	Adams, T.F.
967217	Pte	Dickenson, C.V.			

Wounded:

No.	Rank	Name	No.	Rank	Name
5949711	Pte	Carr, K.	5959979	Pte	Kimpton, R.F.S.
5989704	Pte	Goddard, A.E.	5961441	Pte	Fletcher, E.R.
5784306	Pte	Giddins, J.	5956897	Cpl	Gleeson, M.
5837641	Pte	Hardwick, E.W.	6017786	Pte	Nurse, L.E.
5837344	Pte	Overton, G.L.	14227430	Pte	Purple, A.L.
5951578	L/Cpl	Taylor, J,	6291101	Pte	Thomas, S.C.
5961610	Pte	Thornhill, T.W.	5956486	Pte	Love, J.E.
5837057	Pte	Bailey, J.	5960129	Pte	Gaffing, G.R.
5958725	Pte	Spinks. G.E.	5784561	Pte	Sweeney, R.
5956403	Pte	Wilsher, E.	5837159	L/Cpl	Baxter, G.
5953470	Cpl	Barnett, T.W.	5989528	Pte	Cast, F.W.
5961580	Pte	Warburton, J.	5341950	L/Cpl	Scott, A.C.B.
5947678	Pte	Meech, D.P.	5950824	Pte	Christopher, W.J.
5961153	Pte	Gibson, W.L.	14227310	Pte	Knights, A.
5989999	Pte	Rowley, J.A.	14227421	Pte	Nash, G.K.
5989870	Pte	Shambrook, R.	5989077	CSM	Austin, C.C.
5836966	Pte	Abell, D.	5949665	Pte	Linnell, H.N.
5961162	Pte	Moores, T.	5947508	Sgt	Northwood, O.S.
5953681	Pte	Radnor, F.G.	5961017	Cpl	Walker, W.J.
5837194	Pte	Burgess, J.	5958436	Pte	Lyons, A.E.
	Major	Kenyon, G.V.		Lieut	Eames, L.
	Capt	Todd, A.T.	5961646	Pte	Briggs, E.
5956313	Pte	Langer, J.C.	5947966	Sgt	Wellerd, F.
5958417	L/Sgt	Averillo, E.W.	5961644	Pte	Bletcher, F.H.
5829724	Pte	Clench, E.S.C.	5952821	Pte	Cook, H.
1786374	Pte	Kelt, F.J.	5833821	Pte	Last. C.J.
5961578	L/Cpl	Taylor, J	14227424	Pte	Oakley, A.
5118742	Pte	Doidge, W.J.	5961373	L/Cpl	Fensome, F.S.
5989543	L/Cpl	Gardner, D.H.	5118790	L/Cpl	Gibson, A.C.W.
5837591	Pte	Le Beau, R.G.	5961449	L/Cpl	Newell, R.J.
5827482	Pte	Newman, R.L.P.	5961654	Pte	Quarterman, S.
5833872	Pte	Sherlock, P.R.	5954061	Cpl	Smith, L.C.H.
5989837	Pte	Gardiner, W.J.	5955562	Pte	Gibson, F.
5962162	Pte	James, F.	5961561	L/Cpl	Halton, N.
5962183	L/Cpl	Hudson, R.	5837384	Pte	Staff, P.S.
5961666	Pte S	ugo, E.	7918243	Pte	Murray, L.J.
5989988	L/Cpl	Marshall, F.	5961620	L/Cpl	Hopton, T.
5961910	Pte	Newton, G.W.	5837560	L/Cpl	Oakey, A.
593706	Pte	Emmott, W.	5961627	Pte	Saville, A.
	Major	Scales, W.E, DCM.	5954012	Cpl	Griffith, G.E.
5837507	L/Cpl	Leathers, R.W.	10580089	Pte	Pinckney, C.J.
5954376	Cpl	Busby, E.R.	5961166	Pte	Steadman, F.C.
5837520	Pte	Parish, H.A.	14227438	Pte	Shepherd, F.
5954893	Pte	Gardner, S.J.	5837518	Pte	Vince, C.A.
7954277	Pte	Alexander, E.	5118752	Pte	Edwards, W.J.
5837101	Pte	Jones, W.	5961567	Pte	Melia, A.
5957518	L/Sgt	Murphy, F.J.	5946854	Pte	Collett, L.
5962184	Pte	Johnston, A.E.	5833872	Pte	Sherlock, P.R.
5954356	Pte	Pettitt, G.H.	14555994	Pte	Massey, J.F.

5961314	Pte	Ball, R.	14217438	Pte	Pearce, E.H.
5961455	Pte	Tompkins, M.D.	5837654	Pte	Torr, H.
5989216	Cpl	Hayden, J.E.	5988883	Pte	Head, R.J.
5960485	Pte	Harrison, K.	5961200	Pte	Haynes, E.J.
5956651	Pte	Lovell, P	5959718	Pte	Sole, F.J.
5961386	Pte	Mills, W.	5961172	Pte	Ward, K.C.
1831372	Pte	Stiff, A.J.	14354489	Pte	Hayward, P.
5961436	Cpl	Chamberlain, N.L.			
5837494	Pte	Bloom, R.F.	14250586	Pte	Sharpe, H.G.N.
6026964	L/Cpl	Williams, W.	5959577	Pte	Acres, G.H.
5952830	Sgt	Collins, R.J.	5953615	Pte	Durbar, J.T.
5952902	Cpl	Rowe, V.W.	5989927	L/Sgt	Page, L.S.
5961968	Pte	Bates, R.B.	5784550	Pte	Horth, G.
5833612	Pte	Milton, F.C.	5342121	Pte	Payne, J.J.
5834835	L/Cpl	White, P.H.	5888541	Pte	Wint, H.
454863	Pte	Johnson, H.	5952809	Cpl	Lewis, V.R.
5961652	Pte	Hardy, H.	5342159	Pte	Oliver, G.E.
5955055	Pte	Gargett, D.	5955262	Pte	Haman, R.G.
5988945	Pte	Haines, S.A.	5961211	Pte	Crouch, B.T.
5836982	Pte	Bridger, A.E.	5961666	Pte	Sugo, E.
5956486	Pte	Love, J.E.	5962190	L/Cpl	Naldrett, R.W.
5961572	Pte	Rimmer, T.H.	5954374	Pte	Buck, P.J.
5950035	Cpl	Shotbolt, R.J.W.	5954260	A/Cpl	Young, A.J.
5960158	Pte	Meinertzhagen, G.E.			
5961612	Pte	Vince, R.	14215743	L/Cpl	Smith, M.
5989945	Pte	Youngs, A.	14227424	Pte	Oakley, A.
5833710	Pte	Femsom, T.J.	14215672	Pte	Deamer, F.G.
5962162	Pte	James, F.	14227307	Pte	Hall, R.W.F.
5837466	Pte	Mann, N.A.	5961554	Pte	Armitage, A.
5953556	Pte	Goldsmith, K.C.	5961412	Pte	Harper, G.B.
5953496	Pte	New, S.	5959678	Pte	Marriot, E.G.
5954239	Sgt	Oliver, J.L.	5951570	Cpl	Nicolson, A.
5961157	Pte	Howard, W.S.	5954079	Pte	White, R
5961368	A/Cpl	Arnold, T.	5837427	Pte	Gardiner, A.W.
5961403	Pte	Chainey, B.W.	14217302	Pte	Longthorn, J.
5837650	Pte	Pepper, D.C.	5961665	Pte	Smith, A.J.
5837582	L/Sgt	Gibb, H.V.R.	5947786	Pte	Clarke, A.C.
878303	Pte	Bowen, E.	5836982	Pte	Bridger, A.E.
5837180	Pte	Halls, J.	5955278	Pte	Izzard, F.L.
5952506	Pte	Essam, N.C.	5961653	Pte	Gosling, S.
5954031	Pte	Mellish, L.V.	5988879	Sgt	Game, D.
2653196	RSM	Robinson, G.	5953534	Pte	Roberts, L.D.
5955309	Pte	Pedlar, R.F.	14227412	Pte	Levy, W.
5962174	L/Cpl	Cleverly, H.T.	1588762	Pte	Dysart, W.
5837063	Pte	Emmett, W.	5957220	Pte	Cocklin, C.
5961421	Pte	Turney, T.	5950406	Sgt	Cracknell, F.E.S.
5961444	Pte	Jones, R.R.	5989765	Cpl	Mowbray, R.K.
5954234	Pte	Lythaby, J.	5950663	L/Cpl	Hill, E.H.
5735350	Cpl	Gess, R.	14227414	Pte	Mann, E.
5727811	Cpl	Miles, R.	14227410	Pte	Mickelsen, D.
245757	Lieut	Tait, D.	14281048	Pte	Hollingworth, A.
5731075	Pte	Kirschenbaum, S.	900261	Pte	Anderson, W.A.

909265	Pte	Goodwin, J.	14583631	Pte	Jones, J.
5837440	Pte	Self, J.G.	288248	Lieut	Sutton, P.G.F.
5833710	L/Cpl	Fensome, F.J.	5988788	Pte	Gray, G.G.
6012770	Pte	Law, W.	14359583	Pte	Salmon, V.H.
5831115	L/Cpl	Jarred, E.	5254384	Pte	Righton, E.
5344181	Pte	Biggs, J.H.	5961611	L/Cpl	Twist, J.
5989876	Pte	Barber, A.J.A.	14746624	Pte	Hamlett, H.
6024411	Sgt	Reed, W.J.	14547101	Pte	Stevens, A.E.
5961379	Pte	Hall, J.W.	5961386	Pte	Mills, W.

Missing:

	Lieut	Young, L.W.	5956301	Pte	Hartwell, B.C.
5837595	Pte	McFarlane, C.H.		Capt	Currin, R.A.
6017778	L/Sgt	Williams, V.	5961192	Cpl	Moody, D.
5955064	Pte	Bradford, J.N.	5972987	Pte	Dorsett, W.F.
5833936	Pte	Goodyear, C.	5837585	Pte	Gregory, H.
5956013	Pte	Grugeon, A.E.	6017759	Pte	Harrington, M.
5734368	Pte	Leavy, T.	14284336	Pte	Paterson, E.
6293182	Pte	Pook, F.J.	5961638	Pte	Woodcock, C.V.
5837518	Pte	Vince, C.A.		Lieut	Jackson, R.
6024325	Sgt	Goodfellow, J.R.	5831280	Pte	Hanchett, D.J.
5837732	Pte	Rush, F.J.	5837646	Pte	Law, S.J.
7954935	Pte	Youles, J.	7959641	Pte	Loveridge. W.
5990058	Pte	Thurgood, E.W.	14217368	Pte	McLaughlin, L.
5837159	L/Cpl	Baxter, G.	14241333	L/Cpl	Green, R.J.
5961410	Pte	Meadows, E.E.	14216688	Pte	Luya, R.J.
5837615	Pte	Webster, N.E.	5962193	Cpl	Prescott, R.V.
5837163	Pte	Collins, G.F.	5953598	Pte	Cook, F.
6017776	Pte	Wheeler, G.K.	5948383	Pte	Cooper, A.G.
5961391	Pte	Shorten, J.V.	5836833	Pte	Bendall, S.C.
3384630	Pte	Harrison, J.	5962222	L/Cpl	Emery, A.
5952838	L/Cpl	Parker, W.T.	5953892	Pte	Lucas, S.A.
5949592	Pte	Price, H.G.	5962194	Pte	Salmon, S.T.
5961012	Pte	Robinson, E.E.	5832734	A/Sgt	Norman, T.
5961591	Pte	Cunliffe, W.E.	5837589	Pte	Jenkins, J.A.
5953615	Pte	Durber, J.F.	14588542	Pte	Winfindale, J.

APPENDIX III

LETTER FROM FIELD MARSHAL
MONTGOMERY TO THE COMMANDER

CONFIDENTIAL.

21AGp/1059/C-in-C.

TAC HEADQUARTERS,
21 ARMY GROUP,
No. 1 APDC,
LONDON, W.1.

11 July, 1944.

Dear Harper

      By the end of this month we shall be running short of infantry reinforcements and there are not sufficient in sight for some time to come. At the same time the battle will have reached a crucial phase during which it will be essential to keep the battalions in the divisions up to strength.

      No one is more fully aware than I of the magnitude of the contribution made by you and the officers and men under your command to the success of this operation, or of the outstanding efforts which you and they have made during training. It is therefore with the very greatest regret that I have had to decide that, when the time comes, drafts shall be taken from the battalion under your command to make good deficiencies in divisional units.

      I have given orders that in carrying out this drafting every regard, possible in the circumstances, shall be paid to regimental affiliations and that, where possible, officers and men will be posted together to units in parties approximating to a platoon in size. In effecting this you will be consulted.

      Please convey to all your officers and men my thanks for the splendid work which they performed during the assault and in the days which followed and my regret at the necessity for having to draft so many from your battalion.

Yrs. sincerely,

B. L. Montgomery.

Lt-Col. J.R. Harper,
O.C., 2 Herts.

APPENDIX IV

NUMBER 9 BEACH GROUP

Headquarters:

Commander	Lt Colonel J.R.Harper
Second in Command	Major P.J. Chambers
Staff Captain	Captain A.G.Scott-Joynt
Staff Captain (Camouflage)	Captain D.L.Dick, R.E.
Intelligence Officer	Captain J.D.Cuthbertson
M.L.O.	Major Marshall
A.M.L.O.	Captain G.H.Hum, R.E.
A.M.L.O.	Captain G.E.L.Manley, R.E.

INFANTRY ELEMENT – 2nd Battalion
The Hertfordshire Regiment.

Commanding Officer	Lt Colonel J.R.Harper
Second in Command	Major P.J.Chambers
Adjutant	Captain H.Martell
Intelligence Officer	Captain J.D.Cuthbertson

"A" Company and "B" Company

		"A" Company		"B" Company
O.C.	Major	W.R.Nichols	Major	H.C. Allen
2 i.c	Captain	G.R.Pack	Captain	R.D.Cleare
Pl Comd	Lieut	A.G.Sindall	Lieut	R.P.Wassell
Pl Comd	Lieut	R.J.Hingston	Lieut	F.A.E.Bonney
Pl Comd	2nd Lieut	D.J.Webber	Lieut	A.W.Eyre

"C" Company and "D" Company

		"C" Company		"D" Company
O.C.	Major	D.C.Slemeck	Major	I.W.S.Grey
2 i.c	Captain	J.F.Fripp	Captain	D.C.Franklin
Pl Comd	Lieut	A.S.Cranston	Lieut	D.C.Franklin
Pl Comd	Lieut	R.B.Broadbent	Lieut	C.W.Moxham
Pl Comd	Lieut	R.B.Morley	2nd Lieut	Middlebrook

"H" Company

O.C.	Captain	H.C.Weatherill	Signals	Lieut	C.E.Marvin
Q.M.	Lieut	(QM) S.A.Ames	M.T.O	Lieut	R.H.Smith
M.O.	Lieut	J.Maughan	Chaplain	Capt	J.Scott
		R.A.M.C.			R.A.Ch.D.

"S" Company

O.C.   Captain R.G.Newell

Mortars   Lieut   B.F.Power   Pioneers   Lieut   G.N.Wise

Carrier Platoon

O.C.   Lieut   D.B.Waterhouse   2 i.c   Lieut   D. O'Brian.

Anti-tank Platoon.

O.C.   Captain   H.L Hodson   2 i.c   Lieut   R.J.G.Duns

APPENDIX V

5th BATTALION THE BEDFORDSHIRE AND HERTFORDSHIRE REGIMENT (TA)

LIST OF CASUALTIES

Killed in Action – Singapore Island February 1942

13th February

Capt S.H.Thrussell	Lieut.	D.B.Jackson	
5953071	Pte	Harris.L.	5955612. Pte Jones.D.J.

14th February

	Major	T.C.Wells		Lieut	W.E.Thewles
	2/Lt	G.W.Star	5950688	Pte	Austin.A.J.
5952756	CQMS	Bagshaw.H.	5947372	L/Sgt	Collingridge. R.
5953030	Pte	Coombs.S.	5953037	Pte	Darch.A.
5950521	Pte	Davis.F	5956263	Pte	Dean.C.
5955554	Pte	Ford.L	5954689	Pte	Lawrence.V.A.
5944175	Pte	Whitbread. H.J.	5955678	Pte	Winup.T.
5956407	Cpl	Young.R.			

15th February

5949374	Pte	Billings.E.M.	5952642	Pte	Brightman. A.C.
5950602	Pte	Fulford.E.J.	5945933	Pte	Rolf.E.S.
5946540	Pte	Thurston.A.J.			

Died of Wounds Sustained in Action – Singapore Island

5949518	Pte	Blount.E.O.B.	5956226	Pte	Bloxham.J.A.
5956619	Pte	Denton.A.M.	5951315	Cpl	Hollyee.A.F.
5952623	Cpl	Lay.W.	5952010	Pte	Rackley.E.A.C.
5952018	Pte	Stokes.F.			

Wounded in Action – Presumed Dead

	2/Lt	F.Hall	59555788	Pte	Haysman.D.
2060055	Pte	Jones.A.S.	955070	Pte	Wilson.H.
5952926	Pte	Gilchrist.D.J.			

6024272	Pte	Chammings.G.H.F.	5951044	Pte	Dunham.O.C.
5949152	Pte	Farmer.A.E.	5950973	Pte	Foley.H.C.
5955273	Pte	Howard.A.L.	5953090	Pte	Irons.W.C.
5947770	Pte	Quantrell.W.	5947983	Sgt	Thompson.W.H.
5952667	Pte	Walker.G.W.			

Escaped from Singapore, Subsequently missing in action in Sumatra

Capt H.F.L.Sladen

Died in Captivity
Thailand

5950225	Sgt	Ainsworth.F.E.	5952585	Pte	Angell.D.M.
5956214	Pte	Auger.D.H.	5951963	L/Cpl	Avey. E.L.
2210825	Pte	Ball.K.O.	5956170	Pte	Bamsey.E.
5953335	Cpl	Bardell.A.H.	5949335	Pte	Barker.F.A.
5945846	Pte	Barnard.F.C.	5951312	Pte	Bartlett.A.
5858718	Pte	Beadle.J.	5952687	Pte	Bell.A.H.
5953195	Pte	Biggs.R.D.	5955497	Pte	Bilner.R.J.
5952296	Pte	Birch.C.A.	5956345	Sgt	Bloss.G.
5952598	Pte	Blyth.R.	5953930	Pte	Bonathon.H.
5952560	Pte	Bond.J.	5955505	Pte	Bone.F.
5956240	Pte	Bozier.W.D.	5959184	Pte	Brant.A. J.
5956235	Pte	Bray.F.J.	5956849	Pte	Braysher.A.
5952603	Pte	Bruce.A.	5951789	Pte	Burch.J.O.R.
5951958	Pte	Burnage.S.G.	5952703	Pte	Burns.W.P.
5956256	Pte	Cannon.H.M.	5952707	Pte	Carruthers.L.G.
5955750	Pte	Catlin.H.A.	5953028	Pte	Chambers.A.E.
5951349	Pte	Cherry.D.F.	5950198	Pte	Clark.F.W.H.
5950056	Pte	Clark.H.C.	5950308	Pte	Clark.C.
5956259	Pte	Clark.S.M.	5956248	Pte	Clark.B.J.
5953824	Pte	Clews.C.	5953025	Cpl	Coath.R.F.
5953027	Pte	Cobbald.G.A.	5955776	Pte	Collier.J.
5955777	Pte	Collins.L.J.	5950460	Pte	Cook.A.
6004971	Pte	Cox.H.W.	5951976	Pte	Cox.R.J.
5950719	Pte	Crane.L.K.	5953036	Pte	Daly.D.
5956265	Pte	Davies.A.	5958868	Pte	Dawson.F.C.
5950976	Pte	Dawson.S.A.	5951061	Pte	Day.W.J.
5949633	Cpl	Deacon.R.W.	5951350	Pte	deacon.W.
5955532	Pte	Denny.D.	5955535	Pte	Devonshire.C.S.
5950552	Pte	Dudley.F.W.	5955547	Pte	Fagg.W.H.
5956269	Pte	Farnham.H.J.	5953050	Pte	Farrington.E.L.
5953051	Pte	Faughnan.F.	5952198	Pte	Fellows.R.F.
5955321	Pte	Fensome.C.	5955557	Pte	Free.L.
5956273	Pte	Freeman.P.J.	5956968	Pte	Freeman.J.
5953052	Pte	Finegan.L.	5951092	Pte	Fisher.H.J.
5953055	Pte	Franklin.J.D.	5951987	Pte	Game.J.W.
5955559	Pte	Geary.L.	5953058	Pte	Geeves.H.F.
595561	Pte	Gibbs.H.	5956283	Pte	Gomme.J.H.
5950172	Pte	Gooch.G.S.	5950332	Pte	Goode.L.F.

595564	Pte	Goode.L.G.	5960329	Pte	Goody.R.
5945810	Cpl	Goodwin.C.W.	5951369	Pte	Grace.A.C.H.
5951682	L/Cpl	Gray.R.F.	5951376	Pte	Gurney.F.
595570	Pte	Gurney.L.	5953065	Pte	Hall.S.J.
5951991	Pte	Harpur.R.A.	5950327	Pte	Harris, W.C.
5950975	Pte	Harvey.C.	5950612	Pte	Harwood.R.W.
5952464	Pte	Haughton.D.B.	5950421	Cpl	Hawes.H.E.
5945674	L/Cpl	Hillson.J.T.H.	5951385	Pte	Hillyard.S.
5955585	Pte	Holden.J.	5951387	Pte	Hollier.C.
5959068	Pte	Holliman.E.C.	5949698	L/Cpl	Hornsby.L.C.
5956291	Pte	Hull.J.	5951388	Pte	Humphrey. F.W.J.
5951891	Pte	Hummerstone B.W.	5955609	Pte	Janes.A.W.
5951998	Pte	Jenkins.E.C.	5950957	Pte	Johnson.A.
5953644	Pte	Jones.A.	5953098	Pte	Keirle.R.
5955624	Pte	Kirby.M.	5955139	Pte	Knight.D.F.
5949684	Pte	Lane.A.G.	5952653	Pte	Lane.C.T.
5946227	Sgt	Langston.F.	5950136	Pte	Large.G.
5952341	Sgt	Larman.C.E.	5953106	Pte	Lee.T.J.
5952004	Cpl	Lewin.J.	5950012	Pte	Loss.H.
5955490	Pte	Maddams.P.	5950951	Pte	Mannall.A.L.
5959250	Pte	Marks.G.	5950987	Pte	Martin.L.
5959684	Pte	Mills.H.	5955144	Pte	Milton.H.W.
5950944	Pte	Moorby.A.C.	5953706	Pte	Morris.L.C.
5951398	Pte	Nash.J.	5959689	Pte	Newell.E.H.
5953124	Pte	Norton.T.W.	5950607	Pte	O'Connor.P.
5947386	Sgt	Owen.L.	5952654	Pte	Page.A.C.
5951254	Pte	Parker.V.G.	5950109	L/Sgt	Parrott.L.J.
5953129	Pte	Patterson.K.	5952345	Pte	Payne.J.
5951407	L/Sgt	Perryman.E.	5949064	Pte	Pettit.E.J.
5950016	Pte	Phair.S.A.	5953131	Pte	Phillips.K.W.
5946267	Pte	Phillipson.H.	5955317	Pte	Pope.D.G.
5956691	Pte	Priestley.H.	5950155	Pte	Pupplett.R.
2201226	Pte	Purser.F.A.E.	5950736	Sgt	Pycock.A.L.
5950023	L/Cpl	Quenby.R.	5952550	Pte	Rayment.H.E.
5950954	Pte	Roberts.J.W.G.	5947992	Pte	Robinson.F.J.
5951409	L/Cpl	Robinson.W.	5950175	Cpl	Rogers.N.C.O.
5956449	Pte	Rowe.A.J.	5951943	Pte	Saunders.C.
329890	Pte	Scholes.J.	5951961	Pte	Scrutton.G.F.
5955850	Pte	Sear.J.T.	5955351	Pte	Searle.J.D.
5944178	Pte	Slingo.F.E.	5953160	L/Cpl	Smith.R.C.S.
6024448	Pte	Smith.W.	5952950	Pte	Smith.J.W.
5953159	Pte	Smith.H.C.	5951935	Pte	Smith. J.
5951937	Pte	Smy.W.G.	5951415	Pte	Spavins.R.E.
5955748	Pte	Stephenson.C.	5952285	Pte	Stonton.F.E.
5952263	Cpl	Thody.J.T.	5951723	Pte	Timpson.R.J.
5960212	Pte	Tobin.J.F.	5953172	Pte	Turney.E.
5959118	Pte	Varney.W.	5950170	Pte	Watts.T.G.
5953180	Pte	Wheatley.J.W.	5952635	Pte	White.W.
5952577	Pte	White.S.	5951416	Pte	Whitehead. S.G.R.

5953184	Pte	Wickens.C.	5955651	Pte	Wilder.J.G.
5951421	Pte	Wildman.A.	5950044	Pte	Wiles.E.C.
5956749	Pte	Willoughby.A.W.	5955661	Pte	Williams.R.E.
5955659	Pte	Williams.G.	5952302	Pte	Williams.A.
5955656	Pte	Willett.A.D.	5952669	Pte	Wilson.G.E.P.
5946198	Sgt	Wood.A.	5950048	Sgt	Wright.A.G.
5947588	Pte	Wright.R.A.V.	5955705	Pte	Yirrell.B.R.
5953194	Pte	Young.O.A.	5952672	Cpl	York.D.L.G.

Burma

5951341	L/Cpl	Bacon.R.J.	5953207	Pte	Chambers.D.
5951265	Pte	Clark.S.	5950135	Pte	Cook.A.F.
5949272	Pte	Cox.C.A.	5951125	L/Cpl	Evinson.H.T.
5960359	Pte	Fortnum.R.E.	5956297	Pte	Hall.C.
5950043	Pte	Hamblin.F.J.	5951383	L/Sgt	Hayday.T.V.A.
5951380	Pte	Higgins.S.	1733854	Pte	Hinks.J.
5948816	L/Sgt	Jacobs.H.A.	5950166	L/Cpl	Knight.D.E.
5952002	Pte	Law.J.F.	5955460	Pte	Mean.L.
5950941	Pte	Monk.A.F.			

Singapore

5950218	Pte	Barker.F.H.	5952710	Pte	Diprose.P.D.
5955560	Cpl	George.W.F.	5950468	Pte	Onione.F.
5950117	Pte	Rainbird.L.	5951256	Pte	Wingfield.W.E.
5959743	Pte	Young.B.			

Formosa

5951657	Pte	Bannister.A.	5946549	L/Cpl	Crisford.W.
5945841	Pte	Fishpool.L.H.	5945090	L/Sgt	Flemming.S.
5956310	Pte	Kempster.C.	5953154	Pte	See.A.H.

Japan

5950368	Pte	Bivans.R.S.	5951917	Pte	Brace.H.
5955778	Pte	Collison.D.J.	5950575	Pte	Humphries.A.
50949245	Pte	Ingram.R.W.	5951392	L/Cpl	Knight.A.E.
5949709	Pte	Savage.J.H.	5955695	Pte	Worster.F.H.

Sumatra

5952618	Pte	Cousins.J.

Manila

5955631	Pte	Leach.W.L.	5989149	Pte	Rolph.D.F.
5955682	Pte	Winter.H.W.			

Presumed drowned in captivity
Men of No II Group on board SS Hofoku Maru sunk 21 Sept, 1944

5951842	Pte	Angell.L.	5950134	Pte	Bambridge.A.S.
5952179	Pte	Burns.T.A.	5951972	Pte	Calleweart.A.
5952182	Pte	Cato.F.	5956862	Pte	Catterall.A.
5952645	Pte	Catterall.J.	5952722	Pte	Cawthorn.M.
5955761	Pte	Chamberlain.E.J.	5955225	Pte	Chorlton.G.S.
5953024	Pte	Clark.J.H.	5956613	Pte	Cooper.S.G.
5953032	Pte	Cox.R.H.	5951900	Pte	Crawley.A.E.
5950551	Pte	Dimmock.F.J.	5955494	Pte	Dines.A.E.
5953045	Pte	Edwards.F.	5951983	Pte	Emerton.J.
5951363	Pte	Evans.S.	5951112	Cpl	Gayler.E.F.
5950591	Pte	Gilfillan.A.	5950230	Pte	Hall.R.W.
5956299	Pte	Hand.W.	5950453	Pte	Hanlon.P.
5949809	Pte	Healey.T.	5951830	Pte	High.H.W.S.
5951955	Cpl	Hornett.J.B.	5955606	Pte	Ives.R.H.
5956643	Pte	Jarvis.R.	5952942	L/Sgt	Johnson.A.C.F.
5950118	Cpl	Karmy.J.J.	5951726	Pte	Lawrence.G.
5952003	Pte	Lawrence.R.C.	5955634	Pte	Lemmon.D.J.W.
5951396	Pte	MacDonald.A.	5942925	Pte	Mayne.F.
5951754	Pte	McCue.B.	5952006	L/Cpl	Norman.H.G.
5953125	Pte	Nugent.E.	5949716	Cpl	Odell.E.
5951403	Pte	Peasnall.W.	5950095	Pte	Perry M.A.
5950318	Pte	Plum.A.G.H.J.	5950196	Pte	Prior.J.G.
5956692	Pte	Rabone.T.W.	5952012	Pte	Richardson.W.
5951056	Pte	Sullivan.T.A.	5946692	Sgt	Welham.R.E.
5953196	Pte	Wiley.S.	5951422	Cpl	Wilton.L.
5946307	Sgt	Wright.W.			

Men of IV Group on board SS Rakuyo Maru sunk 12 Sept 1944

5950963	Pte	Absom.J.W.	5950867	Pte	Carter.J.D.H.
5950050	Pte	Cockburn.W.	5952616	Pte	Cole.W.H.
5951977	Pte	Craxford.W.G.	5950980	Pte	Cross.A.E.
5950041	Pte	Donavon.P.	5956262	Pte	Dunbabin.J.
5955645	Pte	Floyd.J.	5956270	Pte	Fuller.A.
5950488	Cpl	Gray.R.	5953352	Cpl	Green.C.
5959900	Pte	Leaney.J.	5951384	Cpl	Hedley.J.
5949464	Pte	MacGregor.J.A.	5950730	Pte	Mapley.J.W.
5953113	Pte	Martin.P.R.	5947537	Pte	Perkins.F.W.
5948397	Cpl	Robinson.E.A.	5956377	L/Cpl	Smith.E.J.
5952485	Cpl	Sell.W.F.	5953170	Pte	Tomlinson.F.
5955166	Pte	Willsher.T.H.			

Men of IV Group on board SS President Harrison sunk 11 Sept 1944

5951821	L/Cpl	Biggs.E.C.	5951971	Pte	Bush.J.
5951193	L/Cpl	Clark.R.	5956609	Pte	Cole.E.
5951123	Pte	Crawley.L.G.	5959739	Pte	Fairman.B.
5949707	Pte	Gardner.J.T.	5951764	Pte	Hale.F.G.
5956982	Pte	Hewitt.H.	5949582	Pte	Izzard.C.W.

5953093	Pte	Jackson.H.	2217764	Sgt	Lett.A.
5822243	Pte	Mumford.S.C.	5946061	CQMS	Richardson.S.J.
5950343	Pte	Taylor.R.	5346830	Pte	Wade.R.J.
5955679	Pte	Winstanley.J.			
5952518	Pte	Crawlet.F.W.	5956293	Pte	Hayes.P.

APPENDIX VI

BEDFORDS WHO SERVED IN
THE ARMY COMMANDOS

The number in brackets denotes the Army Commando/s, + = MM,
* = Killed in Action, HOC – Holding Operation Commando
Wrexham, CBTC – Commando Basic Training Centre,
STC – Submarine Training Centre.

5958457	Pte	Abrahams.C.	(3)	5949273	Pte	Abrahams.A.	(7)
5958160	Pte	Abrahams.W.	(3)	14734834	Pte	Adams.H.	(3)
4974035	Pte	Adderton.V.	(3)+	14879827	Pte	Albon.C.	(3)
5950968	Pte	Alldis.F.	(1)	5886090	Pte	Allen.R.	(3)
5947997	Pte	Allen.R.	(2)	14854465	Pte	Austen.C.	(HOC)
5989153	L/Cpl	Austwich.J.	(2)	5385086	Pte	Bailey.W.	(5)
5951072	L/Cpl	Bandey.R.	(4)	5956234	Pte	Barbour.A.	(3)
14868825	Pte	Bardell.	(3)	14429630	Pte	Barrett.D.	(3)
4453609	L/Cpl	Bates.R.	(2)	5947282	Cpl	Beale.W.	(3 & 7)
5958171	Sgt	Beckett.T.	(3 & 7)+	5954421	Cpl	Benham.D.	(3 & 7)
5949755	Pte	Bennett.G.	(3)	14241728	Pte	Bidwell.	(3)
5950712	Cpl	Bird.B.	(2)	14643796	Pte	Bird.E.	(HOC)
5958184	Pte	Blackman.T.	(4)	4105149	Pte	Bolton.D.	(1)
2049398	Cpl	Booklees.D.	(3)	5958865	Pte	Bowen.J.	(2)
5956867	Pte	Bowman.L.	(2)	5949794	Pte	Bowyer.S.	(3 & 4)
59524076	Pte	Boyce.J.	(3)	14812025	Pte	Boyden.R.	(HOC)
5956518	Pte	Bradbury.T.	(3)	5951445	Pte	Breaverman.S.	(3)
5948422	Pte	Brooks.E.	(3)	5959037	Pte	Brown.W.	(STC)
5989540	Sgt	Bruce.J.	(2)	5949323	L/Cpl	Bygrave.E.	(2)
5858258	Pte	Campbell.N.	(2)	14436414	Pte	Campbell.N.	(2)
5952606	Pte	Campbell.H.	(6)	5952606	Pte	Carnell.H.	(3 & 7)
14734810	Pte	Casewell.R.	(6)	5948494	Cpl	Cate.R.	(1)
5946494	Pte	Cato.R.	(2)	5954316	Pte	Chambers.T.	(3)
5958207	Pte	Chapman.K.	(3)+	5989548	Pte	Child.K.	(3)
5990123	Sgt	Christopher.	(3)+	5948690	L/Cpl	Clark.A.	(3)
5962427	Pte	Clark.L.	(3)	5989664	Cpl	Clarke.S.	(3)+
5930512	Pte	Cockman.W.	(3)	5855773	L/Cpl	Coggins	(3 & 7)
5953029	Pte	Colgrove.	(7)	5951266	Pte	Collins.D.	(2)
5989748	Cpl	Collins.E.	(2)	5948386	L/Cpl	Cooper.H.	(7)
5947825	Cpl	Cooper.H.	(3)	5959026	Pte	Cooper.C.	(2)
5950061	Pte	Cox.C.	(7)	5958303	Pte	Cracknell.L.	(CBTC)
5950610	L/Cpl	Craft.A.	(3)+*	5885281	Pte	Creswell.D.	(3)

5947714	Sgt	Crew, J.	(4 & 7)		5956553	Cpl	Crowden.D.	(5)
5990088	Pte	Culshaw.V.	(2)		5949811	Pte	Curran.P.	(3)
594——	Sgt	Dean.G.	(5)		5953035	Pte	Dale.J.	(4)
5949117	L/Sgt	Dart.F.	(3)+		5051021	Pte	Dawson.H.	(2)
14756324	Pte	Deeman.D.	(6)		5885246	Sgt	Dix.J. (3)	
4104895	Pte	Dobbs.R.	(1)		5948105	Pte	Donovan.J.	(3)
595——	Pte	Drain.F.	(3)		5948538	L/Cpl	Drain.P.	(3)
14756258	Pte	Dudley.R.	(6)		5949213	Cpl	Easton.J.	(4)
5950653	L/Cpl	Eaton.F.	(2)		5958979	L/Sgt	Edwards.R.	(3)
5946317	L/Cpl	Edwards.S.	(3)		5947514	Cpl	Elwood.C.	(4)
4026838	Cpl	Evans.E.	(1)		5957221	L/Cpl	Farnborough.	(4)
5953050	Pte	Farrington.	(7 & 4)		14558054	Pte	Fennessey.I.	(3)
14592817	L/Cpl	Filby.R.	(3)		5958817	Pte	Flecknall.F.	(3)
5952887	Pte	Fleckney.H.	(2)		14489907	Pte	Florence.A.	(HOC)
5948655	Pte	Flynn.D.	(9)		5958550	Cpl	Francis.C.	(3)
5989934	Sgt	Freeman.V.	(2)		5951584	L/Cpl	French.S.	(2)
5959060	Pte	Furness.C.	(STC)		5957857	Sgt	Gadsby.J.	(STC)
5950657	Sgt	Gambriel.S.	(6)		799237	Pte	Gardner.J.	(1)
5775175	L/Cpl	Garwood.E.	(1)		5945661	L/Sgt	Gibbs.A.	(2)
14868773	Pte	Gibbs.W.	(HOC)		5958784	Pte	Gibson.P.	(3)
5956288	Pte	Gilbertson.	(3)		5957538	Pte	Gill.J.	(3)
5946830	CSM	Gimbert.J.	(3)		5951329	Pte	Green.F.	(3)
5952209	Cpl	Gregory.W.	(3)		5959802	Pte	Grey.R.	(CBTC)
5949085	L/Cpl	Grief.G.	(2)		3962016	Pte	Griffiths.T.	(1)
14205785	Pte	Guest.A.	(3)*		4684695	Pte	Hall.F.	(2)
5954903	Pte	Hall.W.	(6)		5946926	Sgt	Hamblin.S.	(4)
5990064	L/Sgt	Hancock.R.	(3)		14591917	Pte	Hancock.H.	(3)
5950794	Pte	Hanlon.D.	(2)		5950275	Pte	Harding.J.	(2)
5888628	Pte	Hargreaves.	(STC)		5990060	Pte	Harman.J.	(3)
5946275	Pte	Harris.S.	(3)		5954087	Cpl	Haydon.A.	(3)
5951098	Pte	Head.P.	(3)		5947229	Pte	Heyman.	(3)
5118848	Pte	Hill.H.	(3)		5953856	L/Cpl	Hill.S.	(2)
5953566	L/Sgt	Hines.E.	(2)		5952216	L/Sgt	Hiscock.G.	(2)
5946959	L/Cpl	Hobson.	(3)		5959068	Pte	Holliman.E.	(STC)
4036113	Pte	Holloway.C.	(1)		5949596	L/Cpl	Holloway.V.	(4)
6024341	Pte	Hope.J.	(2)		5948301	Cpl	Hopkins.F.	(3)+
5948229	L/Sgt	Horne.G.	(4)		5951439	Pte	Howard.G.	(7)
14571346	Pte	Howard.K.	(3)		6010576	L/Sgt	Hughes.C.	(3)*
5952786	Cpl	Hume.W.	(6)		14951851	Pte	Hutchinson.D.	(HOC)
5957598	Pte	Ingram.C.	(STC)		14762965	Pte	Jackson.R.	(6)
5957044	Pte	James.E.	(3)		14646696	Pte	James.A.	(3)
14868812	Pte	Jarvis.C.	(3)		4105449	Pte	Jenkins.E.	(1)
5958758	Cpl	Jennings.T.	(3 & 2)		5960150	Pte	Jeyes.F.	(2)
5955043	Pte	Jones.T.	(3)		5957106	Pte	Jones.W.	(3)
5958432	Pte	Jones.H.S.	(3 & 2)		6687605	RQMS	Kelsey.	(1)
5346738	Pte	Kennedy.H.	(3 & 4)		5952892	Sgt	Kerison.C.	(3)
404846	Pte	Kileen.N.	(2)		5952546	Pte	King.D.	(3)
5958371	Pte	King.R.	(3)		5950896	Pte	Klanavski or	
5947085	Pte	Knight.J.	(3)				Klonowski	(1 & 2)
5958833	Pte	Kysow.G.	(1)		5962088	Pte	Larcombe.L.	(HOC)
5948108	Pte	Lawrence.E.	(3)		5990155	Sgt	Lee.A.	(2)
5948937	CSM	Leech.J.	(3 & 7)+		5957064	Pte	LeFerre.	(1)

Number	Rank	Name		Number	Rank	Name	
6024366	Pte	Leishman.P.	(3)	5958563	Pte	Lewington.W.	(3)
590948	L/Cpl	Lewis.A.	(3)	5956316	Pte	Lewis.H.	(3)
5958476	Pte	Lilley.E.	(3)	5950358	Pte	Littlejohn.G.	(7)
5350008	Cpl	Lowen.B.	(3)	14549713	Pte	Lucas.C.	(3)
14724788	Pte	Luff.A.	(6)	5956829	Pte	Lumm.H.	(2)
5951008	Cpl	Lundgren.P.	(6)	5956562	Cpl	MacDonald.A.	(3)
5958714	L/Cpl	Magnoni.B.	(3)	5958496	Pte	Mallet.E.	(3)
5949269	Cpl	Mapplebeck.	(3)	5953115	Pte	Marshall.G.	(7)
5952848	Pte	Mason.H.	(STC)	5959090	Pte	Mattey.C.	(STC)
14778881	Pte	Mayhew.W.	(HOC)	5947918	Cpl	McConville	(4 & 7)
5958300	Pte	McDonald.T.	(5)	5951561	Pte	McGowan.H.	(2)
5947292	Pte	McGregor.F.	(4)	5959088	Pte	McKinnon.D.	(5)
59895473	Cpl	Mechan.H.	(6)	5951818	L/Cpl	Meninsky.P.	(7)
5958830	Pte	Meredith.F.	(1)	5947499	Pte	Miles.J.	(4)
14731332	Pte	Miles.N.	(HOC)	5957158	Pte	Miller.A.	(4)
5958396	Pte	Miller.L.	(3)	5942738	L/Sgt	Mills.J.	(3)
5959768	Pte	Millward.R.	(3)	5951083	L/Cpl	Monro.J.	(4 & 7)
5350013	Pte	Morgan.J.	(3)	5949820	Cpl	Moxey.E.	(7)
14768822	Pte	Murray.D.	(HOC)	5961985	Cpl	Newman.L.	(3)
14734828	Pte	Neve.K.	(HOC)	14570324	Pte	Nicholl.L.	(3)
5955941	L/Cpl	North.F.	(3)	5383388	Pte	Nutley.W.	(1)
5837560	Pte	Oakey.K.	(2)	5958696	L/Cpl	Oakley.G.	(3)
14854627	Pte	Old.C.	(HOC)	5959801	Cpl	Owen.D.	(CBTC)
5958935	Pte	Page.L.	(3)	5946442	Sgt	Parker.J.	(1)
5959898	Pte	Parker.A.	(3)	5950711	L/Cpl	Parker.C.	(2)
5952876	L/Cpl	Parsons.G.	(2)	5956678	L/Sgt	Parsons.T.	(2)
5859862	Pte	Parsons.A.	(3)	5955083	Pte	Pegram.J.	(3)
59890779	Sgt	Penn.H.	(2)	811703	Pte	Pepper.R.	(4)
5952655	Pte	Peters.A.	(7)	5884387	Pte	Pettel.E.	(2)
14965686	Pte	Phypers	(HOC)	5888719	Pte	Poole.J.	(3)
5952348	Cpl	Porter.J.	(2)	5346789	Sgt	Priest.C.	(2)
5949801	Pte	Pugh.P.	(4)	5947479	L/Cpl	Quarman.G.	(3)
5951029	Pte	Quinne.P.	(3)*	5989608	Pte	Ralph.V.	(2)
14766079	Pte	Raynor.R.	(6)	5950322	Sgt	Redman.J.	(3)
5956694	Pte	Rhodes.J.	(3)	5955044	Pte	Rice.L.	(7)
5884746	Pte	Roberts.E.	(3)	5949874	Pte	Roberts.J.	(4)
5952268	Pte	Robins.G.	(2)	5949049	Pte	Rollings.R.	(3)
5956389	Pte	Routledge.S.	(3)	14927517	Pte	Ryan.J.	(HOC)
5952271	Pte	Salisbury.G.	(2)	5952683	Pte	Salter.J.	(2)
5952682	Sgt	Sarguison.E.	(2)	14950554	Pte	Seaman.J.	(HOC)
14764125	Pte	Shaw.A.	(HOC)	14849068	Pte	Shelley.	(HOC)
14819595	Pte	Shepherd.E.	(HOC)	5951108	Cpl	Shields.J.	(1)
5957047	Pte	Shipp.I.	(1)	59149184	Pte	Short.L.	(3)
5957109	Pte	Smart.V.	(3)	756754	Cpl	Smith.S.	(1)
5956795	Pte	Smith.R.	(3)	5947667	Pte	Stacey.L.	(3)
5951036	Pte	Stevens.H.	(3)	14455863	Pte	Stickley.R.	(6)
5950066	Pte	Stratford.M.	(7)	14872401	Pte	Summers.F.	(HOC)
820959	Pte	Taylor.H.	(3)	5950681	L/Cpl	Teagle.W.	(2)
7013391	Pte	Thurger.F.	(3)	14403533	Pte	Tilson.A.	(3)
14577057	Pte	Titchmarsh.D.	(3)	5990289	L/Cpl	Trustham.D.	(3)
14734890	Pte	Tuck.V.	(HOC)	5948415	Pte	Tupper.J.	(3)*
5951593	Sgt	Turney.W.	(2)	5961168	L/Cpl	Turnock.C.	(3)

14409810	Pte	Turpin.S.	(3)	5956544	Pte	Underwood.L.	(3)
14461636	Pte	Unsworse	(HOC)	5958448	L/Cpl	Venn.F.	(3)
14427389	Pte	Vickery.E.	(4)	5960542	Pte	Walker.F.	(3)
5948722	Sgt	Warburton.C.	(3)	5951286	Cpl	Ward.A.	(7)
5946789	RQMS	Watkins.S.	(3 & 4)	5989899	L/Sgt	Watson.R.	(2)
5948357	L/Cpl	Watts.F.	(3)	5958178	Pte	Webb.R.	(4)
5990006	Sgt	Weedon.J.	(6)	14494249	Pte	Wellman.	(HOC)
5950877	Pte	Wells.	(2)	5958490	Pte	Wells.	(4)
5383381	Pte	Wells.T.	(2)	59519869	Sgt	Westlake.T.	(4)
5950224	Cpl	Whaley.J.	(7)	14959007	Pte	Whant.F.	(HOC)
5948438	Pte	Wheatley.J.	(1)	5958390	Sgt	White.J.	(3)
14965696	Pte	Whybarn.C.	(HOC)	3950750	L/Sgt	Wickson.L.	(2)
5957050	Lieut	Wilkinson	(3)+	5950129	Pte	Wilson.R.	(1)
14862513	Pte	Wilson	(HOC)	5958950	L/Cpl	Winkworth.	(3)
1561949	Pte	Winter.F.	(2)	————	Pte	Warren.	(3)
60876708	Pte	Wood.P..	(3)	5955706	Pte	Young.D.	(7)

APPENDIX VII

HONOURS AND AWARDS

THE BEDFORDSHIRE AND HERTFORDSHIRE REGIMENT AND THE HERTFORDSHIRE REGIMENT (TA) FOR SERVICE IN THE SECOND WORLD WAR

BAR TO D.S.O.

Major	H.J.Nagle		12th Apr 1945
T/Lt Col	R.P. McMullen	M.B.E.(Herts)	4th Oct 1945

D.S.O

Lt Col J.C.A.Birch	France	28th May 1940
Major R.A.W.Stevenson	N.Africa	1941
Major H.C.R.Hose	N.Africa	1941
T/Major P.Young. M.C.	Dieppe	1942
T/Major H.Hollick	Cassino	24th Aug 1944
T/Major E.Jenkins	Italy	1944
Brigadier E.C.Pepper		21st Dec 1944
Major H.J.Nangle		21st Dec 1944
Major A.Andrews	Italy	1944
T/Major G.Bone (Herts)	Italy	1944
T/Lt Col G.W.H.Peters M.C.	Italy	8th Mar 1945
T/Lt Col T.M.Barrow	Burma	26th Apr 1945
T/Lt Col B.A.Burke (Kings Own)	Italy	1945
T/Lt Col R.P. McMullen (Herts)		

BAR and 2nd BAR TO M.C.

T/Lt Col P.Young	Sicily and Italy	1943

M.C.

Capt G.W.H.Peters	France	28th May 1940
2/Lt B.C.Pincombe	France	28th May 1940
2/Lt P.Young	France	28th May 1940
T/Capt T.B.D.McMillen (Att AAC)	Sicily	1943
T/Major J.S.Ross	Burma	Mar/Aug 1944

T/Capt J.C.Salazar	Burma	Mar/Aug 1944
T/Capt L.J.Stevens	Burma	Mar/Aug 1944
T/Capt J.Devlin	Burma	Mar/Aug 1944
Lt A.D.Pond	Burma	Mar/Aug 1944
T/Capt F Sutton	Italy	1944
Lt T.Taylor	Italy	1944
T/Major R.J.Cook	Cassino	1944
T/Major G.H.Sheppard (Herts)	Italy	28th Jun 1945
Lt P.G.F.Sutton (Herts)	Italy	1944
Lt F.Walton (Herts)	Italy	1944
Lt Owen (Herts)	Italy	1944
T/Capt T.F.A.G. Medes		19th Oct 1944
T/Capt B. Williamson		8th Feb 1945
T/Major W.P. Duhan (Att Gold Coast Regt)		
	Burma	8th Feb 1945
Lt R.J.Hingston		10th Jul 1945
T/Major G.O.Watkins		12th Jul 1945
Lt R.W.Satchell		23rd Aug 1945
Lt B.G.R.Stille		13th Sep 1945
T/Major G.W.Croker		13th Dec 1945

KNIGHT COMMANDER OF THE BRITISH EMPIRE

Major General R.F.S. Denning. C.B.	May 1946

C.B.E.

Brigadier E.C.Pepper	June 1944
Brigadier J.A. Longmore M.B.E., T.D.	1st Jan 1946

O.B.E.

T/Col The Hon L.O. Russell	June 1944
T/Lt Col M.C.D.L. Reynolds	22nd Feb 1945
T/Col C.A.Dixon	14th Jun 1945
T/Lt Col M.R.L. Robinson (Herts)	2nd Aug 1945
T/Lt Col B. Passingham (Herts)	20th Sep 1945
T/Major R.E. Mitchell (Herts)	20th Sep 1945
T/Lt Col A.C. Clarke 1st	Jan 1945
T/Lt Col F. Wilson (Herts)	24th Jan 1946
Capt G.G.A. Barkham	18th Oct 1945

M.B.E.

Capt H.E.I. Phillips	1942/1945
Major G.L Sprunt	2nd Mar 1944
T/Major W.N. Jones	24th Aug 1944
Lt J.C. Crowne (Att R.W.A.F.F.)	Mar/Aug 1944

T/Major C.F. Russell		21st Dec 1944
Lt S.N. Drewer		1st Feb 1945
T/Major J.D. Paybody		1st Feb 1945
T/Major I.A. Campbell		19th Apr 1945
T/Capt J.E.Douglas		28th Jun 1945
T/Capt C.J.Miles		28th Jun 1945
2653196 WO I G. Robinson		28th Jun 1945
Capt (QM) W.F. Sandys		13th Dec 1945
WO I H. Roberts		1st Jan 1946
Major J.S, Falkner		Jun 1946
5950322 WO I J. Redman		Jun 1946
5946830 WO II J.H. Gimbert		Jun 1946

KNIGHT OFFICER OF THE ORDER OF ORANGE NASSAU

Lt Col R.H.H. Osborne

UNITED STATES SILVER STAR

Major A. Andrews	1945

CROIX DE GUERRE

5950180 Sgt W.J. Hicks (With Palm)	France	1940
Lieut T. Taylor	Italy	1944

FRENCH BRONZE STAR MEDAL

Capt A.E.Ames	8th Nov 1945

D.C.M.

WO III W.E.Scales	France	1st Jun 1940
WO III L.G.Warren	France	1st Jun 1940
WO II W.Harrison	France	1st Jun 1940
5952486 Sgt F. Snape	Italy	26th Oct 1944
5953381 Sgt A. Hough	Burma	26th Apr 1945
——— Sgt A.G. Branch (Herts)		1944/1945
Cpl F.J.Darts	Sicily	28th Feb 1946

BAR TO M.M.

5948937	Sgt J.E.Leech	Normandy	31st Aug 1944

M.M.

5949252	Pte G. Johnson	France	11th Jul 1940
5947606	Pte R. Lambert	France	11th Jul 1940
5953382	Pte R.R. Hucklesbee	Middle East	24th Feb 1942

5948931	Pte J.T. Walker	Middle East	24th Feb 1942
5948930	Sgt L.W. Cannon	East Africa	16th Apr 1942
5989664	Pte S.G. Clark	Dieppe	2nd Oct 1942
5950610	Pte A.J. Craft	Dieppe	2nd Oct 1942
4974035	Pte V. Adderton	Dieppe	2nd Oct 1942
5948301	Pte F.W. Hopkins	Dieppe	2nd Oct 1942
5948937	Pte J.E.Leech	Italy	13th Jan 1944
5957086	L/Sgt J.W. Wilkinson	Italy	13th Jan 1944
5958297	Pte K.H. Chapman	Italy	27th Jan 1944
5886002	Pte L.R.E. Savage	Italy	26th Oct 1944
5951139	Cpl J.F. Evans	Belgium	4th Jan 1945
14205793	Pte W.J.F. Kirby	Italy	8th Feb 1945
5958758	Cpl T. Jennings	NWE	1st Mar 1945
13020903	L/Cpl E.J. Slade	Italy	8th Mar 1945
5947276	Sgt A.J.Waller	Italy	19th Apr 1945
3656585	Pte R. Boyd	Belgium	26th Apr 1945
5950750	Sgt C. Wickson	St Nazaire	28th Jun 1945
———	Sgt C.D. Parsons	Italy	23rd Aug 1945
5953487	Sgt A.C. Hart (Herts)	Italy	13th Dec 1945
5952830	Sgt J.R. Collins(Herts)	Italy	12th Apr 1945
5115951	Sgt F.W. Ellard (Herts)	Italy	12th Apr 1945
5952969	Cpl T. McGinnis (Herts)	Italy	12th Apr 1945
5954260	Cpl A.J. Young (Herts)	Italy	12th Apr 1945
14215743	L/Cpl M . Smith (Herts)	Italy	12th Apr 1945
5947796	Pte A.C. Clarke (Herts)	Italy	12th Apr 1945
5958171	Sgt T. Beckett	Middle East	1945
5990123	Cpl R.W. Christopher	Middle East	29th Nov 1945
———	Pte E. Jones	Italy	13th Dec 1945
———	Cpl A.G.Church	Normandy	31st Aug 1944

BRITISH EMPIRE MEDAL

5947056	Sgt C.E. Pettit	1st Feb 1945
5949331	Sgt J.C. Grummitt	26th Apr 1945
5949593	Cpl R. French	26th Apr 1945
5956177	L/Cpl H.D. Cousins	Jun 1946

MENTIONED IN DESPATCHES

One hundred and forty three Officers and men were
'Mentioned in Despatches'

APPENDIX VIII

BATTALIONS SERVING 1939–1946

1st (Regular)	Egypt, Palestine, Lemnos, Syria, Tobruk, Burma.
2nd (Regular)	France 1940, North Africa, Italy, Greece.
1st Herts (TA)	UK, Gibraltar, Italy, Palestine.
2nd Herts (TA)	UK, 'D' Day Normandy.
5th Bedfs Herts (TA)	UK, Singapore.
6th Bedfs Herts (TA)	UK, disbanded August 1944.
8th Bedfs Herts	Raised August 1940, became 14 Medium Regt RA.
30th Bedfs Herts	UK, North Africa, Italy, disbanded June 1946.
50th (Later 9th)	UK, Raised October, 1940; became PTC and ITC, disbanded June 1946.
70th (Young Soldiers)	UK, Raised April 1941, disbanded August 1943.
71st (Young Soldiers)	UK, Raised December 1940, disbanded December 1942.

BIBLIOGRAPHY

Atkin, Ronald.   Pillars of Fire – Dunkirk 1940. Sidgwick and Jackson
                              Limited, London.

Briant, Keith.   Fighting with the Guards. Evans Brothers Ltd London.

Bryant, Arthur.   The Turn of the Tide – 1939 to 1943. Grafton Books,
                              London.

Churchill, Winston   The Second World War Volumes I to VI. Cassel and
                              Co Ltd, London.

Divine, David.   The Nine Days of Dunkirk. Faber and Faber, London.

Dupuy, Ernest   The Encyclopedia of Military History, (Fourth
and Trevor   Edition). BCA, London Mackeys of Chatham.

Eisenhower, D.,   Crusade in Europe. Heinemann, Windmill Press,
                              Kingswood, Surrey.

Forty, George.   The Fall of France. Guild Publishing, London.

Goutard. Col A.   The Battle of France 1940. Frederick Muller Ltd,
                              London.

Hay, Ian.   The Battle of Flanders – 1940. HMSO London.

Hickey, Michael.   The Unforgettable Army. BCA, London.

Holmes, Richard.   The World Atlas of Warfare. Guild Publishing,
                              London.

Horrocks, Sir Brian.   Corps Commander. Sidgwick and Jackson, London.

Howarth, David.   Dawn of "D" Day. Collins, London.

Macdonald, John.   Great Battles of World War II. Guild Publishing
                              London.

Medley. R.H.   Five Days to Live – France 1939 – 1940. Dover Press,
                              Abergavenny.

Montgomery of   El Alamein to the River Sangro. Hutchinson, London
Alamein, Field Marshal
the Viscount

Peters, G.W.H.   Famous Regiments – The Bedfordshire and
                              Hertfordshire Regiment. Leo Cooper, London.

Sainsbury. J.D.   The Hertfordshire Regiment. Castlemead Pub-
                              lications, Ware. Herts.

Slim, Viscount.   Defeat into Victory. The Reprint Society, London.

Smith. E.D.   The Battles for Cassino, Charles Seribras and Sons,
                              New York.

Turner, John.   Invasion 44. George. G.Harrap and Co, London.

324

Westlake, Ray.	The Territorial Battalions. Guild Publishing London.
Whiting, Charles.	Slaughter over Sicily. Leo Cooper, London.
Williamson, Hugh.	The Fourth Division 1939 – 1945. Newman Neame, London.

The Story of The Bedfordshire and Hertfordshire Regiment (The 16th Regiment of Foot) Volume II 1914 – 1958.
Hertfordshire Field Gazette – Italian Campaign August 1944 to January 1945.
The Wasp – The Regimental Journal of The Bedfordshire and Hertfordshire Regiment.

INDEX